Legendlore

VOLUME TWO   **THE REALM CHRONICLES**

CALIBER
COMICS

VOLUME TWO   THE REALM CHRONICLES

PLOT & WRITTEN BY
RALPH GRIFFITH
STUART KERR

PENCILS
GUY DAVIS

INKS
SANDY SCHREIBER
DIRK JOHNSTON
RANDY ZIMMERMAN

LETTERS
VINCE LOCKE
LEX MORRIS
RANDY ZIMMERMAN

THIS BOOK CONTAINS *THE REALM* VOLUME ONE ISSUES 6 -7
LEGENDLORE: TALE OF THE REALM SERIES
Originally published by Arrow Comics

A REVISIT TO THE REALM

~ RALPH GRIFFITH

I want to start by saying thank you for supporting our comic. If you were a fan of both comics and Dungeons and Dragons in the 1980's, I'm sure you've seen our books around. If you are a new reader, welcome to The Realm, a fantastical land populated by strange and wondrous creatures that, in many cases, would be more than happy to impale you, grind your bones, or simply lop off your head. We hope you have a pleasant stay. Don't mind the cold and damp accommodations. It's not quite the civilized place of any of your previous vacation stops.

The land of Azoth is the mythical continent where the events of The Realm comic book series played out. It is a world with all the classic fantasy elements: dwarves, elves, shape shifters, demons and dragons; wondrous cities and deep, dark forests; peaceful valleys and the plains of battle. In short, everything D&D players like us would want to see in a comic book. The only thing missing was to be able to go there ourselves. Hence, the creation of four characters from our own dear Earth who manage to find themselves transported to The Realm, when they originally had a different vacation destination in mind.

As a Dungeon Master for over ten years, and a life-long comics fan, I noticed a lack of fantasy comics with that Dungeons and Dragons vibe to them. The various Conan titles and a few other sword and sorcery books used many of the same elements, and told stories that easily could have been adapted into scenarios and campaigns. However, they did not have that sense of light and fun adventure that even the most serious player understands. Our little D&D group began in high school and stayed together for some time after. We had so many cool adventures played in someone or other's basement until we noticed the sun starting to creep in those little windows. That is the particular excitement I wanted to capture in comic form.

Our heroes were college freshmen, young and inexperienced, and totally unprepared for what fate brought their way. Still teens, the foursome were thrust into the middle of a vast campaign, where kings and emperors vied for power, often in the most brutal of ways. Fortunately, we sent them some allies in the form of Silverfawn, an Elf who had escaped from slavery; the battled-proven Dwarf Diggoruss Gorey; and even the Halfling Grappo Pilden with his sneaky skills. Yes, indeed, a classic band of D&D adventurers, if ever there was one. Many of our character names, including Diggy and Grappo, were the actual names of characters our D&D group created for our late night adventures.

Although there were many dangers for the party to face, such as Night Creatures, slavers, Orcs, brigands, Ogres, and Trolls, it was the central villain Lord Darkoth who orchestrated the domination of Azoth, and used the Earthers as lynchpins in his plan. Darkoth and his generals constantly plotted and schemed to gain political and military advantage over the known world of Ardonia and its various nations. Each issue focused on the immediate plight of our heroes, while revealing more about the larger world about them. The action often ranged from a simple yet potentially deadly barroom brawl, to a battle of armies with hundreds or even thousands of warriors clashing.

The world grew in scope and detail, because that is what happens with a D&D campaign. That first scenario where the various characters begin to interact becomes a campaign as players developed those characters and the relationships between them. The characters gained levels and added new skills and abilities. The players learned how best to work together. They soon demanded more dangerous opponents and more intricate puzzles to work out. This was another of the key elements of fantasy role-playing that I wanted to translate into comics.

As the plotter of The Realm, I was very much in Dungeon master mode. I had to supply an engaging tale and just the right level of danger. No D&D group stays together long when the DM sets about to crush them at every turn. Nor do they stay with a DM who lets them walk unimpeded through monsters and traps. Players want to feel some sense of risk in their actions. When they manage, just barely, to escape that cavern full of goblins, carrying a chest of gold and a magic item or two, they leave the gaming session with a sense of accomplishment. And they want to come back for more.

This is what we so desperately wanted to bring to The Realm. And even though it was our first published comic book title and shows some of that inexperience at times, I believe that we more often than not reached what we were striving for: a comic that was fun, lighthearted, yet with sense of danger and risk, and a dash of humor. I truly hope you enjoy this second volume of Realm stories. I guess you must have found something worthwhile in the first volume to stay with us.

On a final note, I would like to thank the good folks at Caliber for bringing these tales back into the hands of many new readers that might have missed it the first time around. As far as where things go from here, well, you can start by ordering more of our books if you enjoyed this one. Let our publisher know how much you enjoyed The Realm and all of its characters. Who knows, maybe some new tales are waiting to be told.

Catch ya later!

Ralph Griffith
February 2017

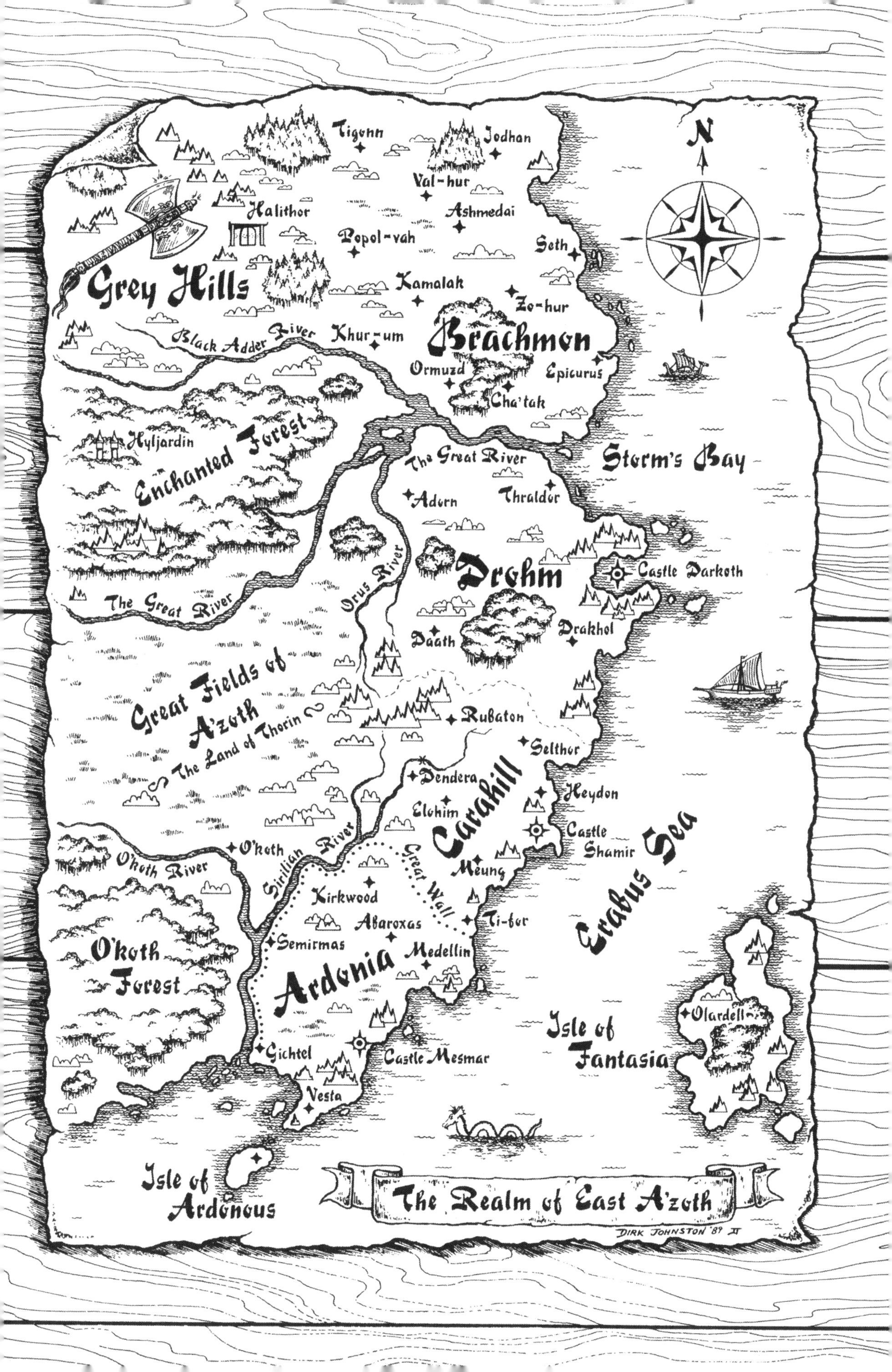

N
Tigonn
Jodhan
Val-hur
Halithor
Ashmedai
Popol-vah
Seth
Grey Hills
Kamalak
Zo-hur
Black Adder River
Khur-um
Brachmon
Ormuzd
Epicurus
Cha'tak
Hyljardin
Enchanted Forest
The Great River
Storm's Bay
Thraldor
Adorn
Orus River
Drohm
Castle Darkoth
The Great River
Daath
Drakhol
Great Fields of A'zoth
The Land of Thorin
Rubaton
Selthor
Dendera
Carahill
Heydon
Elohim
Castle Shamir
O'koth
O'koth River
Sirilian River
Great Wall
Meung
Erabus Sea
Kirkwood
Abaroxas
Ti-for
O'koth Forest
Semirmas
Medellin
Ardonia
Olardell
Isle of Fantasia
Gichtel
Castle Mesmar
Vesta
Isle of Ardonous
The Realm of East A'zoth
DIRK JOHNSTON '89 II

LEGENDLORE

THE REALM - VOLUME ONE

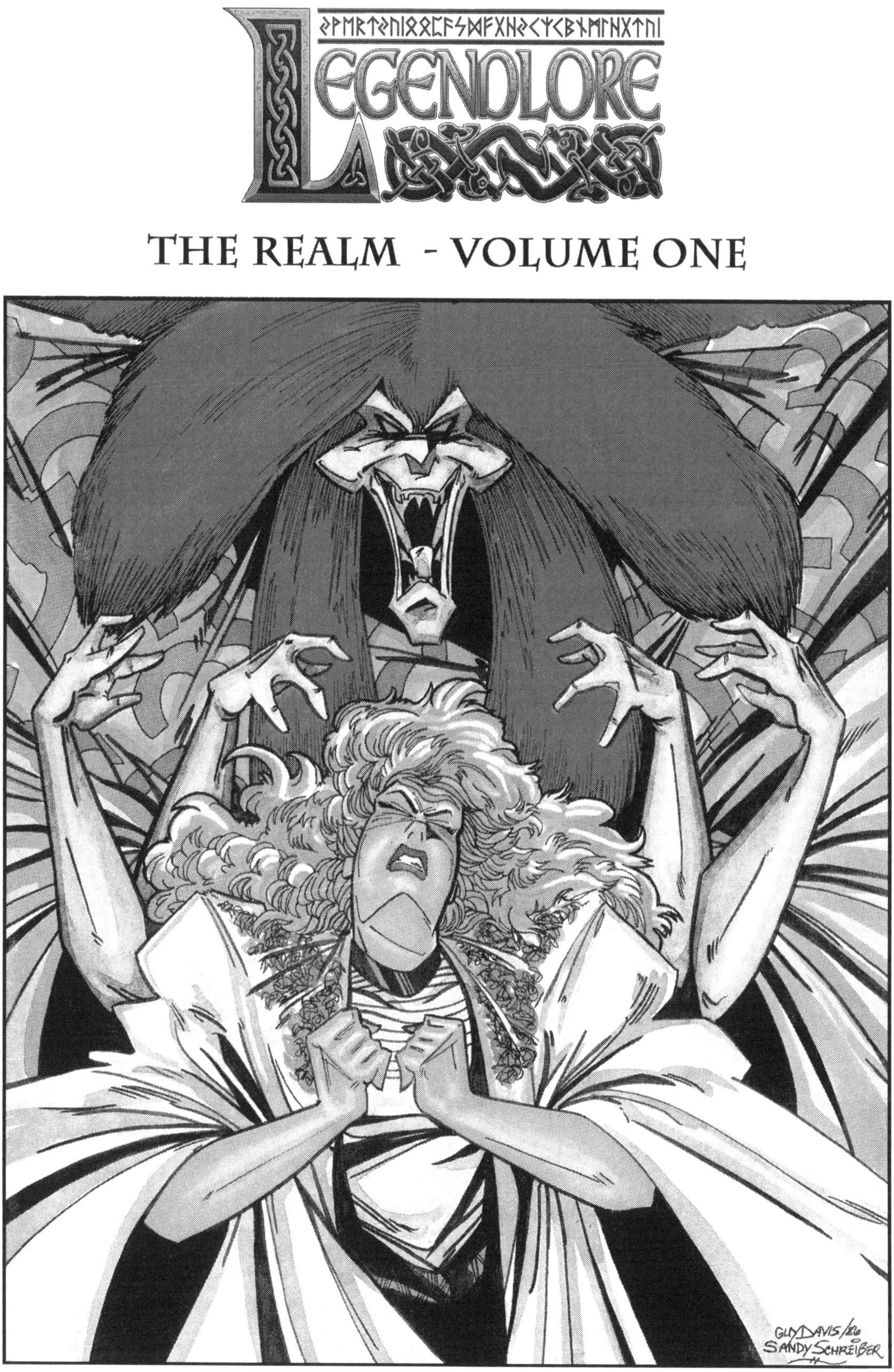
GUY DAVIS/86
SANDY SCHREIBER

ISSUE SIX

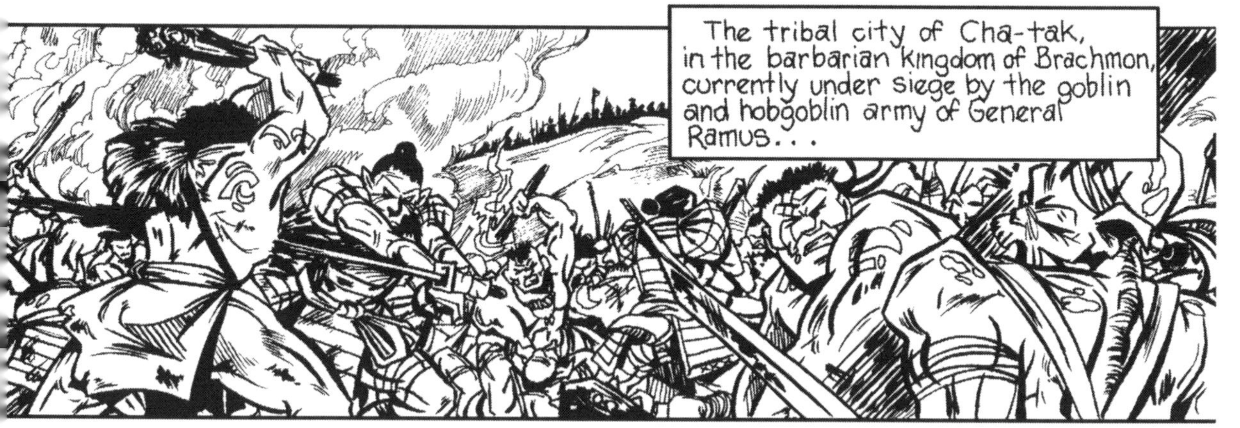
The tribal city of Cha-tak, in the barbarian kingdom of Brachmon, currently under siege by the goblin and hobgoblin army of General Ramus...

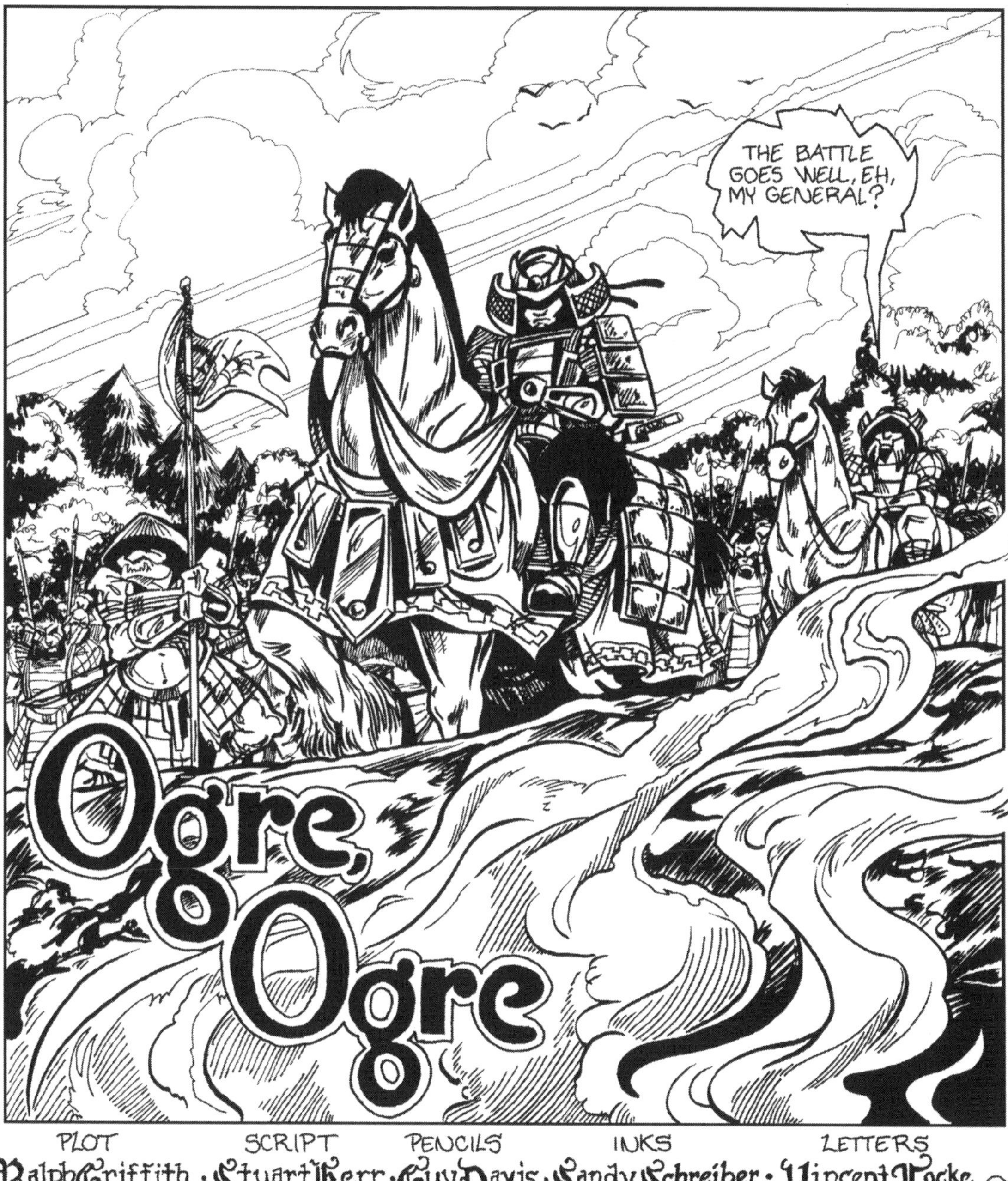
THE BATTLE GOES WELL, EH, MY GENERAL?
Ogre, Ogre

PLOT Ralph Griffith · SCRIPT Stuart Kerr · PENCILS Guy Davis · INKS Sandy Schreiber · LETTERS Vincent Locke

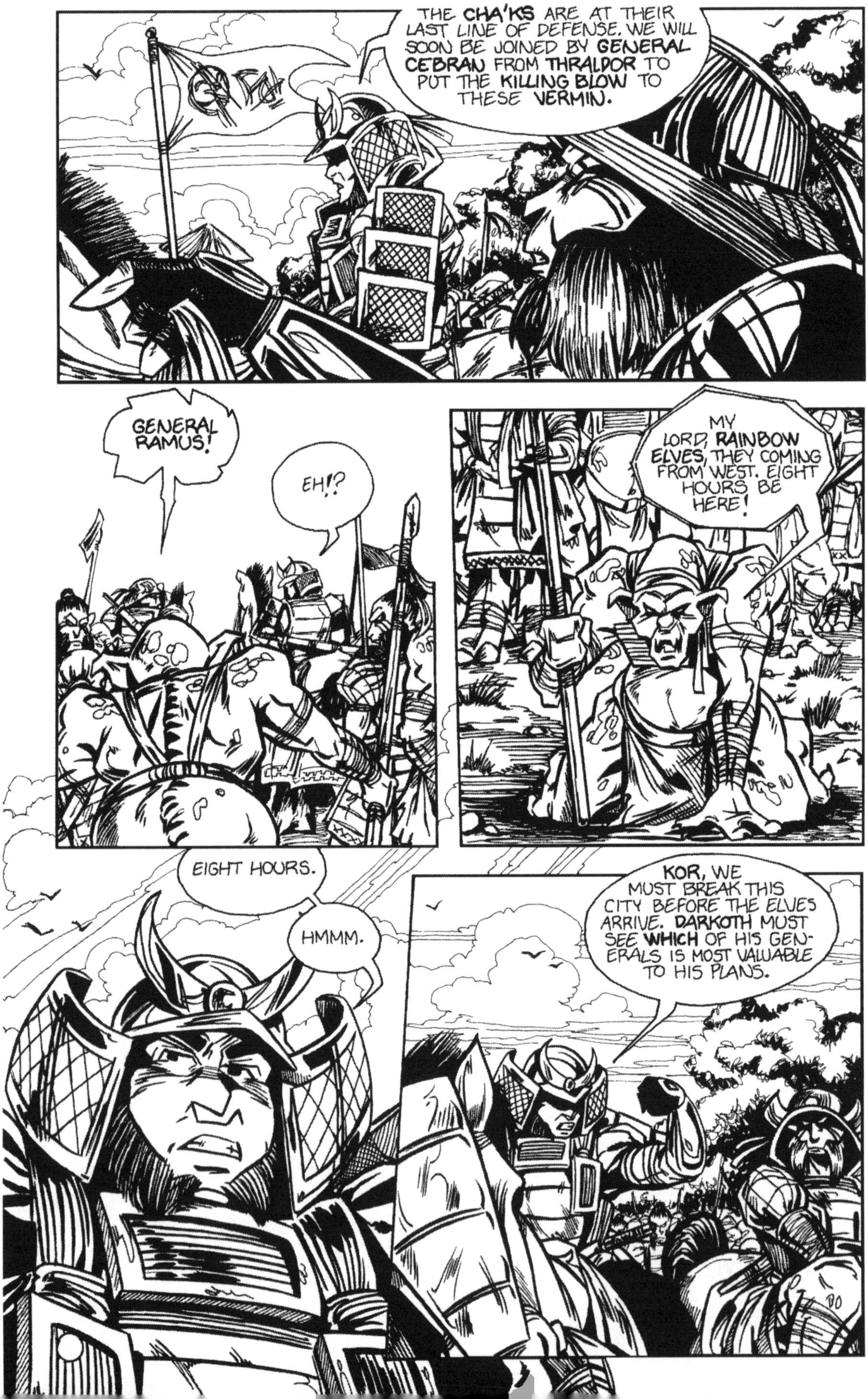
THE CHA'KS ARE AT THEIR LAST LINE OF DEFENSE. WE WILL SOON BE JOINED BY GENERAL CEBRAN FROM THRALDOR TO PUT THE KILLING BLOW TO THESE VERMIN.
GENERAL RAMUS!
EH!?
MY LORD, RAINBOW ELVES, THEY COMING FROM WEST. EIGHT HOURS BE HERE!
EIGHT HOURS.
HMMM.
KOR, WE MUST BREAK THIS CITY BEFORE THE ELVES ARRIVE. DARKOTH MUST SEE WHICH OF HIS GENERALS IS MOST VALUABLE TO HIS PLANS.

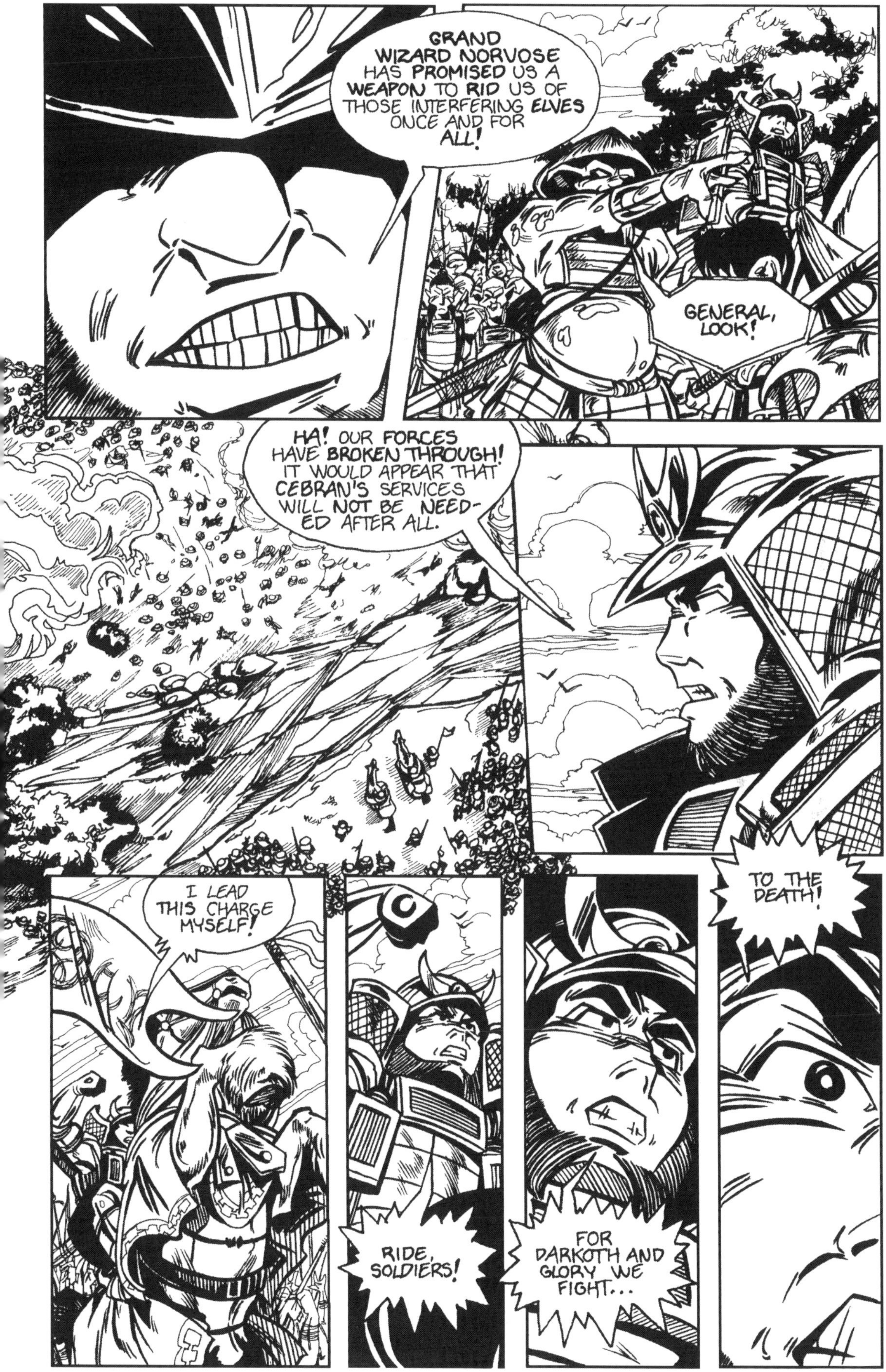
GRAND WIZARD NORVOSE HAS PROMISED US A WEAPON TO RID US OF THOSE INTERFERING ELVES ONCE AND FOR ALL!
GENERAL, LOOK!
HA! OUR FORCES HAVE BROKEN THROUGH! IT WOULD APPEAR THAT CEBRAN'S SERVICES WILL NOT BE NEED-ED AFTER ALL.
I LEAD THIS CHARGE MYSELF!
RIDE, SOLDIERS!
FOR DARKOTH AND GLORY WE FIGHT...
TO THE DEATH!

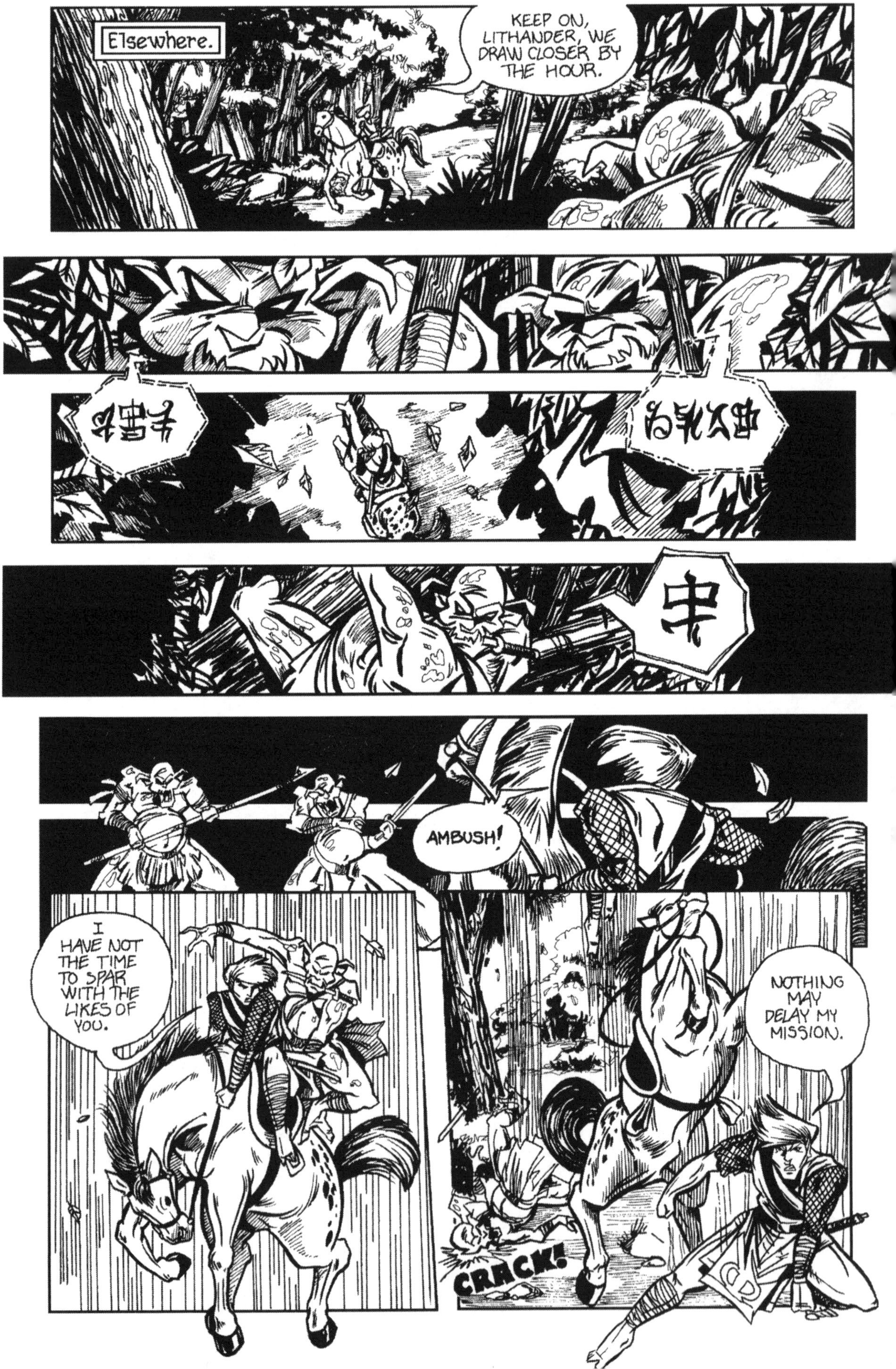
Elsewhere.
KEEP ON, LITHANDER, WE DRAW CLOSER BY THE HOUR.
AMBUSH!
I HAVE NOT THE TIME TO SPAR WITH THE LIKES OF YOU.
NOTHING MAY DELAY MY MISSION.
CRACK!

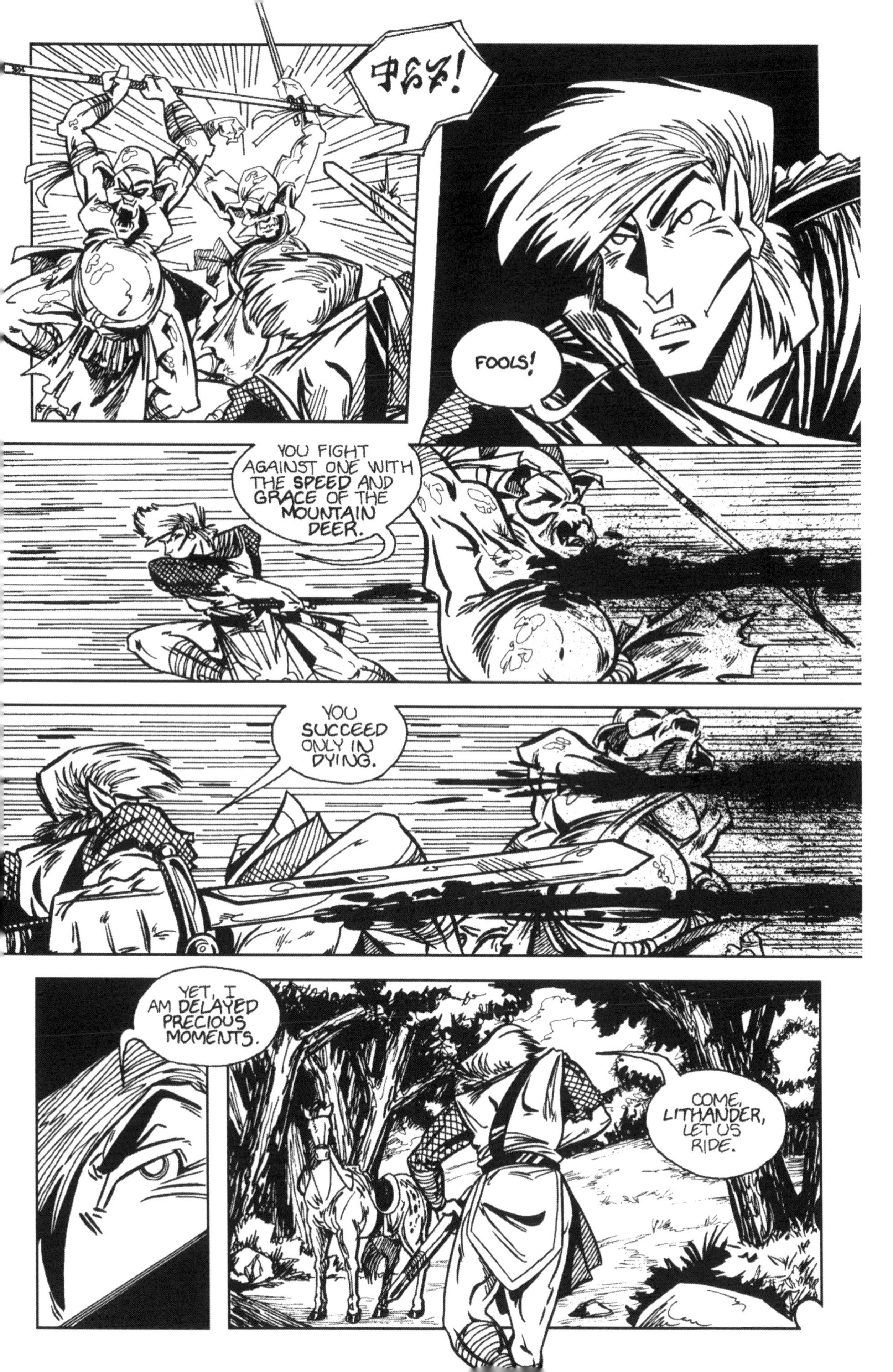
FOOLS!
YOU FIGHT AGAINST ONE WITH THE SPEED AND GRACE OF THE MOUNTAIN DEER.
YOU SUCCEED ONLY IN DYING.
YET, I AM DELAYED PRECIOUS MOMENTS.
COME, LITHANDER, LET US RIDE.

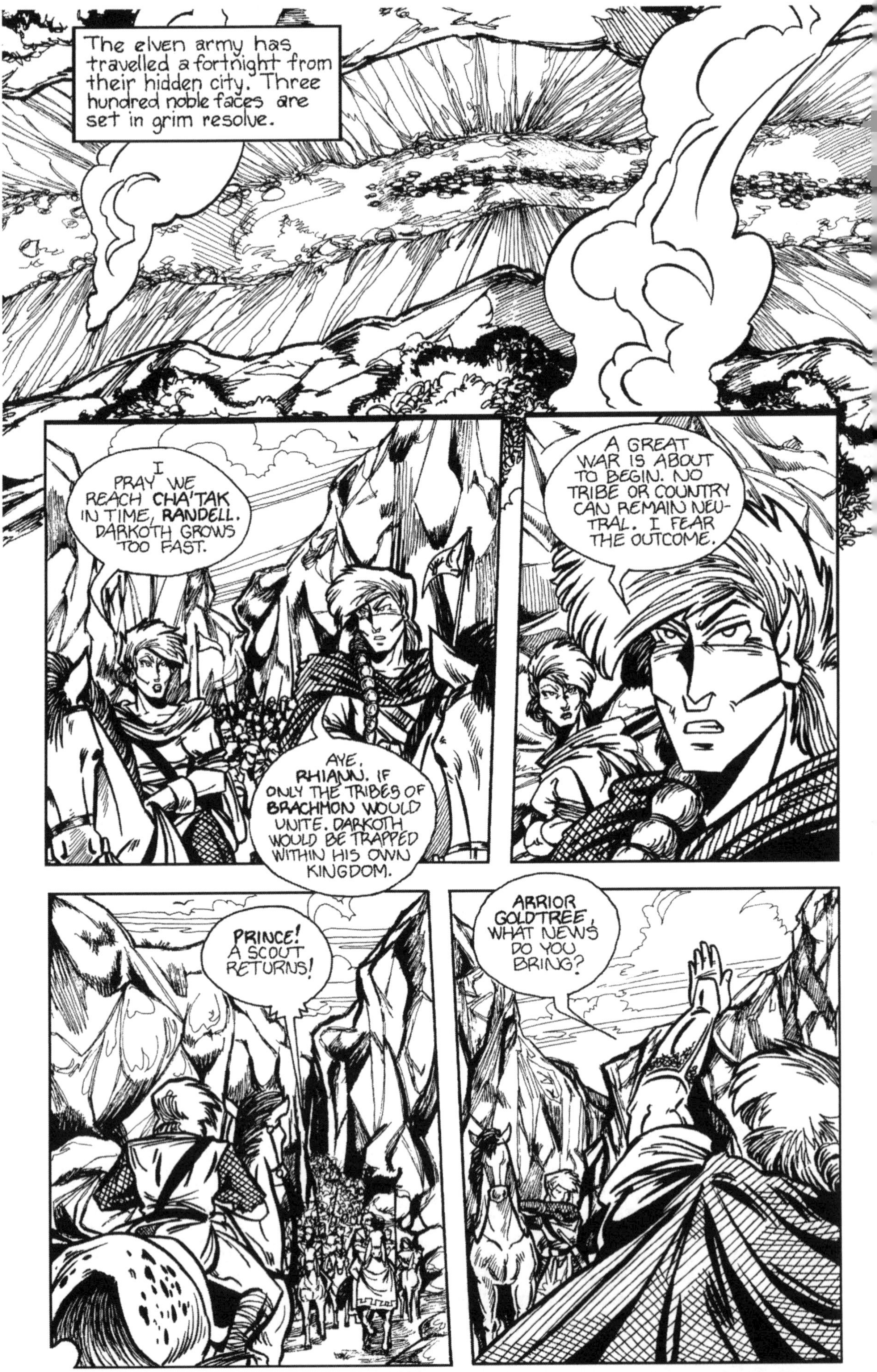
The elven army has travelled a fortnight from their hidden city. Three hundred noble faces are set in grim resolve.
I PRAY WE REACH CHA'TAK IN TIME, RANDELL. DARKOTH GROWS TOO FAST.
AYE, RHIANN. IF ONLY THE TRIBES OF BRACHMON WOULD UNITE. DARKOTH WOULD BE TRAPPED WITHIN HIS OWN KINGDOM.
A GREAT WAR IS ABOUT TO BEGIN. NO TRIBE OR COUNTRY CAN REMAIN NEUTRAL. I FEAR THE OUTCOME.
PRINCE! A SCOUT RETURNS!
ARRIOR GOLDTREE, WHAT NEWS DO YOU BRING?

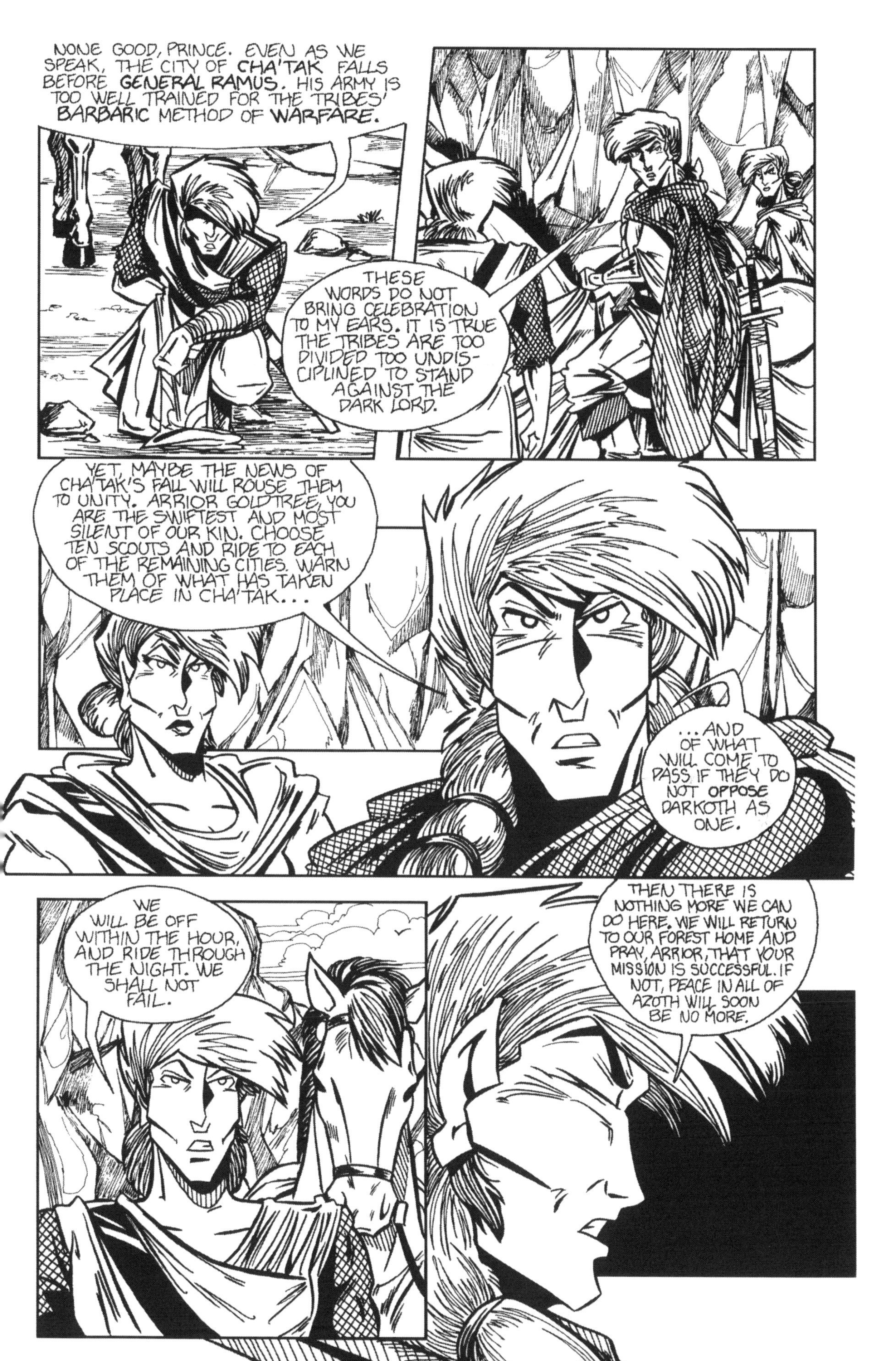
NONE GOOD, PRINCE. EVEN AS WE SPEAK, THE CITY OF CHA'TAK FALLS BEFORE GENERAL RAMUS. HIS ARMY IS TOO WELL TRAINED FOR THE TRIBES' BARBARIC METHOD OF WARFARE.
THESE WORDS DO NOT BRING CELEBRATION TO MY EARS. IT IS TRUE THE TRIBES ARE TOO DIVIDED TOO UNDISCIPLINED TO STAND AGAINST THE DARK LORD.
YET, MAYBE THE NEWS OF CHA'TAK'S FALL WILL ROUSE THEM TO UNITY. ARRIOR GOLDTREE, YOU ARE THE SWIFTEST AND MOST SILENT OF OUR KIN. CHOOSE TEN SCOUTS AND RIDE TO EACH OF THE REMAINING CITIES. WARN THEM OF WHAT HAS TAKEN PLACE IN CHA'TAK...
...AND OF WHAT WILL COME TO PASS IF THEY DO NOT OPPOSE DARKOTH AS ONE.
WE WILL BE OFF WITHIN THE HOUR, AND RIDE THROUGH THE NIGHT. WE SHALL NOT FAIL.
THEN THERE IS NOTHING MORE WE CAN DO HERE. WE WILL RETURN TO OUR FOREST HOME AND PRAY, ARRIOR, THAT YOUR MISSION IS SUCCESSFUL. IF NOT, PEACE IN ALL OF AZOTH WILL SOON BE NO MORE.

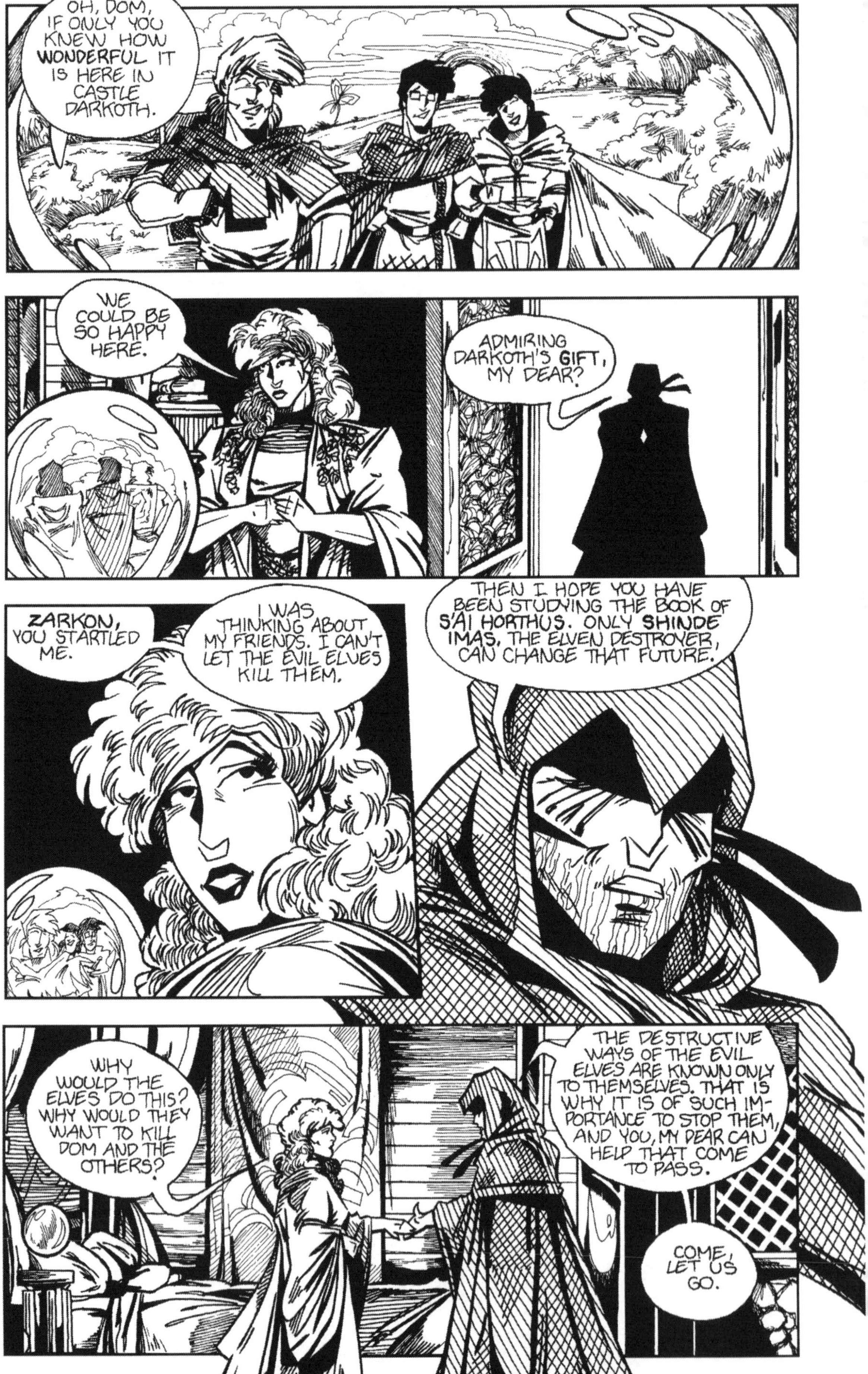

OH, DOM, IF ONLY YOU KNEW HOW WONDERFUL IT IS HERE IN CASTLE DARKOTH.
WE COULD BE SO HAPPY HERE.
ADMIRING DARKOTH'S GIFT, MY DEAR?
ZARKON, YOU STARTLED ME.
I WAS THINKING ABOUT MY FRIENDS. I CAN'T LET THE EVIL ELVES KILL THEM.
THEN I HOPE YOU HAVE BEEN STUDYING THE BOOK OF S'AI HORTHUS. ONLY SHINDE IMAS, THE ELVEN DESTROYER, CAN CHANGE THAT FUTURE.
WHY WOULD THE ELVES DO THIS? WHY WOULD THEY WANT TO KILL DOM AND THE OTHERS?
THE DESTRUCTIVE WAYS OF THE EVIL ELVES ARE KNOWN ONLY TO THEMSELVES. THAT IS WHY IT IS OF SUCH IMPORTANCE TO STOP THEM, AND YOU, MY DEAR CAN HELP THAT COME TO PASS.
COME, LET US GO.

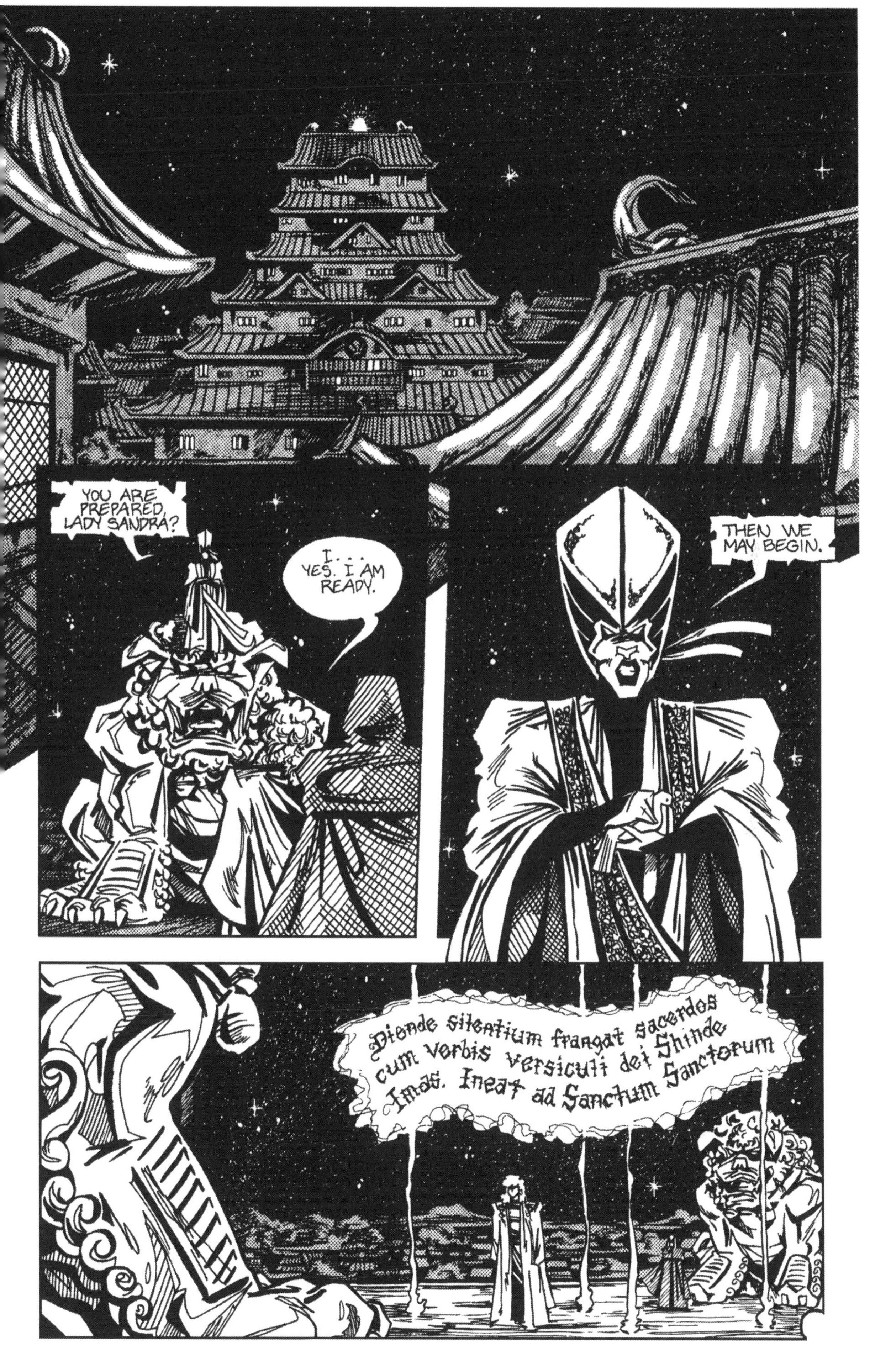
YOU ARE PREPARED, LADY SANDRA?
I . . . YES. I AM READY.
THEN WE MAY BEGIN.
Diende silentium frangat sacerdos cum verbis versiculi dei Shinde Imas. Ineat ad Sanctum Sanctorum

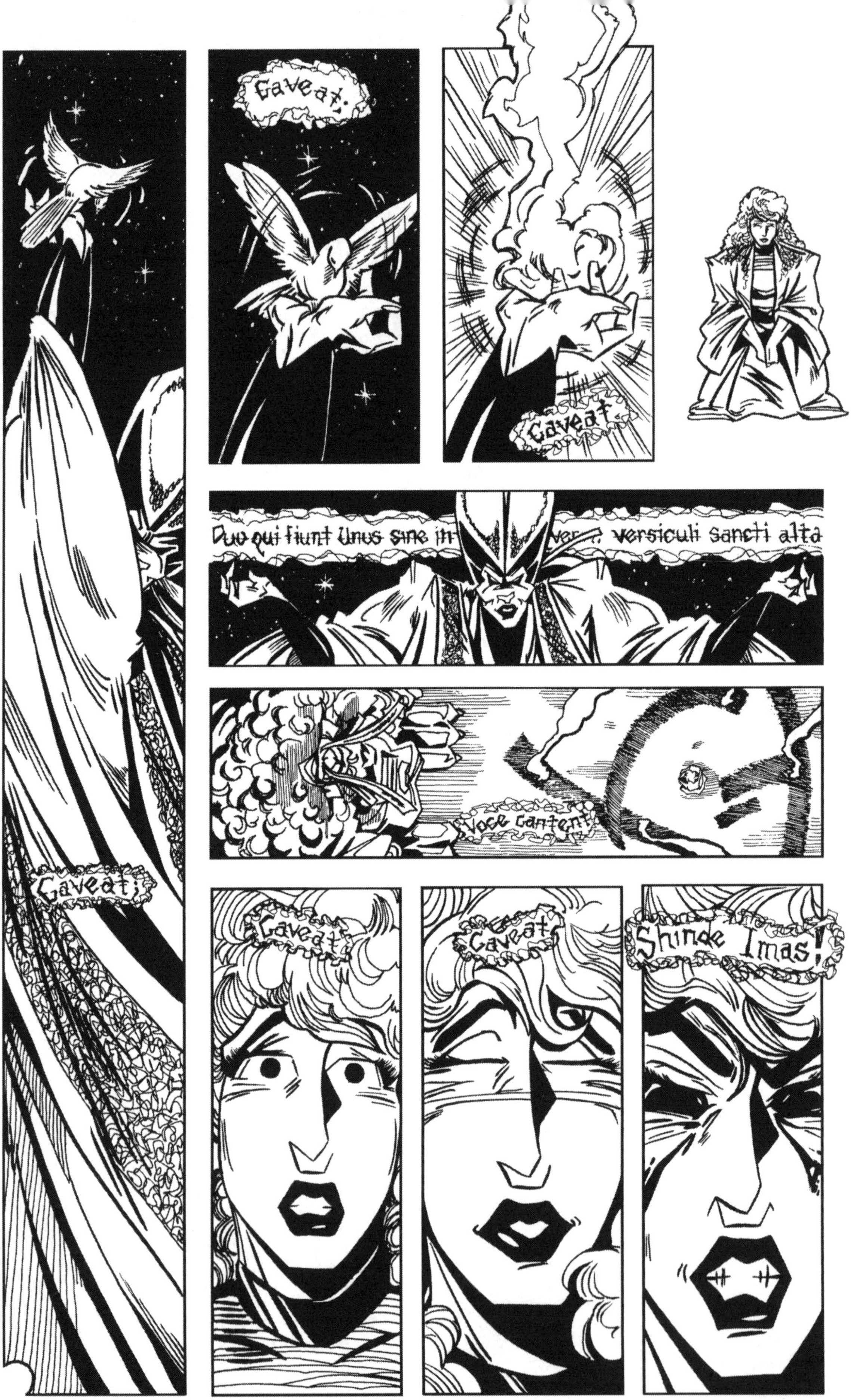
Caveat;
Caveat
Duo qui fiunt Unus sine in
versiculi sancti alta
Voce cantent!
Caveat;
Caveat
Caveat
Shinde Imas!

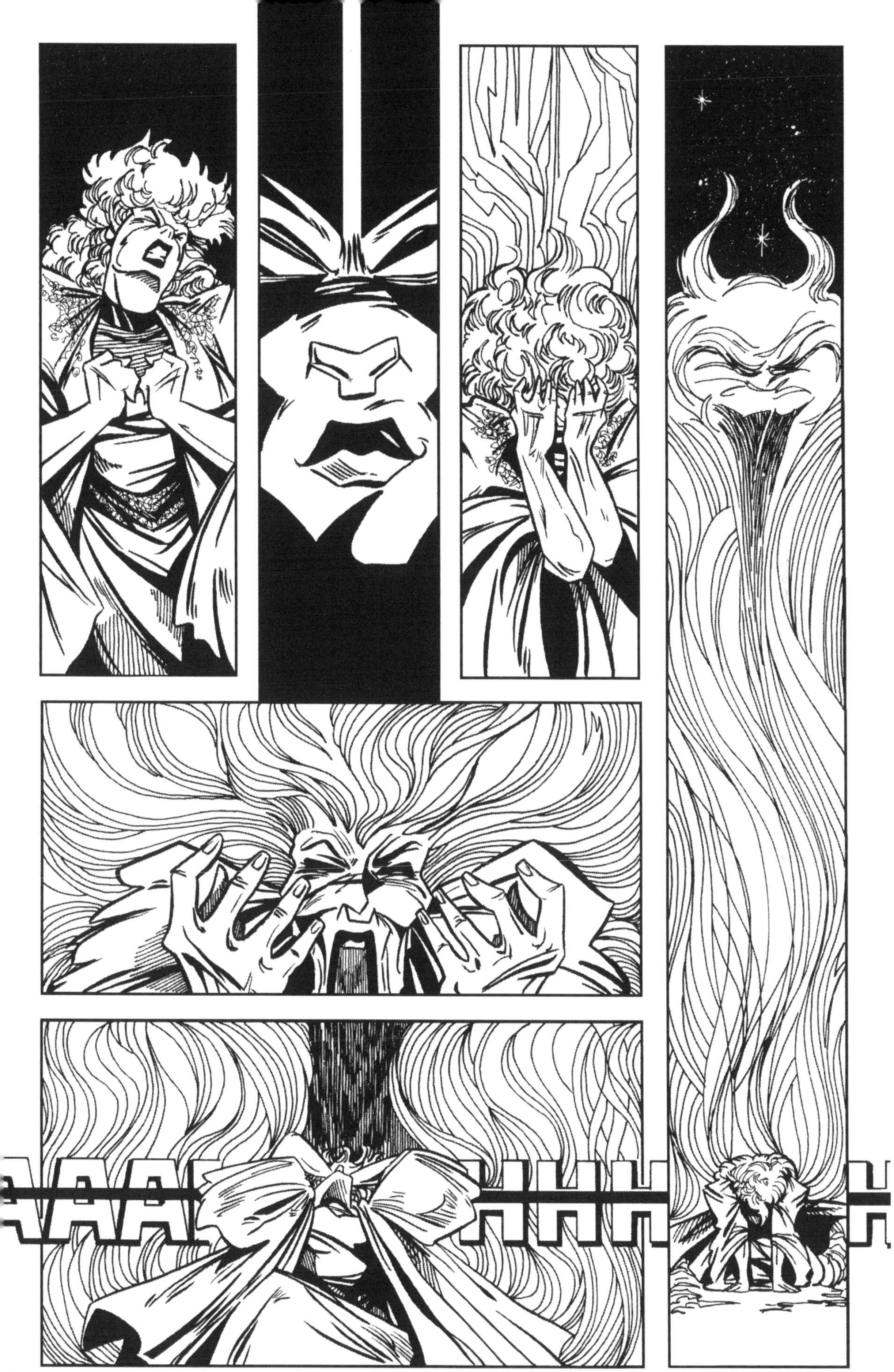
AAAHHHH

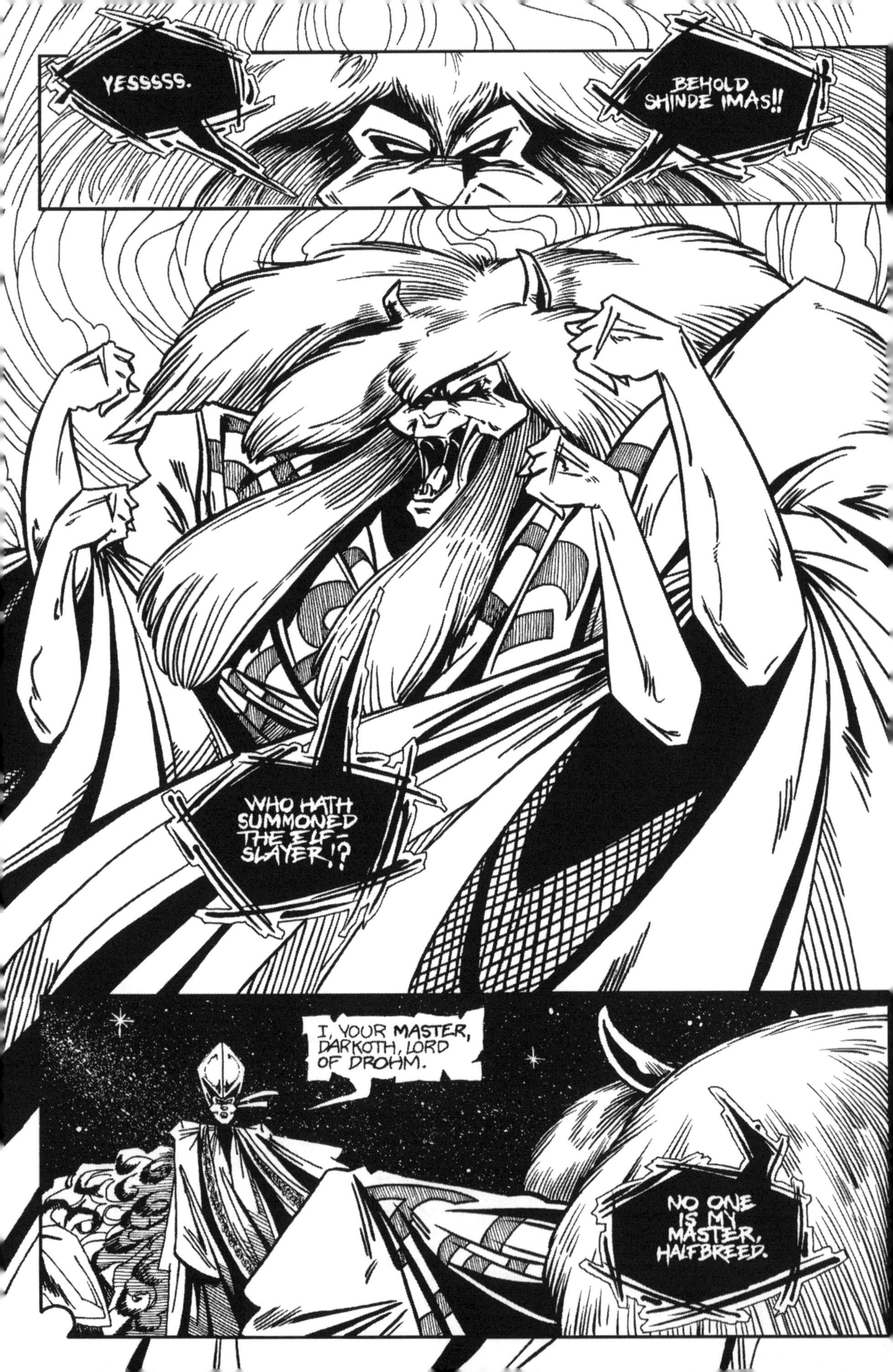
YESSSSS.
BEHOLD SHINDE IMAS!!
WHO HATH SUMMONED THE ELF-SLAYER!?
I, YOUR MASTER, DARKOTH, LORD OF DROHM.
NO ONE IS MY MASTER, HALFBREED.

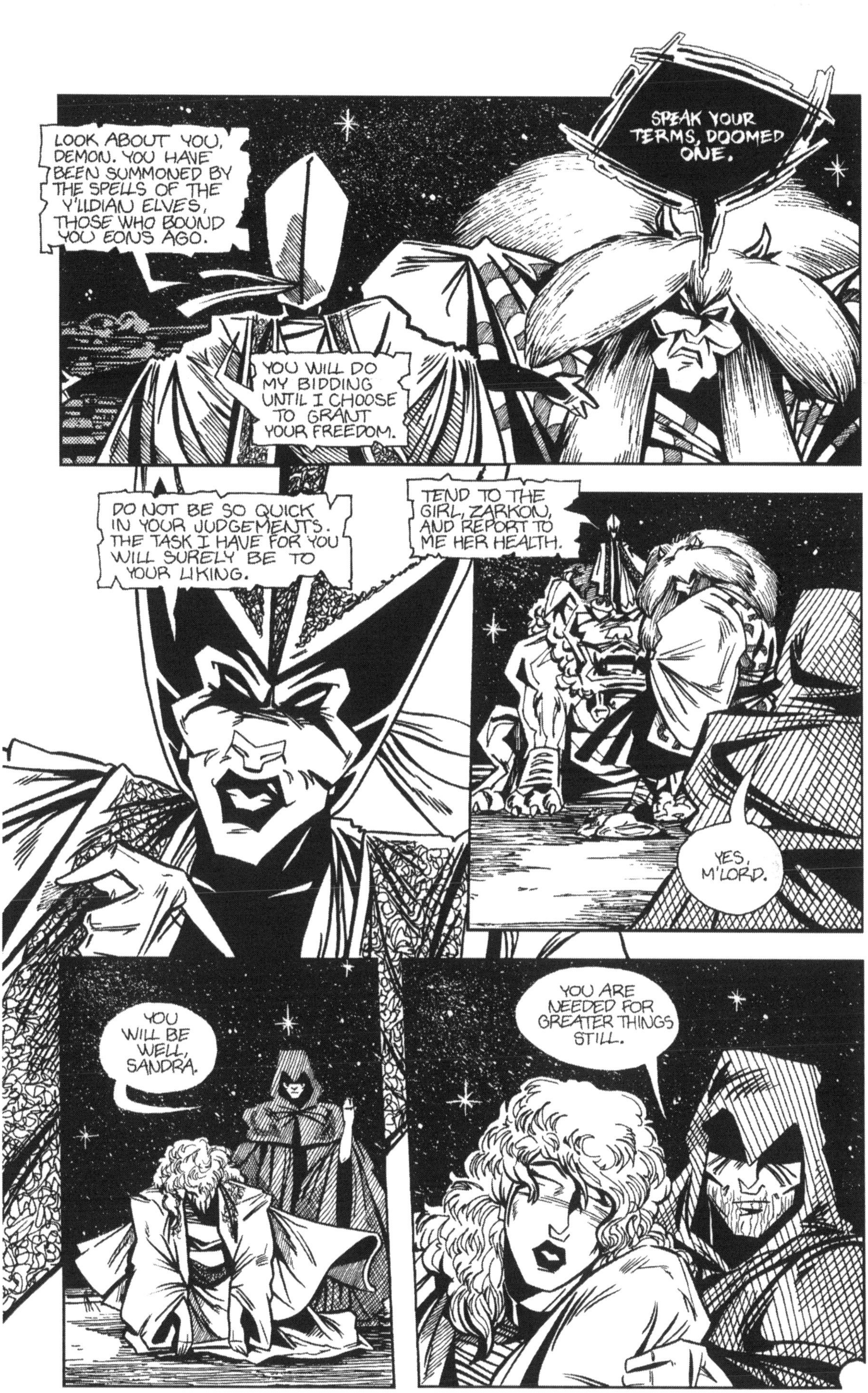
LOOK ABOUT YOU, DEMON. YOU HAVE BEEN SUMMONED BY THE SPELLS OF THE Y'ILDIAN ELVES, THOSE WHO BOUND YOU EONS AGO.
SPEAK YOUR TERMS, DOOMED ONE.
YOU WILL DO MY BIDDING UNTIL I CHOOSE TO GRANT YOUR FREEDOM.
DO NOT BE SO QUICK IN YOUR JUDGEMENTS. THE TASK I HAVE FOR YOU WILL SURELY BE TO YOUR LIKING.
TEND TO THE GIRL, ZARKON, AND REPORT TO ME HER HEALTH.
YES, M'LORD.
YOU WILL BE WELL, SANDRA.
YOU ARE NEEDED FOR GREATER THINGS STILL.

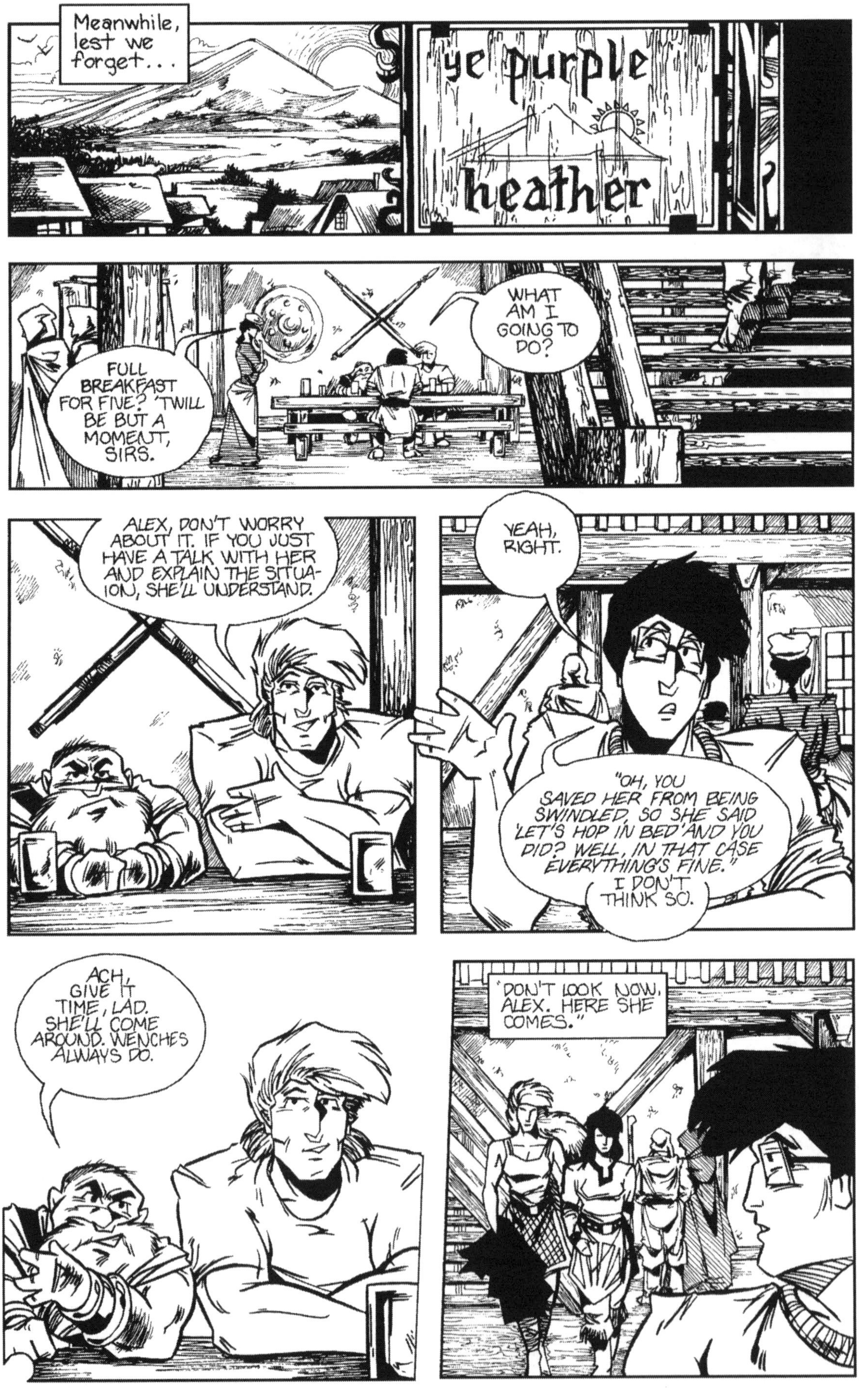
Meanwhile, lest we forget...
ye purple heather
FULL BREAKFAST FOR FIVE? 'TWILL BE BUT A MOMENT, SIRS.
WHAT AM I GOING TO DO?
ALEX, DON'T WORRY ABOUT IT. IF YOU JUST HAVE A TALK WITH HER AND EXPLAIN THE SITUATION, SHE'LL UNDERSTAND.
YEAH, RIGHT.
"OH, YOU SAVED HER FROM BEING SWINDLED, SO SHE SAID 'LET'S HOP IN BED' AND YOU DID? WELL, IN THAT CASE EVERYTHING'S FINE."
I DON'T THINK SO.
ACH, GIVE IT TIME, LAD. SHE'LL COME AROUND. WENCHES ALWAYS DO.
"DON'T LOOK NOW, ALEX. HERE SHE COMES."

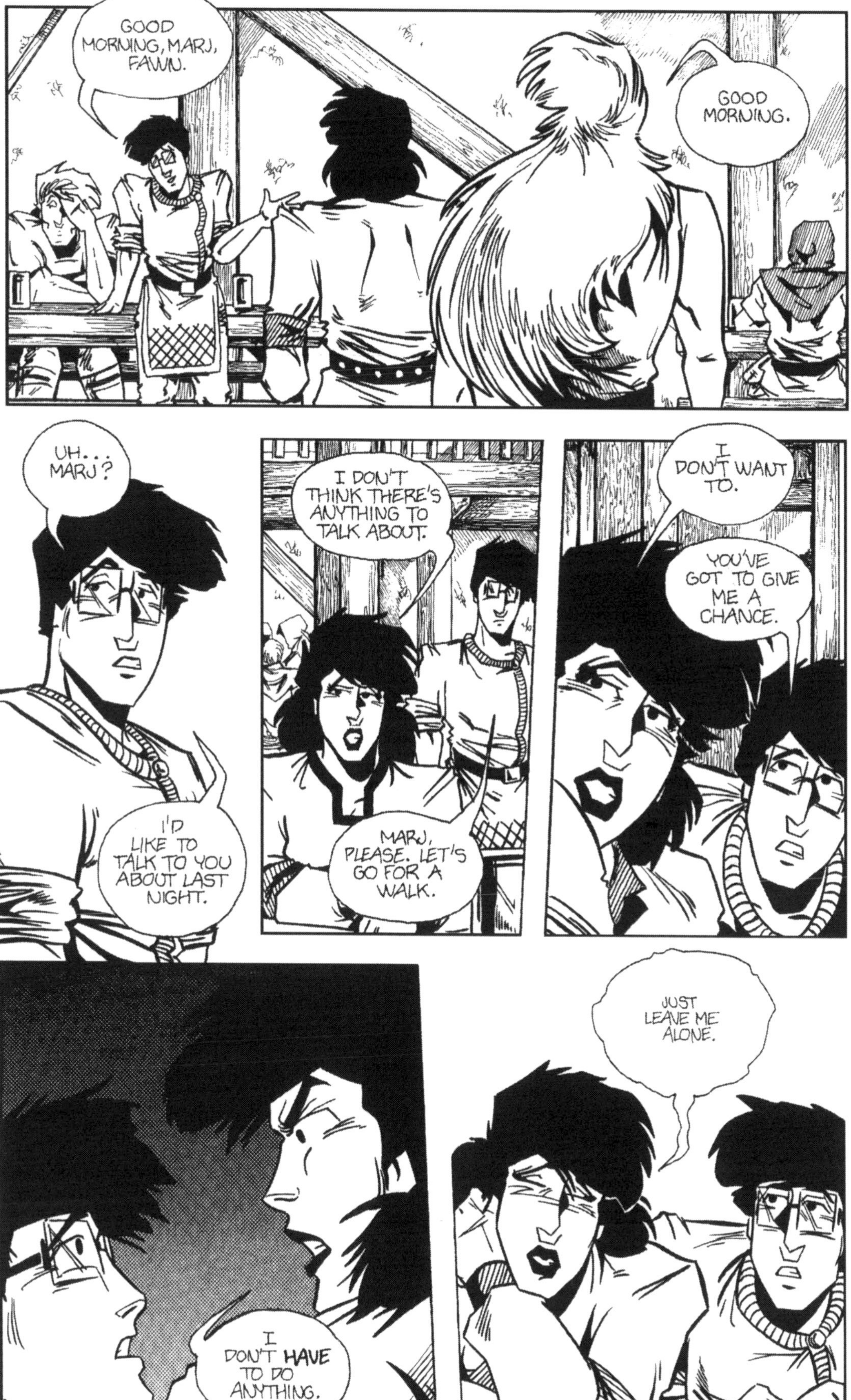
GOOD MORNING, MARJ, FAWN.
GOOD MORNING.
UH... MARJ?
I'D LIKE TO TALK TO YOU ABOUT LAST NIGHT.
I DON'T THINK THERE'S ANYTHING TO TALK ABOUT.
MARJ, PLEASE. LET'S GO FOR A WALK.
I DON'T WANT TO.
YOU'VE GOT TO GIVE ME A CHANCE.
I DON'T **HAVE** TO DO ANYTHING.
JUST LEAVE ME ALONE.

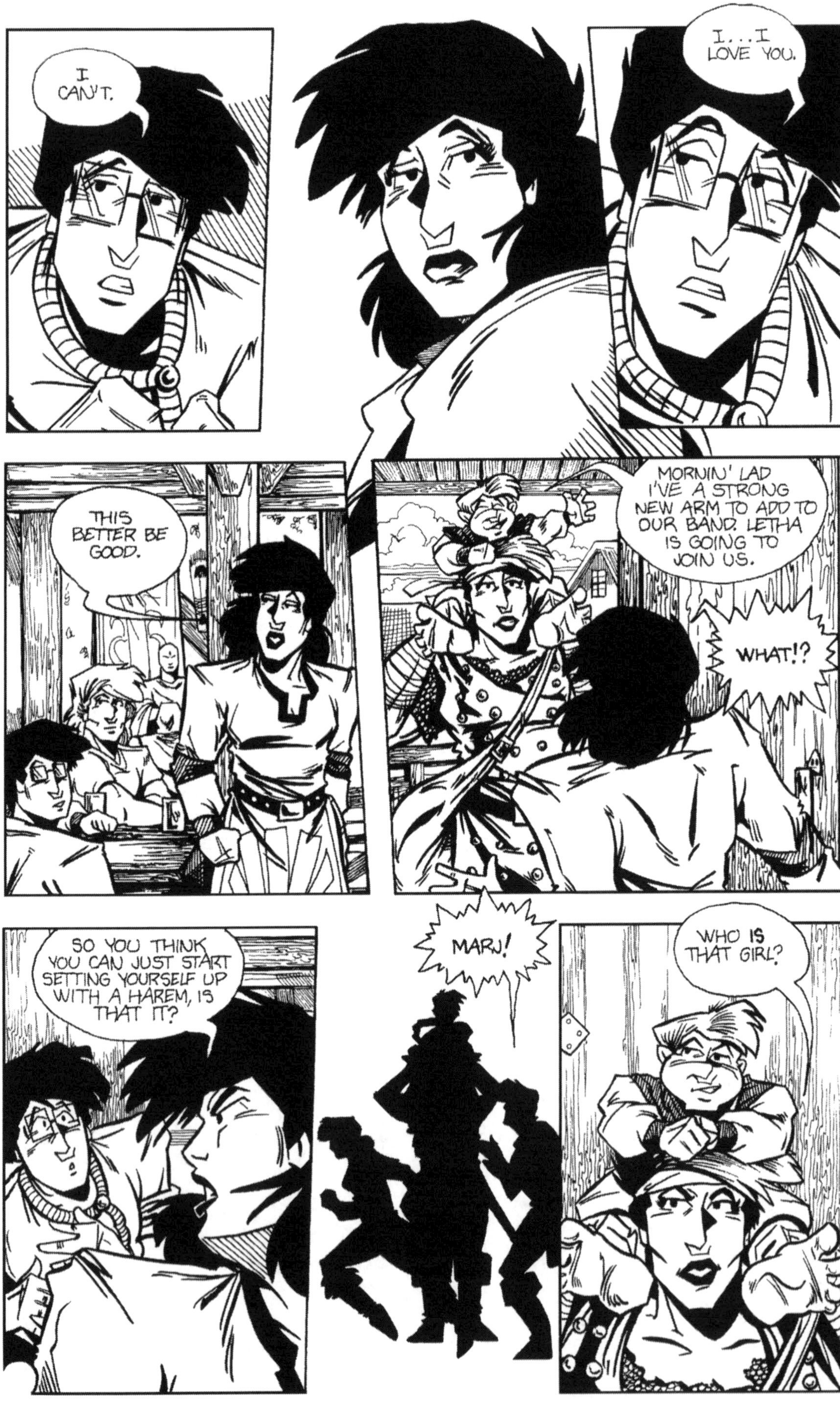
I CAN'T.
I... I LOVE YOU.
THIS BETTER BE GOOD.
MORNIN' LAD I'VE A STRONG NEW ARM TO ADD TO OUR BAND. LETHA IS GOING TO JOIN US.
WHAT!?
SO YOU THINK YOU CAN JUST START SETTING YOURSELF UP WITH A HAREM, IS THAT IT?
MARJ!
WHO IS THAT GIRL?

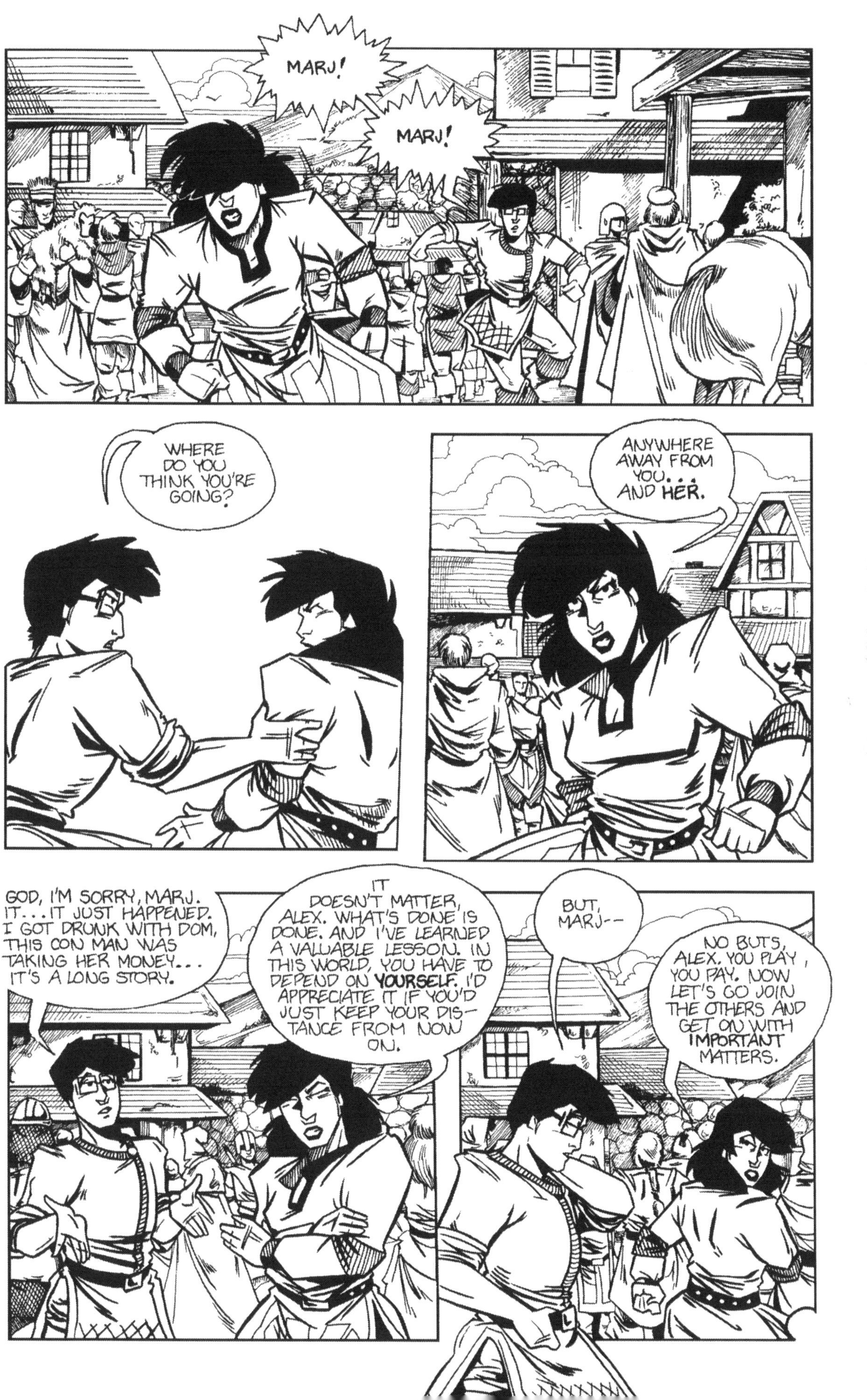
MARJ!
MARJ!
WHERE DO YOU THINK YOU'RE GOING?
ANYWHERE AWAY FROM YOU. . . AND **HER.**
GOD, I'M SORRY, MARJ. IT. . . IT JUST HAPPENED. I GOT DRUNK WITH DOM, THIS CON MAN WAS TAKING HER MONEY. . . IT'S A LONG STORY.
IT DOESN'T MATTER, ALEX. WHAT'S DONE IS DONE. AND I'VE LEARNED A VALUABLE LESSON. IN THIS WORLD, YOU HAVE TO DEPEND ON **YOURSELF**. I'D APPRECIATE IT IF YOU'D JUST KEEP YOUR DISTANCE FROM NOW ON.
BUT, MARJ--
NO BUTS, ALEX. YOU PLAY, YOU PAY. NOW LET'S GO JOIN THE OTHERS AND GET ON WITH **IMPORTANT** MATTERS.

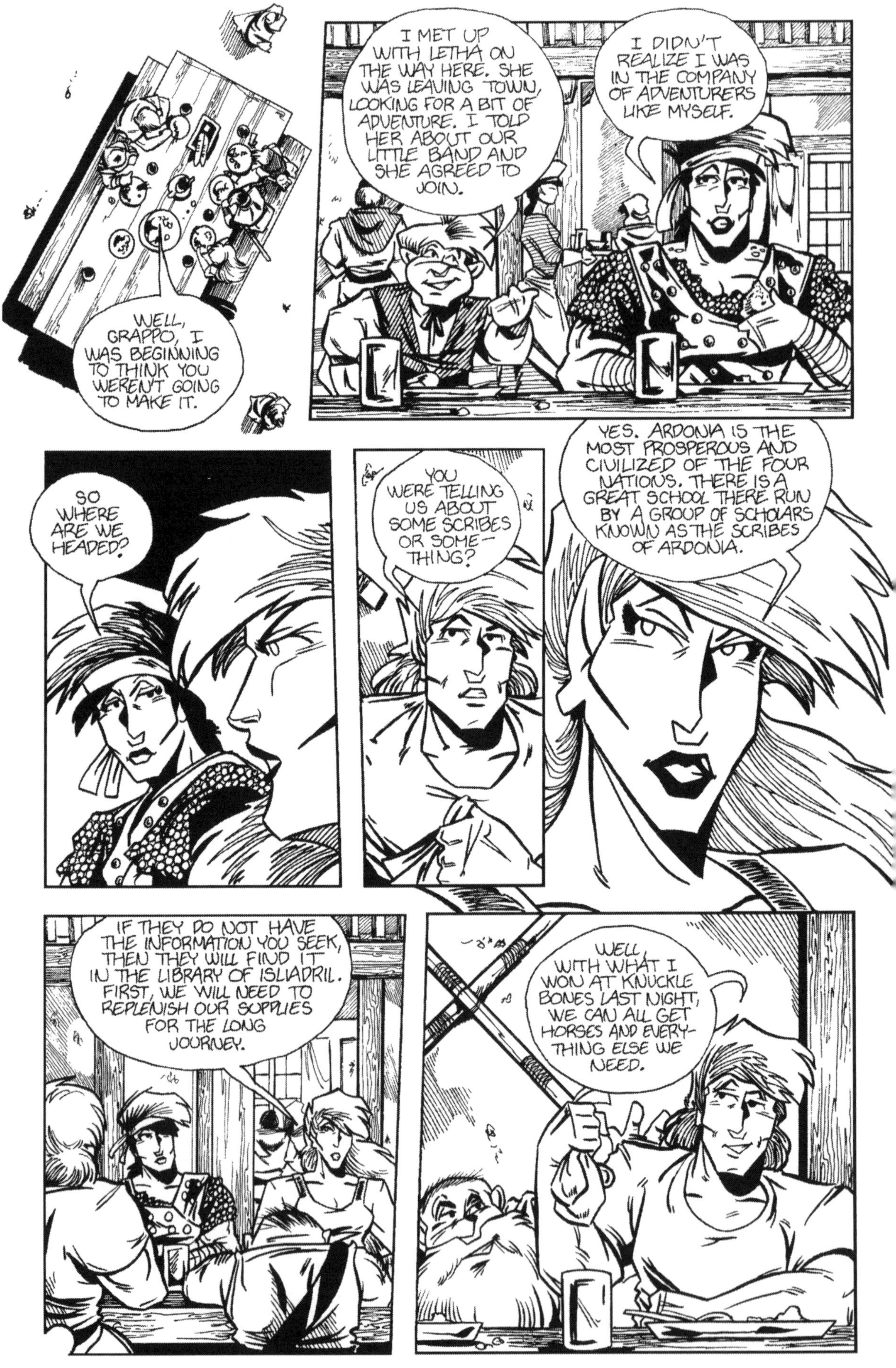
WELL, GRAPPO, I WAS BEGINNING TO THINK YOU WEREN'T GOING TO MAKE IT.
I MET UP WITH LETHA ON THE WAY HERE. SHE WAS LEAVING TOWN, LOOKING FOR A BIT OF ADVENTURE. I TOLD HER ABOUT OUR LITTLE BAND AND SHE AGREED TO JOIN.
I DIDN'T REALIZE I WAS IN THE COMPANY OF ADVENTURERS LIKE MYSELF.
SO WHERE ARE WE HEADED?
YOU WERE TELLING US ABOUT SOME SCRIBES OR SOME-THING?
YES. ARDONIA IS THE MOST PROSPEROUS AND CIVILIZED OF THE FOUR NATIONS. THERE IS A GREAT SCHOOL THERE RUN BY A GROUP OF SCHOLARS KNOWN AS THE SCRIBES OF ARDONIA.
IF THEY DO NOT HAVE THE INFORMATION YOU SEEK, THEN THEY WILL FIND IT IN THE LIBRARY OF ISLIADRIL. FIRST, WE WILL NEED TO REPLENISH OUR SUPPLIES FOR THE LONG JOURNEY.
WELL, WITH WHAT I WON AT KNUCKLE BONES LAST NIGHT, WE CAN ALL GET HORSES AND EVERY-THING ELSE WE NEED.

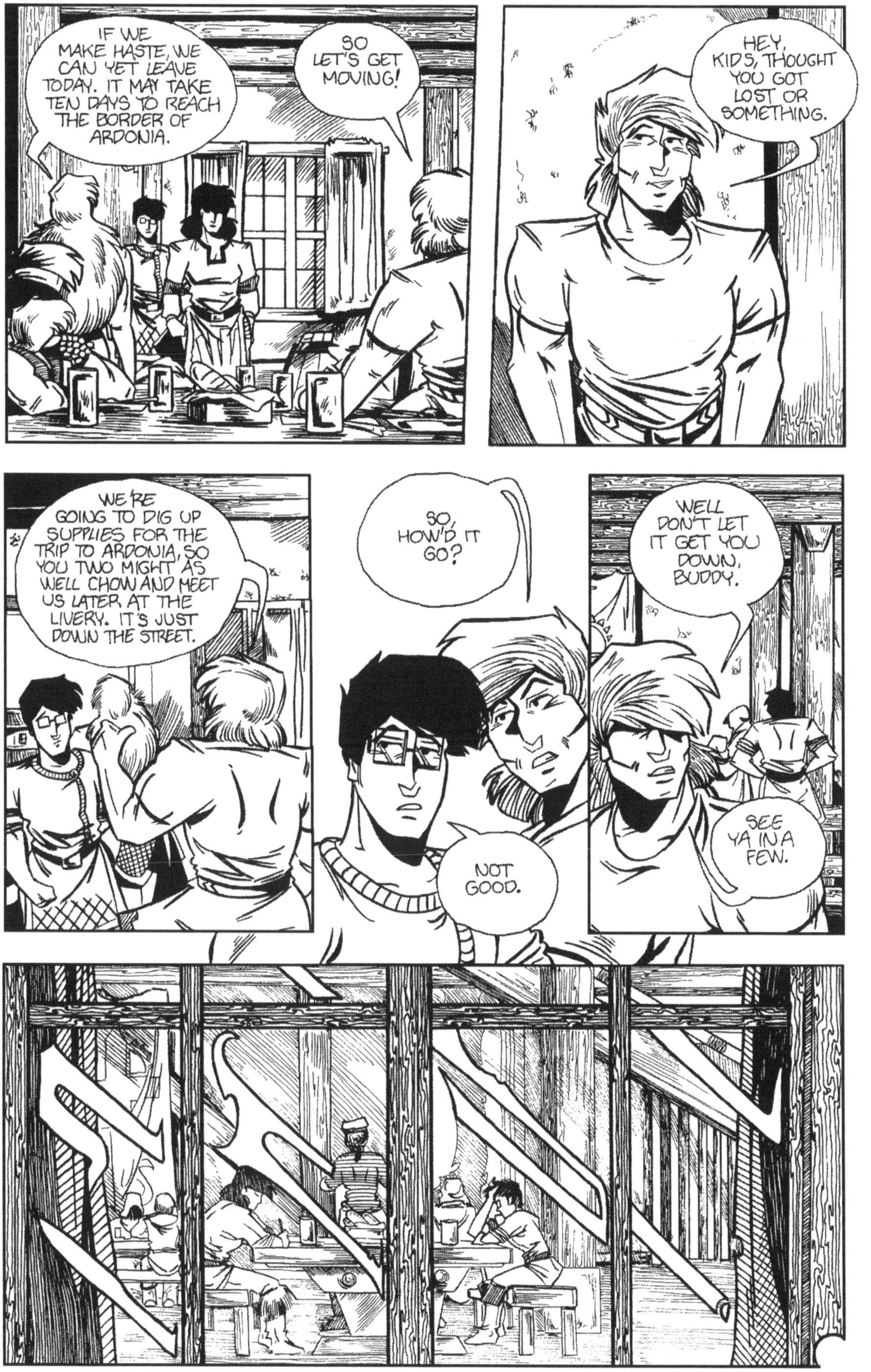
IF WE MAKE HASTE, WE CAN YET LEAVE TODAY. IT MAY TAKE TEN DAYS TO REACH THE BORDER OF ARDONIA.
SO LET'S GET MOVING!
HEY, KIDS, THOUGHT YOU GOT LOST OR SOMETHING.
WE'RE GOING TO DIG UP SUPPLIES FOR THE TRIP TO ARDONIA, SO YOU TWO MIGHT AS WELL CHOW AND MEET US LATER AT THE LIVERY. IT'S JUST DOWN THE STREET.
SO, HOW'D IT GO?
NOT GOOD.
WELL DON'T LET IT GET YOU DOWN, BUDDY.
SEE YA IN A FEW.

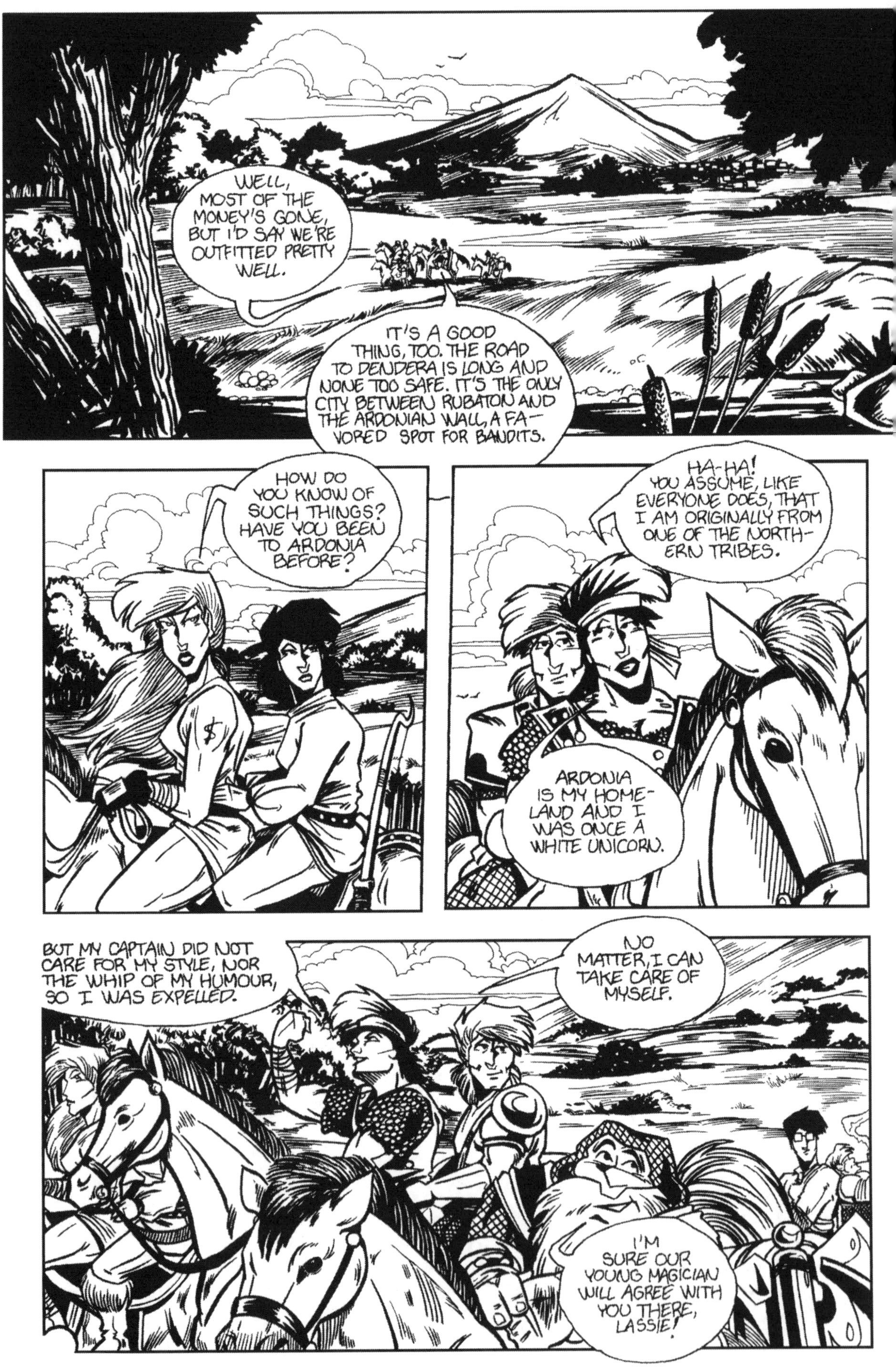
WELL, MOST OF THE MONEY'S GONE, BUT I'D SAY WE'RE OUTFITTED PRETTY WELL.
IT'S A GOOD THING, TOO. THE ROAD TO DENDERA IS LONG AND NONE TOO SAFE. IT'S THE ONLY CITY BETWEEN RUBATON AND THE ARDONIAN WALL, A FA-VORED SPOT FOR BANDITS.
HOW DO YOU KNOW OF SUCH THINGS? HAVE YOU BEEN TO ARDONIA BEFORE?
HA-HA! YOU ASSUME, LIKE EVERYONE DOES, THAT I AM ORIGINALLY FROM ONE OF THE NORTH-ERN TRIBES.
ARDONIA IS MY HOME-LAND AND I WAS ONCE A WHITE UNICORN.
BUT MY CAPTAIN DID NOT CARE FOR MY STYLE, NOR THE WHIP OF MY HUMOUR, SO I WAS EXPELLED.
NO MATTER, I CAN TAKE CARE OF MYSELF.
I'M SURE OUR YOUNG MAGICIAN WILL AGREE WITH YOU THERE, LASSIE!

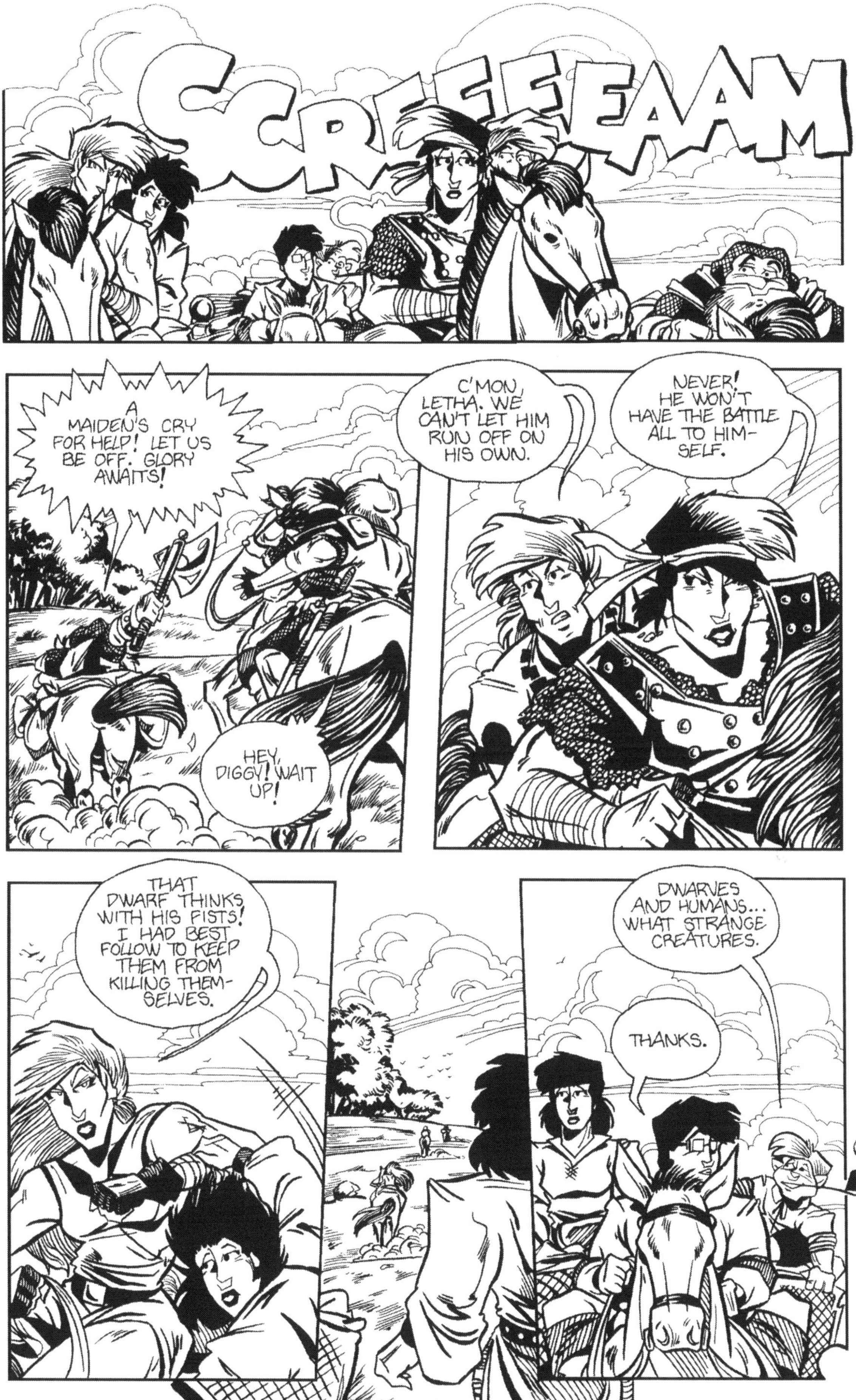
SCREEEAAM
A MAIDEN'S CRY FOR HELP! LET US BE OFF. GLORY AWAITS!
HEY, DIGGY! WAIT UP!
C'MON, LETHA. WE CAN'T LET HIM RUN OFF ON HIS OWN.
NEVER! HE WON'T HAVE THE BATTLE ALL TO HIM-SELF.
THAT DWARF THINKS WITH HIS FISTS! I HAD BEST FOLLOW TO KEEP THEM FROM KILLING THEM-SELVES.
DWARVES AND HUMANS... WHAT STRANGE CREATURES.
THANKS.

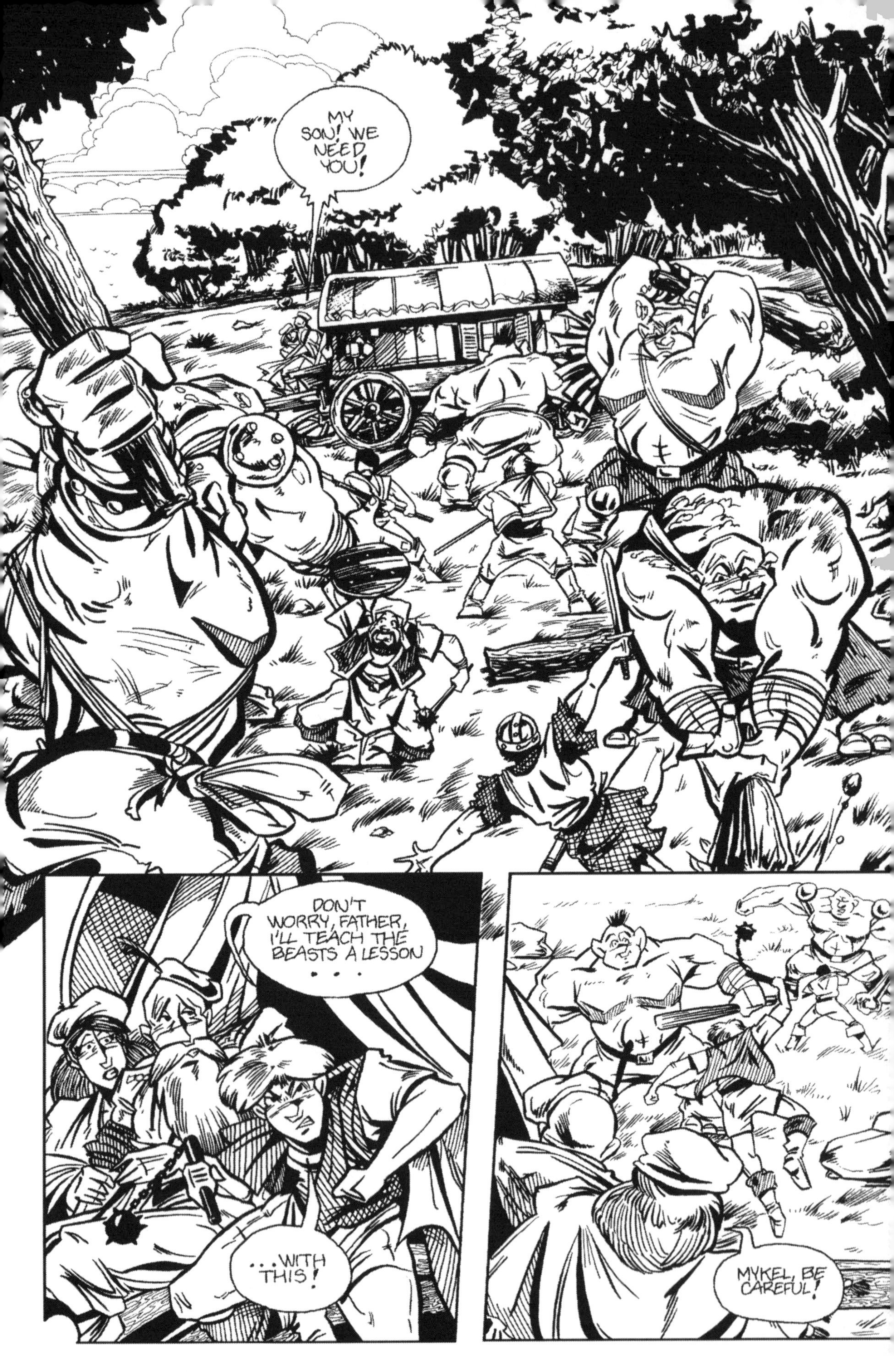
MY SON! WE NEED YOU!
DON'T WORRY, FATHER, I'LL TEACH THE BEASTS A LESSON . . .
. . . WITH THIS!
MYKEL, BE CAREFUL!

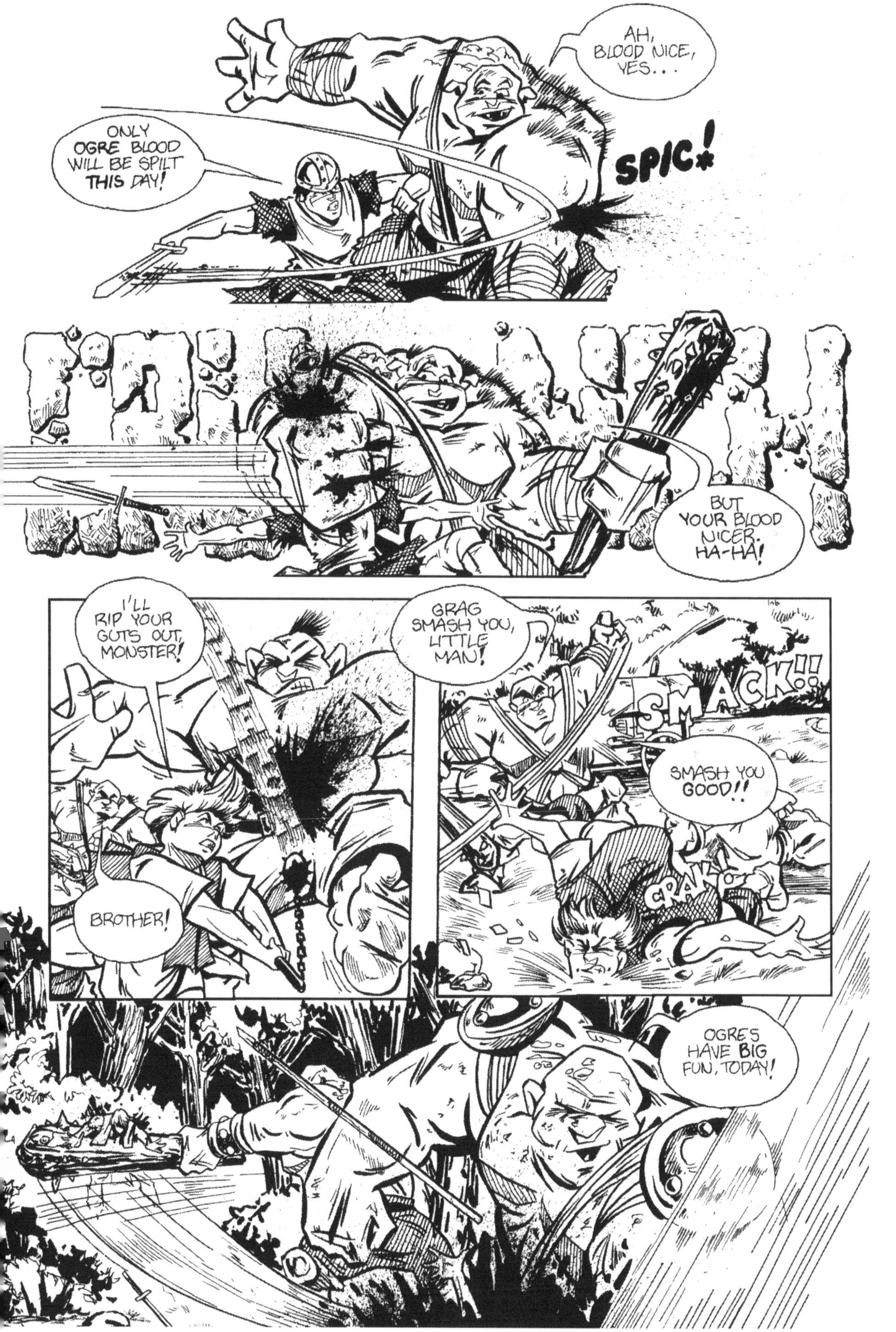
AH, BLOOD NICE, YES...
ONLY OGRE BLOOD WILL BE SPILT THIS DAY!
SPIC*!
BUT YOUR BLOOD NICER. HA-HA!
I'LL RIP YOUR GUTS OUT, MONSTER!
BROTHER!
GRAG SMASH YOU, LITTLE MAN!
SMACK!!
SMASH YOU GOOD!!
OGRES HAVE BIG FUN, TODAY!

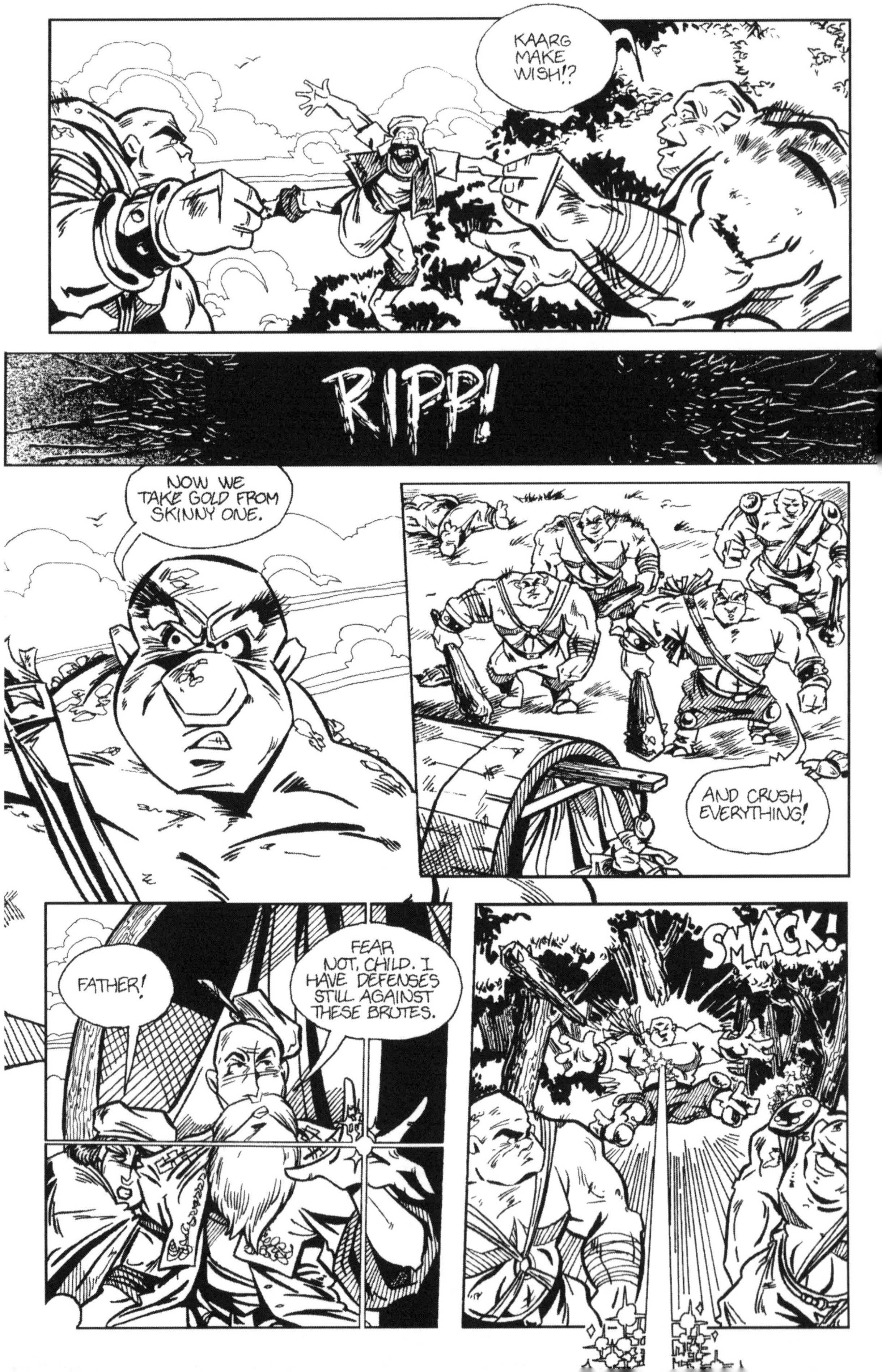
KAARG MAKE WISH!?
RIPP!
NOW WE TAKE GOLD FROM SKINNY ONE.
AND CRUSH EVERYTHING!
FATHER!
FEAR NOT, CHILD. I HAVE DEFENSES STILL AGAINST THESE BRUTES.
SMACK!

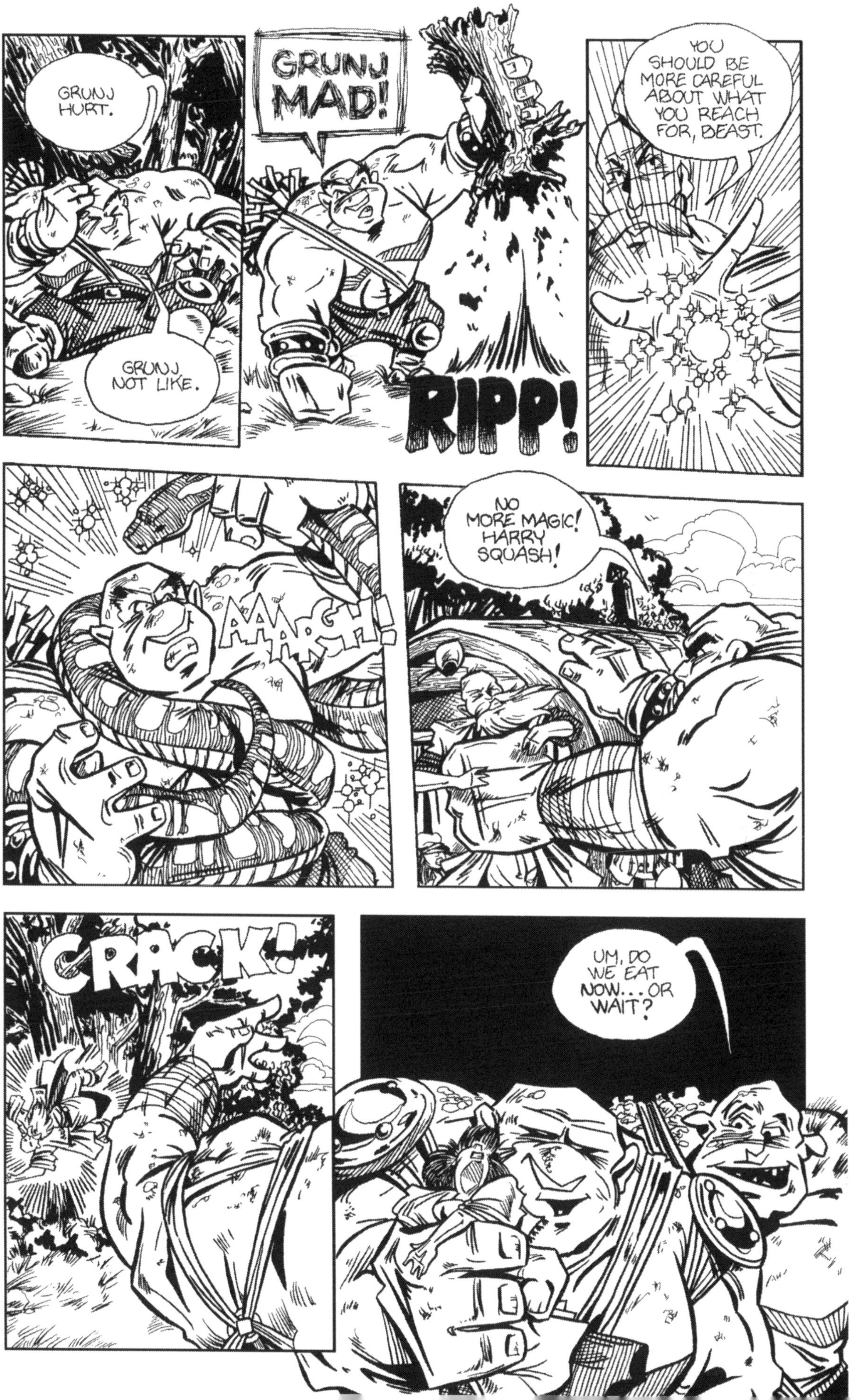
GRUNJ HURT.
GRUNJ NOT LIKE.
GRUNJ MAD!
RIPP!
YOU SHOULD BE MORE CAREFUL ABOUT WHAT YOU REACH FOR, BEAST.
AAARGH!
NO MORE MAGIC! HARRY SQUASH!
CRACK!
UM, DO WE EAT NOW... OR WAIT?

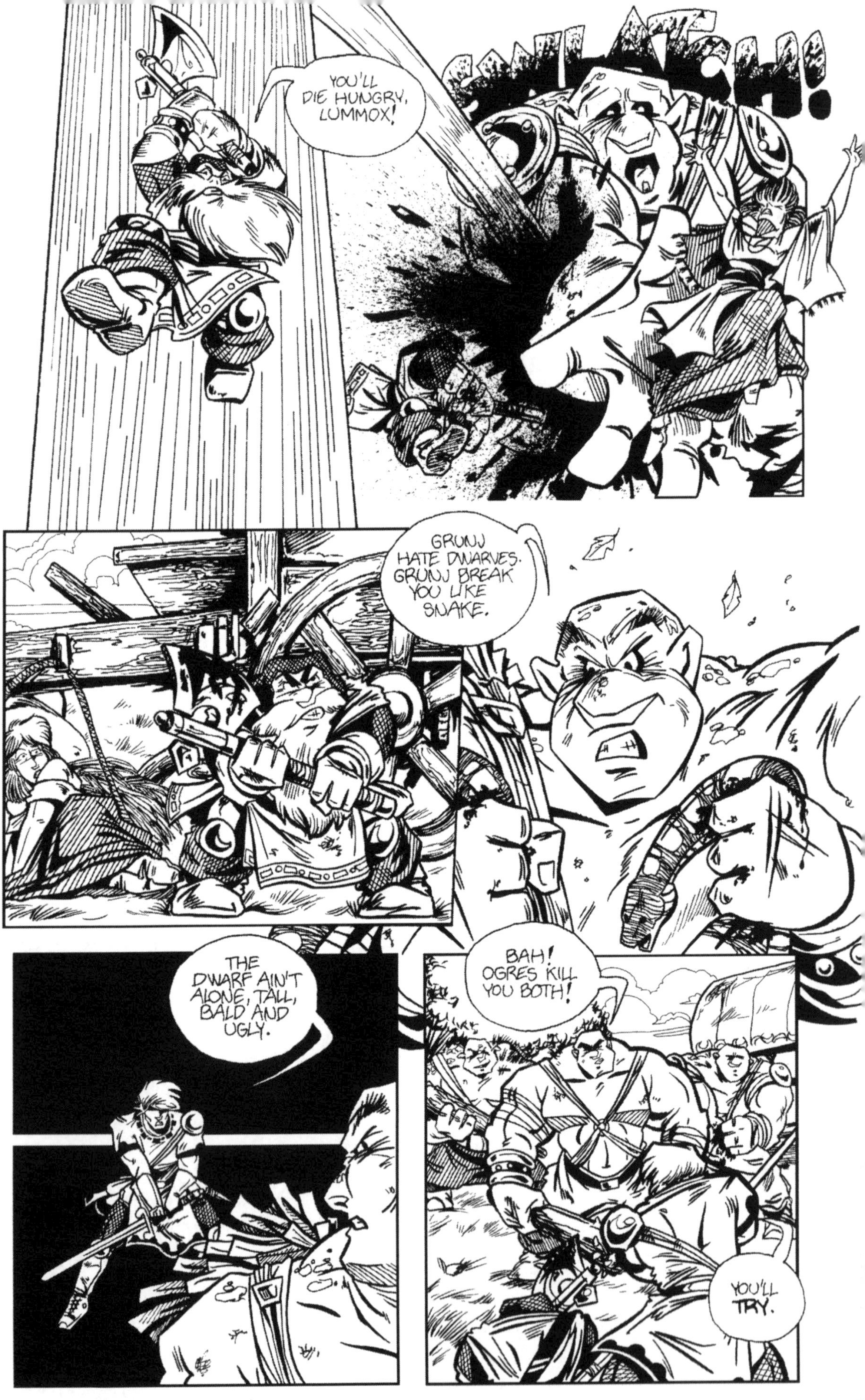
YOU'LL DIE HUNGRY, LUMMOX!
GRUNJ HATE DWARVES. GRUNJ BREAK YOU LIKE SNAKE.
THE DWARF AIN'T ALONE, TALL, BALD AND UGLY.
BAH! OGRES KILL YOU BOTH!
YOU'LL TRY.

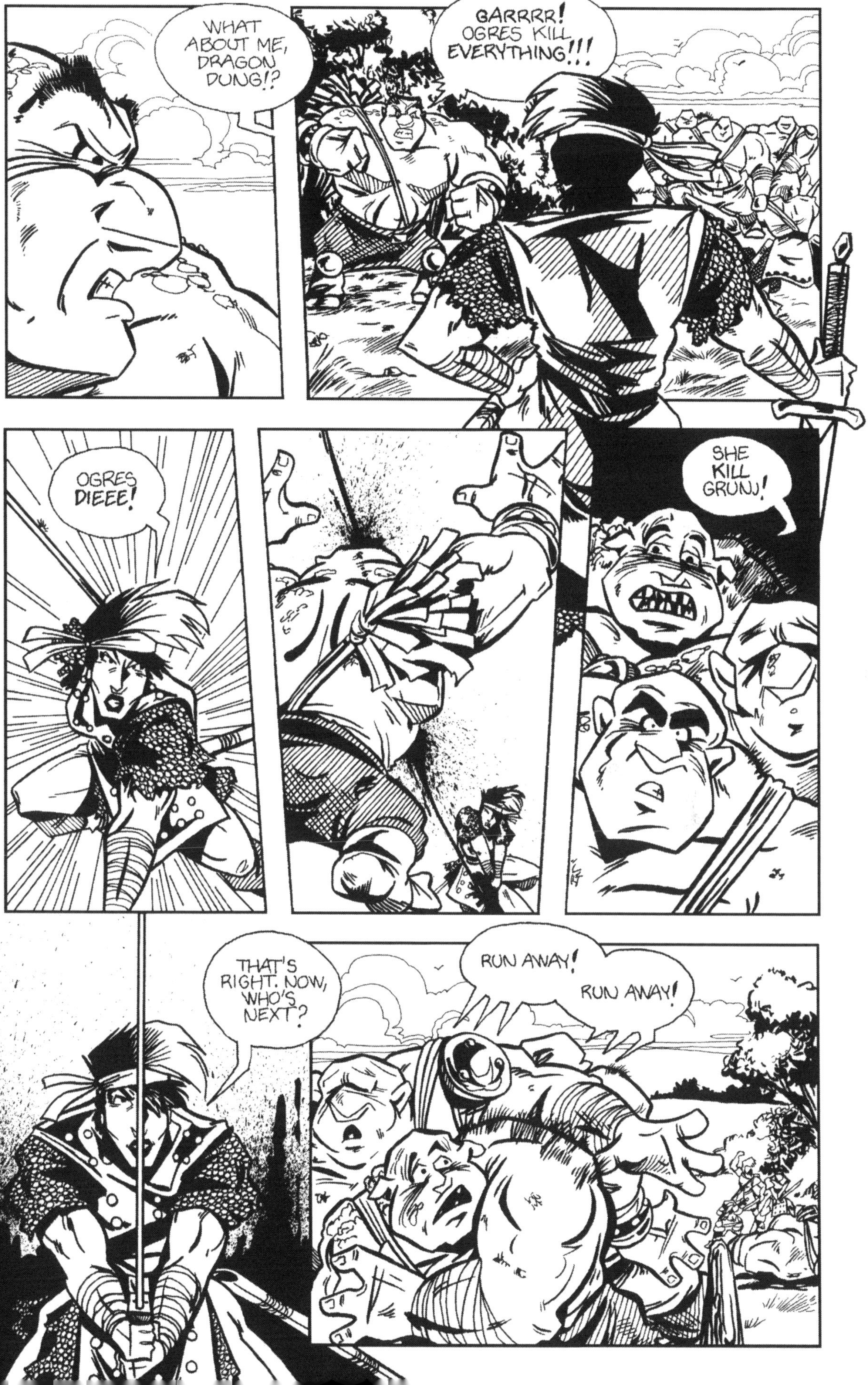
WHAT ABOUT ME, DRAGON DUNG!?
GARRRR! OGRES KILL EVERYTHING!!!
OGRES DIEEE!
SHE KILL GRUNJ!
THAT'S RIGHT. NOW, WHO'S NEXT?
RUN AWAY!
RUN AWAY!

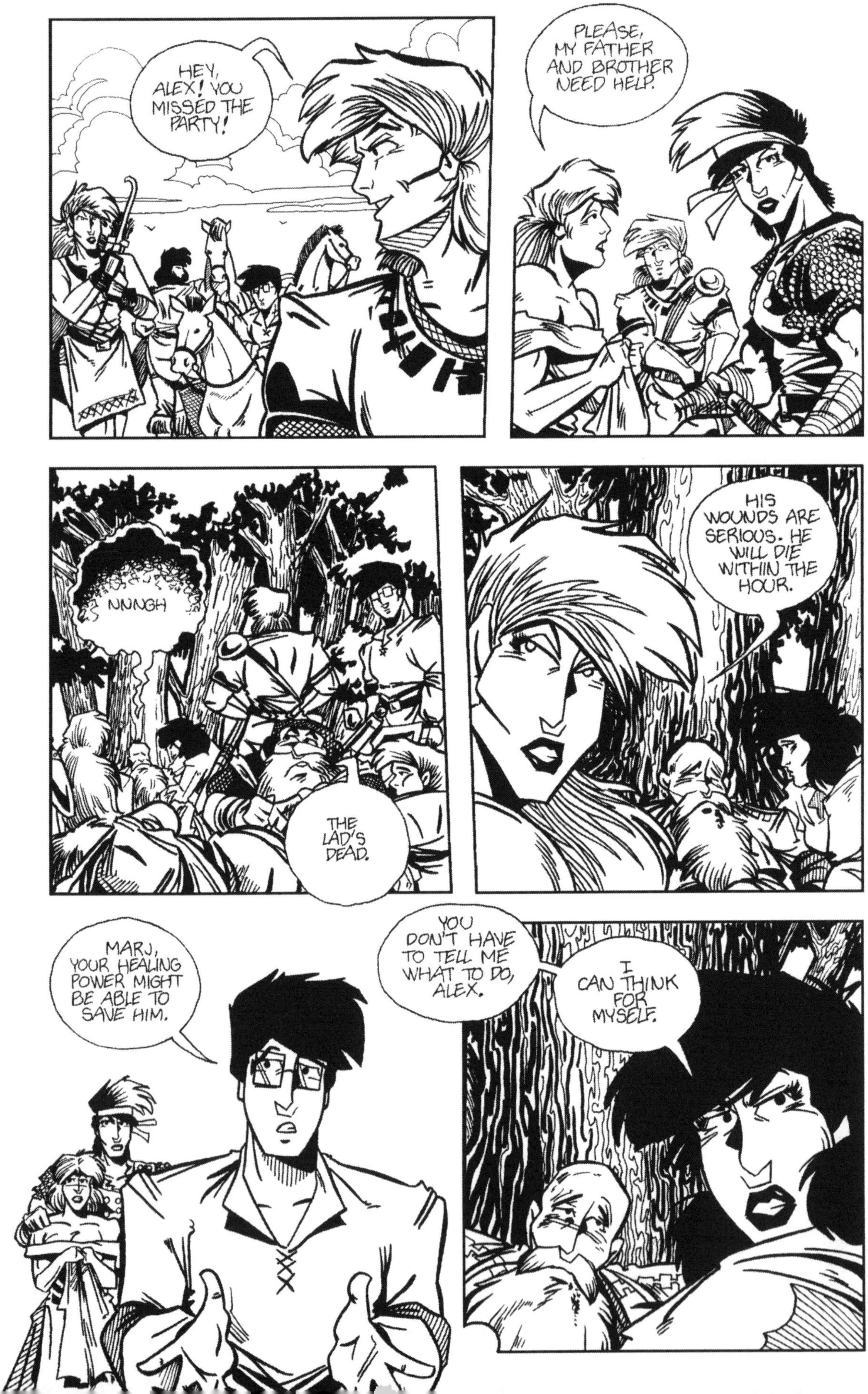
HEY, ALEX! YOU MISSED THE PARTY!
PLEASE, MY FATHER AND BROTHER NEED HELP.
NNNGH
THE LAD'S DEAD.
HIS WOUNDS ARE SERIOUS. HE WILL DIE WITHIN THE HOUR.
MARJ, YOUR HEALING POWER MIGHT BE ABLE TO SAVE HIM.
YOU DON'T HAVE TO TELL ME WHAT TO DO, ALEX.
I CAN THINK FOR MYSELF.

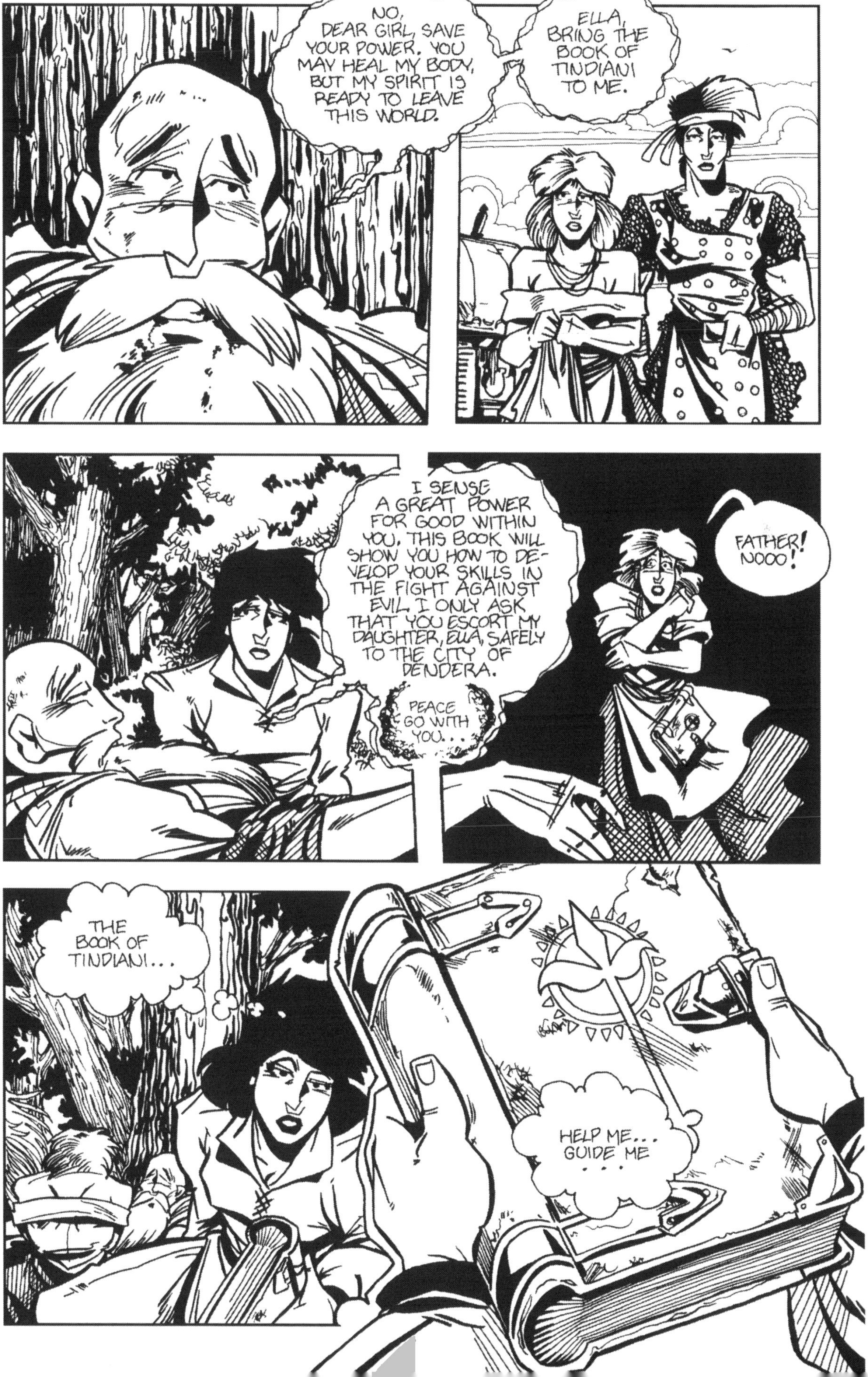
NO, DEAR GIRL, SAVE YOUR POWER. YOU MAY HEAL MY BODY, BUT MY SPIRIT IS READY TO LEAVE THIS WORLD.
ELLA, BRING THE BOOK OF TINDIANI TO ME.
I SENSE A GREAT POWER FOR GOOD WITHIN YOU. THIS BOOK WILL SHOW YOU HOW TO DEVELOP YOUR SKILLS IN THE FIGHT AGAINST EVIL. I ONLY ASK THAT YOU ESCORT MY DAUGHTER, ELLA, SAFELY TO THE CITY OF DENDERA.
PEACE GO WITH YOU...
FATHER! NOOO!
THE BOOK OF TINDIANI...
HELP ME... GUIDE ME ...

LEGENDLORE

THE REALM - VOLUME ONE

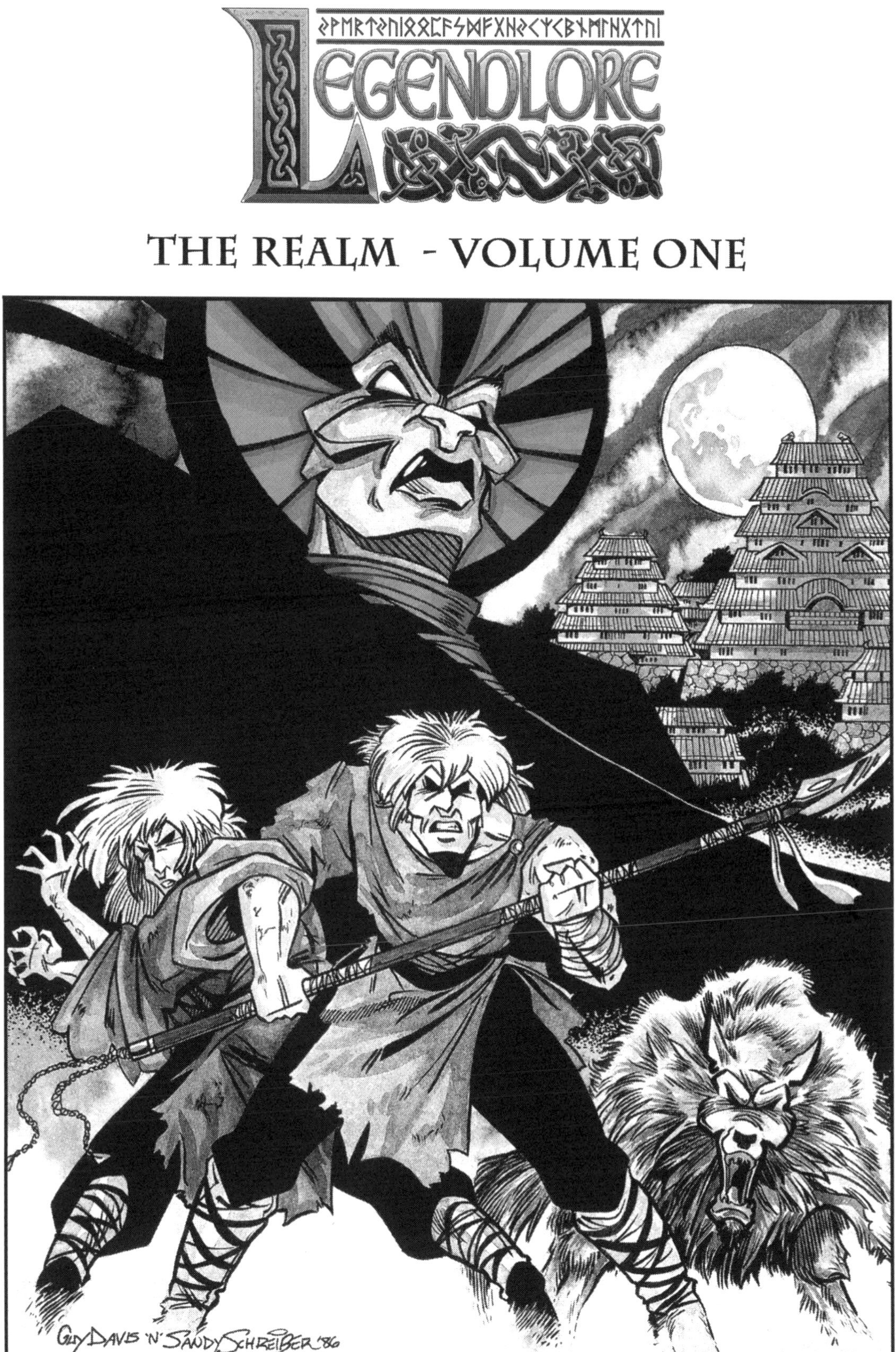
GUY DAVIS 'N' SANDY SCHREIBER '86

ISSUE SEVEN

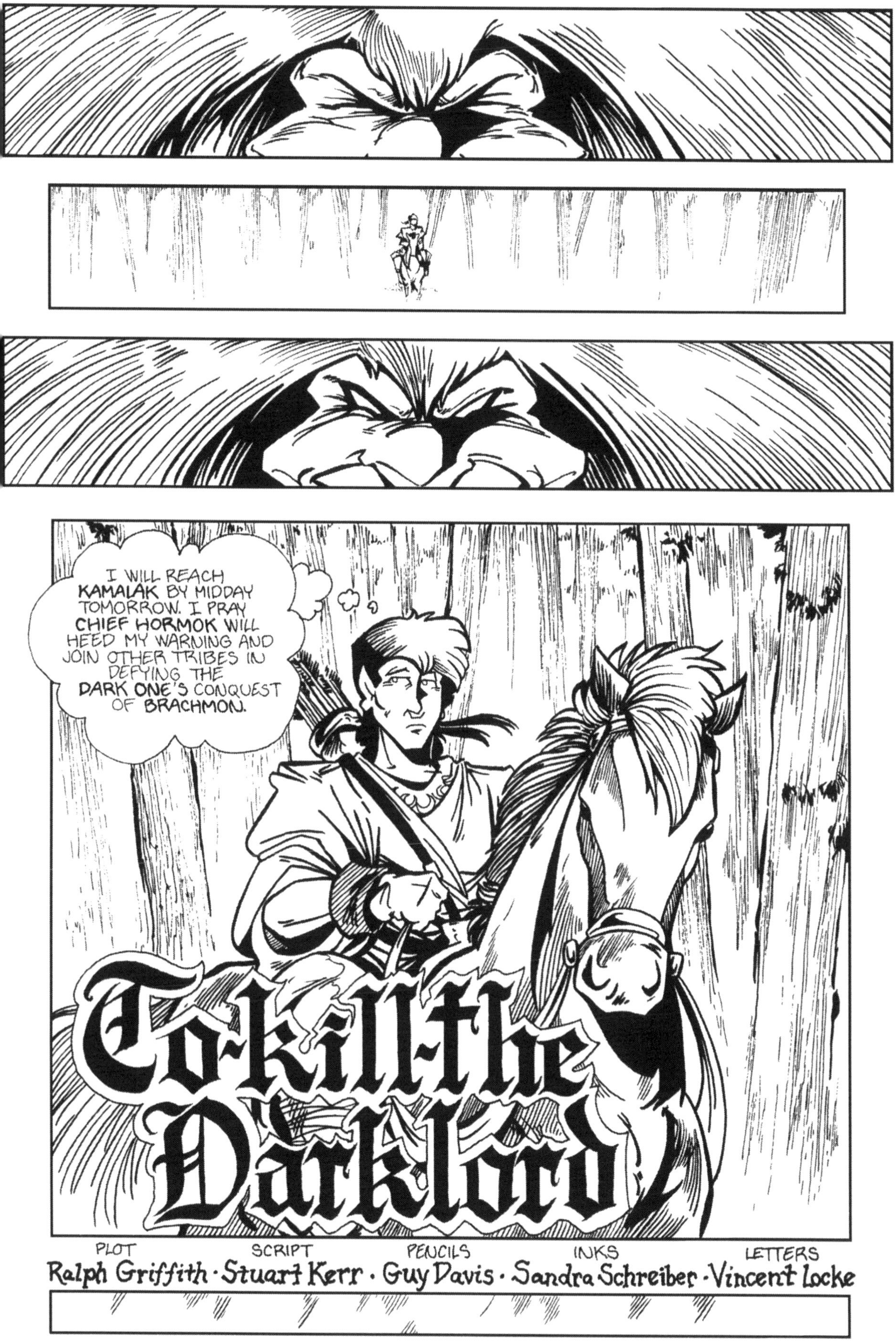
I WILL REACH KAMALAK BY MIDDAY TOMORROW. I PRAY CHIEF HORMOK WILL HEED MY WARNING AND JOIN OTHER TRIBES IN DEFYING THE DARK ONE'S CONQUEST OF BRACHMON.
To Kill the Darklord
PLOT Ralph Griffith · SCRIPT Stuart Kerr · PENCILS Guy Davis · INKS Sandra Schreiber · LETTERS Vincent Locke

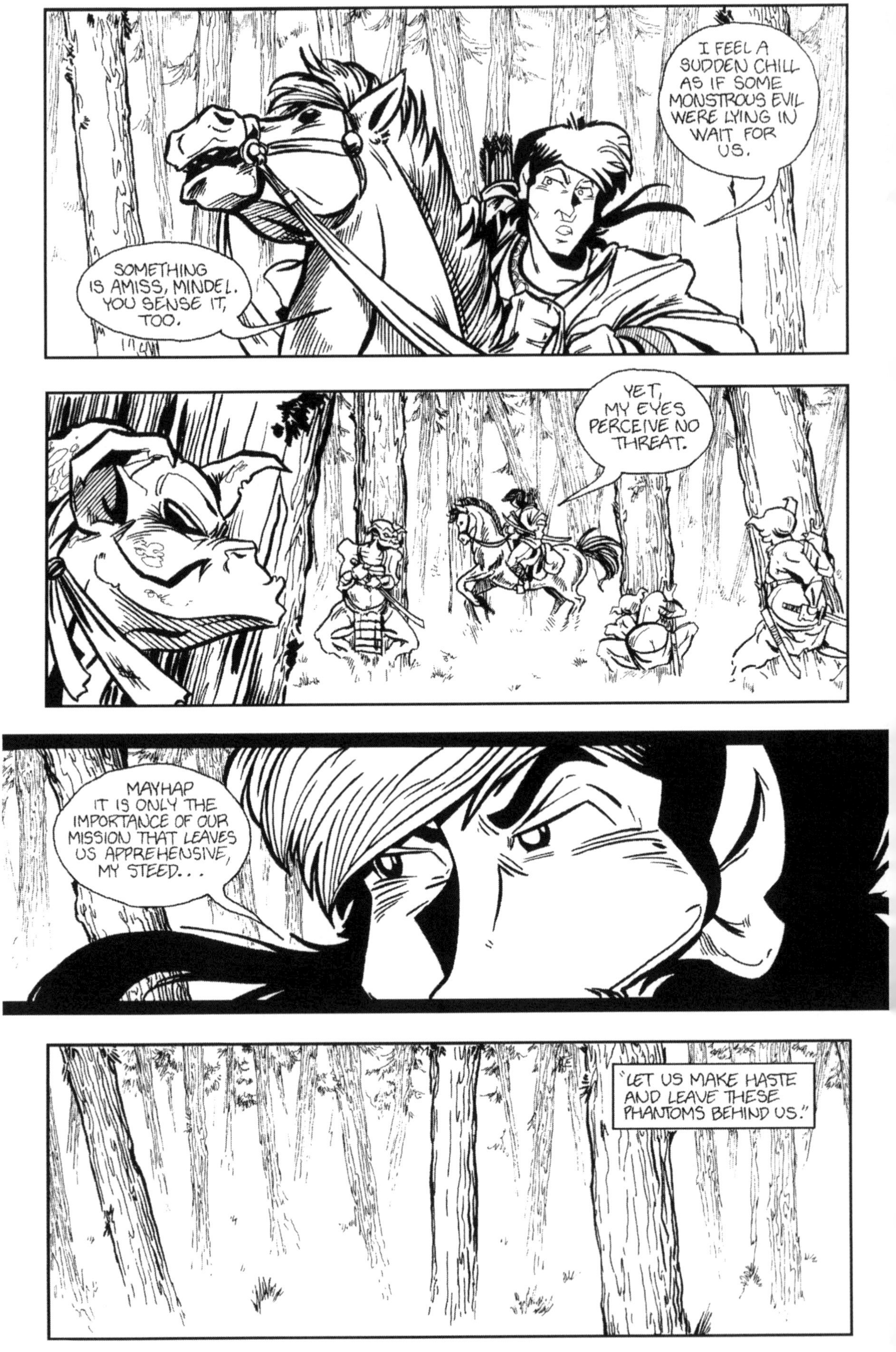
I FEEL A SUDDEN CHILL AS IF SOME MONSTROUS EVIL WERE LYING IN WAIT FOR US.
SOMETHING IS AMISS, MINDEL. YOU SENSE IT, TOO.
YET, MY EYES PERCEIVE NO THREAT.
MAYHAP IT IS ONLY THE IMPORTANCE OF OUR MISSION THAT LEAVES US APPREHENSIVE, MY STEED...
"LET US MAKE HASTE AND LEAVE THESE PHANTOMS BEHIND US."

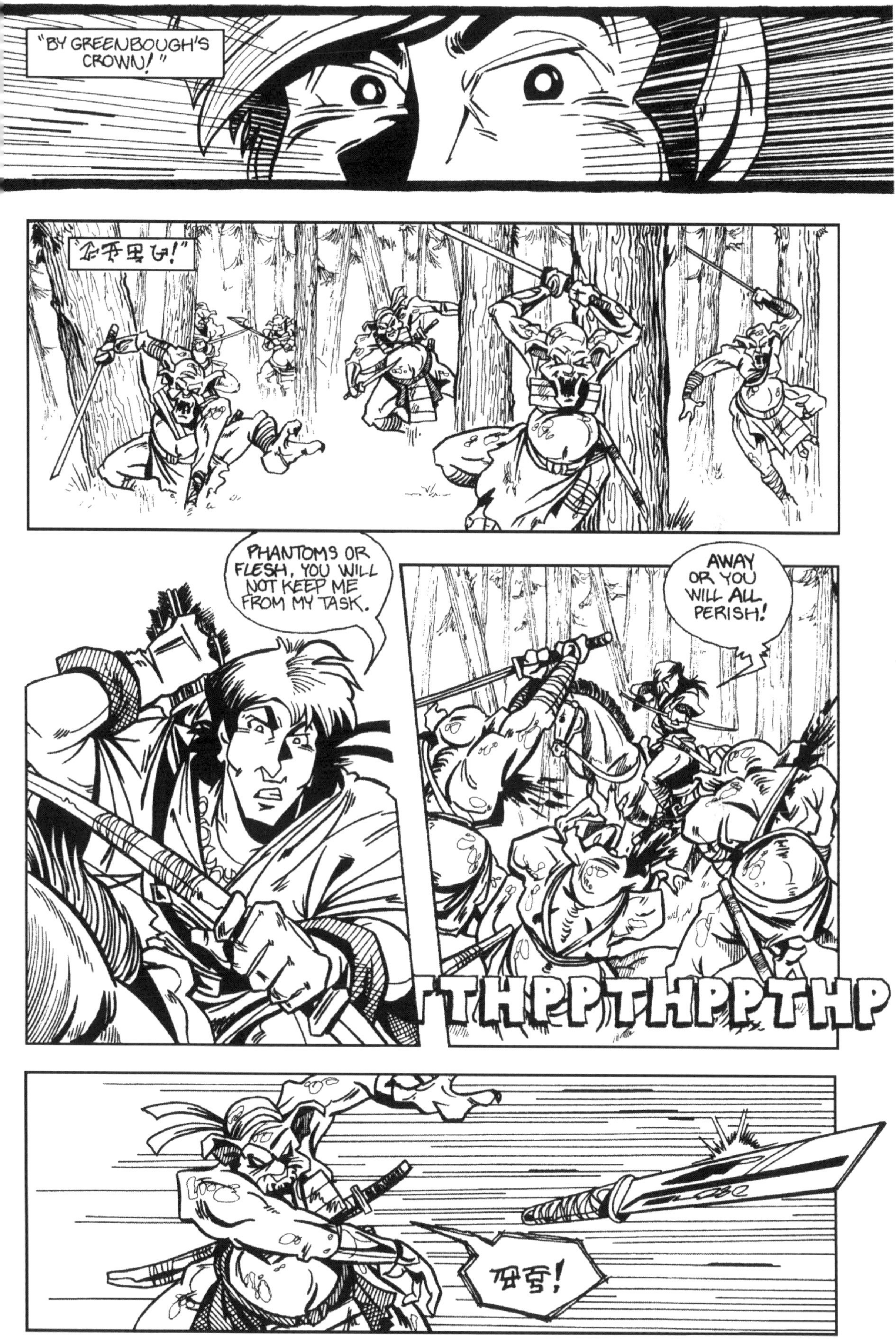
"BY GREENBOUGH'S CROWN!"
PHANTOMS OR FLESH, YOU WILL NOT KEEP ME FROM MY TASK.
AWAY OR YOU WILL ALL PERISH!
THPPTHPPTHP

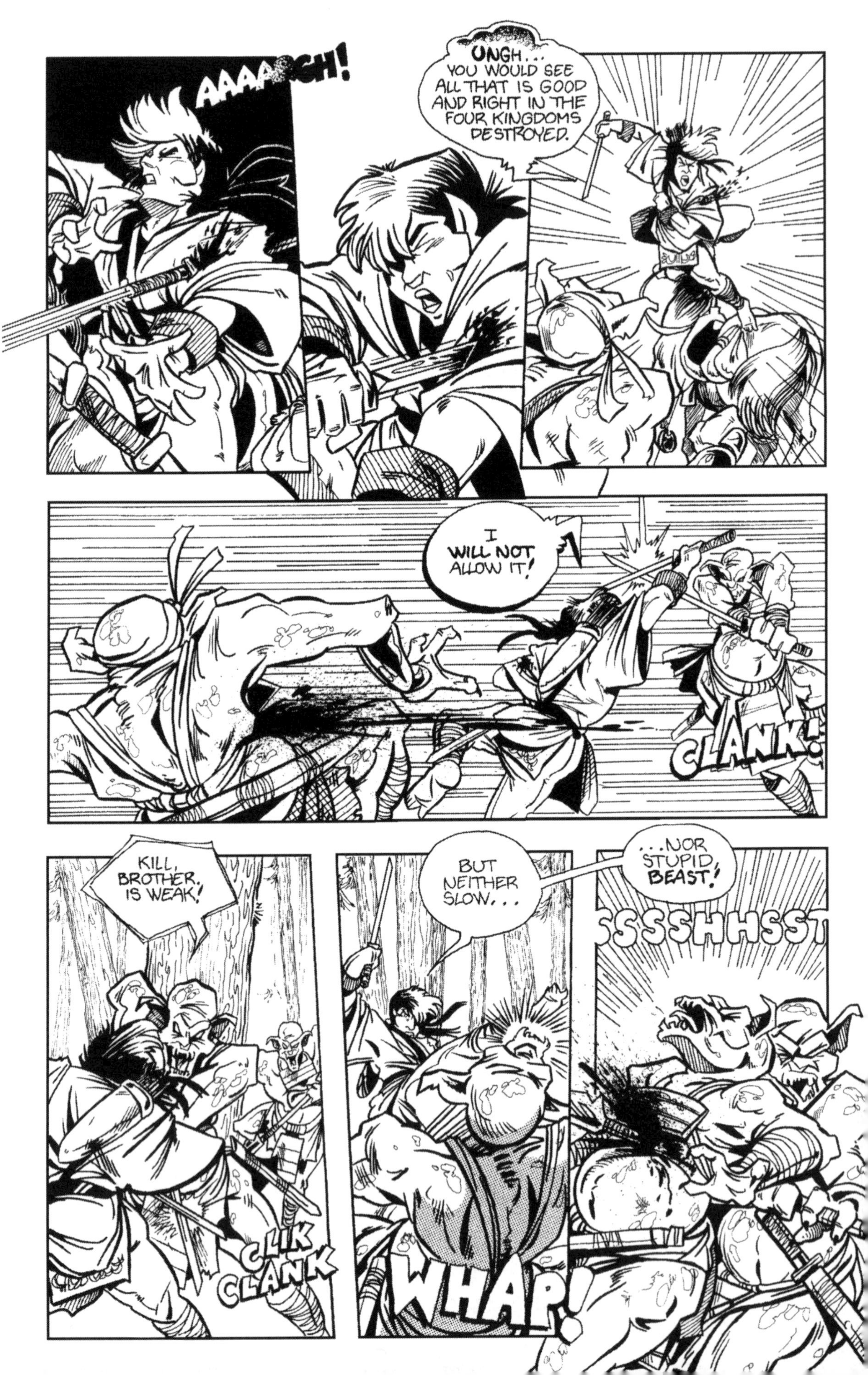
AAAARGH!
UNGH... YOU WOULD SEE ALL THAT IS GOOD AND RIGHT IN THE FOUR KINGDOMS DESTROYED.
I WILL NOT ALLOW IT!
CLANK!
KILL, BROTHER. IS WEAK!
CLIK CLANK
BUT NEITHER SLOW...
...NOR STUPID BEAST!
SSSSHHSST
WHAP!

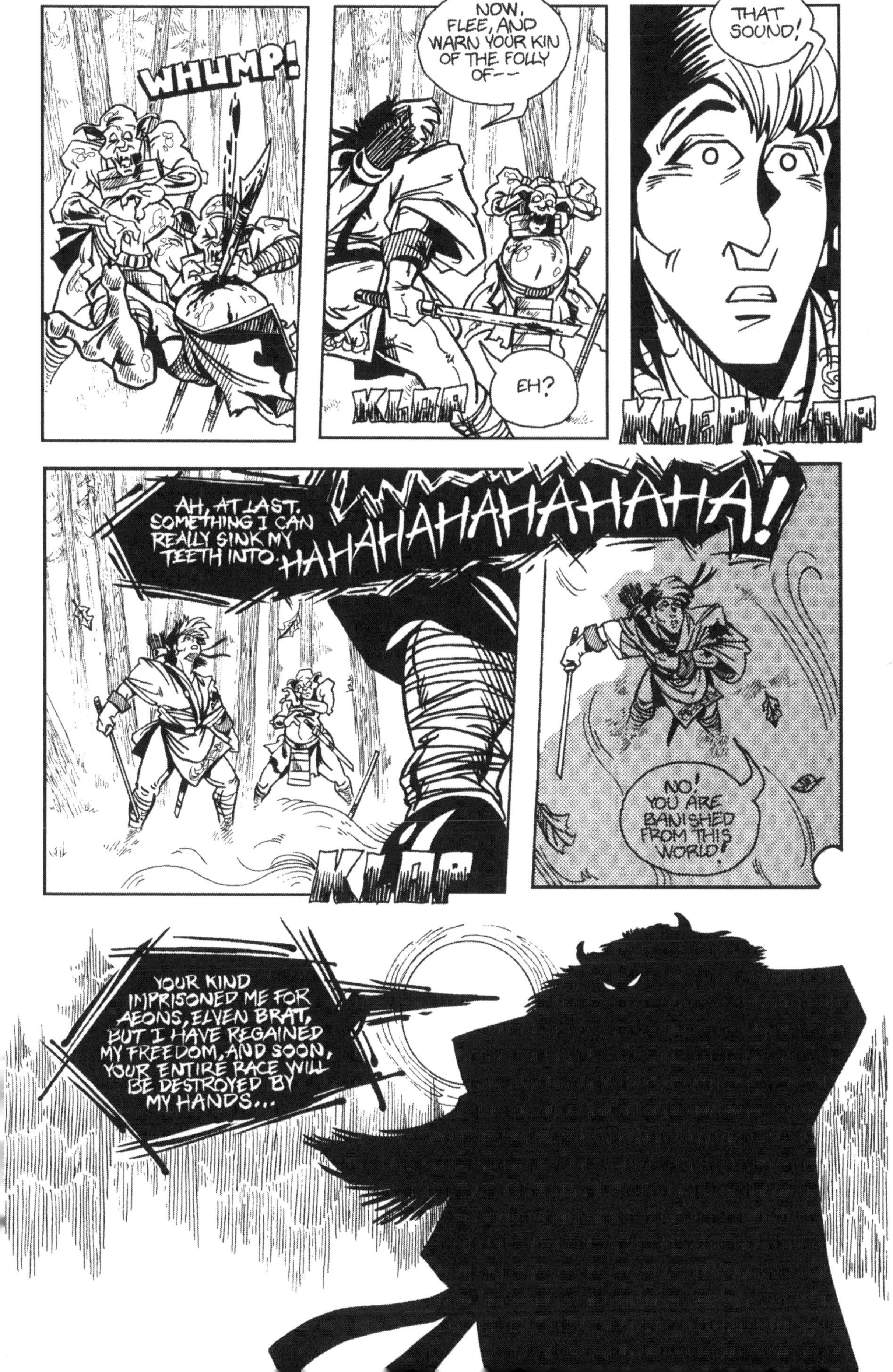
WHUMP!
NOW, FLEE, AND WARN YOUR KIN OF THE FOLLY OF--
KLAP
EH?
THAT SOUND!
KLEPKLAP
AH, AT LAST. SOMETHING I CAN REALLY SINK MY TEETH INTO.
HAHAHAHAHAHAHA!
KLAP
NO! YOU ARE BANISHED FROM THIS WORLD!
YOUR KIND IMPRISONED ME FOR AEONS, ELVEN BRAT, BUT I HAVE REGAINED MY FREEDOM, AND SOON, YOUR ENTIRE RACE WILL BE DESTROYED BY MY HANDS...

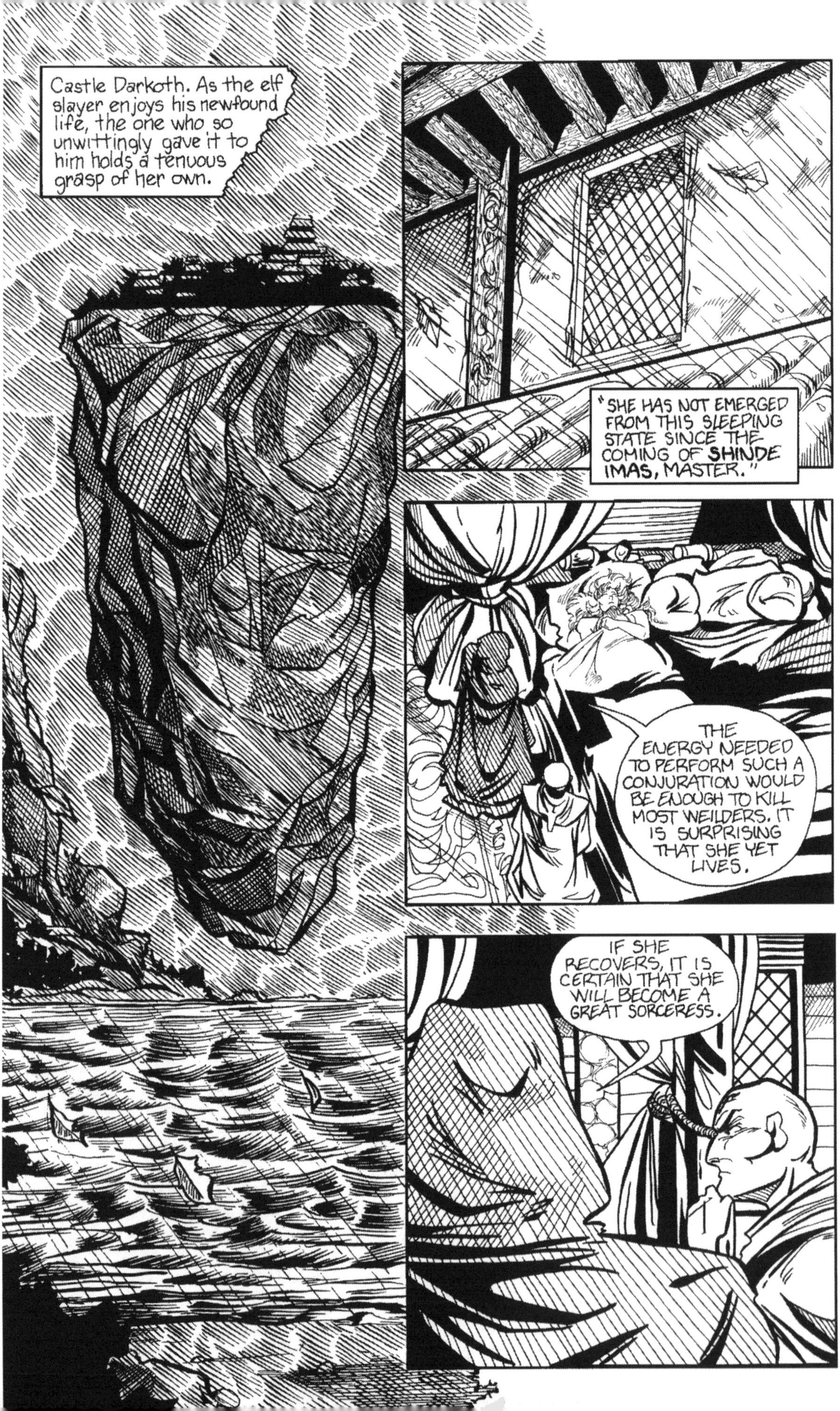
Castle Darkoth. As the elf slayer enjoys his newfound life, the one who so unwittingly gave it to him holds a tenuous grasp of her own.
"SHE HAS NOT EMERGED FROM THIS SLEEPING STATE SINCE THE COMING OF SHINDE IMAS, MASTER."
THE ENERGY NEEDED TO PERFORM SUCH A CONJURATION WOULD BE ENOUGH TO KILL MOST WEILDERS. IT IS SURPRISING THAT SHE YET LIVES.
IF SHE RECOVERS, IT IS CERTAIN THAT SHE WILL BECOME A GREAT SORCERESS.

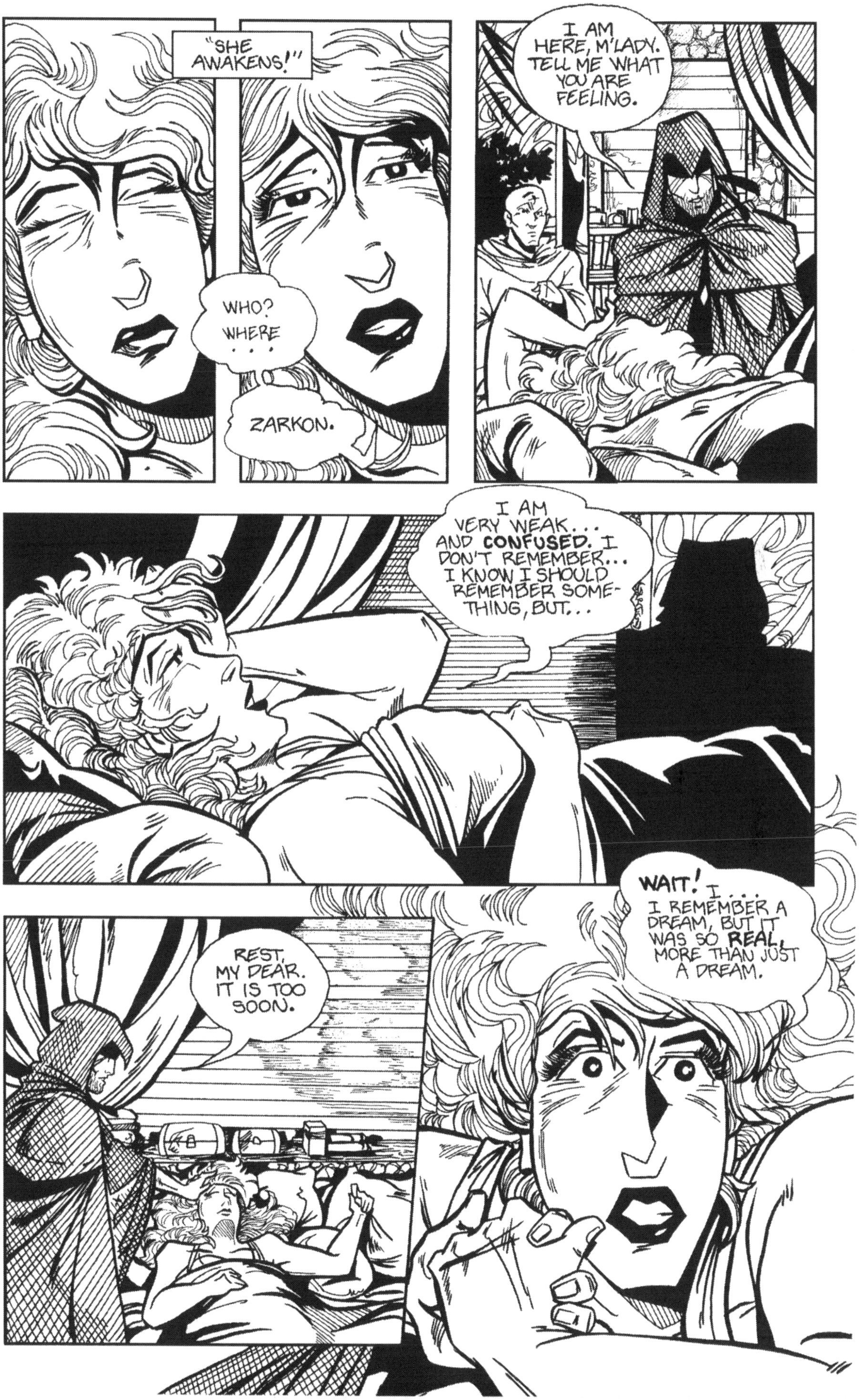
"SHE AWAKENS!"
WHO? WHERE . . .
ZARKON.
I AM HERE, M'LADY. TELL ME WHAT YOU ARE FEELING.
I AM VERY WEAK... AND **CONFUSED**. I DON'T REMEMBER... I KNOW I SHOULD REMEMBER SOME-THING, BUT...
REST, MY DEAR. IT IS TOO SOON.
WAIT! I . . . I REMEMBER A DREAM, BUT IT WAS SO **REAL**, MORE THAN JUST A DREAM.

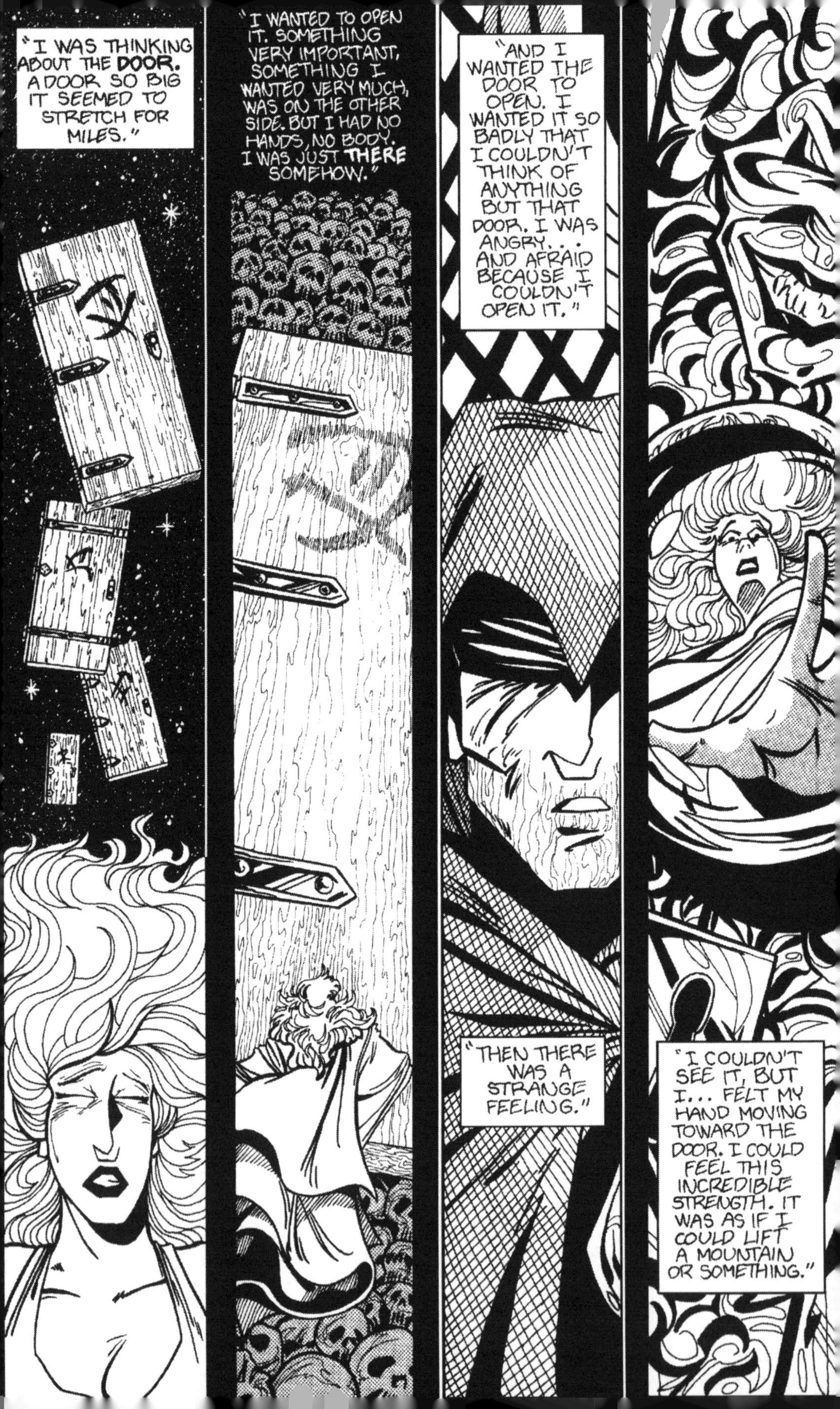
"I WAS THINKING ABOUT THE DOOR. A DOOR SO BIG IT SEEMED TO STRETCH FOR MILES."
"I WANTED TO OPEN IT. SOMETHING VERY IMPORTANT, SOMETHING I WANTED VERY MUCH, WAS ON THE OTHER SIDE. BUT I HAD NO HANDS, NO BODY. I WAS JUST THERE SOMEHOW."
"AND I WANTED THE DOOR TO OPEN. I WANTED IT SO BADLY THAT I COULDN'T THINK OF ANYTHING BUT THAT DOOR. I WAS ANGRY. . . AND AFRAID BECAUSE I COULDN'T OPEN IT."
"THEN THERE WAS A STRANGE FEELING."
"I COULDN'T SEE IT, BUT I... FELT MY HAND MOVING TOWARD THE DOOR. I COULD FEEL THIS INCREDIBLE STRENGTH. IT WAS AS IF I COULD LIFT A MOUNTAIN OR SOMETHING."

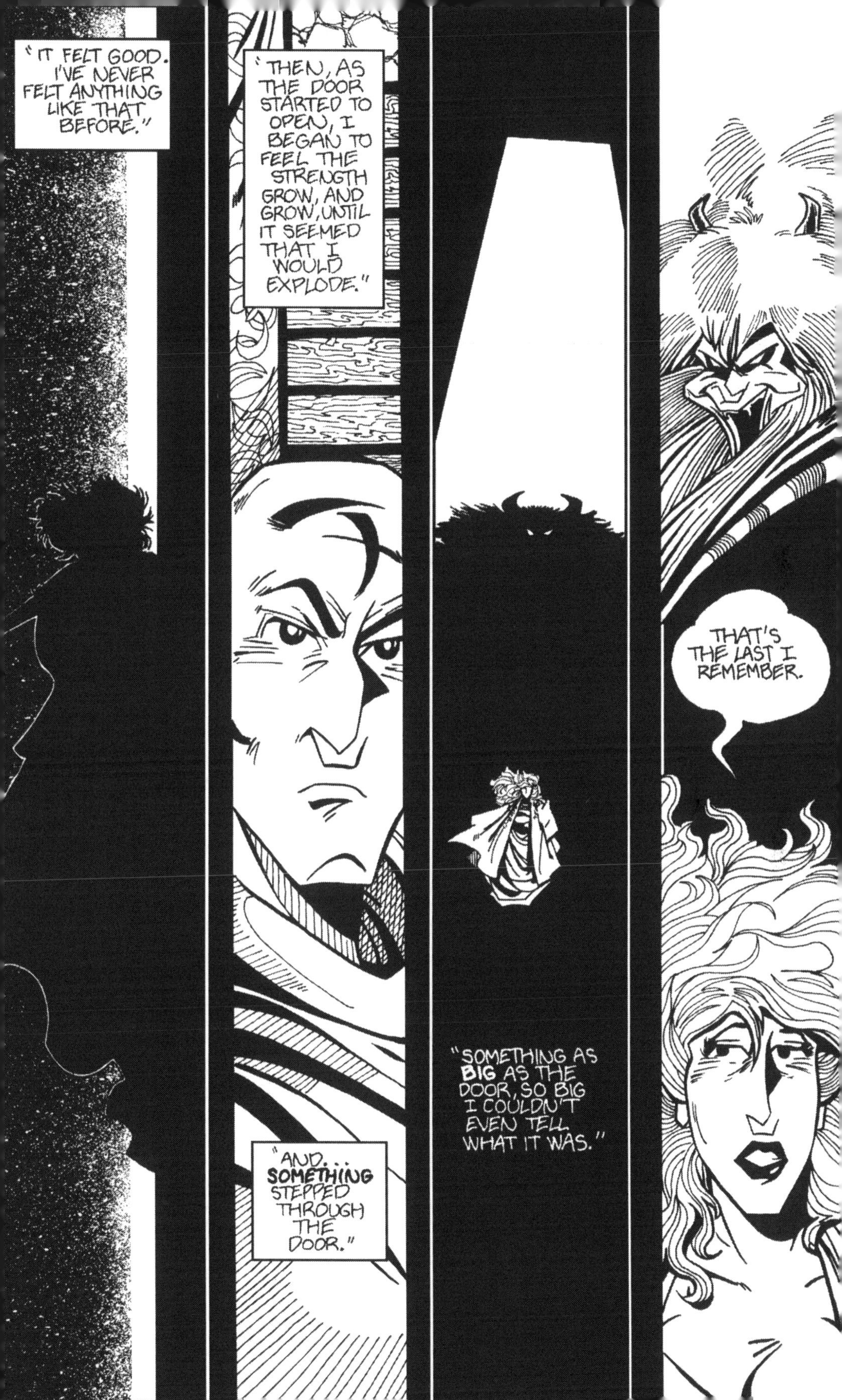
"IT FELT GOOD. I'VE NEVER FELT ANYTHING LIKE THAT BEFORE."
"THEN, AS THE DOOR STARTED TO OPEN, I BEGAN TO FEEL THE STRENGTH GROW, AND GROW, UNTIL IT SEEMED THAT I WOULD EXPLODE."
"AND... **SOMETHING** STEPPED THROUGH THE DOOR."
"SOMETHING AS **BIG** AS THE DOOR, SO BIG I COULDN'T EVEN TELL WHAT IT WAS."
THAT'S THE LAST I REMEMBER.

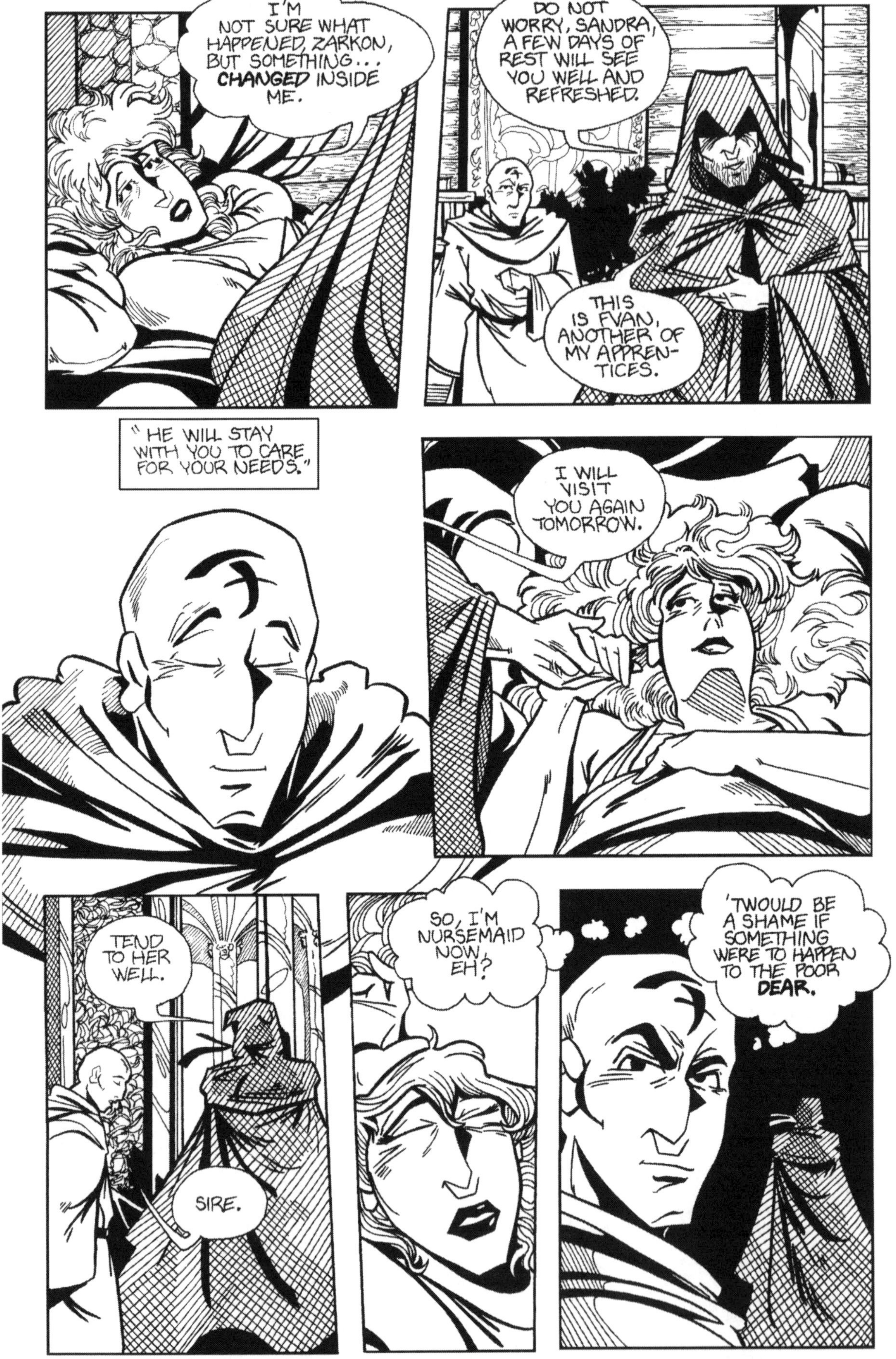
I'M NOT SURE WHAT HAPPENED, ZARKON, BUT SOMETHING... CHANGED INSIDE ME.
DO NOT WORRY, SANDRA, A FEW DAYS OF REST WILL SEE YOU WELL AND REFRESHED.
THIS IS FVAN, ANOTHER OF MY APPRENTICES.
"HE WILL STAY WITH YOU TO CARE FOR YOUR NEEDS."
I WILL VISIT YOU AGAIN TOMORROW.
TEND TO HER WELL.
SIRE.
SO, I'M NURSEMAID NOW, EH?
'TWOULD BE A SHAME IF SOMETHING WERE TO HAPPEN TO THE POOR DEAR.

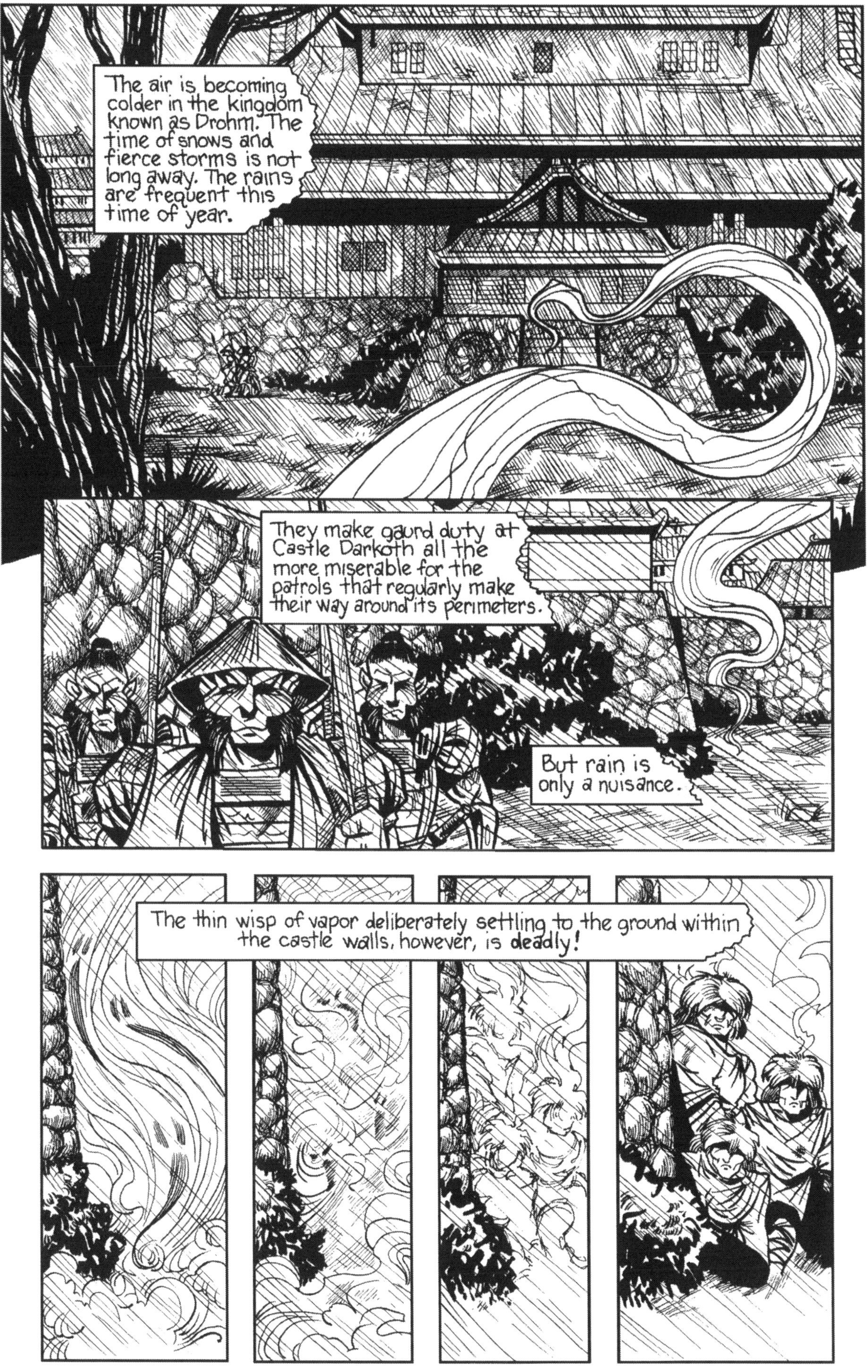
The air is becoming colder in the kingdom known as Drohm. The time of snows and fierce storms is not long away. The rains are frequent this time of year.
They make gaurd duty at Castle Darkoth all the more miserable for the patrols that regularly make their way around its perimeters.
But rain is only a nuisance.
The thin wisp of vapor deliberately settling to the ground within the castle walls, however, is **deadly**!

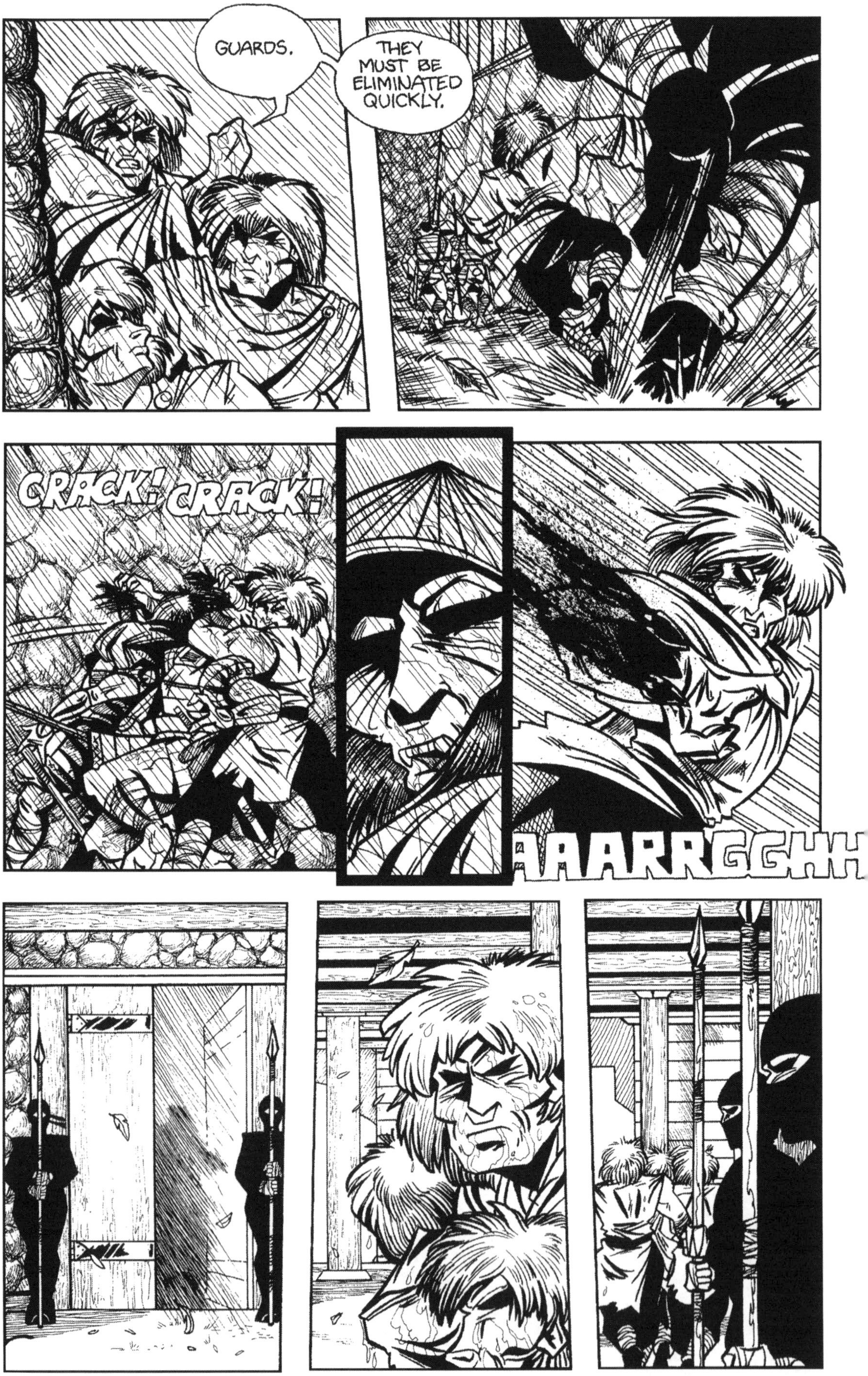
GUARDS.
THEY MUST BE ELIMINATED QUICKLY.
CRACK! CRACK!
AAARRGGHH

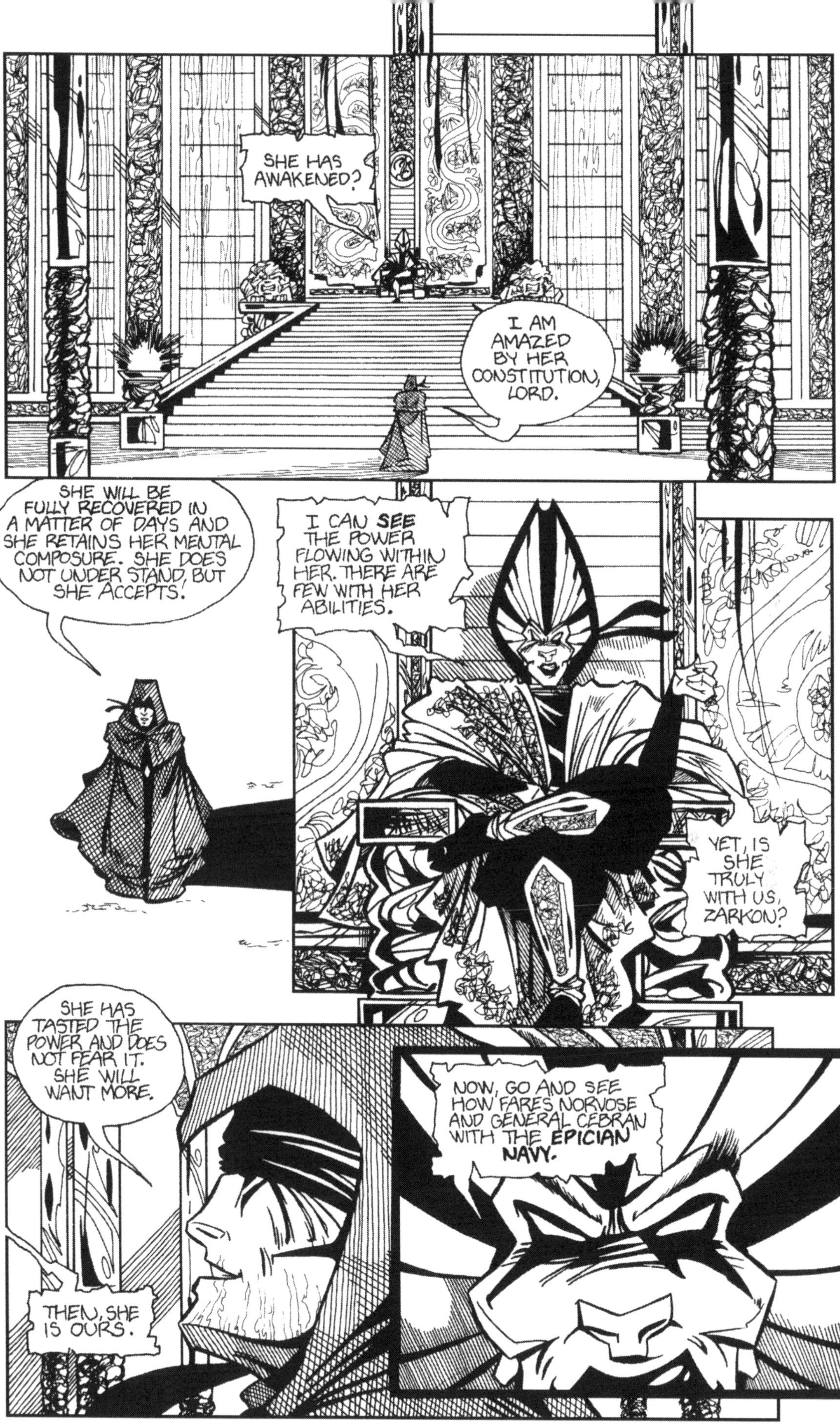
SHE HAS AWAKENED?
I AM AMAZED BY HER CONSTITUTION, LORD.
SHE WILL BE FULLY RECOVERED IN A MATTER OF DAYS AND SHE RETAINS HER MENTAL COMPOSURE. SHE DOES NOT UNDER STAND, BUT SHE ACCEPTS!
I CAN SEE THE POWER FLOWING WITHIN HER. THERE ARE FEW WITH HER ABILITIES.
YET, IS SHE TRULY WITH US, ZARKON?
SHE HAS TASTED THE POWER AND DOES NOT FEAR IT. SHE WILL WANT MORE.
THEN, SHE IS OURS.
NOW, GO AND SEE HOW FARES NORVOSE AND GENERAL CEBRAN WITH THE EPICIAN NAVY.

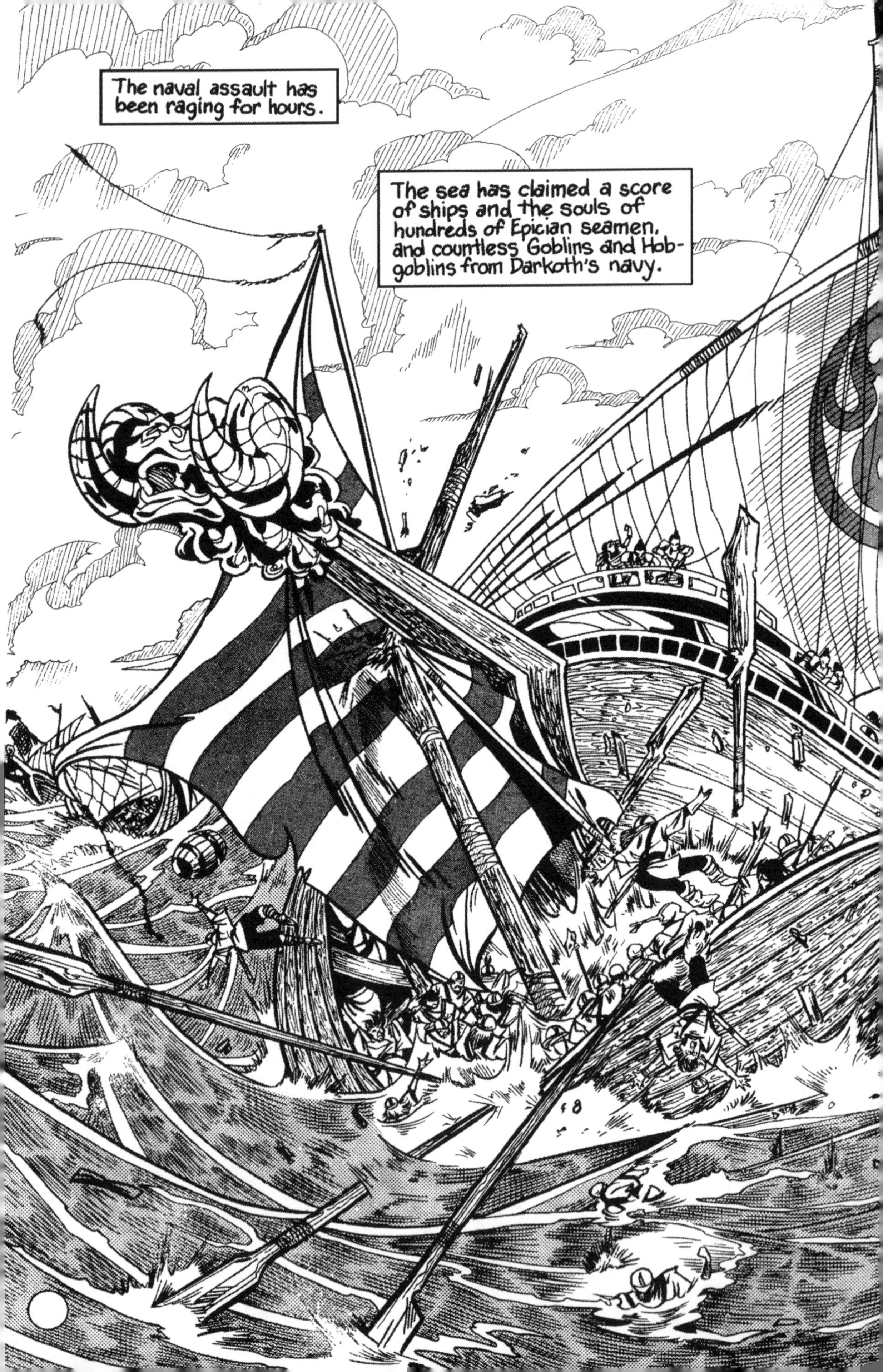
The naval assault has been raging for hours.
The sea has claimed a score of ships and the souls of hundreds of Epician seamen, and countless Goblins and Hobgoblins from Darkoth's navy.

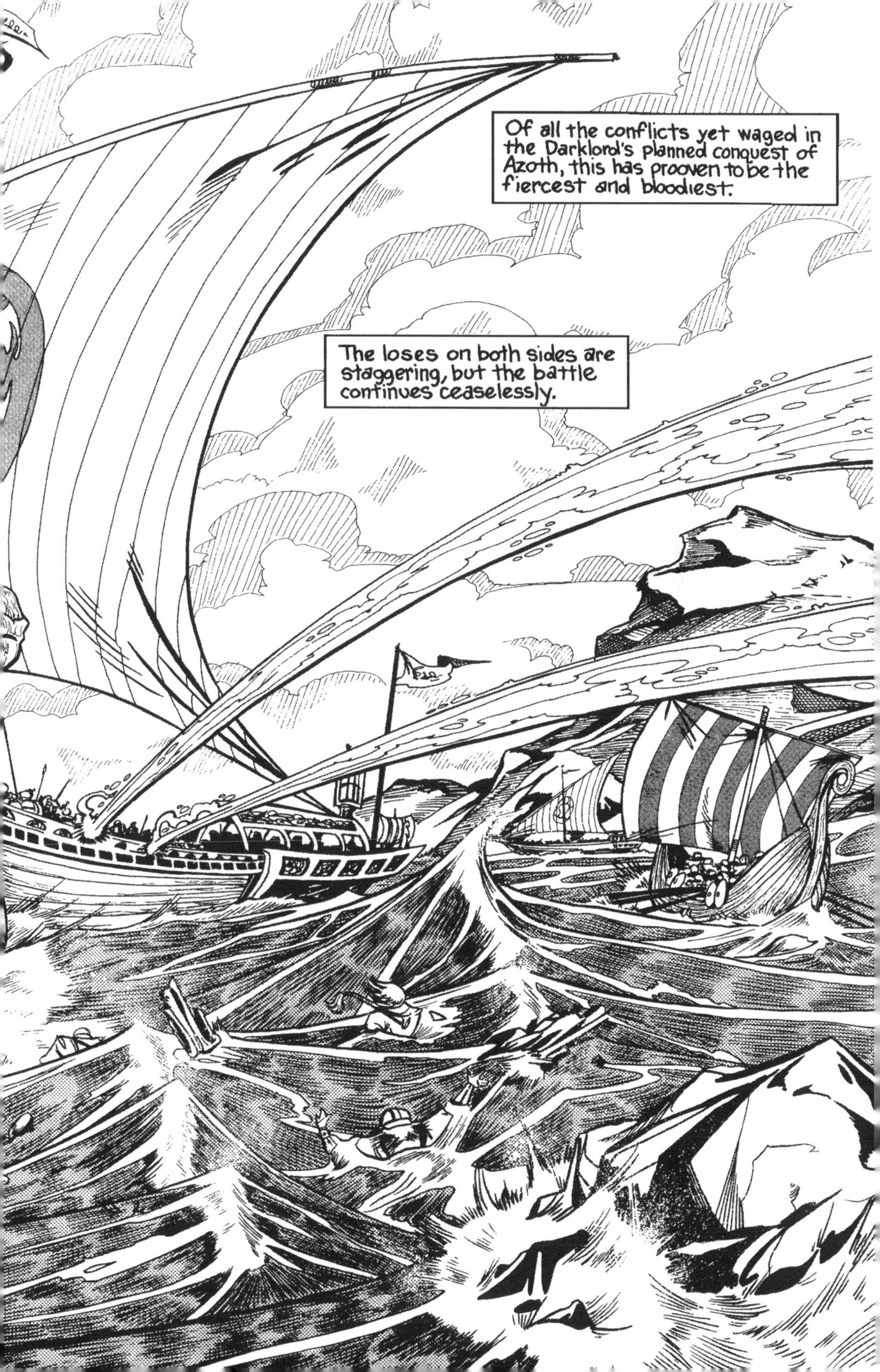
Of all the conflicts yet waged in the Darklord's planned conquest of Azoth, this has prooven to be the fiercest and bloodiest.
The loses on both sides are staggering, but the battle continues ceaselessly.

Sails slap at the air, and waves at the wooden hulls, while boots beat staccato rythms on decks, swords clash against swords and arrows "th-chunk" into living flesh.

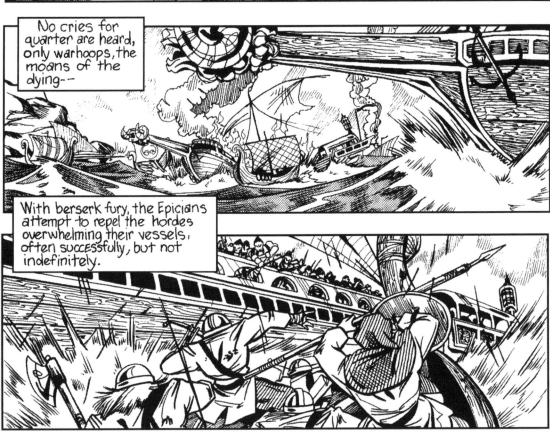

No cries for quarter are heard, only warhoops, the moans of the dying--

With berserk fury, the Epicians attempt to repel the hordes overwhelming their vessels, often successfully, but not indefinitely.

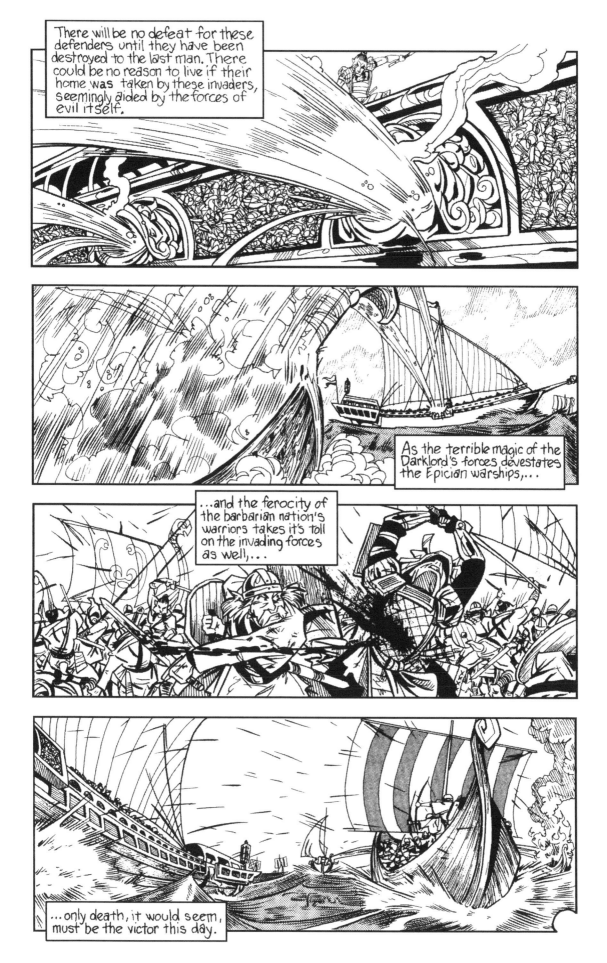

There will be no defeat for these defenders until they have been destroyed to the last man. There could be no reason to live if their home was taken by these invaders, seemingly aided by the forces of evil itself.

As the terrible magic of the Darklord's forces devestates the Epician warships,...

...and the ferocity of the barbarian nation's warriors takes it's toll on the invading forces as well,...

...only death, it would seem, must be the victor this day.

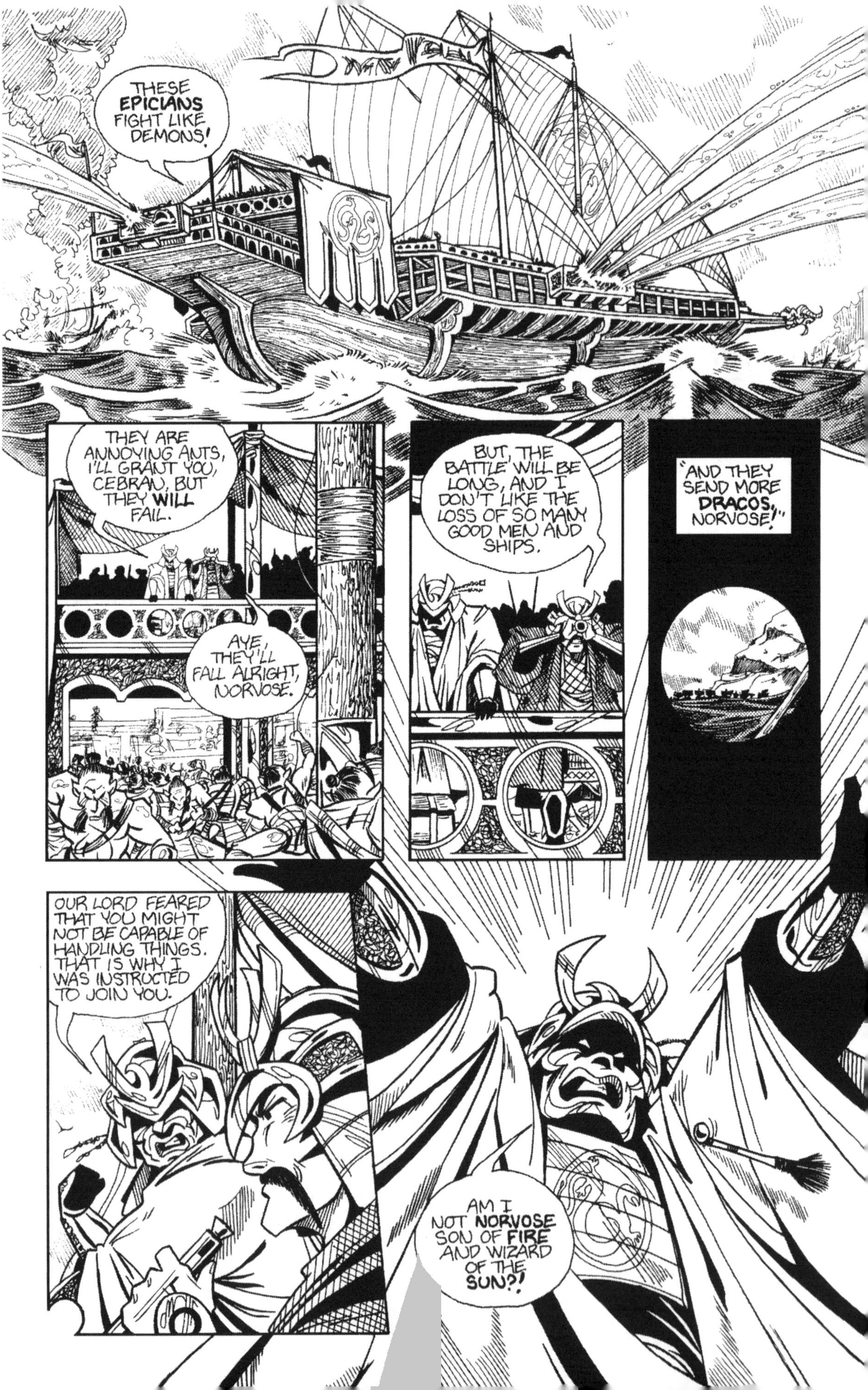
THESE EPICIANS FIGHT LIKE DEMONS!
THEY ARE ANNOYING ANTS, I'LL GRANT YOU, CEBRAN, BUT THEY WILL FAIL.
AYE, THEY'LL FALL ALRIGHT, NORVOSE.
BUT, THE BATTLE WILL BE LONG, AND I DON'T LIKE THE LOSS OF SO MANY GOOD MEN AND SHIPS.
"AND THEY SEND MORE DRACOS, NORVOSE!"
OUR LORD FEARED THAT YOU MIGHT NOT BE CAPABLE OF HANDLING THINGS. THAT IS WHY I WAS INSTRUCTED TO JOIN YOU.
AM I NOT NORVOSE SON OF FIRE AND WIZARD OF THE SUN?!

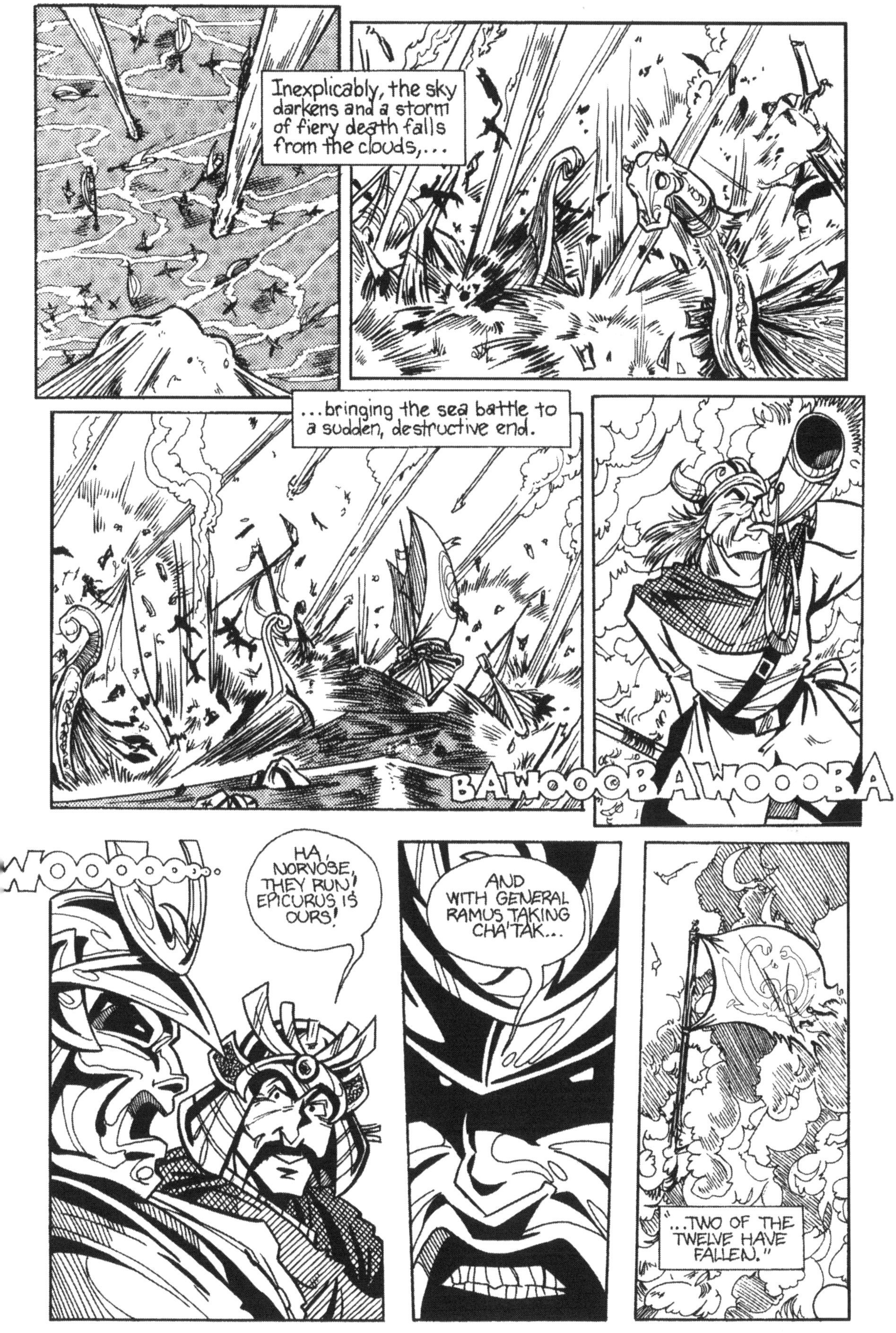
Inexplicably, the sky darkens and a storm of fiery death falls from the clouds,...
...bringing the sea battle to a sudden, destructive end.
BAWOOOBAWOOOBA
WOOOOOO...
HA, NORVOSE, THEY RUN! EPICURUS IS OURS!
AND WITH GENERAL RAMUS TAKING CHA'TAK...
"...TWO OF THE TWELVE HAVE FALLEN."

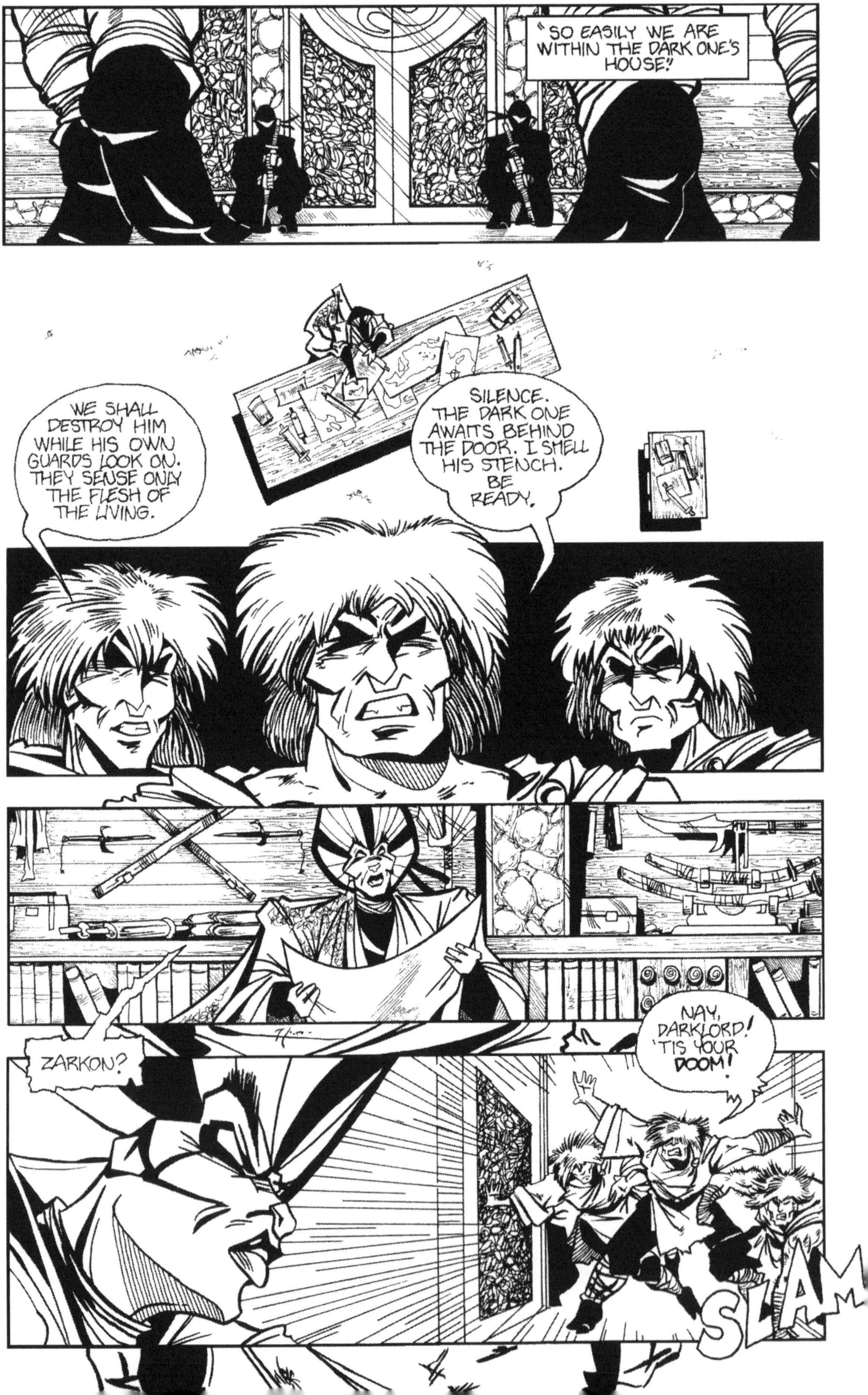
"SO EASILY WE ARE WITHIN THE DARK ONE'S HOUSE!"
WE SHALL DESTROY HIM WHILE HIS OWN GUARDS LOOK ON. THEY SENSE ONLY THE FLESH OF THE LIVING.
SILENCE. THE DARK ONE AWAITS BEHIND THE DOOR. I SMELL HIS STENCH. BE READY.
ZARKON?
NAY, DARKLORD! 'TIS YOUR DOOM!
SLAM

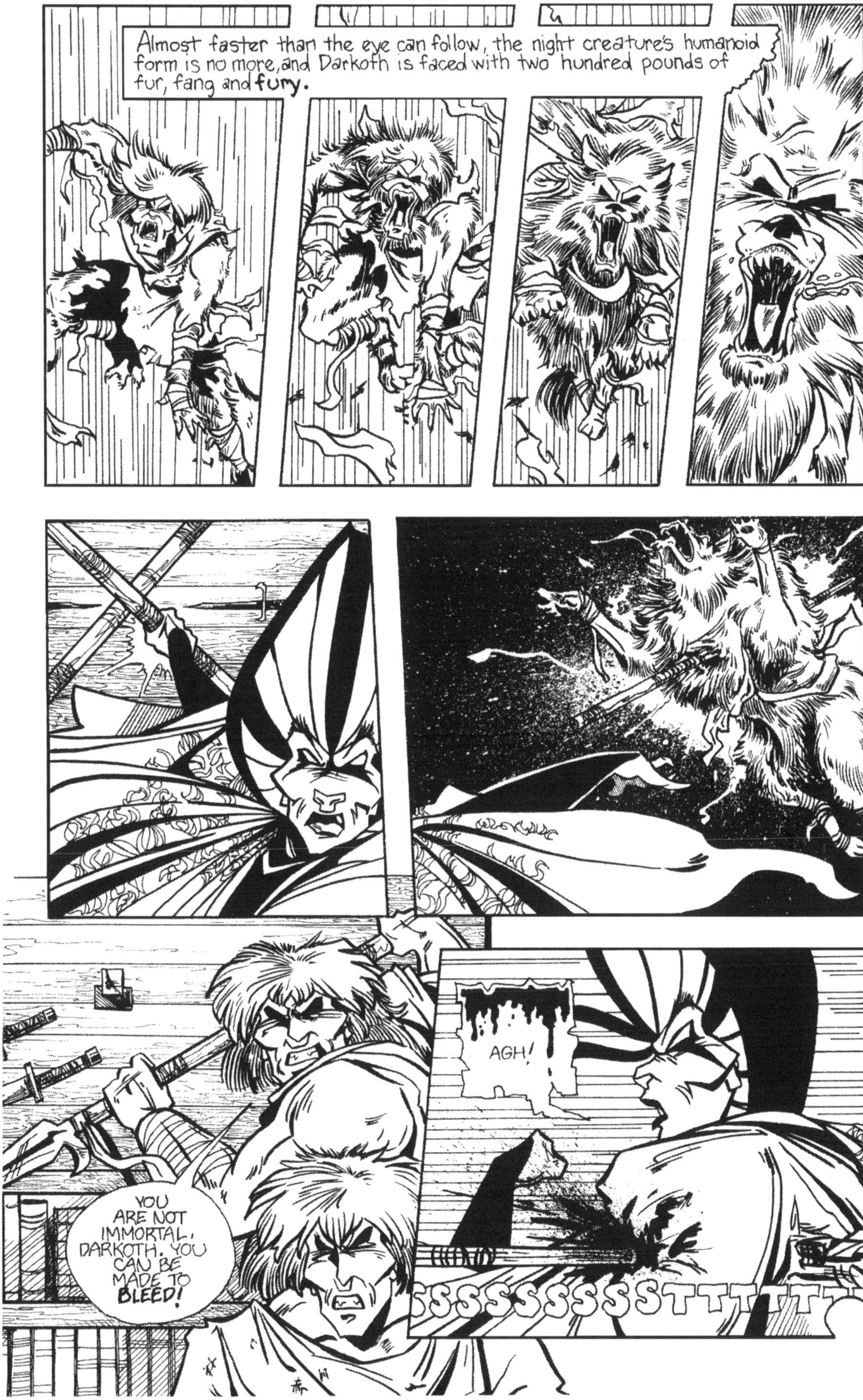
Almost faster than the eye can follow, the night creature's humanoid form is no more, and Darkoth is faced with two hundred pounds of fur, fang and fury.
AGH!
YOU ARE NOT IMMORTAL, DARKOTH. YOU CAN BE MADE TO BLEED!
SSSSSSSSSTTTTTT

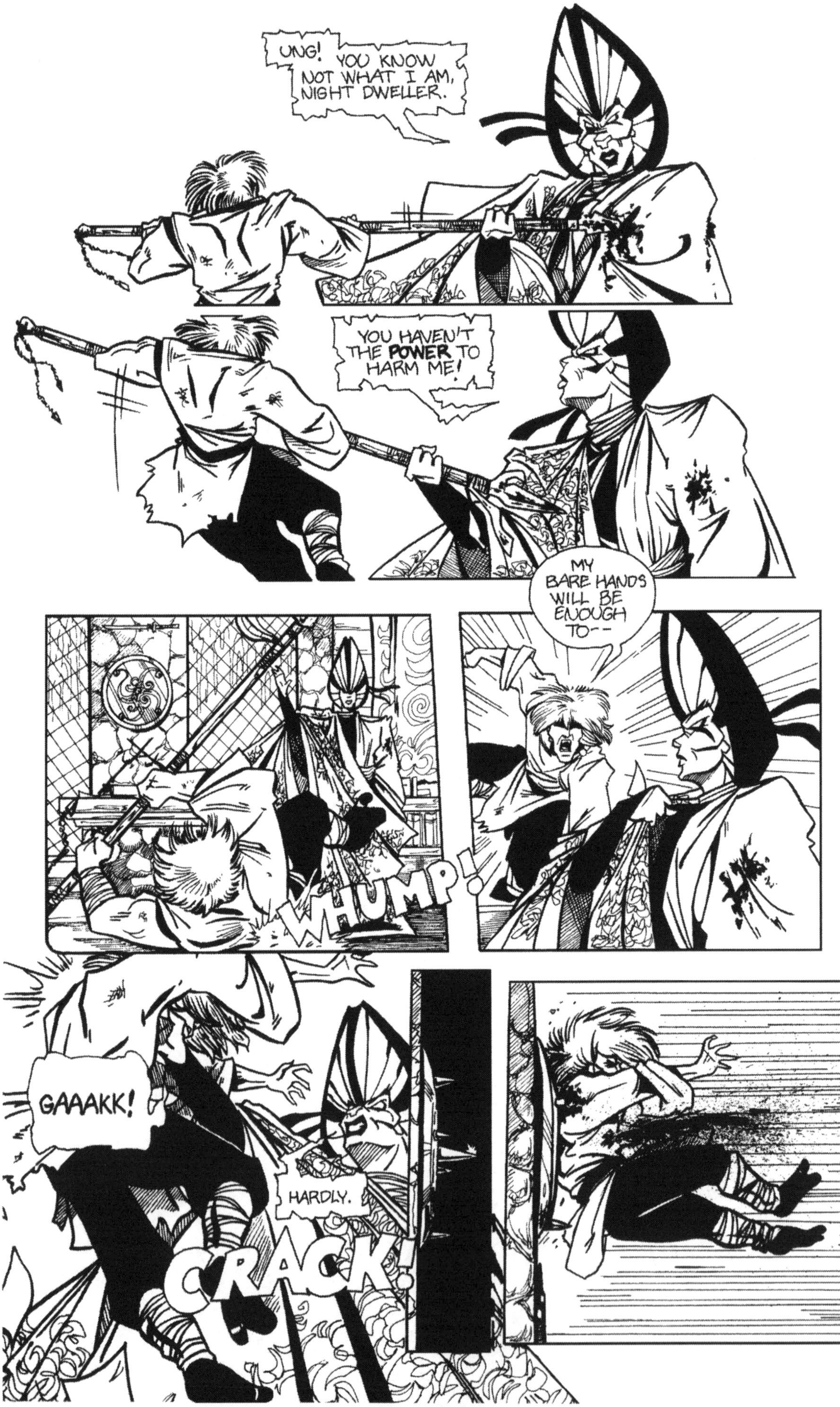
UNG! YOU KNOW NOT WHAT I AM, NIGHT DWELLER.
YOU HAVEN'T THE **POWER** TO HARM ME!
MY BARE HANDS WILL BE ENOUGH TO--
WHUMP!
GAAAKK!
HARDLY.
CRACK!

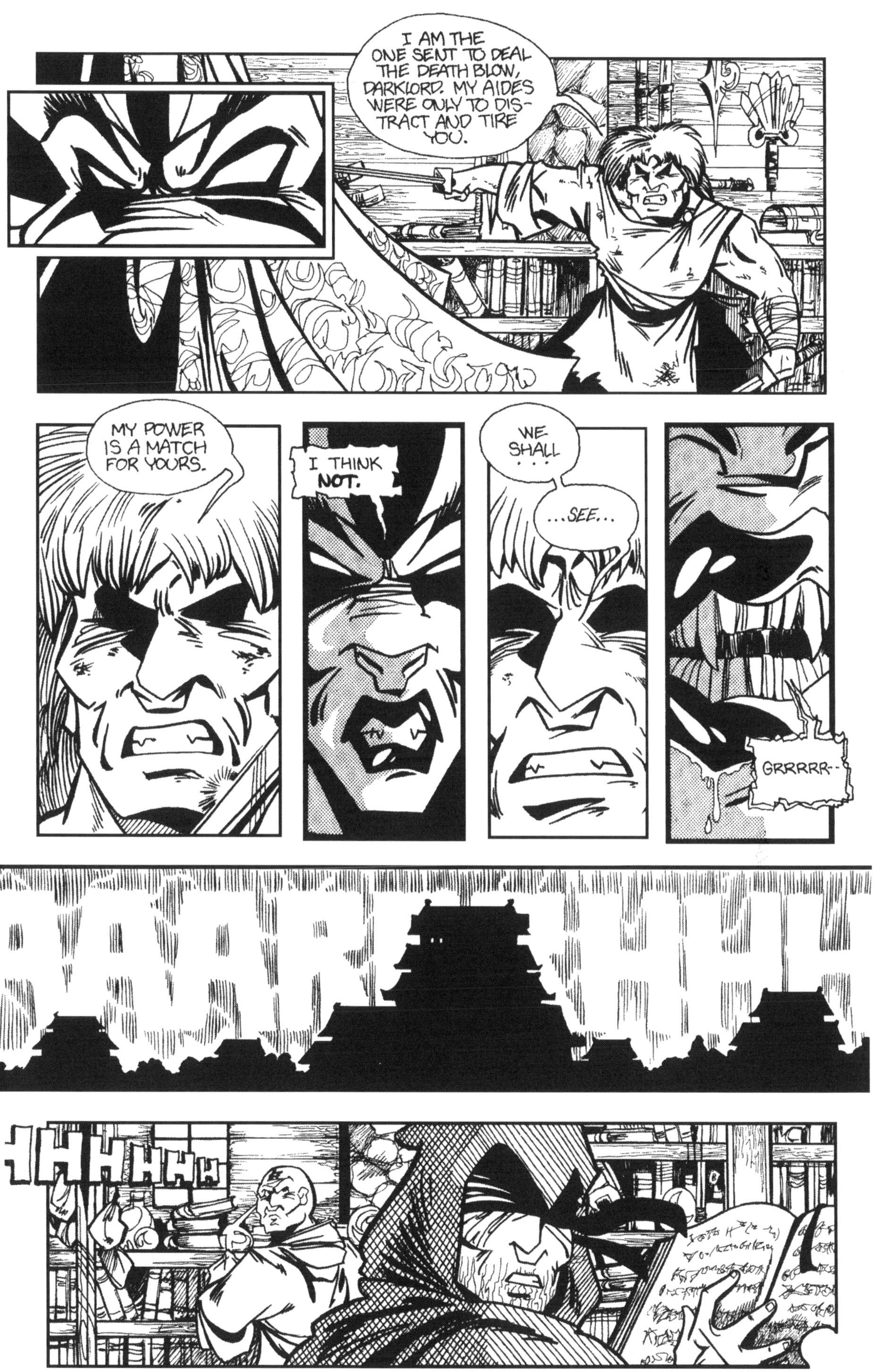
I AM THE ONE SENT TO DEAL THE DEATH BLOW, DARKLORD. MY AIDES WERE ONLY TO DISTRACT AND TIRE YOU.
MY POWER IS A MATCH FOR YOURS.
I THINK **NOT.**
WE SHALL . . .
...SEE...
GRRRRR--
HHHHHH

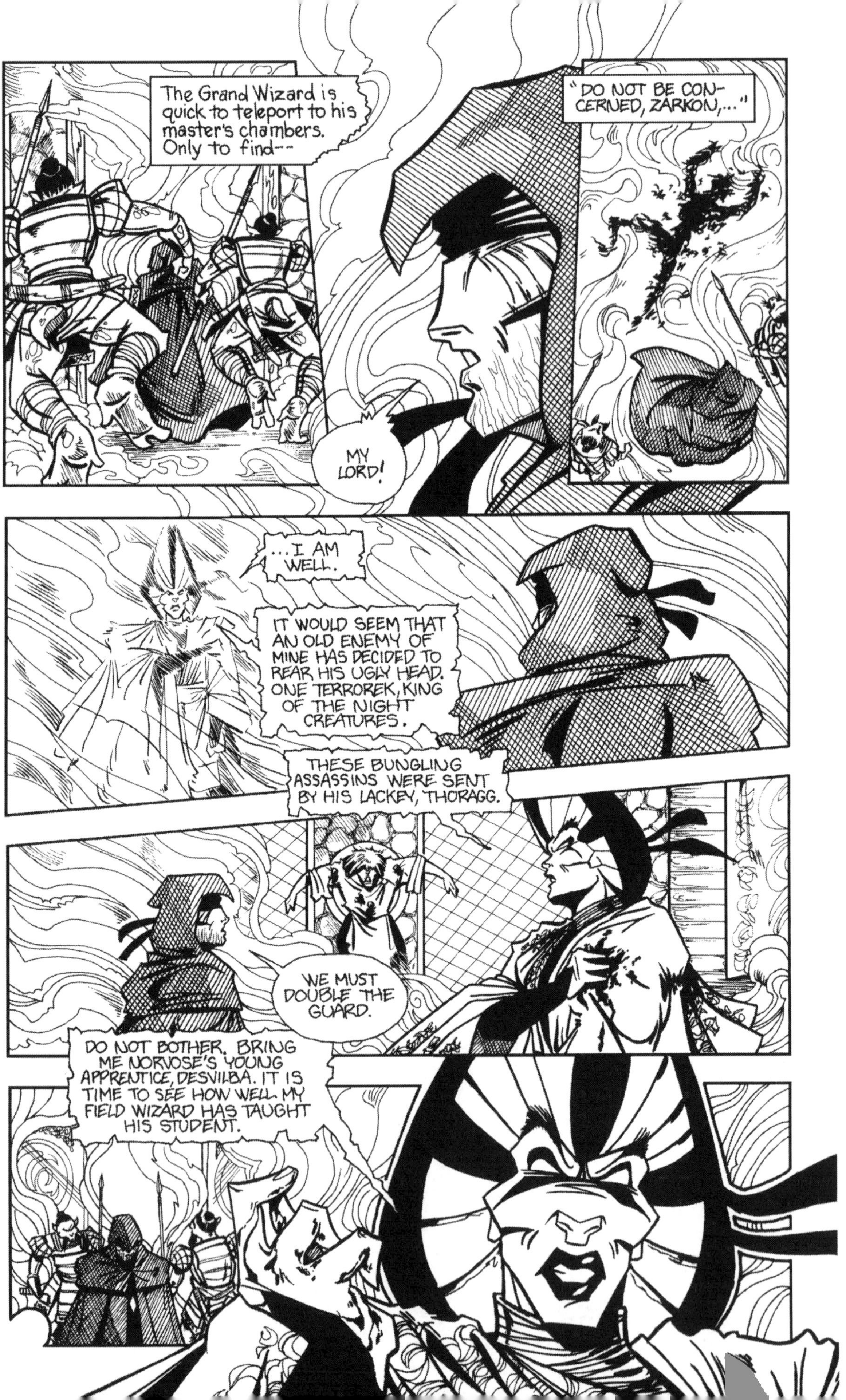
The Grand Wizard is quick to teleport to his master's chambers. Only to find--
MY LORD!
"DO NOT BE CONCERNED, ZARKON,..."
...I AM WELL.
IT WOULD SEEM THAT AN OLD ENEMY OF MINE HAS DECIDED TO REAR HIS UGLY HEAD. ONE TERROREK, KING OF THE NIGHT CREATURES.
THESE BUNGLING ASSASSINS WERE SENT BY HIS LACKEY, THORAGG.
WE MUST DOUBLE THE GUARD.
DO NOT BOTHER. BRING ME NORVOSE'S YOUNG APPRENTICE, DESVILBA. IT IS TIME TO SEE HOW WELL MY FIELD WIZARD HAS TAUGHT HIS STUDENT.

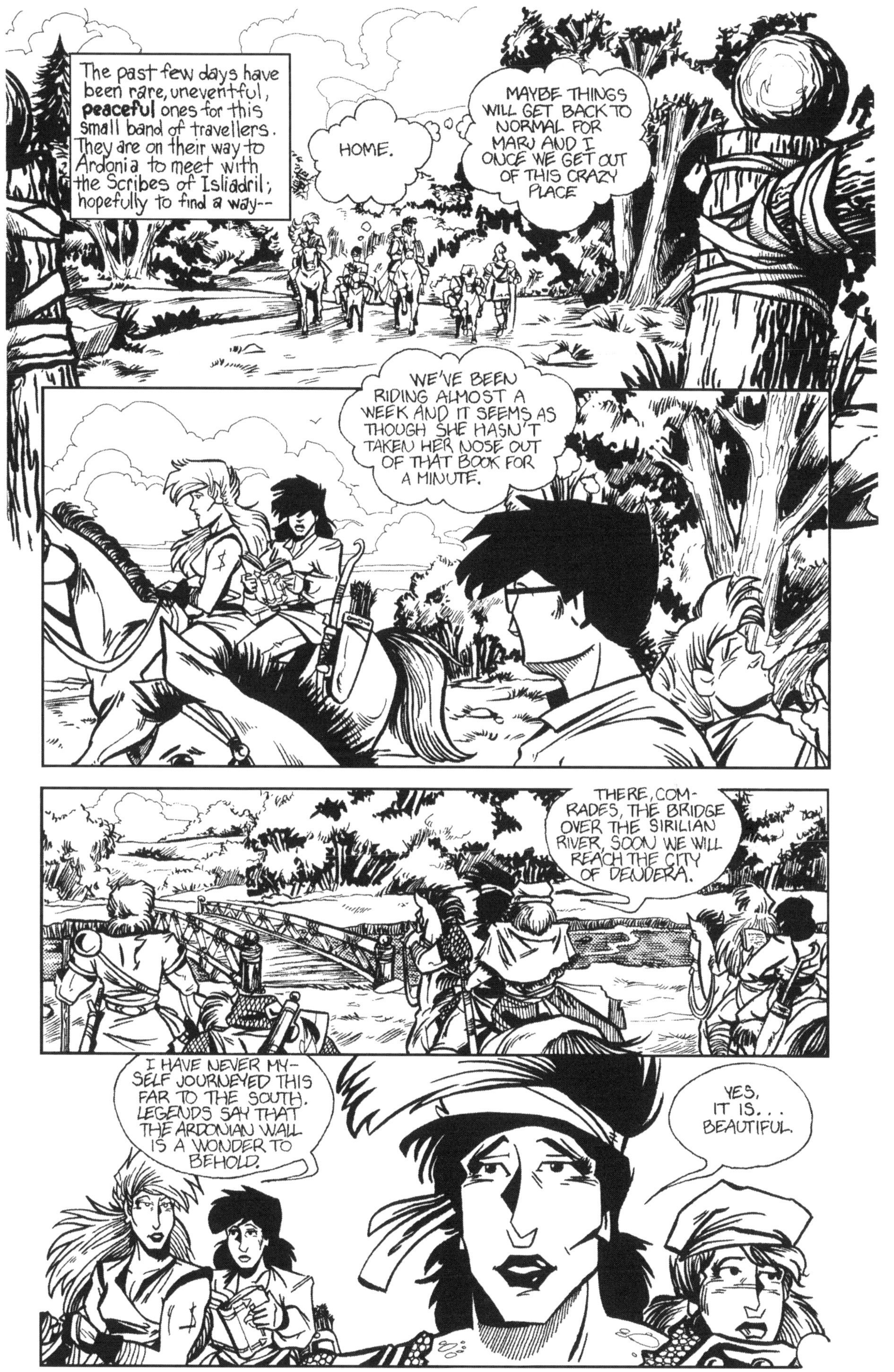
The past few days have been rare, uneventful, **peaceful** ones for this small band of travellers. They are on their way to Ardonia to meet with the Scribes of Isliadril; hopefully to find a way--
HOME.
MAYBE THINGS WILL GET BACK TO NORMAL FOR MARJ AND I ONCE WE GET OUT OF THIS CRAZY PLACE
WE'VE BEEN RIDING ALMOST A WEEK AND IT SEEMS AS THOUGH SHE HASN'T TAKEN HER NOSE OUT OF THAT BOOK FOR A MINUTE.
THERE, COM-RADES, THE BRIDGE OVER THE SIRILIAN RIVER, SOON WE WILL REACH THE CITY OF DENDERA.
I HAVE NEVER MY-SELF JOURNEYED THIS FAR TO THE SOUTH. LEGENDS SAY THAT THE ARDONIAN WALL IS A WONDER TO BEHOLD.
YES, IT IS... BEAUTIFUL.

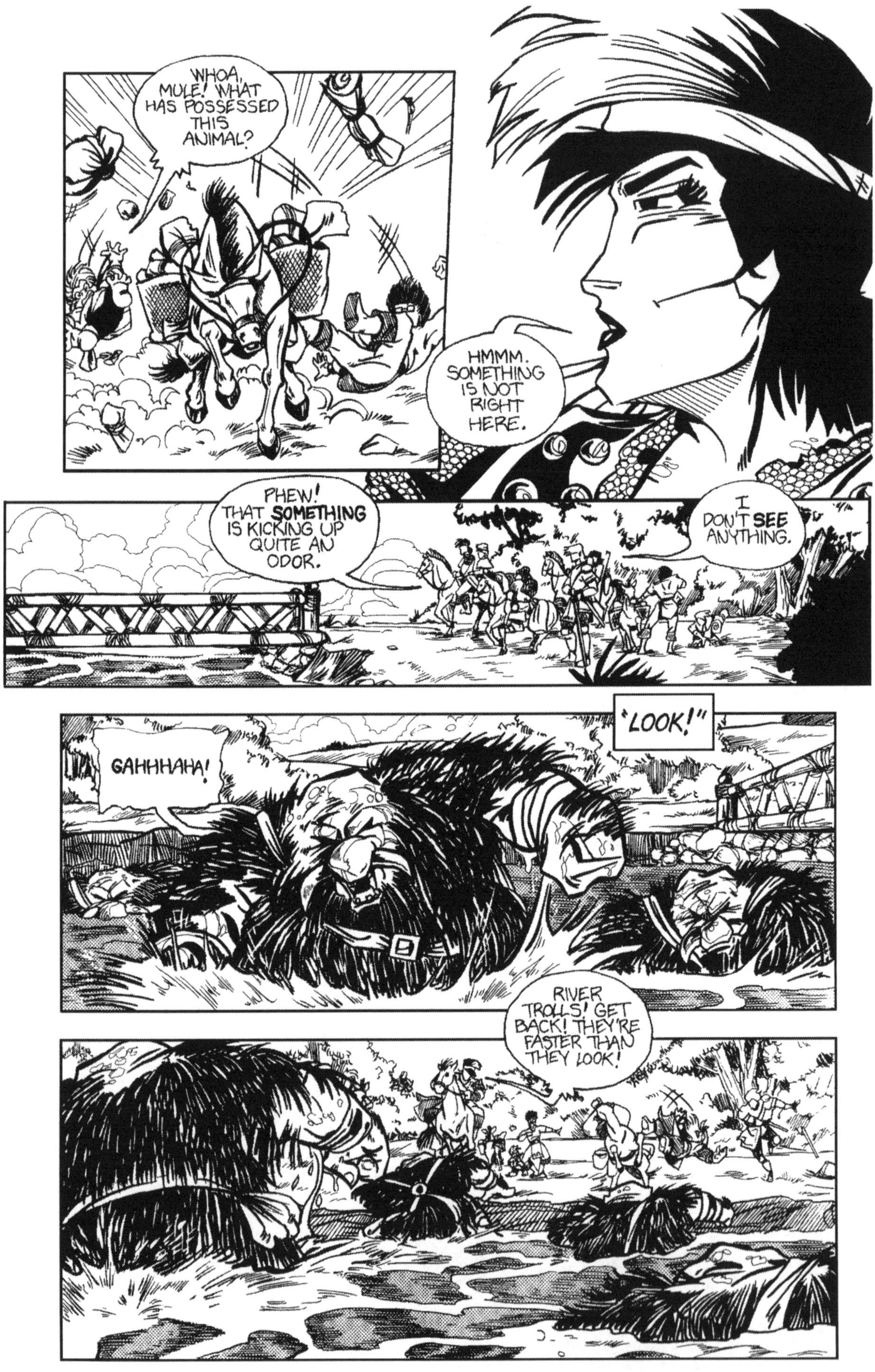
WHOA, MULE! WHAT HAS POSSESSED THIS ANIMAL?
HMMM. SOMETHING IS NOT RIGHT HERE.
PHEW! THAT SOMETHING IS KICKING UP QUITE AN ODOR.
I DON'T SEE ANYTHING.
"LOOK!"
GAHHHAHA!
RIVER TROLLS! GET BACK! THEY'RE FASTER THAN THEY LOOK!

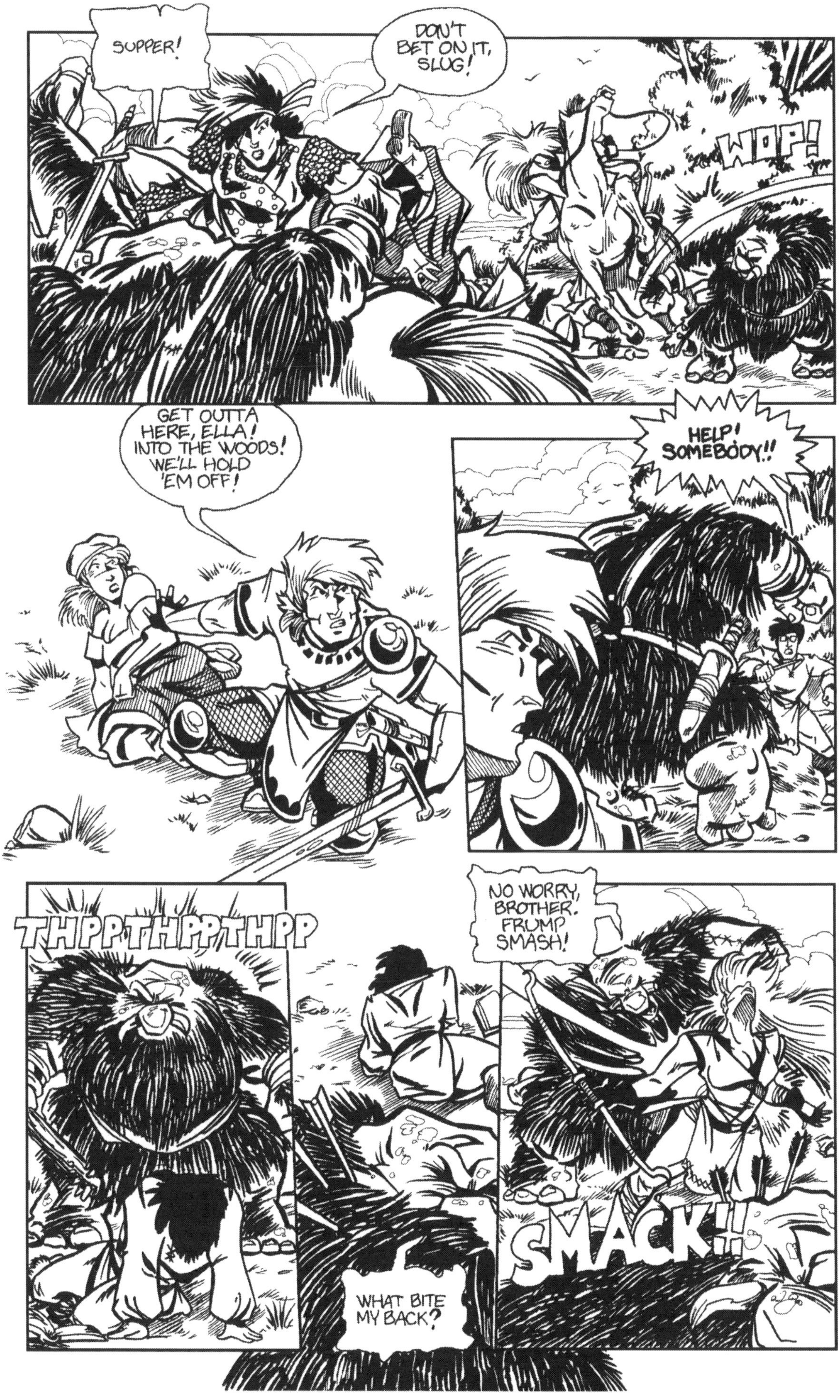
SUPPER!
DON'T BET ON IT, SLUG!
WOP!
GET OUTTA HERE, ELLA! INTO THE WOODS! WE'LL HOLD 'EM OFF!
HELP! SOMEBODY!!
THPPTHPPTHPP
WHAT BITE MY BACK?
NO WORRY, BROTHER. FRUMP SMASH!
SMACK!!

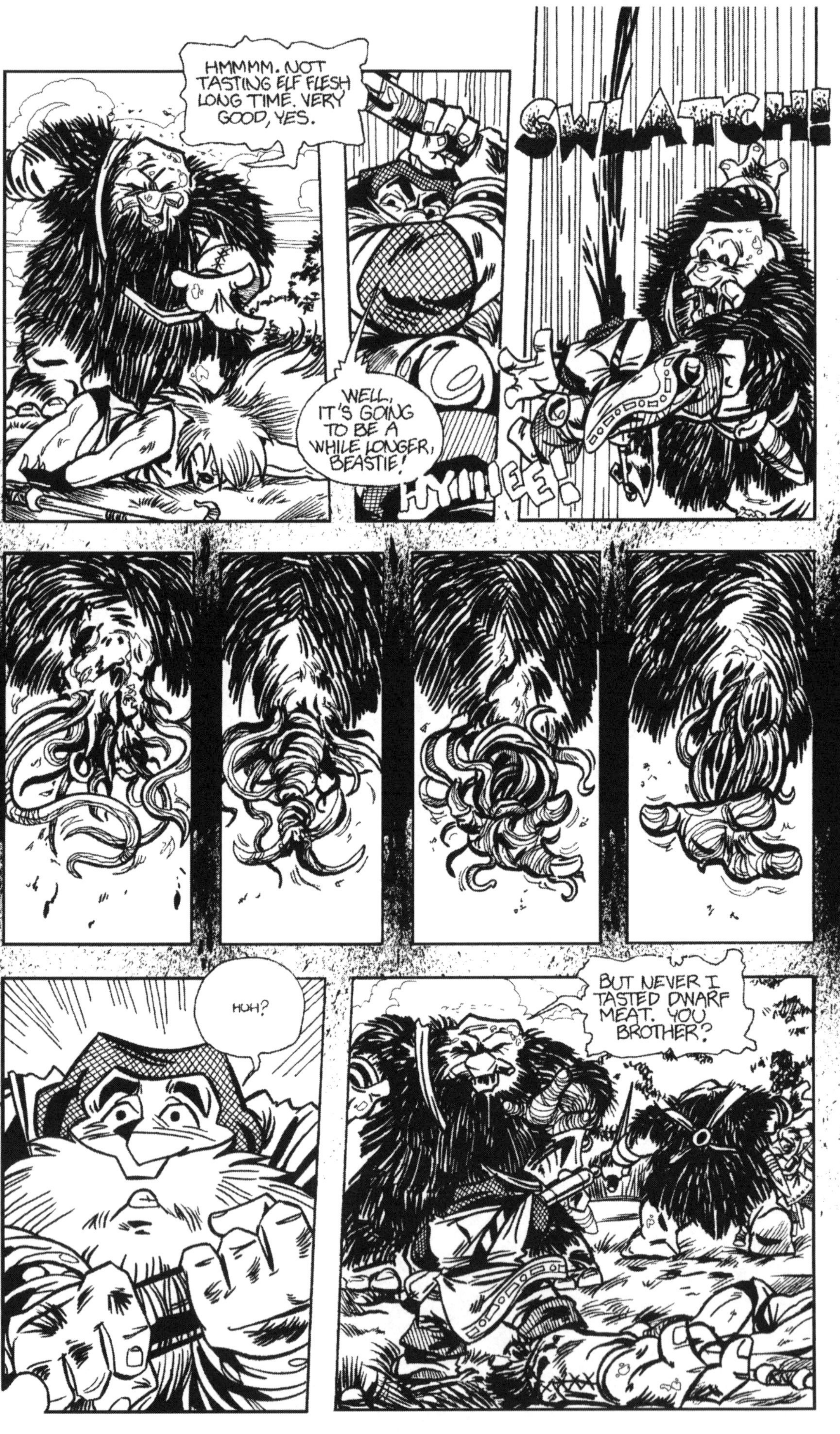
HMMMM. NOT TASTING ELF FLESH LONG TIME. VERY GOOD, YES.
WELL, IT'S GOING TO BE A WHILE LONGER, BEASTIE!
SWLATCH!
HYIIIEE!
HUH?
BUT NEVER I TASTED DWARF MEAT. YOU BROTHER?

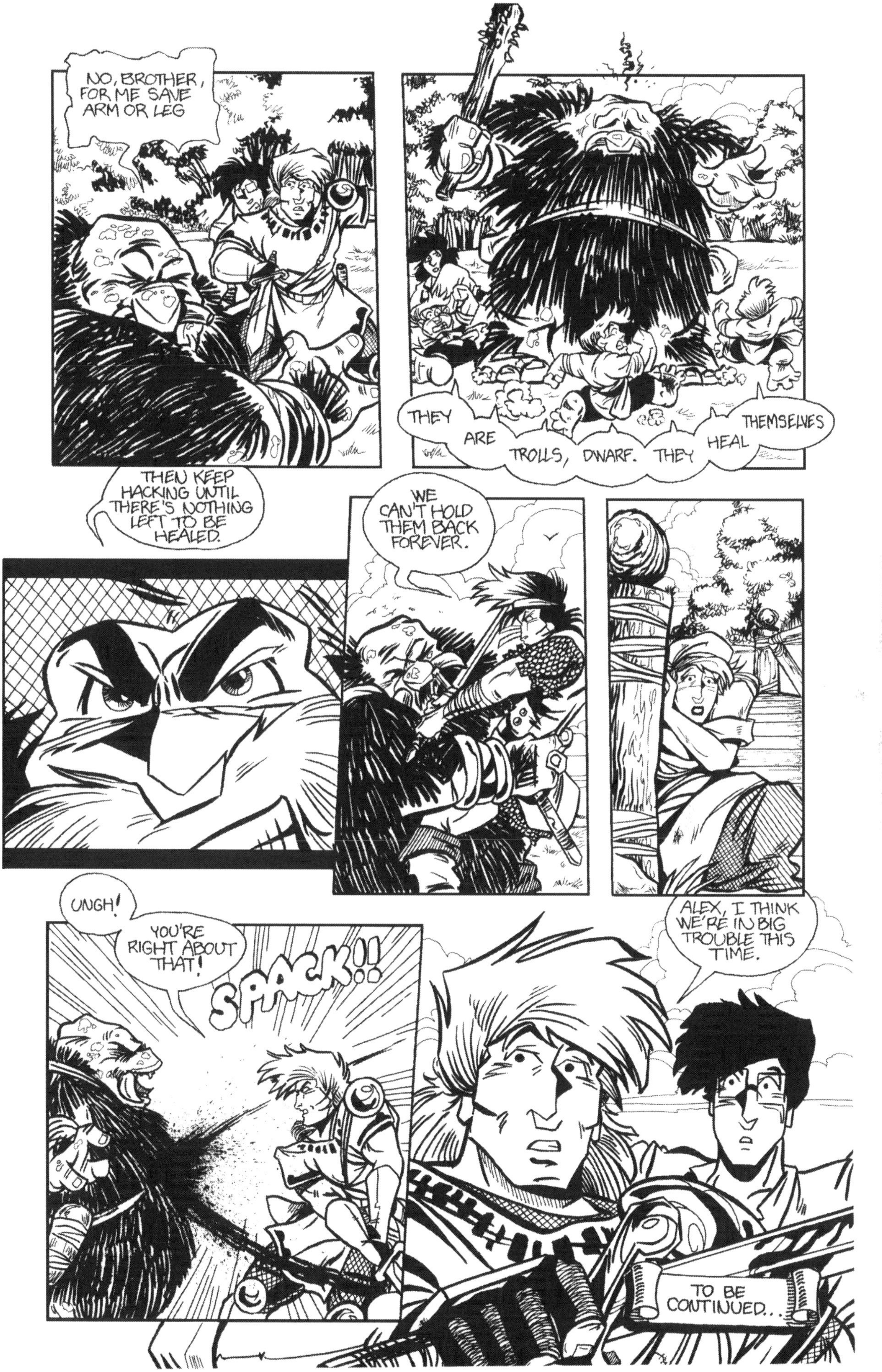
NO, BROTHER, FOR ME SAVE ARM OR LEG
THEY ARE TROLLS, DWARF. THEY HEAL THEMSELVES
THEN KEEP HACKING UNTIL THERE'S NOTHING LEFT TO BE HEALED.
WE CAN'T HOLD THEM BACK FOREVER.
UNGH!
YOU'RE RIGHT ABOUT THAT!
SPACK!!
ALEX, I THINK WE'RE IN BIG TROUBLE THIS TIME.
TO BE CONTINUED...

Legendlore

TALES OF THE REALM

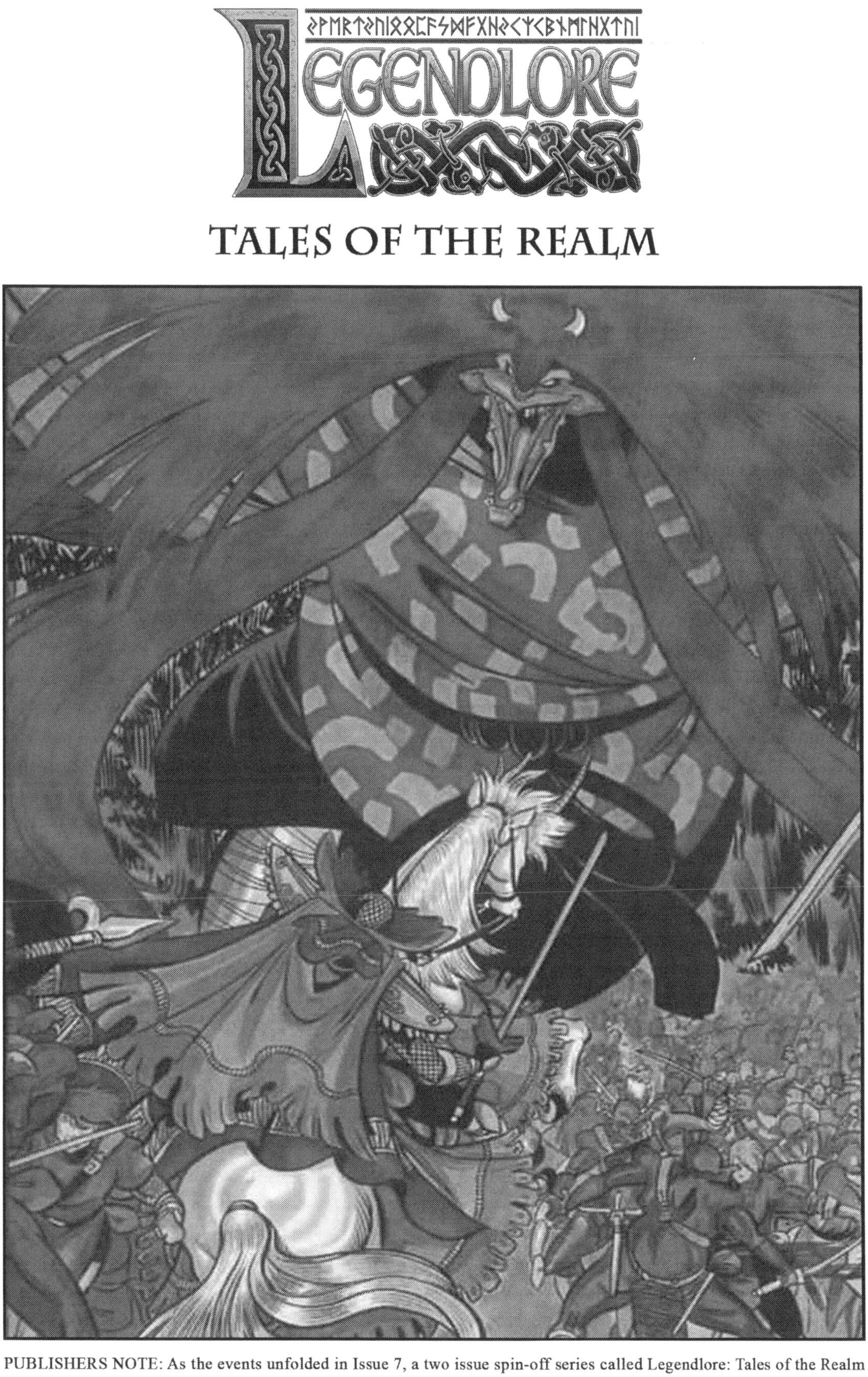

PUBLISHERS NOTE: As the events unfolded in Issue 7, a two issue spin-off series called Legendlore: Tales of the Realm was produced that focused on Lord Darkoth's campaign to conquer the lands of the Enchanted Forest under the rule of Elf King Alieandor Goldtree. This is that tale.

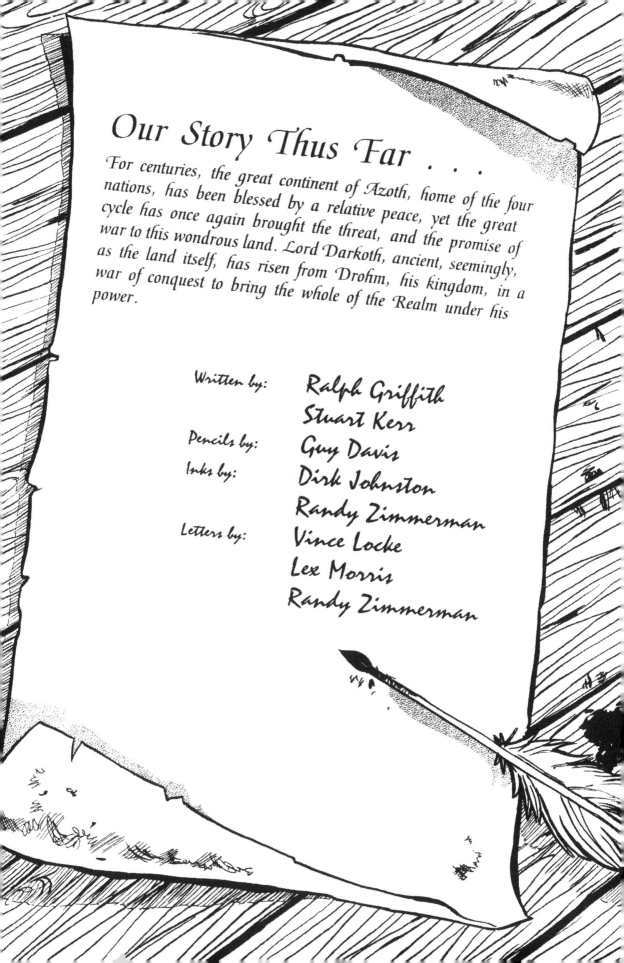

Our Story Thus Far . . .

For centuries, the great continent of Azoth, home of the four nations, has been blessed by a relative peace, yet the great cycle has once again brought the threat, and the promise of war to this wondrous land. Lord Darkoth, ancient, seemingly, as the land itself, has risen from Drohm, his kingdom, in a war of conquest to bring the whole of the Realm under his power.

Written by: Ralph Griffith
                 Stuart Kerr
Pencils by: Guy Davis
Inks by: Dirk Johnston
                 Randy Zimmerman
Letters by: Vince Locke
                 Lex Morris
                 Randy Zimmerman

Introducing. . .

LORD DARKOTH

Darklord of Drohm, who wishes to rule the entire continent of Azoth. The Dark One used the power of he's young queen to gate in the Shinde Imas to assure the defeat of the Rainbow Elves.

SHINDE IMAS

The eleven destroyer, a daemon which ages ago nearly destroyed all of the Rainbow Elves. A feat the Darkload hopes he will accomplish.

ARRIOR GOLDTREE

Adopted son of the elven king, Alieandor Goldtree. Sent by his father to try and enlist the aid of the Grey Hill dwarves against the spreading evil of the Darklord.

RAMSEY FRALEY

Mighty self-proclaimed warrior of the Grey Hills, who in quest for valor and battle skill, has joined forces with the elvin prince.

KING BONECRACK

Lord of the Goblins. Enlisted by the Dark One to aid the Shinde Imas in the attack against the Rainbow Elves.

ALIEANDOR GOLDTREE

Ruler of the Enchanted Forest and king of the Rainbow Elves. Seeing the destruction brought forth by the Darklord, he wishes to unite all races in an effort to stop him.

KING AKMOS KAERON

Leader of the Grey Hill Dwarves, whose large army wishes to remain neutral and let the Darklord battle whomever he wishes as long as he stays away from Warrior's Home.

PRINCE TYROS KAERON

Son of Akmos Kaeron and heir to the throne, who wishes to start a new age of trade relation between all nations.

Prologue...

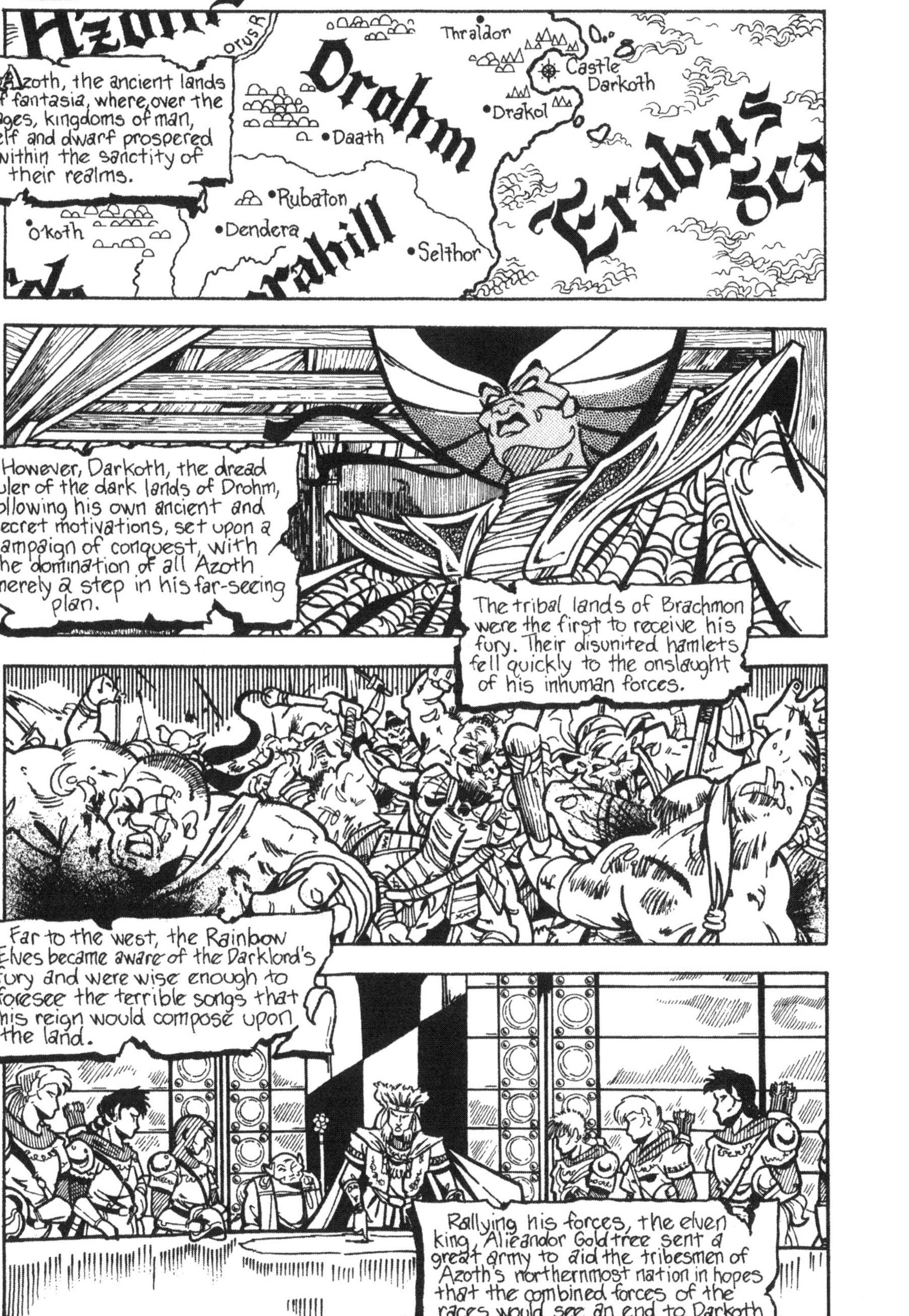
Azoth, the ancient lands of fantasia, where, over the ages, kingdoms of man, elf and dwarf prospered within the sanctity of their realms.
ORUS R
Drohm
Thraldor
Castle Darkoth
Drakol
Daath
Rubaton
Dendera
O'koth
Selthor
Erabus
However, Darkoth, the dread ruler of the dark lands of Drohm, following his own ancient and secret motivations, set upon a campaign of conquest, with the domination of all Azoth merely a step in his far-seeing plan.
The tribal lands of Brachmon were the first to receive his fury. Their disunited hamlets fell quickly to the onslaught of his inhuman forces.
Far to the west, the Rainbow Elves became aware of the Darklord's fury and were wise enough to foresee the terrible songs that his reign would compose upon the land.
Rallying his forces, the elven king, Alieandor Goldtree sent a great army to aid the tribesmen of Azoth's northernmost nation in hopes that the combined forces of the races would see an end to Darkoth and his evil.

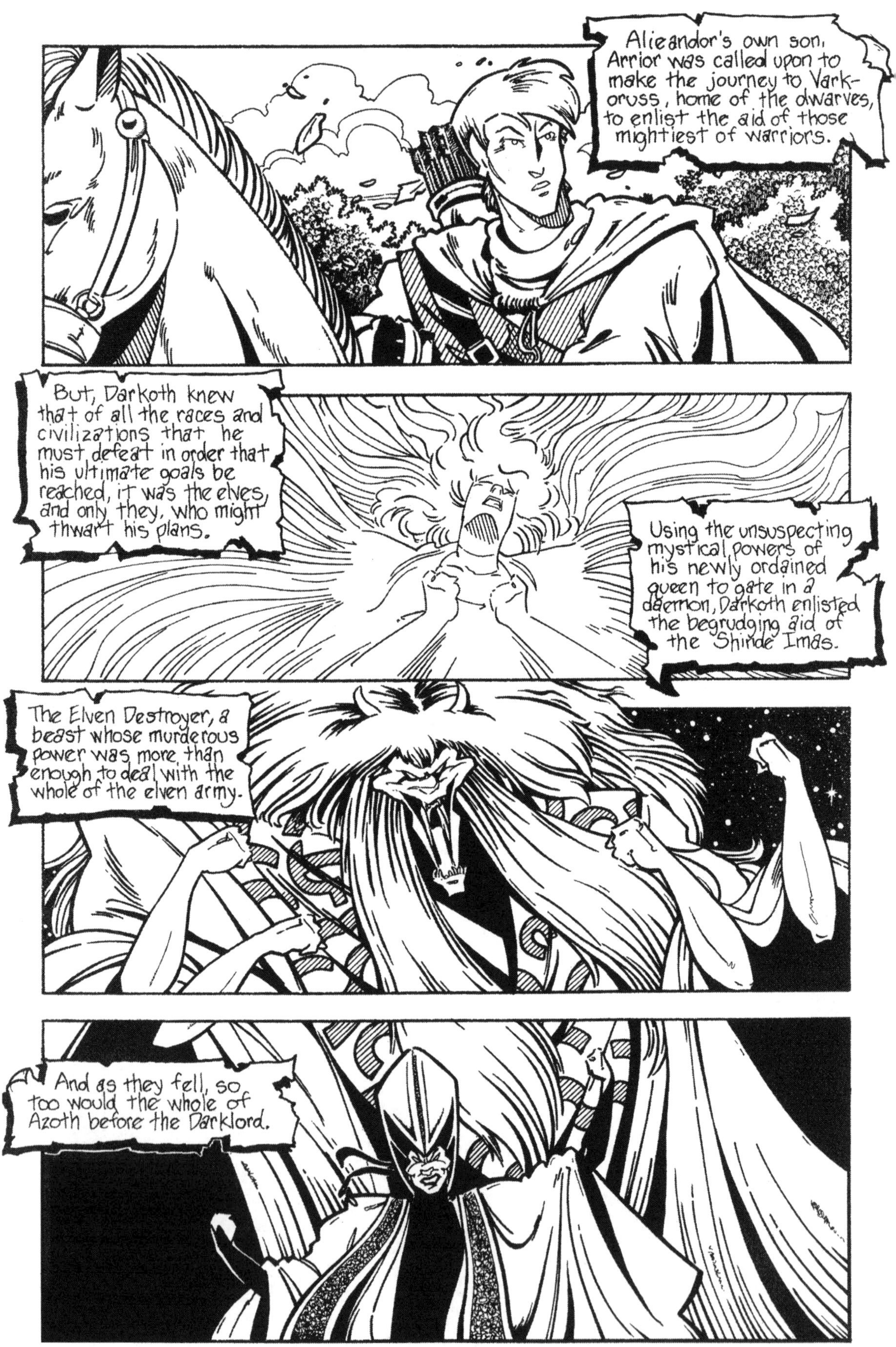
Alieandor's own son, Arrior was called upon to make the journey to Varkoruss, home of the dwarves, to enlist the aid of those mightiest of warriors.
But, Darkoth knew that of all the races and civilizations that he must defeat in order that his ultimate goals be reached, it was the elves, and only they, who might thwart his plans.
Using the unsuspecting mystical powers of his newly ordained queen to gate in a daemon, Darkoth enlisted the begrudging aid of the Shinde Imas.
The Elven Destroyer, a beast whose murderous power was more than enough to deal with the whole of the elven army.
And as they fell, so too would the whole of Azoth before the Darklord.

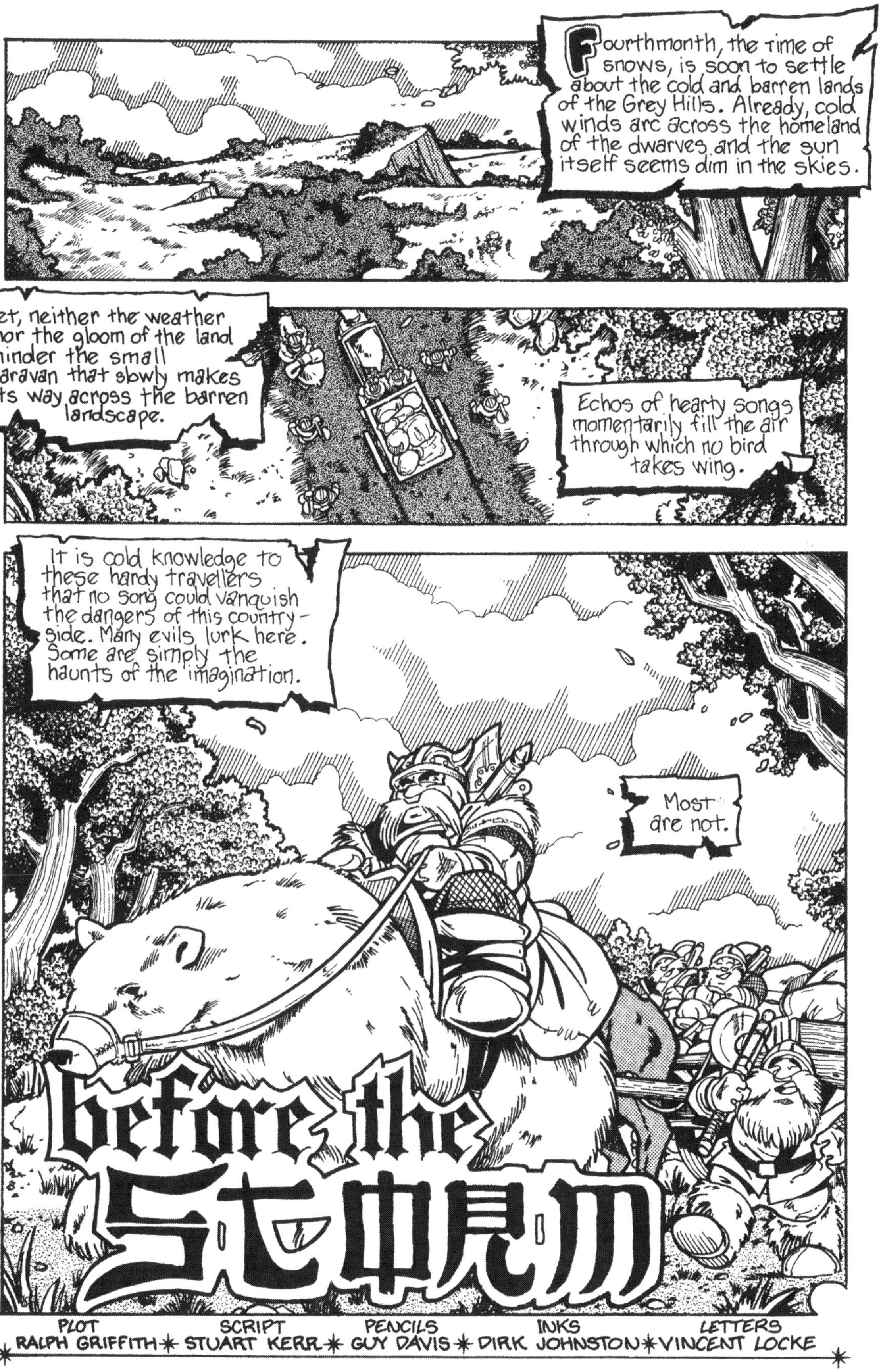
Fourthmonth, the time of snows, is soon to settle about the cold and barren lands of the Grey Hills. Already, cold winds arc across the homeland of the dwarves and the sun itself seems dim in the skies.
Yet, neither the weather nor the gloom of the land hinder the small caravan that slowly makes its way across the barren landscape.
Echos of hearty songs momentarily fill the air through which no bird takes wing.
It is cold knowledge to these hardy travellers that no song could vanquish the dangers of this countryside. Many evils lurk here. Some are simply the haunts of the imagination.
Most are not.
before the STORM

PLOT RALPH GRIFFITH ✶ SCRIPT STUART KERR ✶ PENCILS GUY DAVIS ✶ INKS DIRK JOHNSTON ✶ LETTERS VINCENT LOCKE

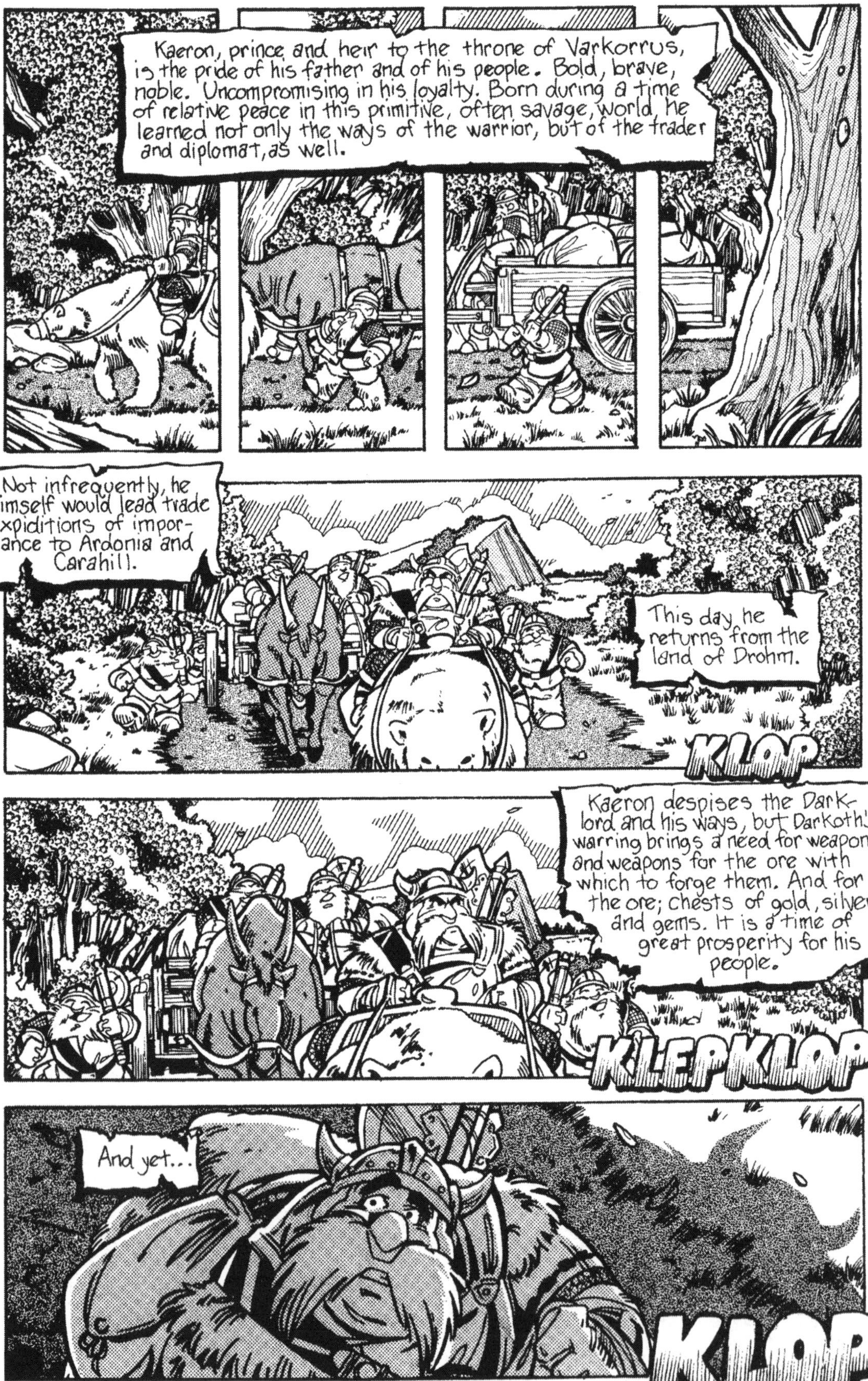
Kaeron, prince and heir to the throne of Varkorrus, is the pride of his father and of his people. Bold, brave, noble. Uncompromising in his loyalty. Born during a time of relative peace in this primitive, often savage, world, he learned not only the ways of the warrior, but of the trader and diplomat, as well.
Not infrequently, he himself would lead trade expiditions of importance to Ardonia and Carahill.
This day, he returns from the land of Drohm.
KLOP
Kaeron despises the Darklord and his ways, but Darkoth's warring brings a need for weapons, and weapons for the ore with which to forge them. And for the ore; chests of gold, silver and gems. It is a time of great prosperity for his people.
KLEPKLOP
And yet...
KLOP

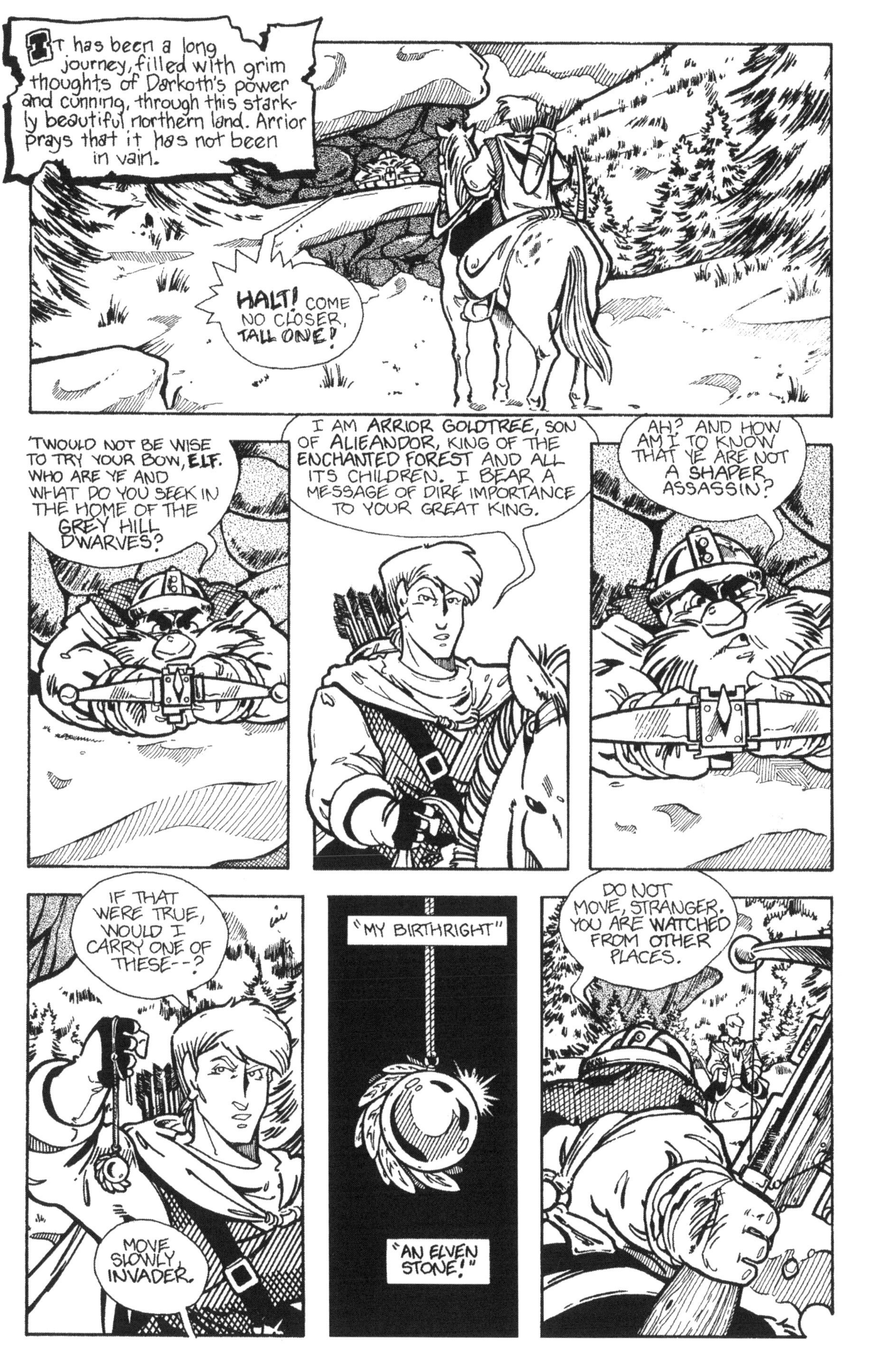
It has been a long journey, filled with grim thoughts of Darkoth's power and cunning, through this starkly beautiful northern land. Arrior prays that it has not been in vain.
HALT! COME NO CLOSER, TALL ONE!
'TWOULD NOT BE WISE TO TRY YOUR BOW, ELF. WHO ARE YE AND WHAT DO YOU SEEK IN THE HOME OF THE GREY HILL DWARVES?
I AM ARRIOR GOLDTREE, SON OF ALIEANDOR, KING OF THE ENCHANTED FOREST AND ALL ITS CHILDREN. I BEAR A MESSAGE OF DIRE IMPORTANCE TO YOUR GREAT KING.
AH? AND HOW AM I TO KNOW THAT YE ARE NOT A SHAPER ASSASSIN?
IF THAT WERE TRUE, WOULD I CARRY ONE OF THESE--?
MOVE SLOWLY, INVADER.
"MY BIRTHRIGHT"
"AN ELVEN STONE!"
DO NOT MOVE, STRANGER. YOU ARE WATCHED FROM OTHER PLACES.

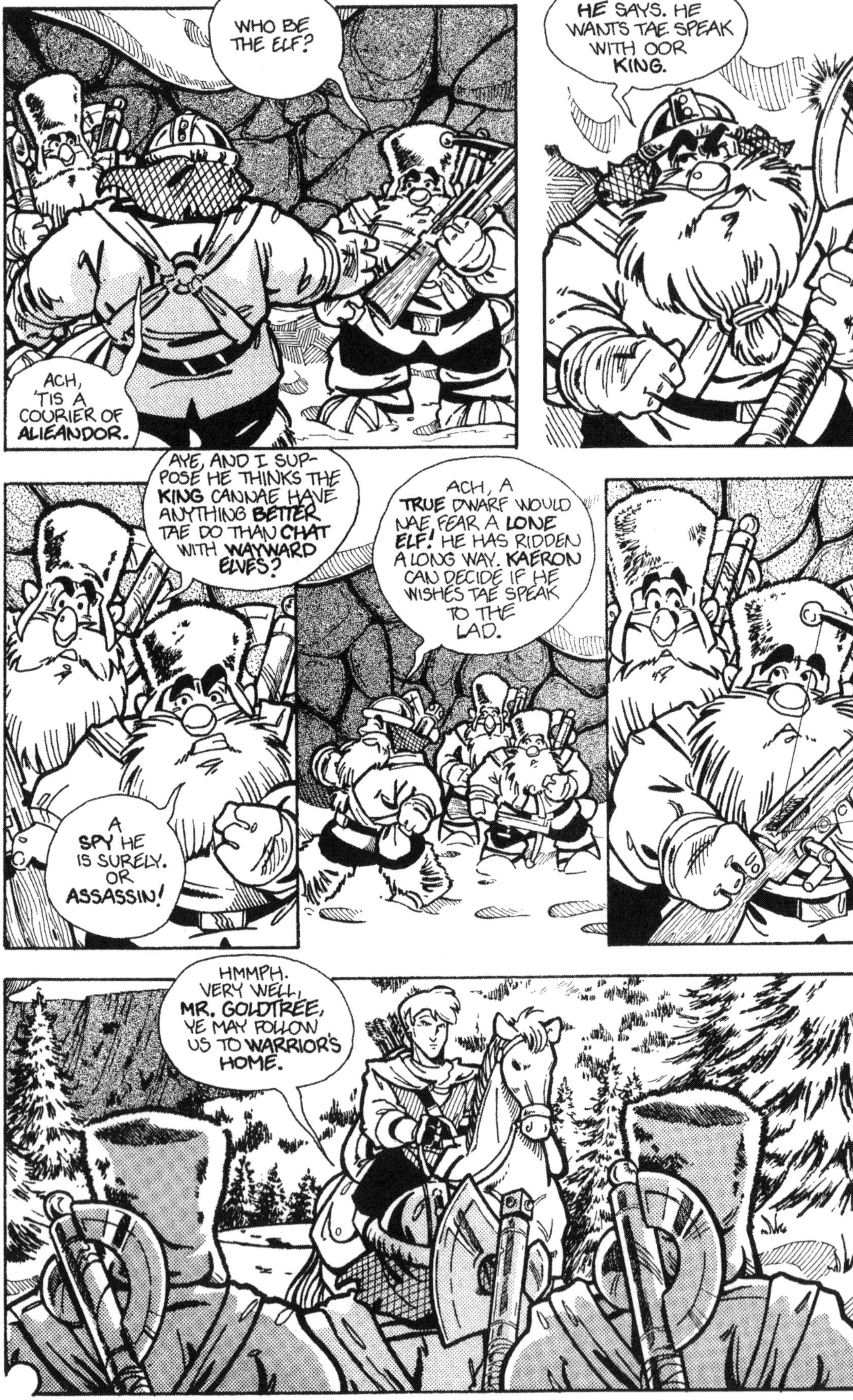
WHO BE THE ELF?
ACH, 'TIS A COURIER OF ALIEANDOR.
OR SO HE SAYS. HE WANTS TAE SPEAK WITH OOR KING.
AYE, AND I SUPPOSE HE THINKS THE KING CANNAE HAVE ANYTHING BETTER TAE DO THAN CHAT WITH WAYWARD ELVES?
A SPY HE IS SURELY. OR ASSASSIN!
ACH, A TRUE DWARF WOULD NAE FEAR A LONE ELF! HE HAS RIDDEN A LONG WAY. KAERON CAN DECIDE IF HE WISHES TAE SPEAK TO THE LAD.
HMMPH. VERY WELL, MR. GOLDTREE, YE MAY FOLLOW US TO WARRIOR'S HOME.

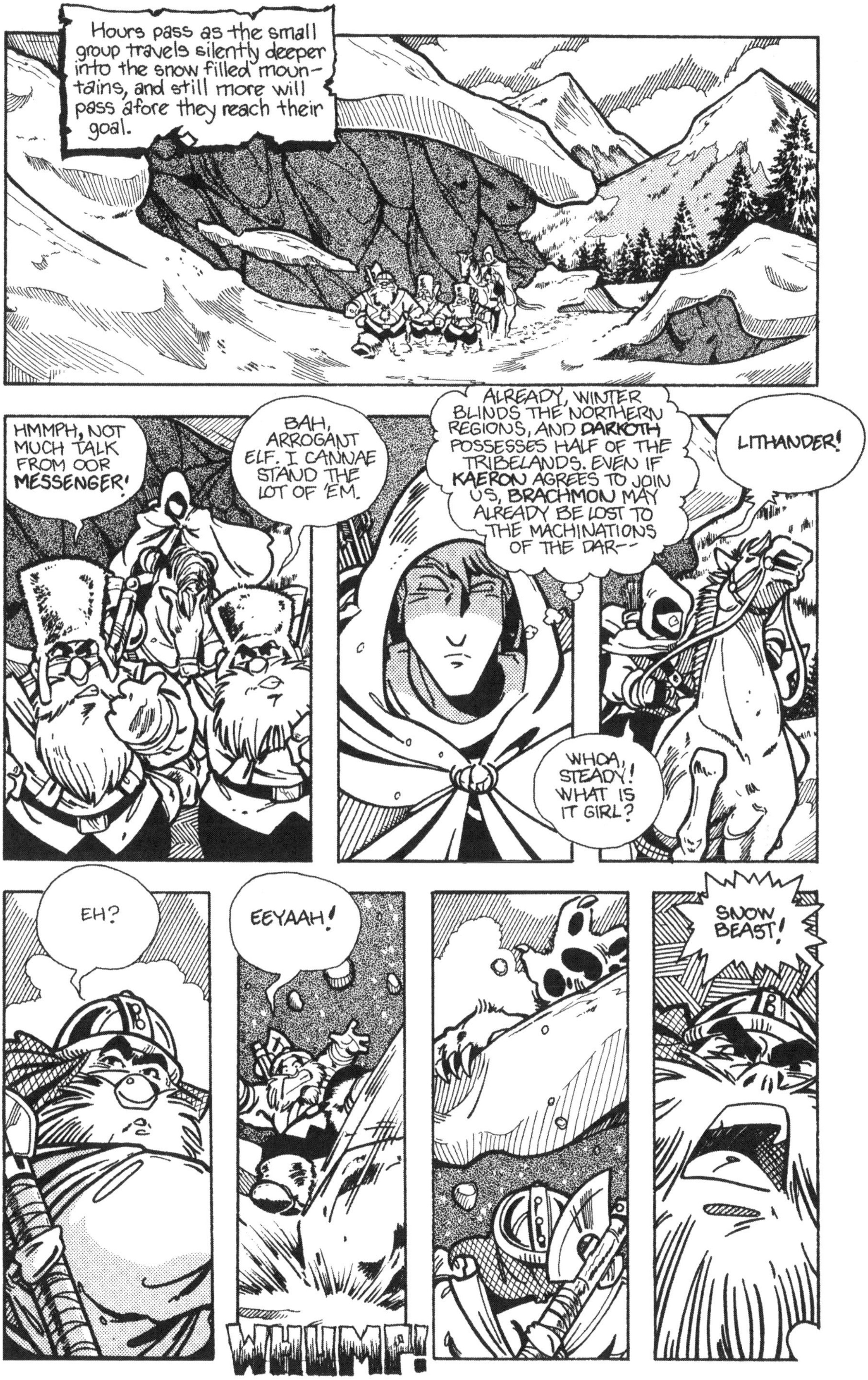
Hours pass as the small group travels silently deeper into the snow filled mountains, and still more will pass afore they reach their goal.
HMMPH, NOT MUCH TALK FROM OOR MESSENGER!
BAH, ARROGANT ELF. I CANNAE STAND THE LOT OF 'EM.
ALREADY, WINTER BLINDS THE NORTHERN REGIONS, AND DARKOTH POSSESSES HALF OF THE TRIBELANDS. EVEN IF KAERON AGREES TO JOIN US, BRACHMON MAY ALREADY BE LOST TO THE MACHINATIONS OF THE DAR--
LITHANDER!
WHOA, STEADY! WHAT IS IT GIRL?
EH?
EEYAAH!
WHUMP!
SNOW BEAST!

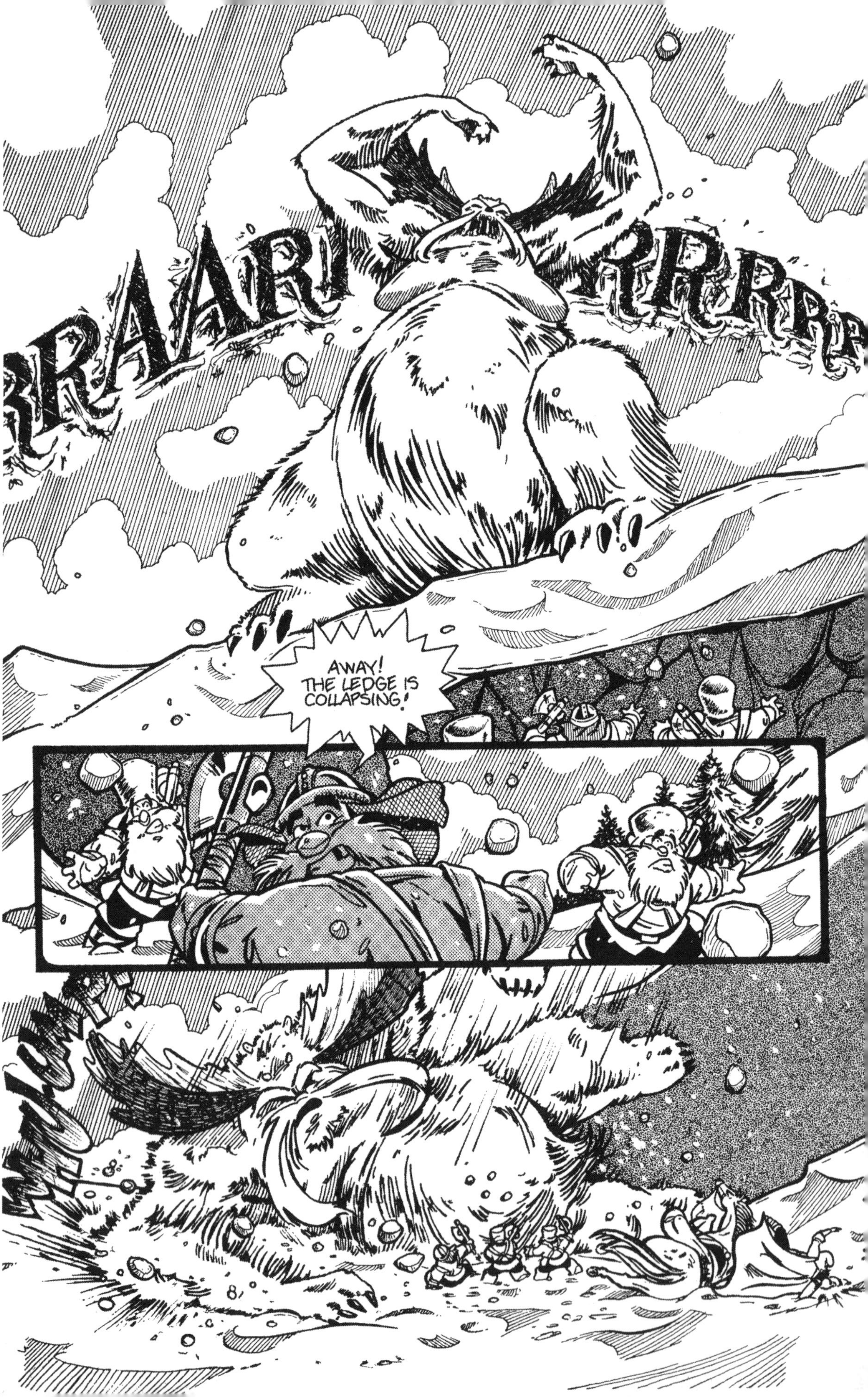
RRAAR! RRRRR
AWAY! THE LEDGE IS COLLAPSING!

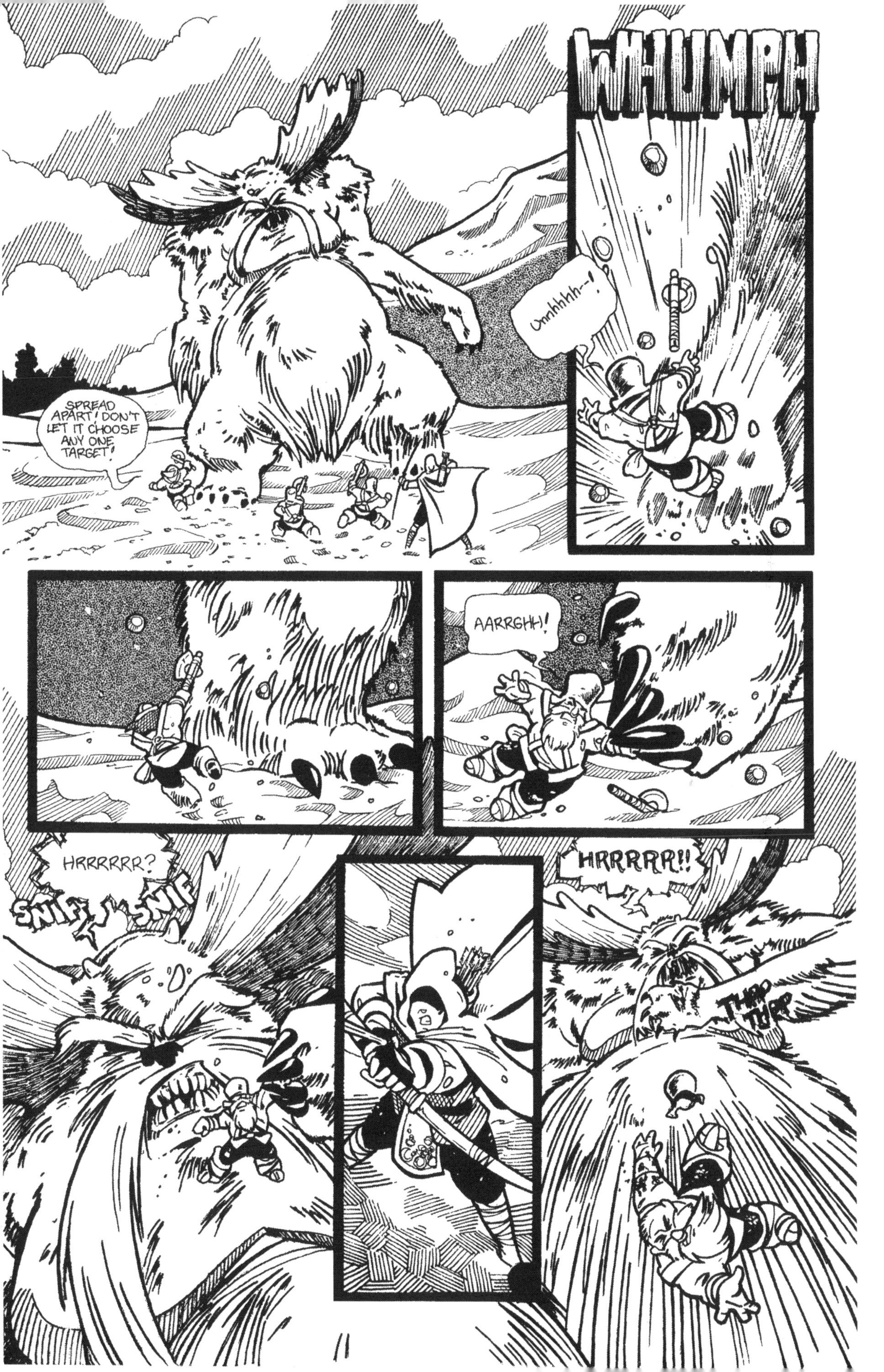

WHUMPH
SPREAD APART! DON'T LET IT CHOOSE ANY ONE TARGET!
Unnhhhh--!
AARRGHH!
HRRRRRR?
SNIF SNIF
HRRRRRR!!
THRP THRP

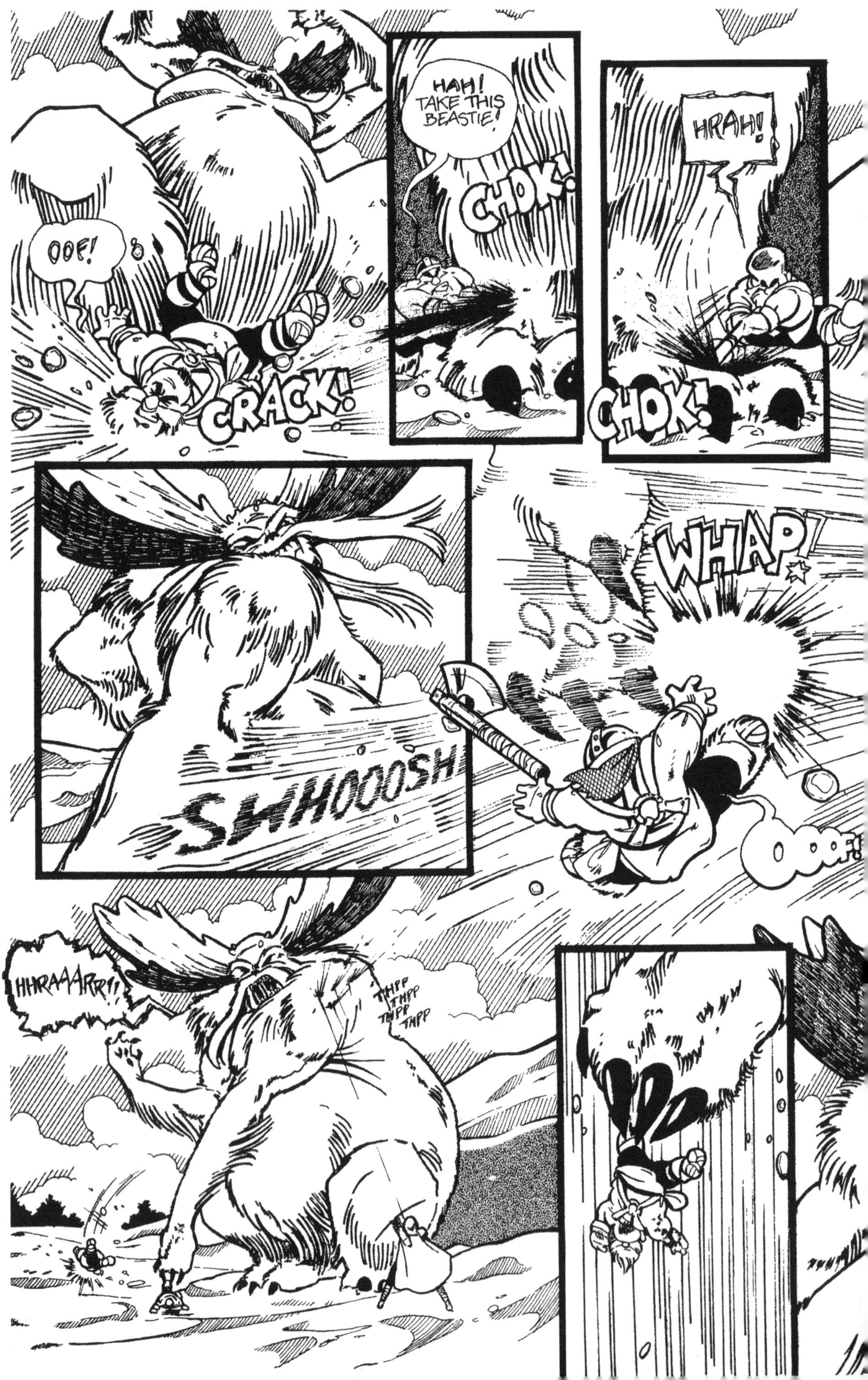
OOF!
CRACK!
HAH! TAKE THIS BEASTIE!
CHOK!
HRAH!
CHOK!
WHAP!
SWHOOOSH
OOOF!
HHRAAARR!!
THPP THPP THPP THPP

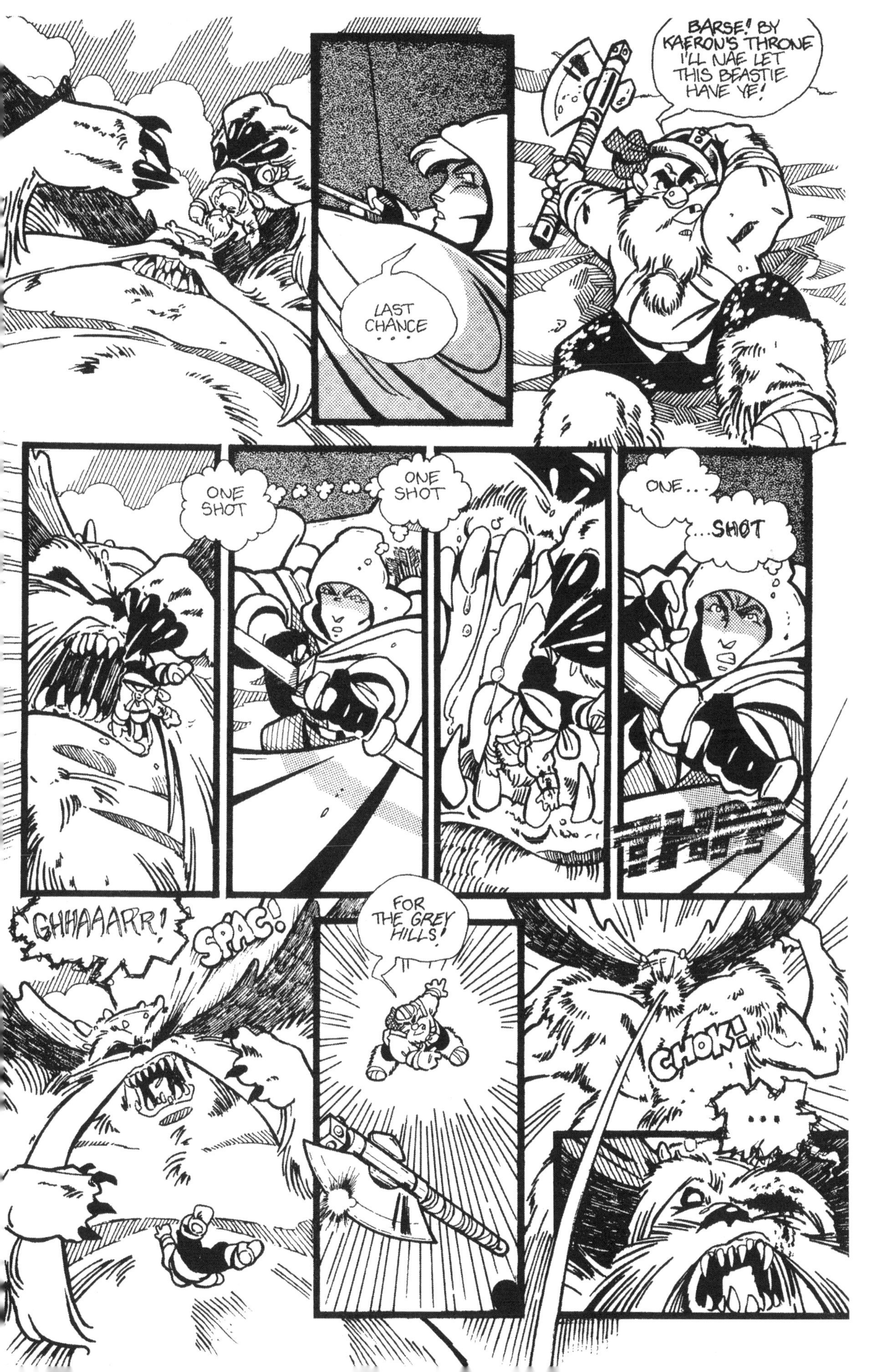
LAST CHANCE . . .
BARSE! BY KAERON'S THRONE I'LL NAE LET THIS BEASTIE HAVE YE!
ONE SHOT
ONE SHOT
ONE...
...SHOT
GHHAAARR!
SPAC!
FOR THE GREY HILLS!
CHOK!
. . .

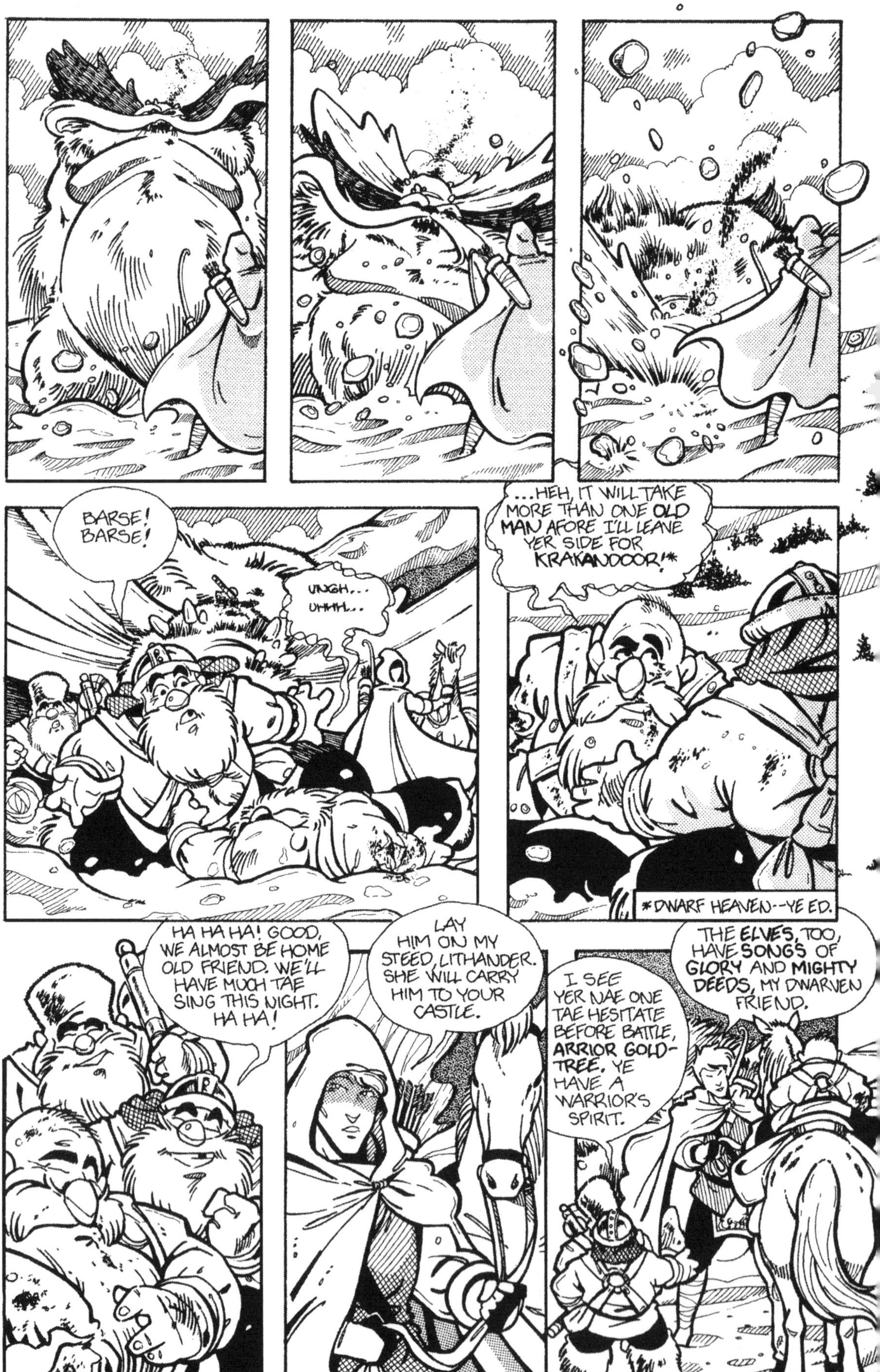
BARSE! BARSE!
UNGH... UHHH...
...HEH, IT WILL TAKE MORE THAN ONE OLD MAN AFORE I'LL LEAVE YER SIDE FOR KRAKANDOOR!*
*DWARF HEAVEN--YE ED.
HA HA HA! GOOD, WE ALMOST BE HOME OLD FRIEND. WE'LL HAVE MUCH TAE SING THIS NIGHT. HA HA!
LAY HIM ON MY STEED, LITHANDER. SHE WILL CARRY HIM TO YOUR CASTLE.
I SEE YER NAE ONE TAE HESITATE BEFORE BATTLE, ARRIOR GOLD-TREE. YE HAVE A WARRIOR'S SPIRIT.
THE ELVES, TOO, HAVE SONGS OF GLORY AND MIGHTY DEEDS, MY DWARVEN FRIEND.

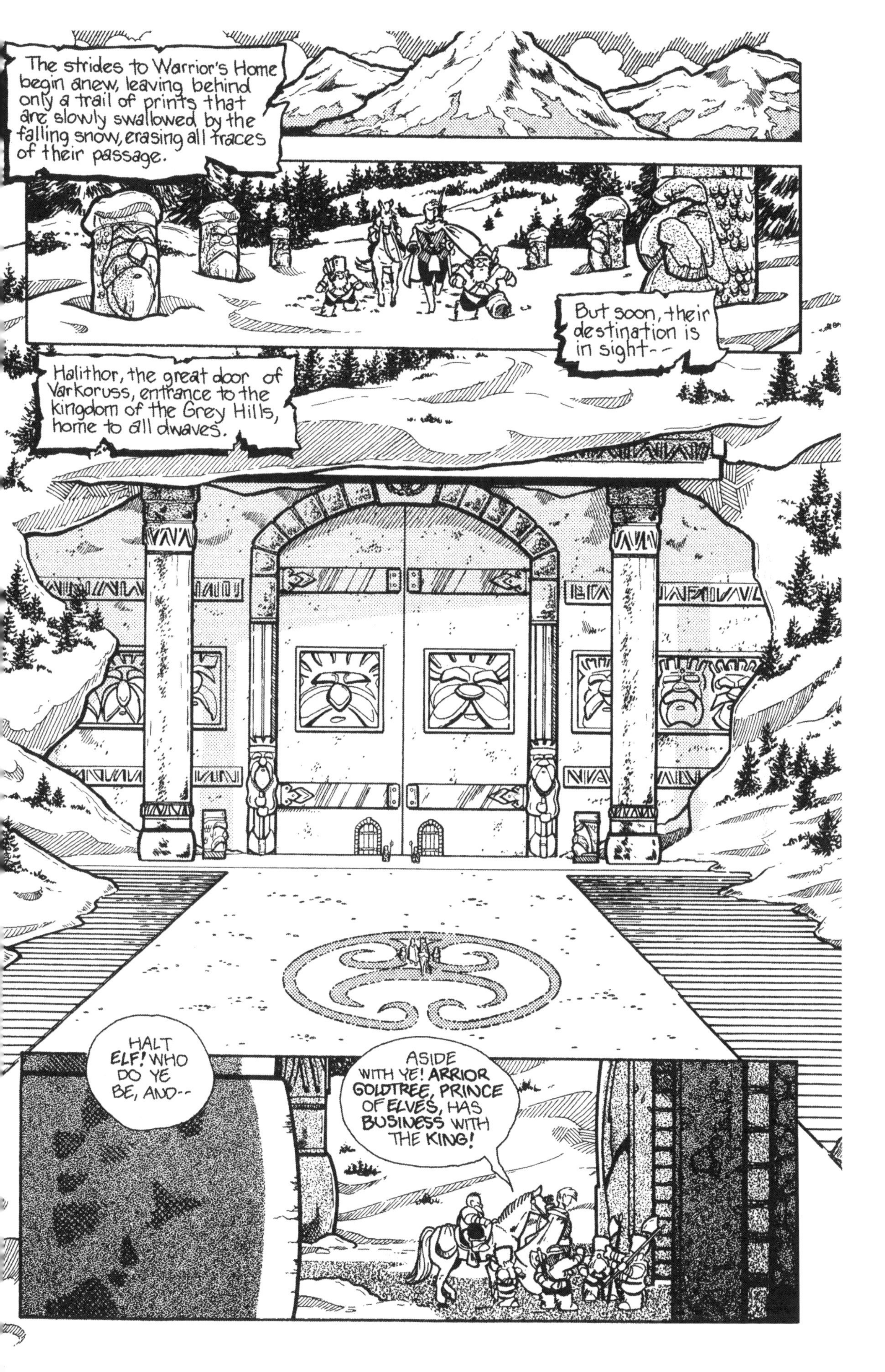
The strides to Warrior's Home begin anew, leaving behind only a trail of prints that are slowly swallowed by the falling snow, erasing all traces of their passage.
But soon, their destination is in sight--
Halithor, the great door of Varkoruss, entrance to the kingdom of the Grey Hills, home to all dwaves.
HALT ELF! WHO DO YE BE, AND--
ASIDE WITH YE! ARRIOR GOLDTREE, PRINCE OF ELVES, HAS BUSINESS WITH THE KING!

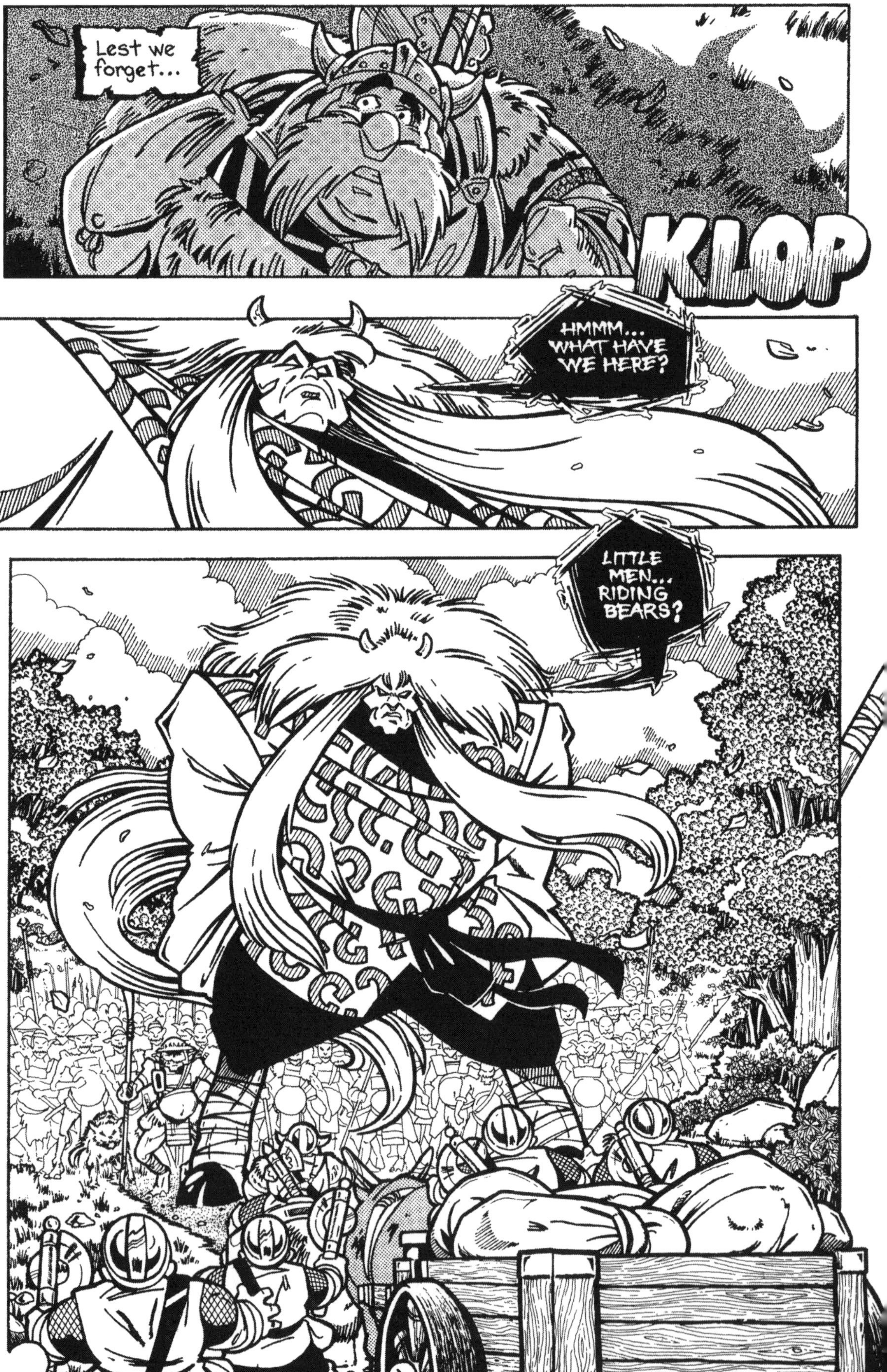
Lest we forget...
KLOP
HMMM... WHAT HAVE WE HERE?
LITTLE MEN... RIDING BEARS?

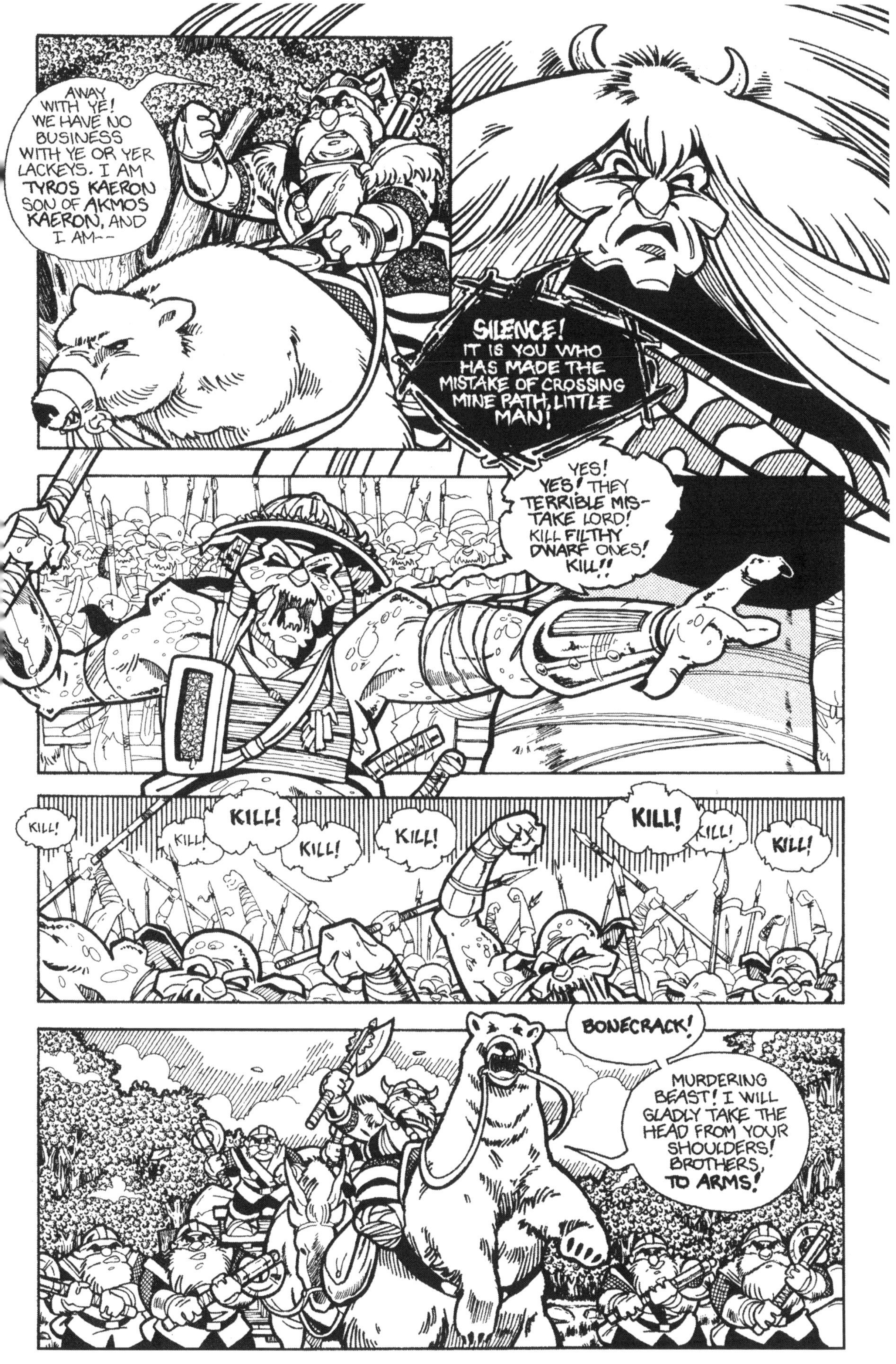
AWAY WITH YE! WE HAVE NO BUSINESS WITH YE OR YER LACKEYS. I AM TYROS KAERON SON OF AKMOS KAERON, AND I AM--
SILENCE! IT IS YOU WHO HAS MADE THE MISTAKE OF CROSSING MINE PATH, LITTLE MAN!
YES! YES! THEY TERRIBLE MISTAKE LORD! KILL FILTHY DWARF ONES! KILL!!
KILL!
KILL!
KILL!
KILL!
KILL!
KILL!
KILL!
KILL!
BONECRACK!
MURDERING BEAST! I WILL GLADLY TAKE THE HEAD FROM YOUR SHOULDERS! BROTHERS, TO ARMS!

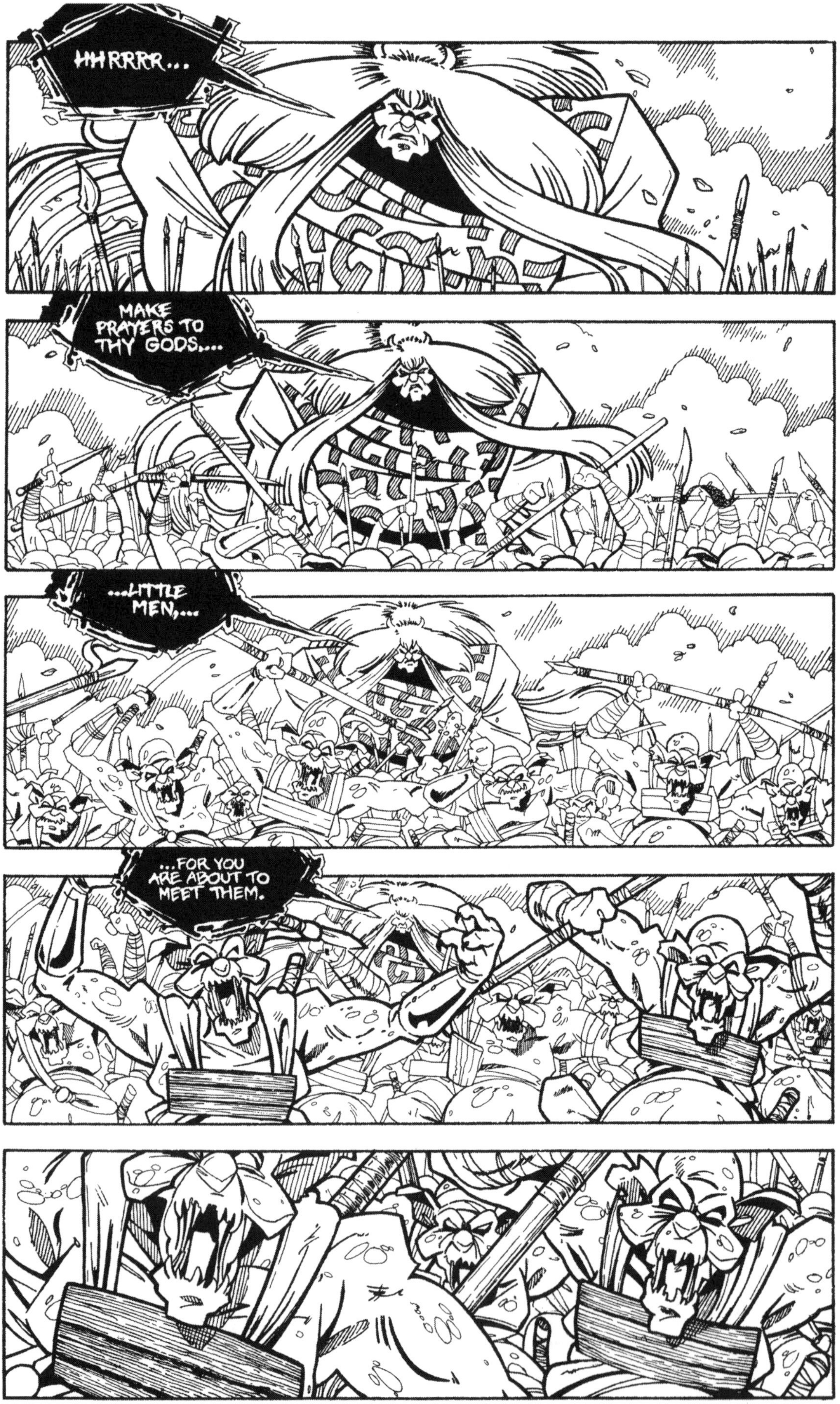
HHRRRR...
MAKE PRAYERS TO THY GODS,...
...LITTLE MEN,...
...FOR YOU ARE ABOUT TO MEET THEM.

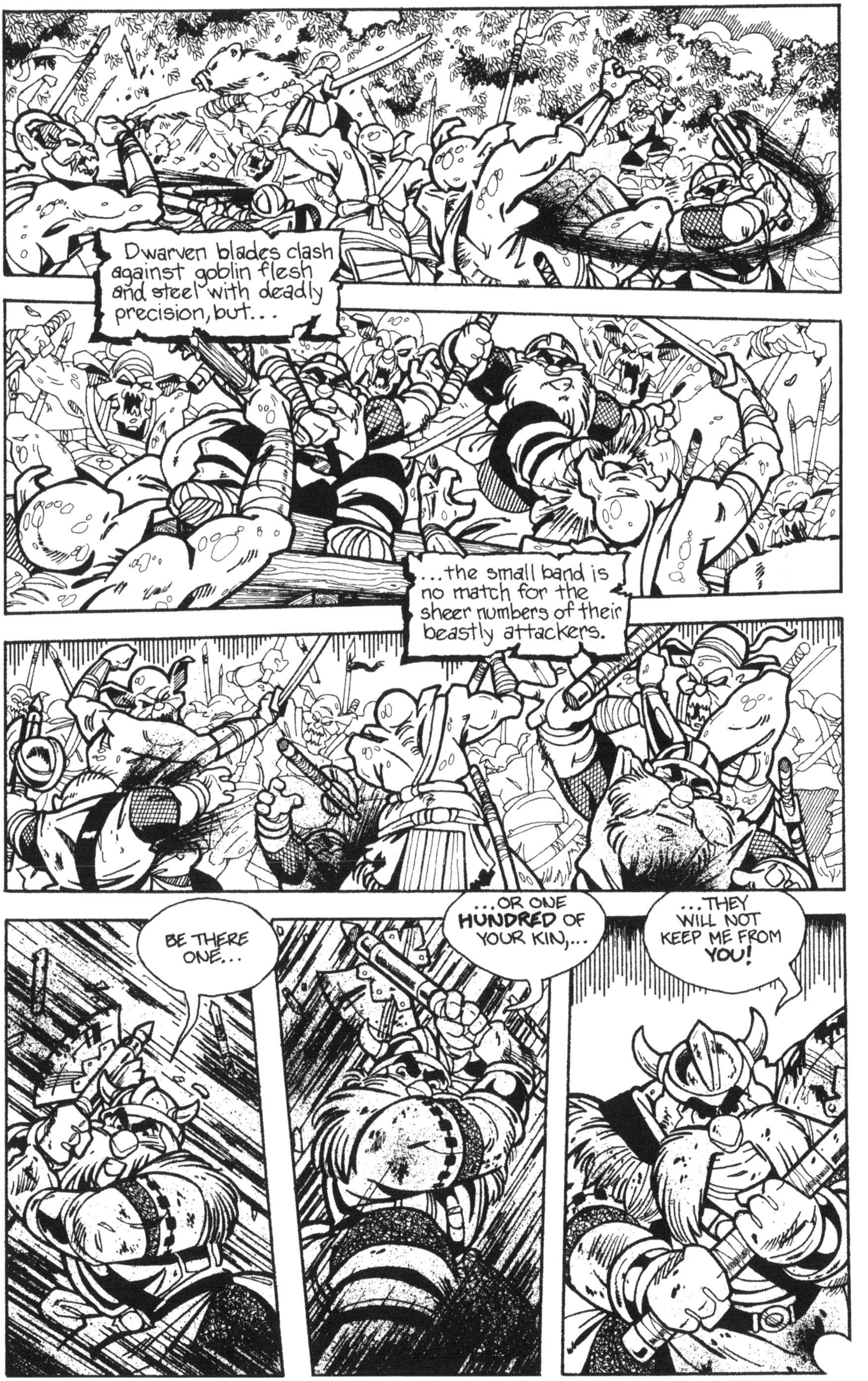

Dwarven blades clash against goblin flesh and steel with deadly precision, but...
...the small band is no match for the sheer numbers of their beastly attackers.
BE THERE ONE...
...OR ONE **HUNDRED** OF YOUR KIN,...
...THEY WILL NOT KEEP ME FROM **YOU**!

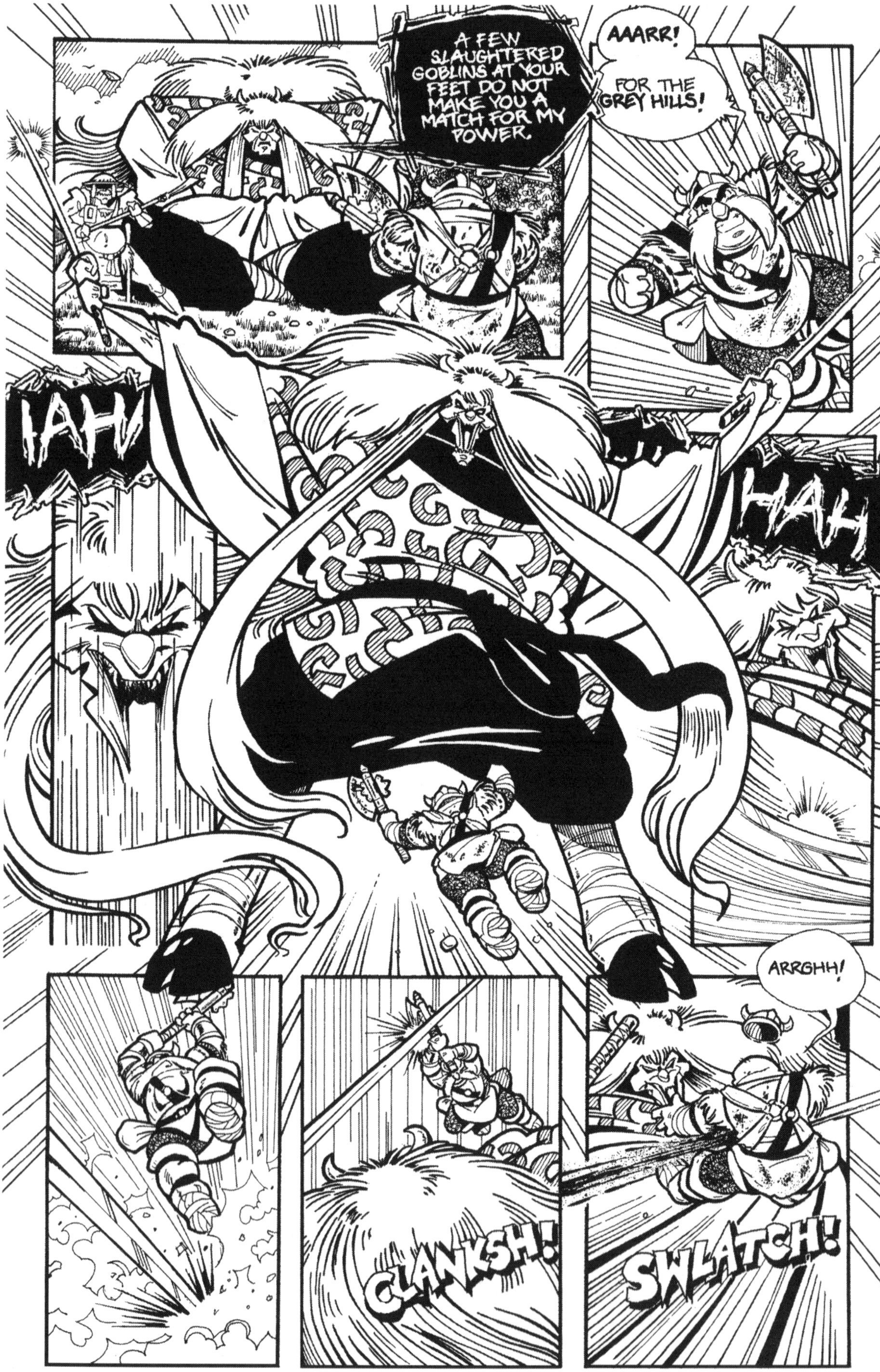
A FEW SLAUGHTERED GOBLINS AT YOUR FEET DO NOT MAKE YOU A MATCH FOR MY POWER.
AAARR!
FOR THE GREY HILLS!
IAH
HAH
ARRGHH!
CLANKSH!
SWLATCH!

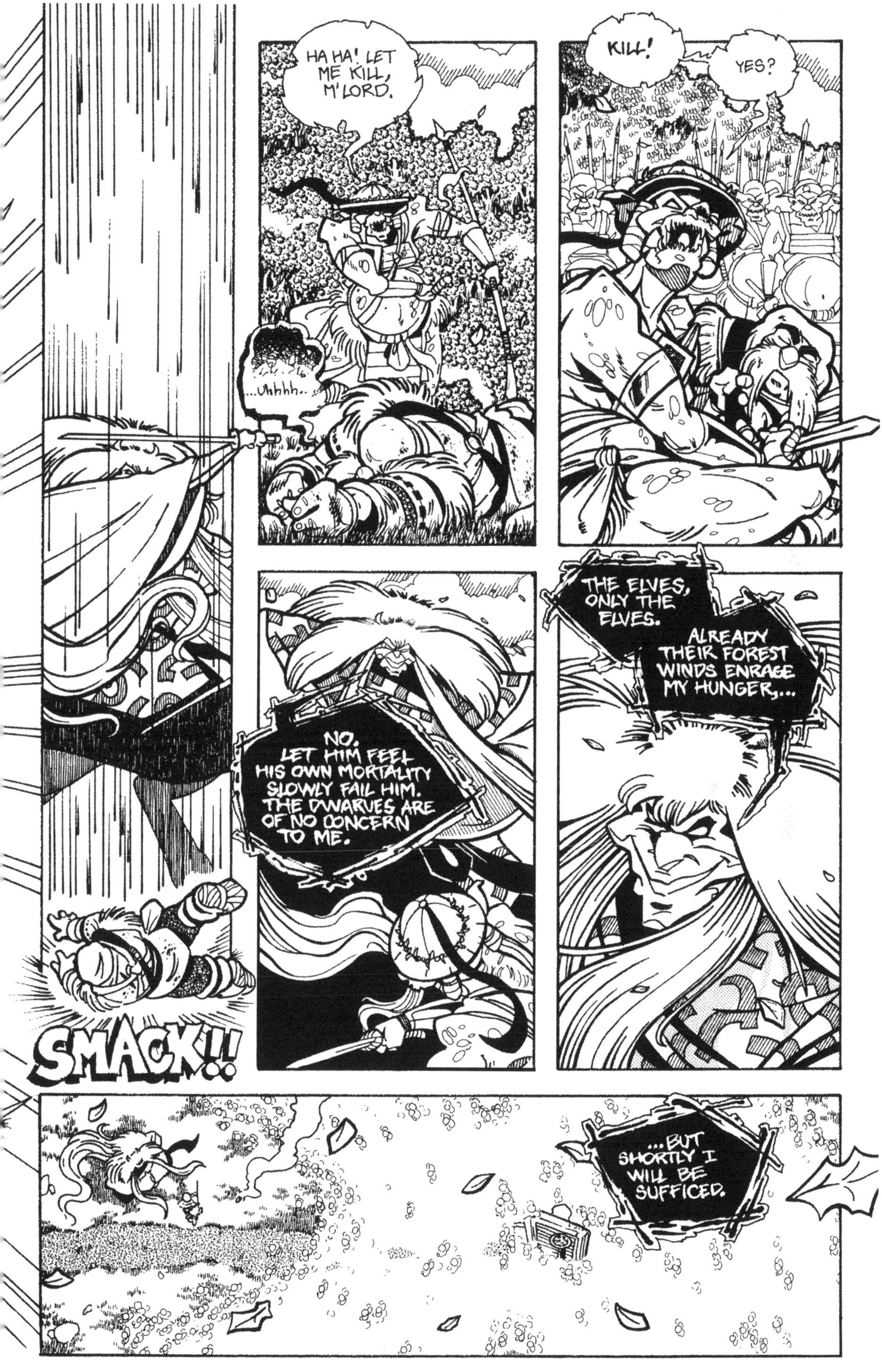

HA HA! LET ME KILL, M'LORD.
...Uhhhh...
KILL!
YES?
SMACK!!
NO. LET HIM FEEL HIS OWN MORTALITY SLOWLY FAIL HIM. THE DWARVES ARE OF NO CONCERN TO ME.
THE ELVES, ONLY THE ELVES.
ALREADY THEIR FOREST WINDS ENRAGE MY HUNGER,...
...BUT SHORTLY I WILL BE SUFFICED.

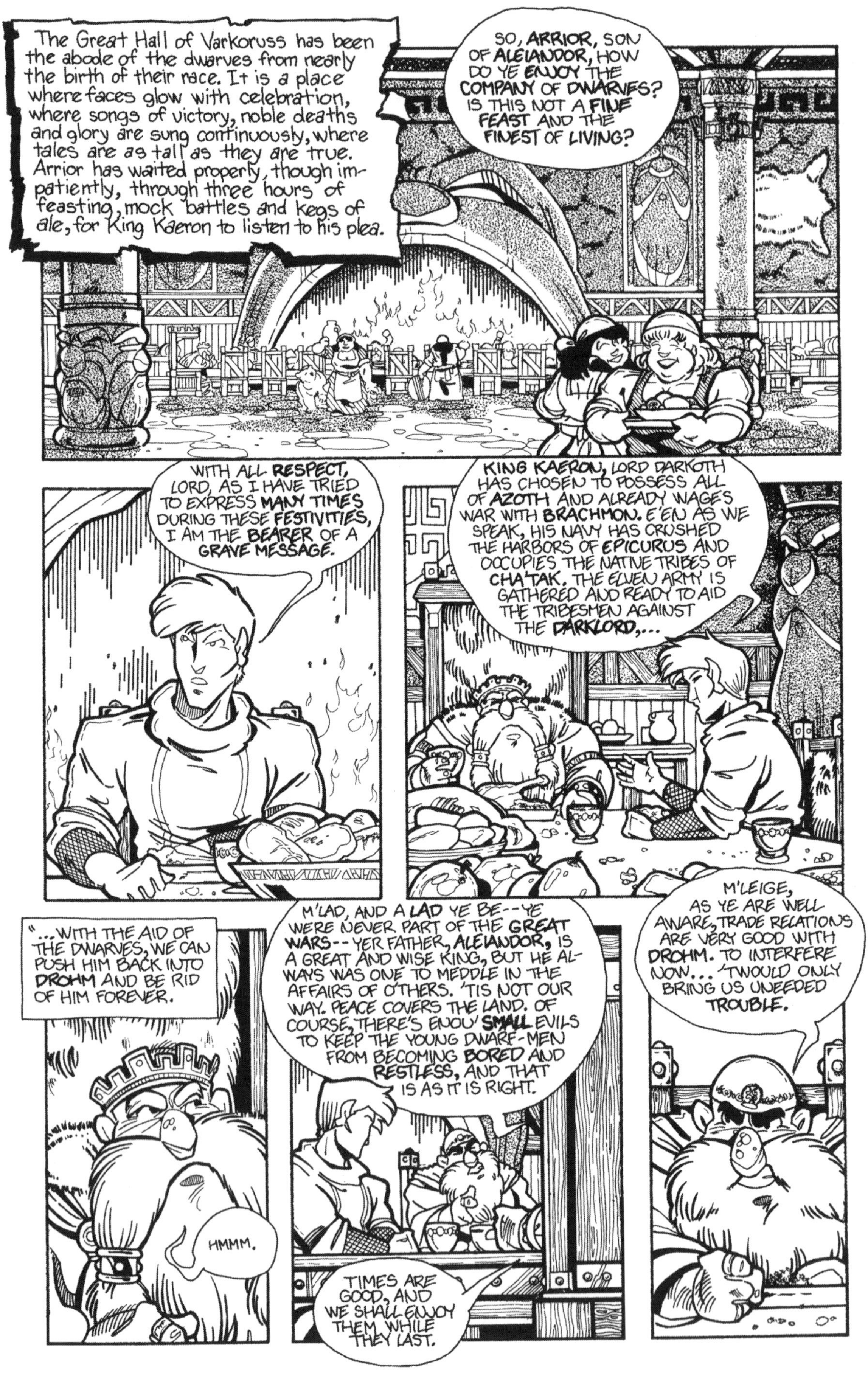
The Great Hall of Varkoruss has been the abode of the dwarves from nearly the birth of their race. It is a place where faces glow with celebration, where songs of victory, noble deaths and glory are sung continuously, where tales are as tall as they are true. Arrior has waited properly, though impatiently, through three hours of feasting, mock battles and kegs of ale, for King Kaeron to listen to his plea.
SO, ARRIOR, SON OF ALEIANDOR, HOW DO YE ENJOY THE COMPANY OF DWARVES? IS THIS NOT A FINE FEAST AND THE FINEST OF LIVING?
WITH ALL RESPECT, LORD, AS I HAVE TRIED TO EXPRESS MANY TIMES DURING THESE FESTIVITIES, I AM THE BEARER OF A GRAVE MESSAGE.
KING KAERON, LORD DARKOTH HAS CHOSEN TO POSSESS ALL OF AZOTH AND ALREADY WAGES WAR WITH BRACHMON. E'EN AS WE SPEAK, HIS NAVY HAS CRUSHED THE HARBORS OF EPICURUS AND OCCUPIES THE NATIVE TRIBES OF CHA'TAK. THE ELVEN ARMY IS GATHERED AND READY TO AID THE TRIBESMEN AGAINST THE DARKLORD,...
"...WITH THE AID OF THE DWARVES, WE CAN PUSH HIM BACK INTO DROHM AND BE RID OF HIM FOREVER.
HMMM.
M'LAD, AND A LAD YE BE--YE WERE NEVER PART OF THE GREAT WARS--YER FATHER, ALEIANDOR, IS A GREAT AND WISE KING, BUT HE ALWAYS WAS ONE TO MEDDLE IN THE AFFAIRS OF O'THERS. 'TIS NOT OUR WAY. PEACE COVERS THE LAND. OF COURSE, THERE'S ENOU' SMALL EVILS TO KEEP THE YOUNG DWARF-MEN FROM BECOMING BORED AND RESTLESS, AND THAT IS AS IT IS RIGHT.
TIMES ARE GOOD, AND WE SHALL ENJOY THEM WHILE THEY LAST.
M'LEIGE, AS YE ARE WELL AWARE, TRADE RELATIONS ARE VERY GOOD WITH DROHM. TO INTERFERE NOW... 'TWOULD ONLY BRING US UNEEDED TROUBLE.

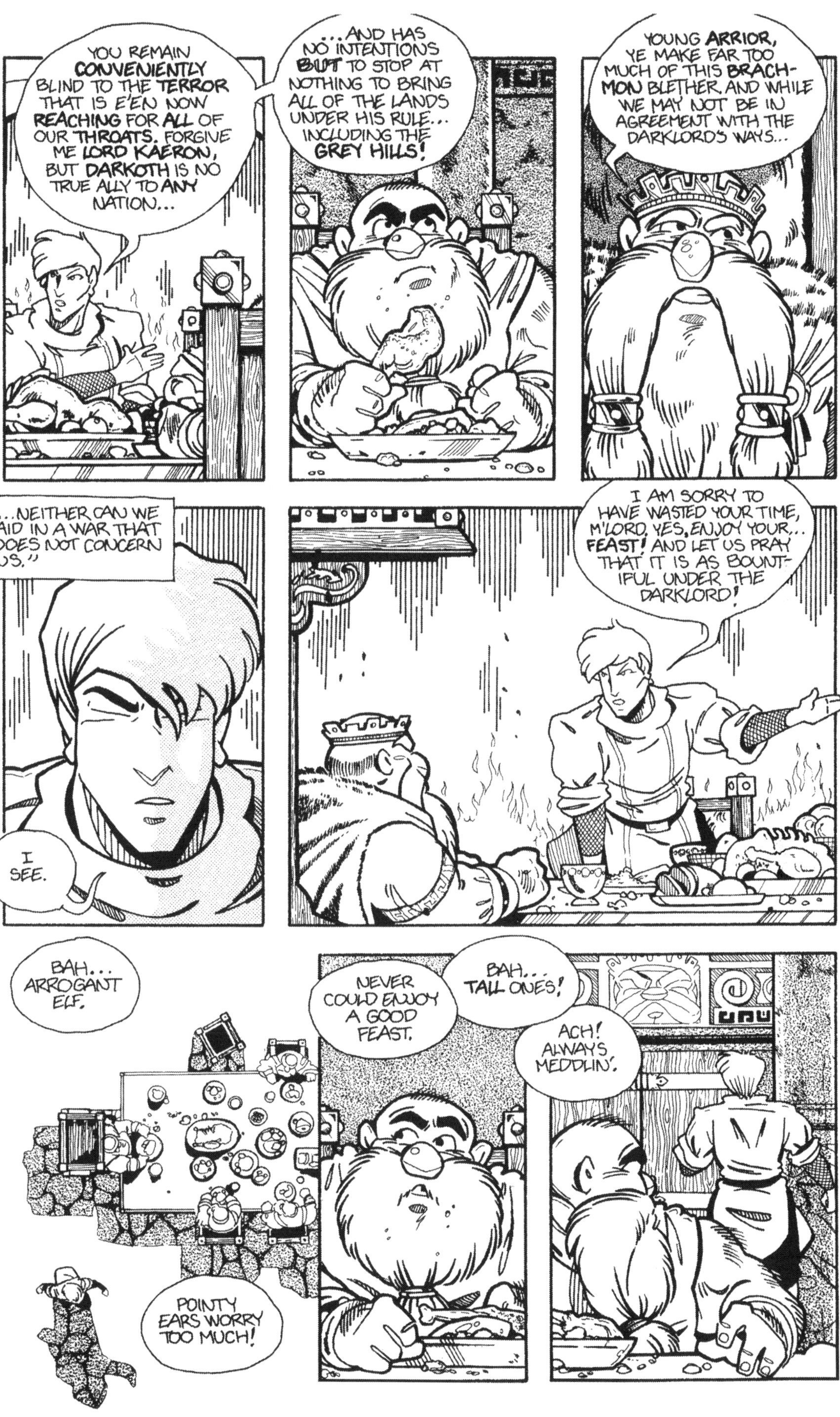

YOU REMAIN CONVENIENTLY BLIND TO THE TERROR THAT IS E'EN NOW REACHING FOR ALL OF OUR THROATS. FORGIVE ME LORD KAERON, BUT DARKOTH IS NO TRUE ALLY TO ANY NATION...
...AND HAS NO INTENTIONS BUT TO STOP AT NOTHING TO BRING ALL OF THE LANDS UNDER HIS RULE... INCLUDING THE GREY HILLS!
YOUNG ARRIOR, YE MAKE FAR TOO MUCH OF THIS BRACHMON BLETHER. AND WHILE WE MAY NOT BE IN AGREEMENT WITH THE DARKLORD'S WAYS...
"...NEITHER CAN WE AID IN A WAR THAT DOES NOT CONCERN US."
I SEE.
I AM SORRY TO HAVE WASTED YOUR TIME, M'LORD. YES, ENJOY YOUR... FEAST! AND LET US PRAY THAT IT IS AS BOUNTIFUL UNDER THE DARKLORD!
BAH... ARROGANT ELF.
POINTY EARS WORRY TOO MUCH!
NEVER COULD ENJOY A GOOD FEAST.
BAH... TALL ONES!
ACH! ALWAYS MEDDLIN'.

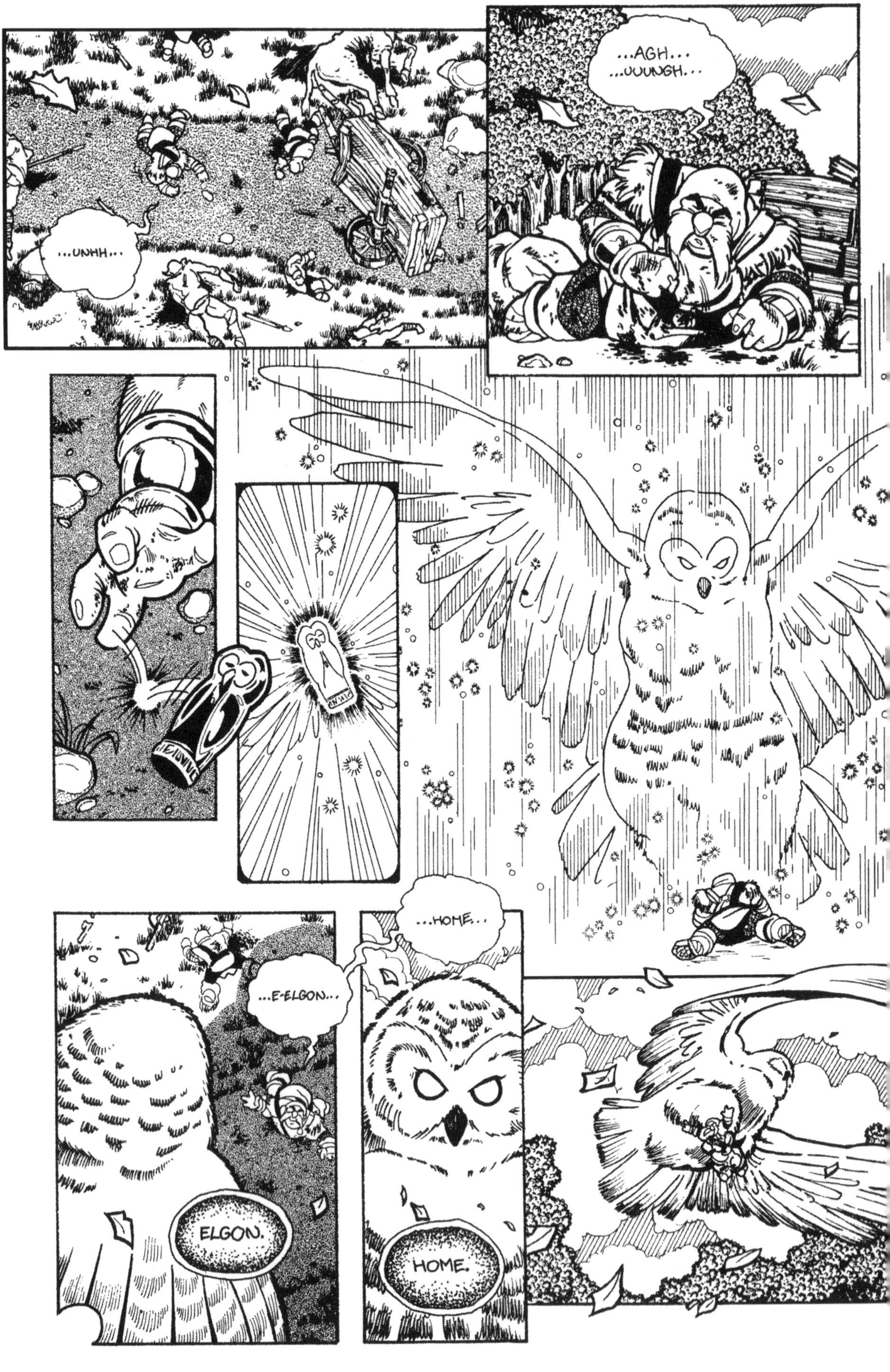
...UNHH...
...AGH...
...UUUNGH...
...E-ELGON...
ELGON.
...HOME...
HOME.

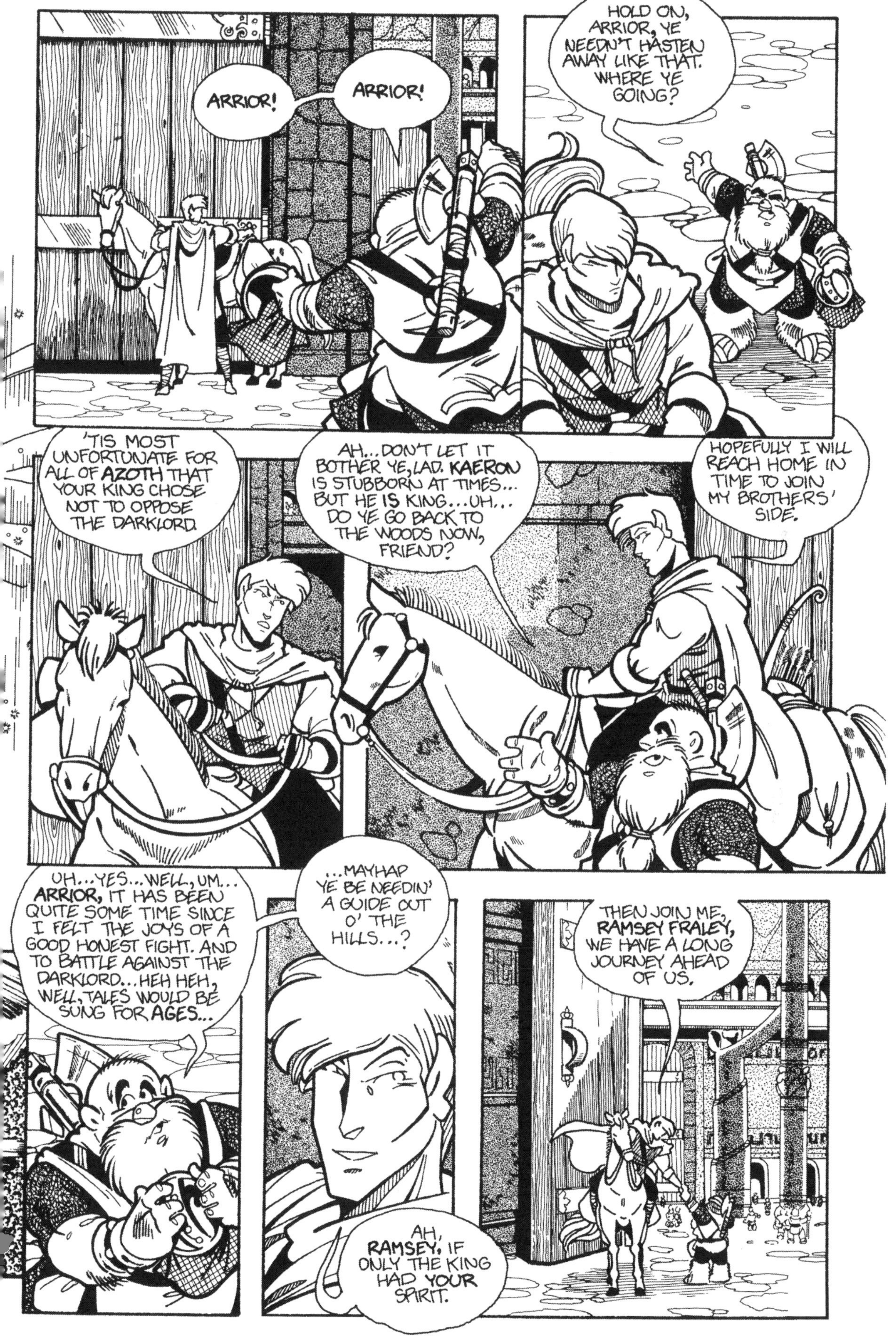
ARRIOR!
ARRIOR!
HOLD ON, ARRIOR, YE NEEDN'T HASTEN AWAY LIKE THAT. WHERE YE GOING?
'TIS MOST UNFORTUNATE FOR ALL OF AZOTH THAT YOUR KING CHOSE NOT TO OPPOSE THE DARKLORD.
AH...DON'T LET IT BOTHER YE, LAD. KAERON IS STUBBORN AT TIMES... BUT HE IS KING...UH... DO YE GO BACK TO THE WOODS NOW, FRIEND?
HOPEFULLY I WILL REACH HOME IN TIME TO JOIN MY BROTHERS' SIDE.
UH...YES...WELL, UM... ARRIOR, IT HAS BEEN QUITE SOME TIME SINCE I FELT THE JOYS OF A GOOD HONEST FIGHT. AND TO BATTLE AGAINST THE DARKLORD...HEH HEH, WELL, TALES WOULD BE SUNG FOR AGES...
...MAYHAP YE BE NEEDIN' A GUIDE OUT O' THE HILLS...?
AH, RAMSEY, IF ONLY THE KING HAD YOUR SPIRIT.
THEN JOIN ME, RAMSEY FRALEY, WE HAVE A LONG JOURNEY AHEAD OF US.

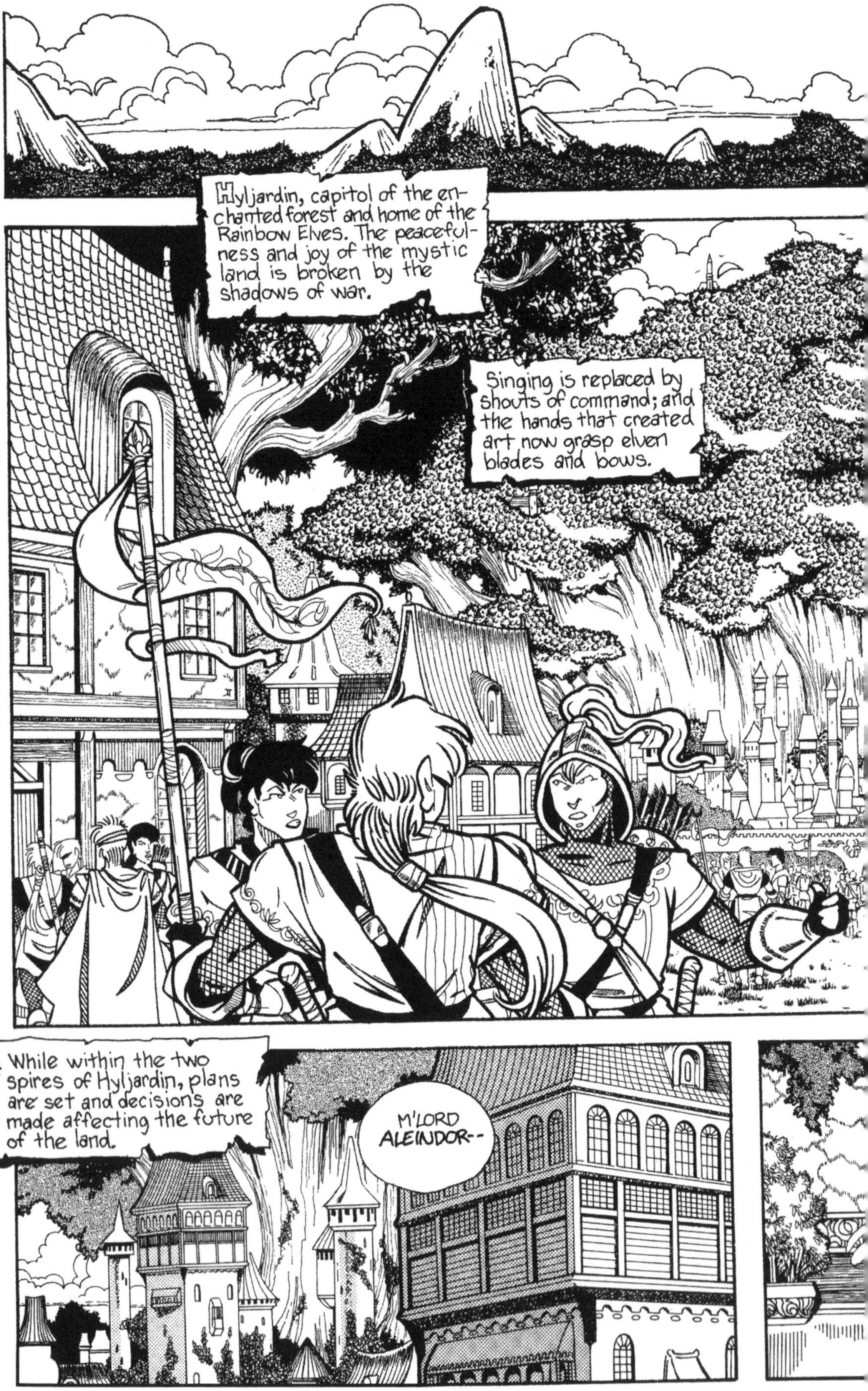
Hyljardin, capitol of the enchanted forest and home of the Rainbow Elves. The peacefulness and joy of the mystic land is broken by the shadows of war.
Singing is replaced by shouts of command; and the hands that created art now grasp elven blades and bows.
While within the two spires of Hyljardin, plans are set and decisions are made affecting the future of the land.
M'LORD ALEINDOR--

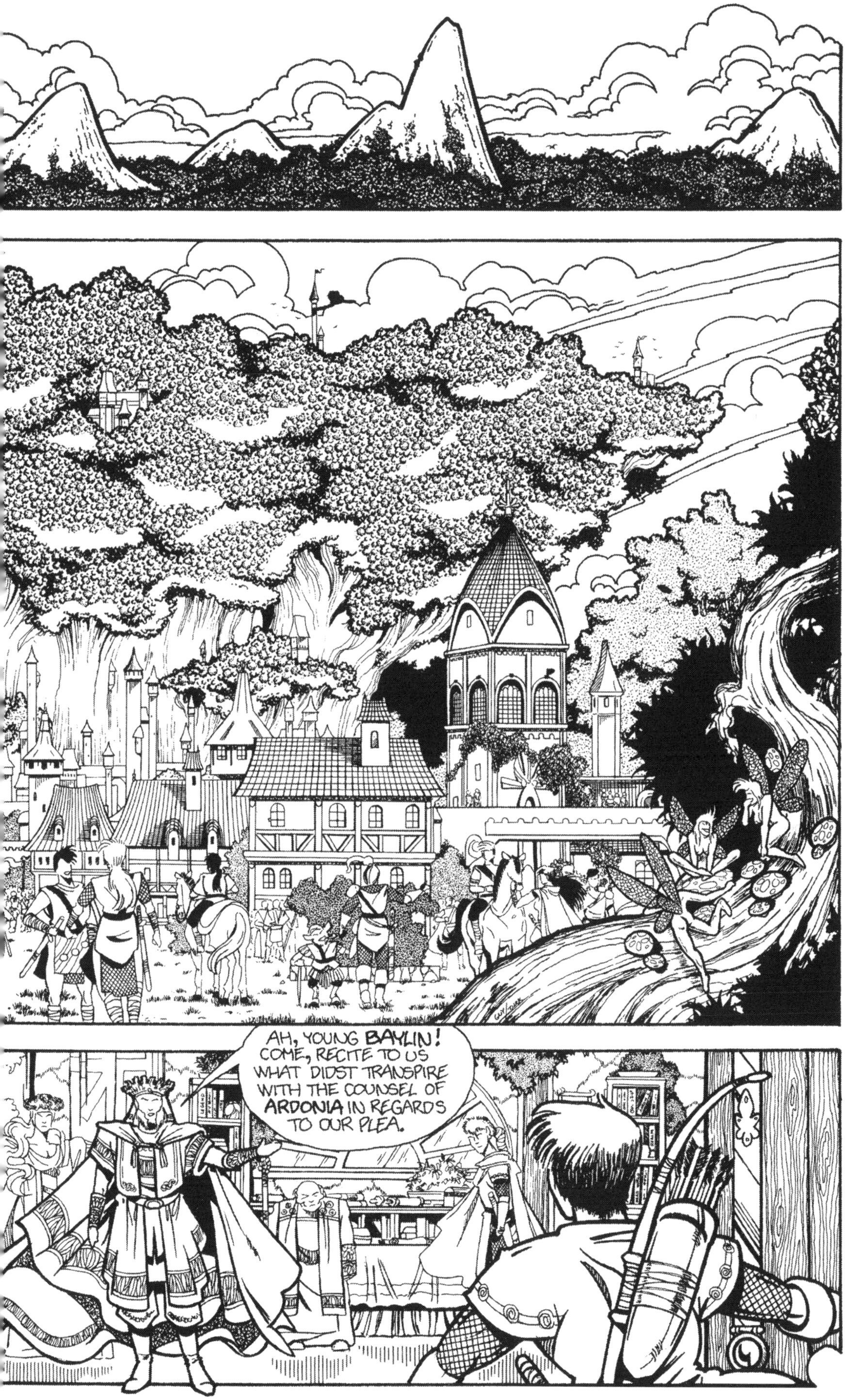
AH, YOUNG **BAYLIN**! COME, RECITE TO US WHAT DIDST TRANSPIRE WITH THE COUNSEL OF **ARDONIA** IN REGARDS TO OUR PLEA.

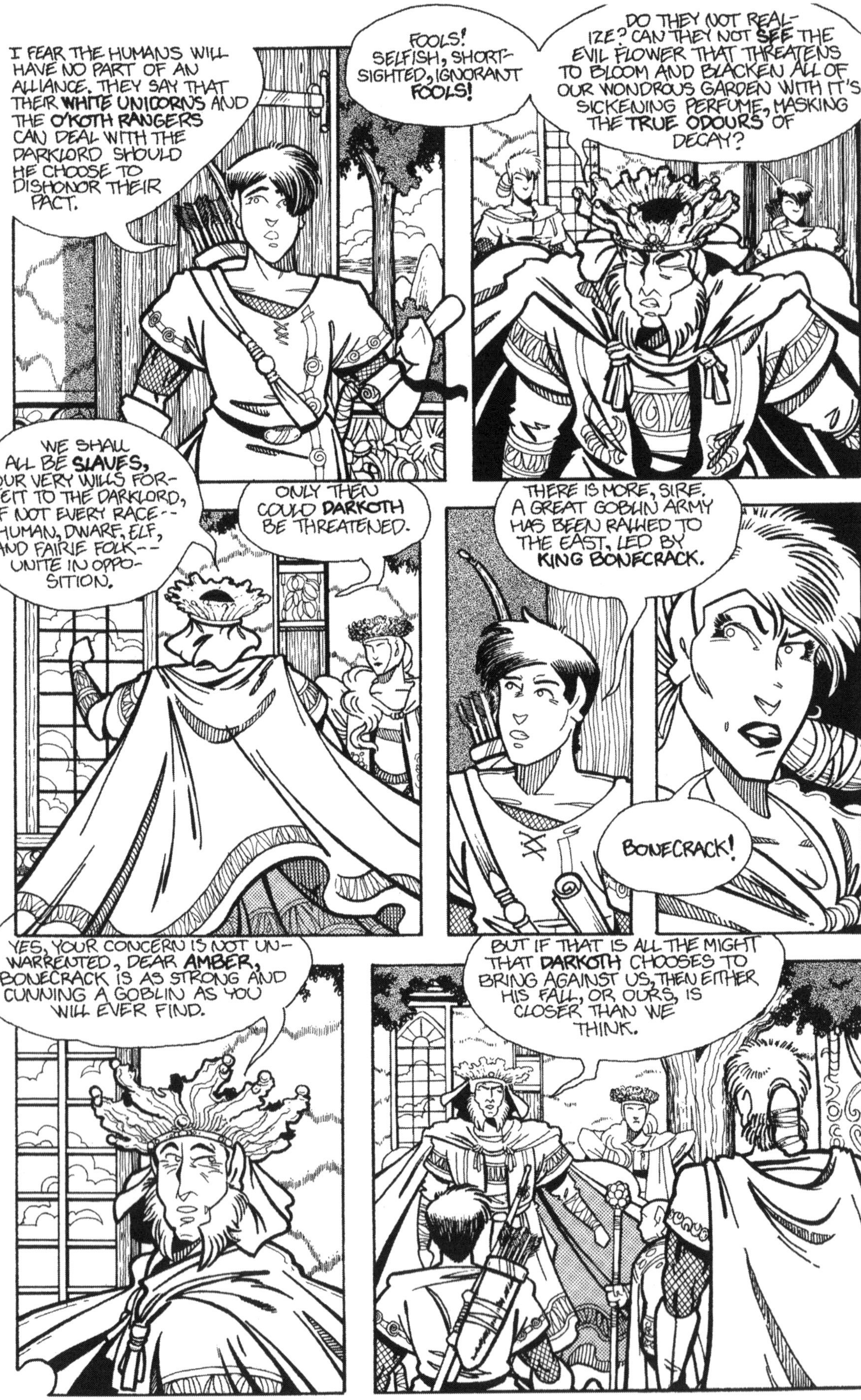

I FEAR THE HUMANS WILL HAVE NO PART OF AN ALLIANCE. THEY SAY THAT THEIR **WHITE UNICORNS** AND THE **O'KOTH RANGERS** CAN DEAL WITH THE DARKLORD SHOULD HE CHOOSE TO DISHONOR THEIR PACT.
FOOLS! SELFISH, SHORT-SIGHTED, IGNORANT **FOOLS!**
DO THEY NOT REALIZE? CAN THEY NOT **SEE** THE EVIL FLOWER THAT THREATENS TO BLOOM AND BLACKEN ALL OF OUR WONDROUS GARDEN WITH IT'S SICKENING PERFUME, MASKING THE **TRUE ODOURS** OF DECAY?
WE SHALL ALL BE **SLAVES,** OUR VERY WILLS FORFEIT TO THE DARKLORD, IF NOT EVERY RACE-- HUMAN, DWARF, ELF, AND FAIRIE FOLK-- UNITE IN OPPOSITION.
ONLY THEN COULD **DARKOTH** BE THREATENED.
THERE IS MORE, SIRE. A GREAT GOBLIN ARMY HAS BEEN RALLIED TO THE EAST, LED BY **KING BONECRACK.**
BONECRACK!
YES, YOUR CONCERN IS NOT UNWARRENTED, DEAR **AMBER**, BONECRACK IS AS STRONG AND CUNNING A GOBLIN AS YOU WILL EVER FIND.
BUT IF THAT IS ALL THE MIGHT THAT **DARKOTH** CHOOSES TO BRING AGAINST US, THEN EITHER HIS **FALL**, OR OURS, IS CLOSER THAN WE THINK.

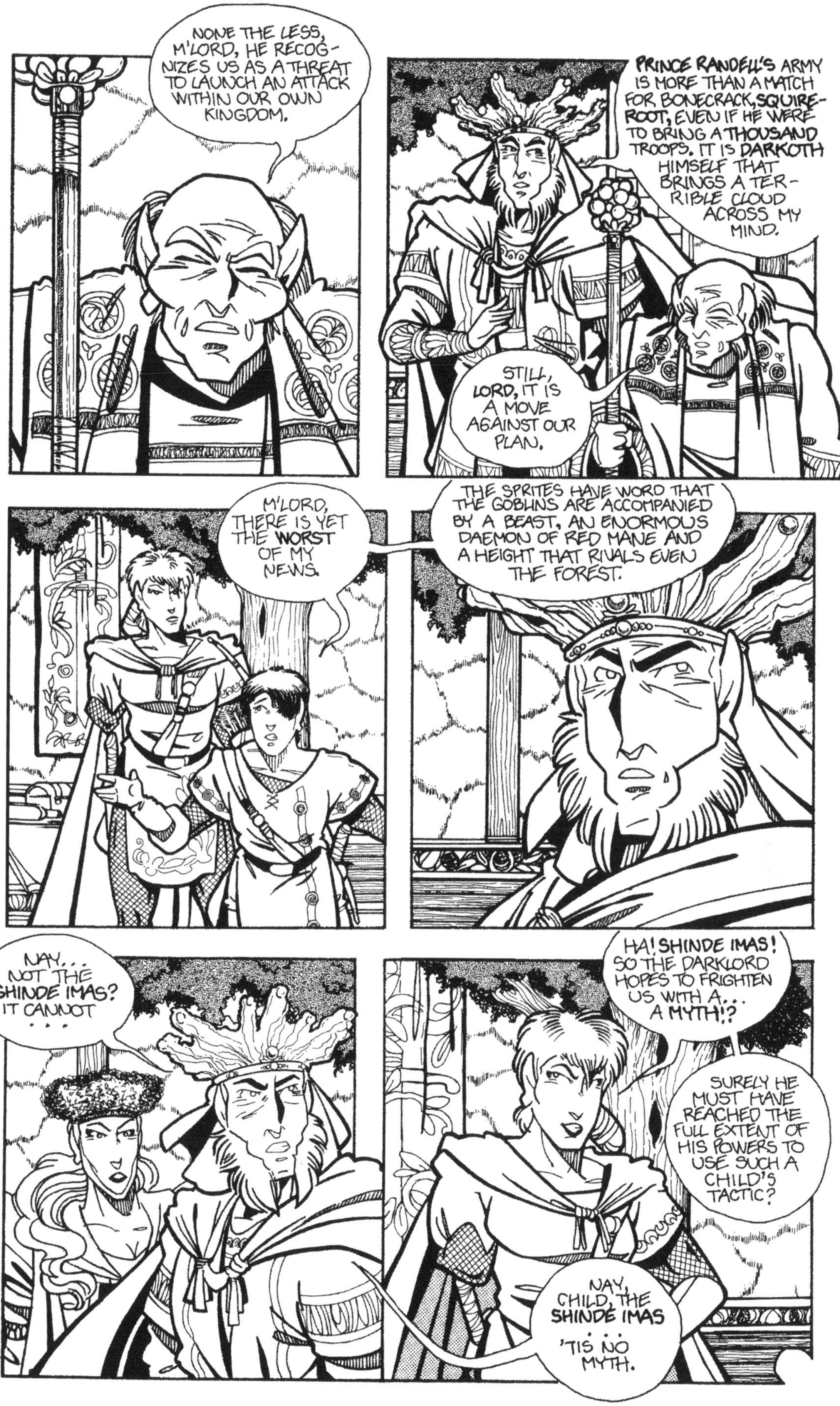
NONE THE LESS, M'LORD, HE RECOGNIZES US AS A THREAT TO LAUNCH AN ATTACK WITHIN OUR OWN KINGDOM.
PRINCE RANDELL'S ARMY IS MORE THAN A MATCH FOR BONECRACK, SQUIRE-ROOT, EVEN IF HE WERE TO BRING A THOUSAND TROOPS. IT IS DARKOTH HIMSELF THAT BRINGS A TERRIBLE CLOUD ACROSS MY MIND.
STILL, LORD, IT IS A MOVE AGAINST OUR PLAN.
M'LORD, THERE IS YET THE WORST OF MY NEWS.
THE SPRITES HAVE WORD THAT THE GOBLINS ARE ACCOMPANIED BY A BEAST. AN ENORMOUS DAEMON OF RED MANE AND A HEIGHT THAT RIVALS EVEN THE FOREST.
NAY... NOT THE SHINDE IMAS? IT CANNOT...
HA! SHINDE IMAS! SO THE DARKLORD HOPES TO FRIGHTEN US WITH A... A MYTH!?
SURELY HE MUST HAVE REACHED THE FULL EXTENT OF HIS POWERS TO USE SUCH A CHILD'S TACTIC?
NAY, CHILD, THE SHINDE IMAS... 'TIS NO MYTH.

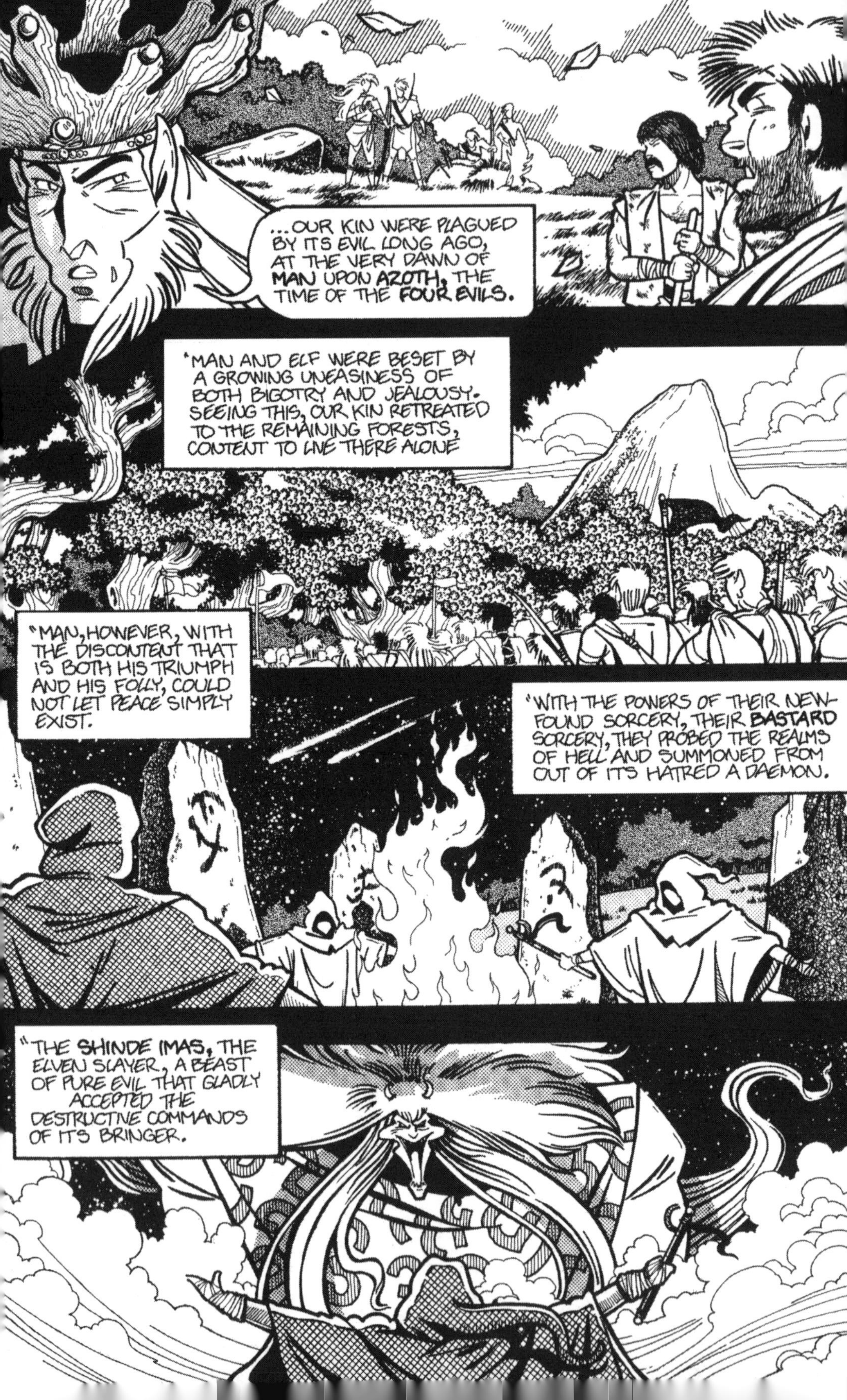
...OUR KIN WERE PLAGUED BY ITS EVIL LONG AGO, AT THE VERY DAWN OF MAN UPON AZOTH, THE TIME OF THE FOUR EVILS.
"MAN AND ELF WERE BESET BY A GROWING UNEASINESS OF BOTH BIGOTRY AND JEALOUSY. SEEING THIS, OUR KIN RETREATED TO THE REMAINING FORESTS, CONTENT TO LIVE THERE ALONE
"MAN, HOWEVER, WITH THE DISCONTENT THAT IS BOTH HIS TRIUMPH AND HIS FOLLY, COULD NOT LET PEACE SIMPLY EXIST.
"WITH THE POWERS OF THEIR NEW-FOUND SORCERY, THEIR BASTARD SORCERY, THEY PROBED THE REALMS OF HELL AND SUMMONED FROM OUT OF ITS HATRED A DAEMON.
"THE SHINDE IMAS, THE ELVEN SLAYER, A BEAST OF PURE EVIL THAT GLADLY ACCEPTED THE DESTRUCTIVE COMMANDS OF ITS BRINGER.

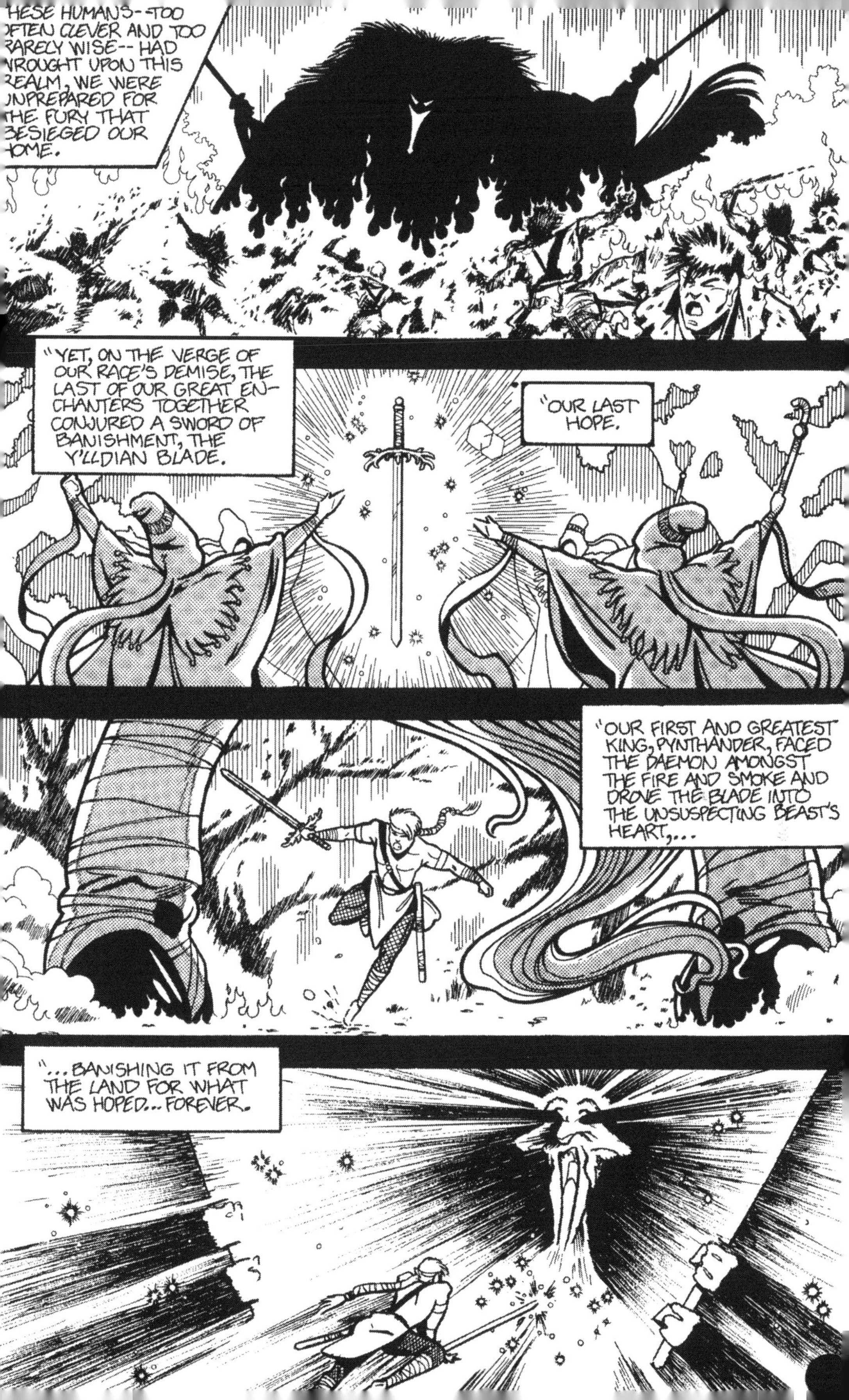
THESE HUMANS--TOO OFTEN CLEVER AND TOO RARELY WISE-- HAD WROUGHT UPON THIS REALM, WE WERE UNPREPARED FOR THE FURY THAT BESIEGED OUR HOME.
"YET, ON THE VERGE OF OUR RACE'S DEMISE, THE LAST OF OUR GREAT ENCHANTERS TOGETHER CONJURED A SWORD OF BANISHMENT, THE Y'LLDIAN BLADE.
"OUR LAST HOPE.
"OUR FIRST AND GREATEST KING, PYNTHANDER, FACED THE DAEMON AMONGST THE FIRE AND SMOKE AND DROVE THE BLADE INTO THE UNSUSPECTING BEAST'S HEART,...
"...BANISHING IT FROM THE LAND FOR WHAT WAS HOPED...FOREVER.

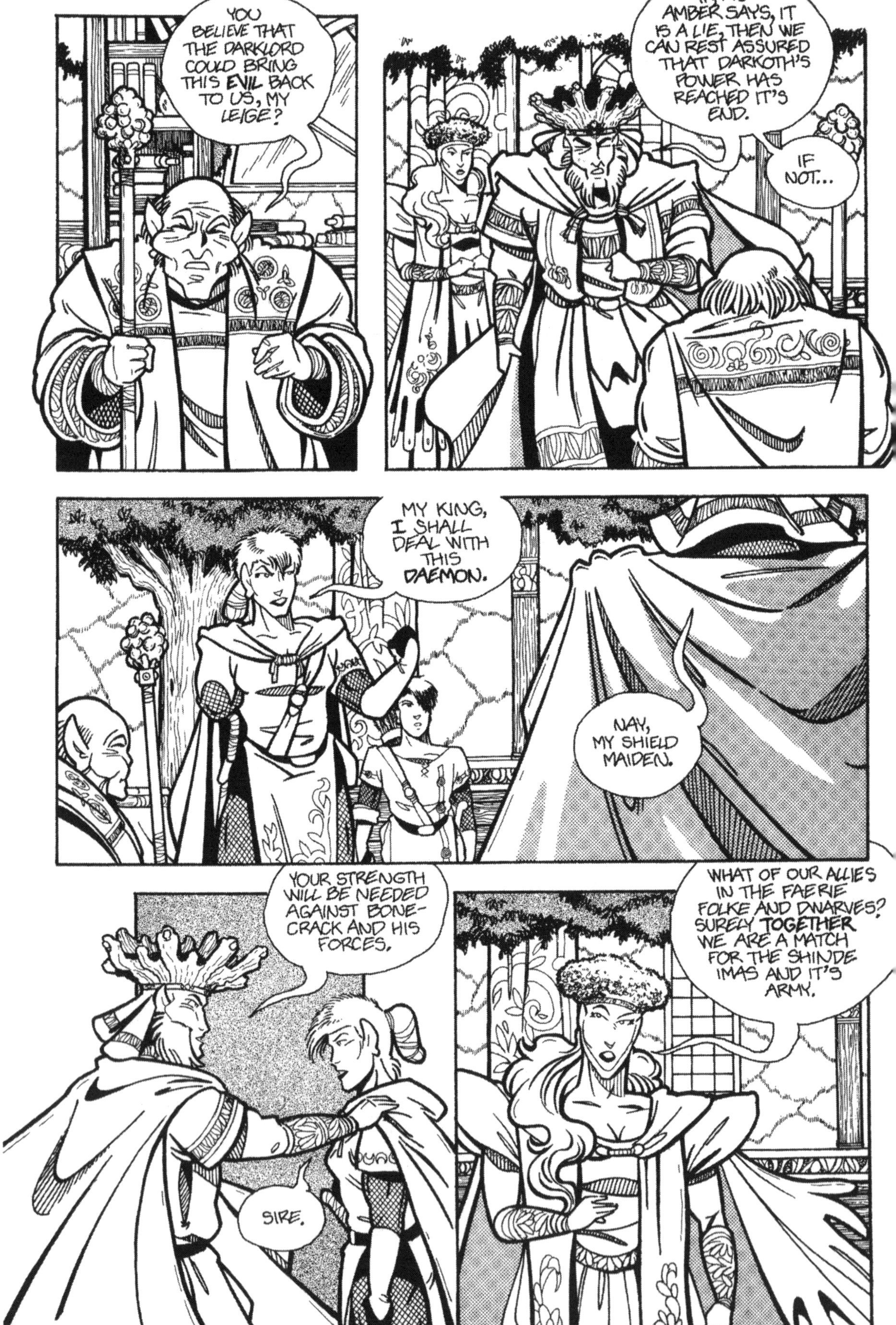
YOU BELIEVE THAT THE DARKLORD COULD BRING THIS EVIL BACK TO US, MY LEIGE?
IF, AS AMBER SAYS, IT IS A LIE, THEN WE CAN REST ASSURED THAT DARKOTH'S POWER HAS REACHED IT'S END.
IF NOT...
MY KING, I SHALL DEAL WITH THIS DAEMON.
NAY, MY SHIELD MAIDEN.
YOUR STRENGTH WILL BE NEEDED AGAINST BONE-CRACK AND HIS FORCES.
SIRE.
WHAT OF OUR ALLIES IN THE FAERIE FOLKE AND DWARVES? SURELY TOGETHER WE ARE A MATCH FOR THE SHINDE IMAS AND IT'S ARMY.

MY QUEEN, THE FAERIE FOLKE ARE HIGH SPIRITED, YES, BUT **HARDLY** WARRIORS ENOUGH AGAINST A GOBLIN ARMY.

MY COUNCIL IS CORRECT, MYLINTHIA. AND AS OF YET, WE CANNOT COUNT THE DWARVES AMONG OUR NUMBERS UNTIL OUR SON RETURNS. FOR NOW, THIS BATTLE IS OUR OWN.

MY LORD, I WILL CALL BACK RANDELL'S ARMY TO THE FOREST'S EDGE.

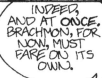

INDEED, AND AT ONCE. BRACHMON, FOR NOW, MUST FARE ON ITS OWN.

I WILL RALLY OUR REMAINING FORCES AND SEND SCOUTS TO THE FOUR CORNERS.

LET US MAKE HASTE BEFORE THE STORM IS UPON US.

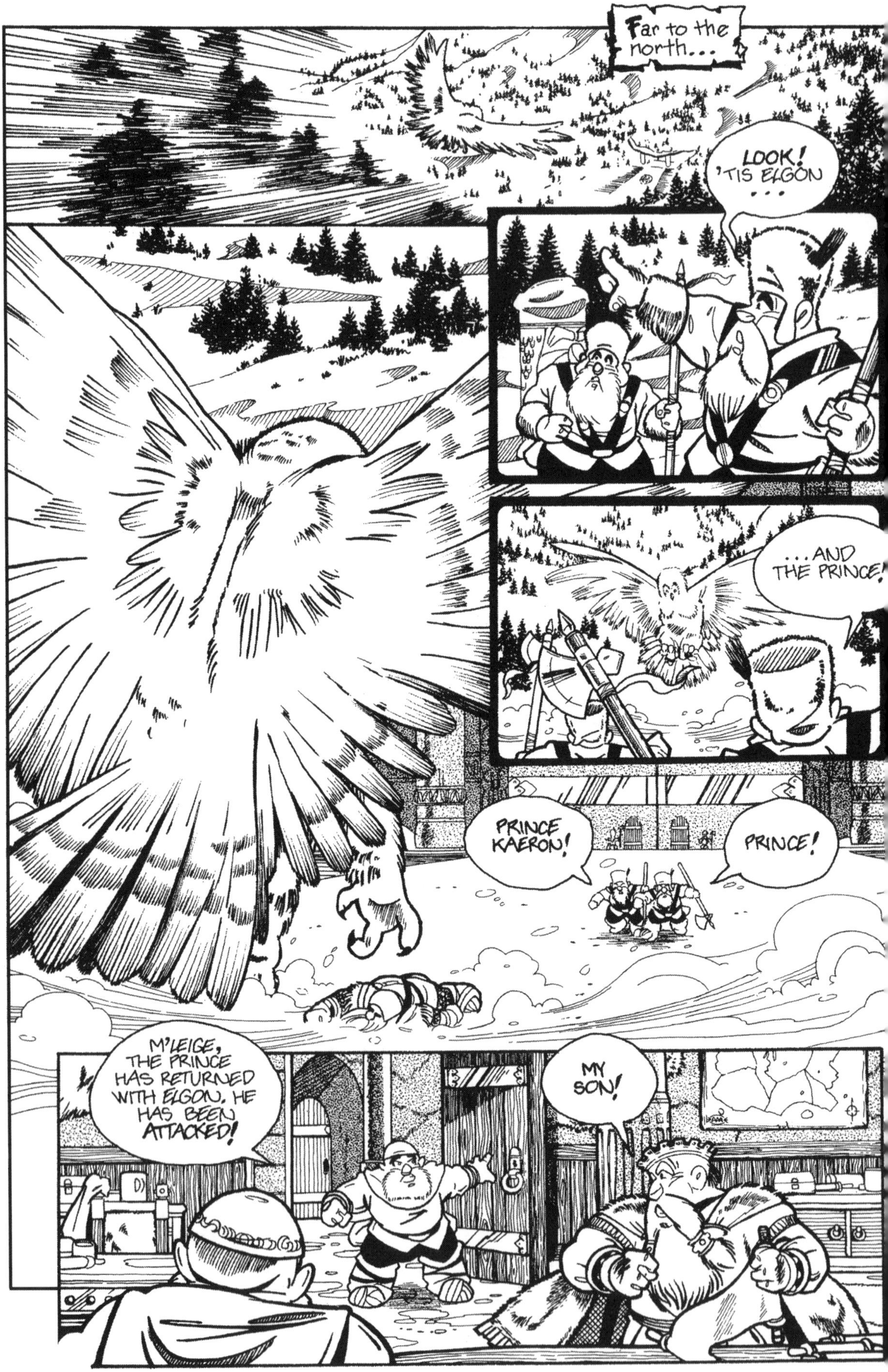
Far to the north...
LOOK! 'TIS ELGON ...
...AND THE PRINCE!
PRINCE KAERON!
PRINCE!
M'LEIGE, THE PRINCE HAS RETURNED WITH ELGON. HE HAS BEEN ATTACKED!
MY SON!

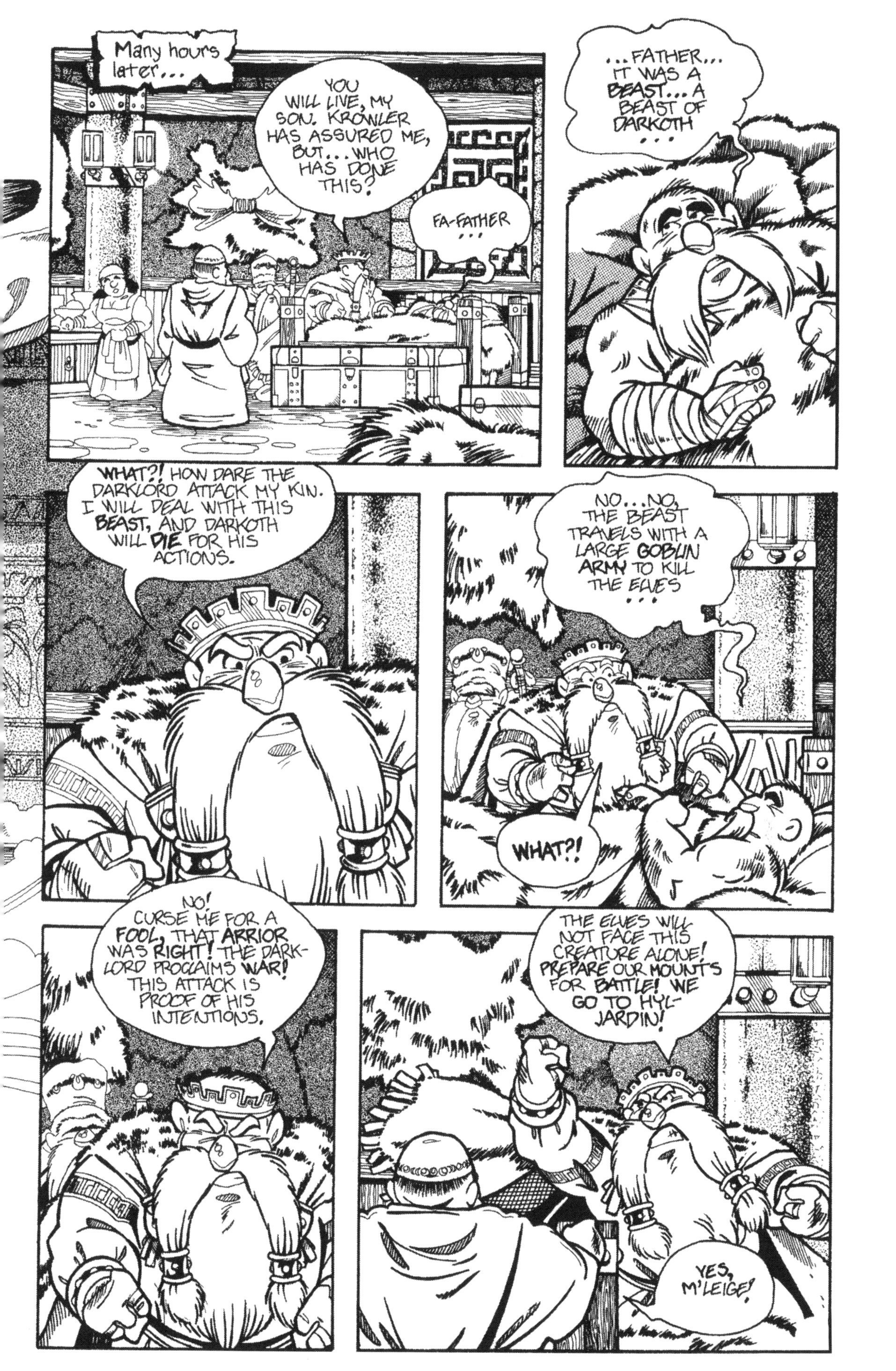
Many hours later...
YOU WILL LIVE, MY SON. KROWLER HAS ASSURED ME, BUT... WHO HAS DONE THIS?
FA-FATHER ...
...FATHER... IT WAS A BEAST... A BEAST OF DARKOTH ...
WHAT?! HOW DARE THE DARKLORD ATTACK MY KIN. I WILL DEAL WITH THIS BEAST, AND DARKOTH WILL DIE FOR HIS ACTIONS.
NO...NO, THE BEAST TRAVELS WITH A LARGE GOBLIN ARMY TO KILL THE ELVES ...
WHAT?!
NO! CURSE ME FOR A FOOL, THAT ARRIOR WAS RIGHT! THE DARK-LORD PROCLAIMS WAR! THIS ATTACK IS PROOF OF HIS INTENTIONS.
THE ELVES WILL NOT FACE THIS CREATURE ALONE! PREPARE OUR MOUNT'S FOR BATTLE! WE GO TO HYL-JARDIN!
YES, M'LEIGE!

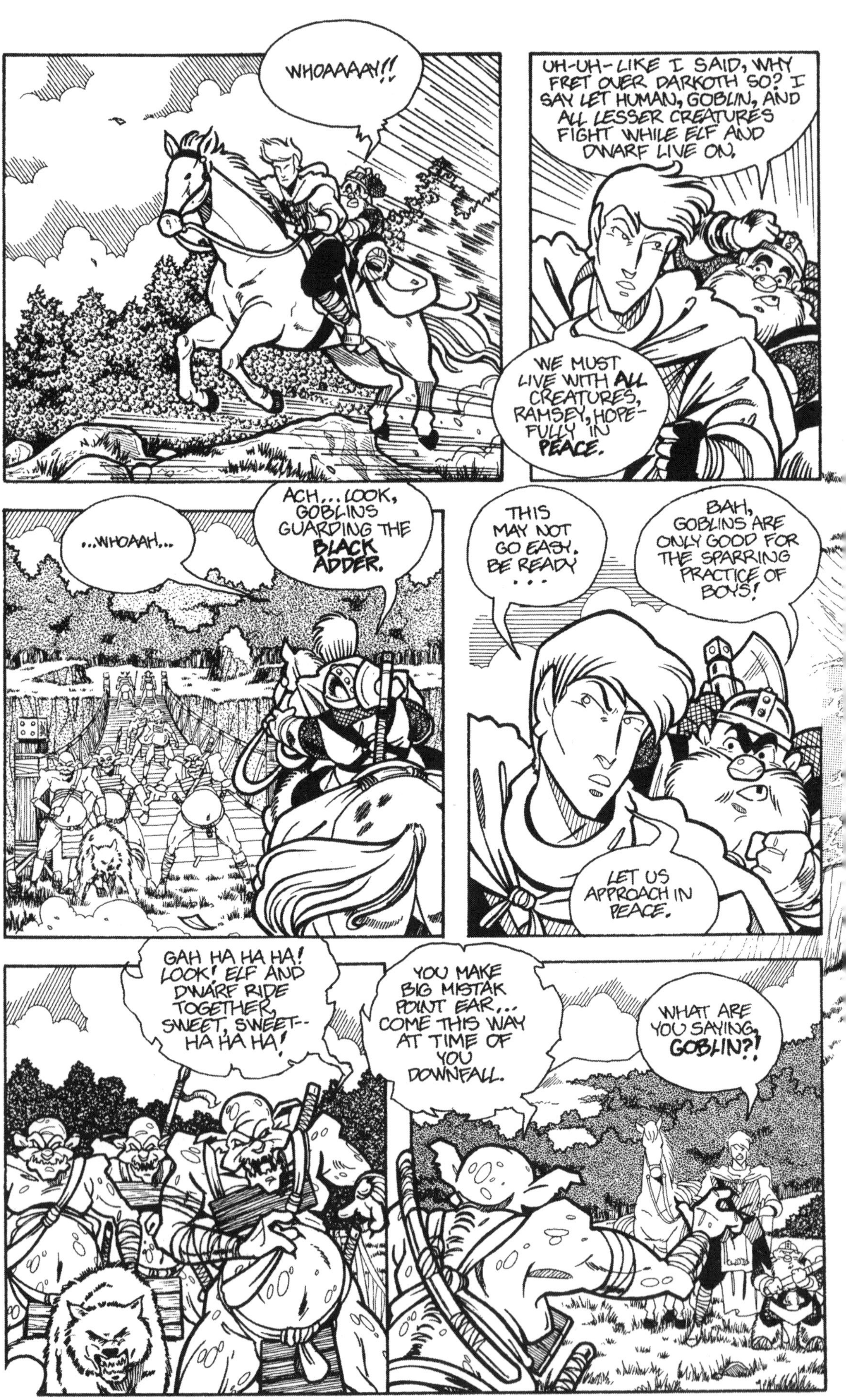
WHOAAAAY!!
UH-UH-LIKE I SAID, WHY FRET OVER DARKOTH SO? I SAY LET HUMAN, GOBLIN, AND ALL LESSER CREATURES FIGHT WHILE ELF AND DWARF LIVE ON.
WE MUST LIVE WITH ALL CREATURES, RAMSEY, HOPE-FULLY IN PEACE.
...WHOAAH...
ACH... LOOK, GOBLINS GUARDING THE BLACK ADDER.
THIS MAY NOT GO EASY. BE READY . . .
BAH, GOBLINS ARE ONLY GOOD FOR THE SPARRING PRACTICE OF BOYS!
LET US APPROACH IN PEACE.
GAH HA HA HA! LOOK! ELF AND DWARF RIDE TOGETHER, SWEET, SWEET-- HA HA HA!
YOU MAKE BIG MISTAK POINT EAR... COME THIS WAY AT TIME OF YOU DOWNFALL.
WHAT ARE YOU SAYING, GOBLIN?!

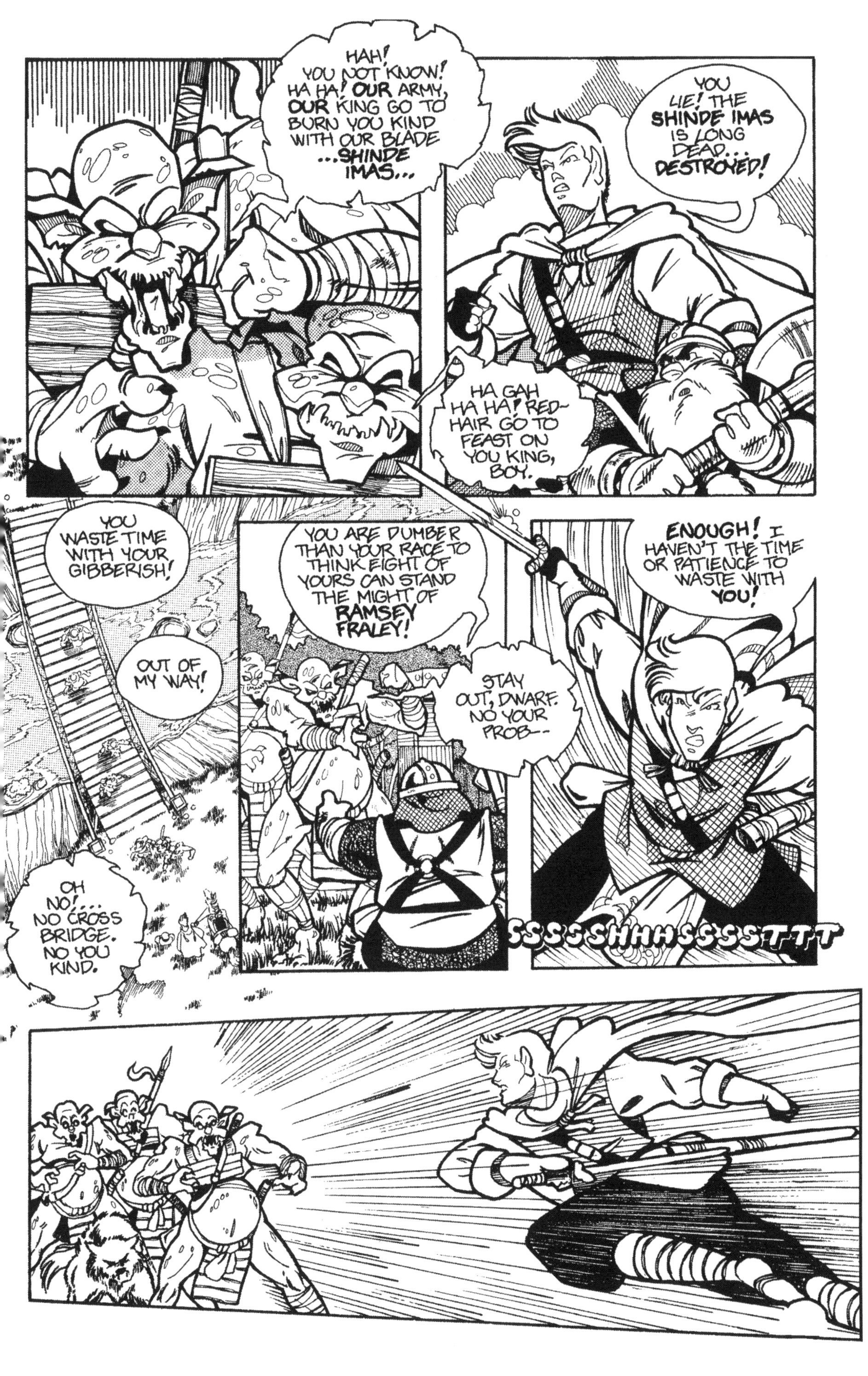
HAH! YOU NOT KNOW! HA HA! OUR ARMY, OUR KING GO TO BURN YOU KIND WITH OUR BLADE ...SHINDE IMAS...
YOU LIE! THE SHINDE IMAS IS LONG DEAD... DESTROYED!
HA GAH HA HA! RED-HAIR GO TO FEAST ON YOU KING, BOY.
YOU WASTE TIME WITH YOUR GIBBERISH!
OUT OF MY WAY!
OH NO!... NO CROSS BRIDGE. NO YOU KIND.
YOU ARE DUMBER THAN YOUR RACE TO THINK EIGHT OF YOURS CAN STAND THE MIGHT OF RAMSEY FRALEY!
STAY OUT, DWARF. NO YOUR PROB--
ENOUGH! I HAVEN'T THE TIME OR PATIENCE TO WASTE WITH YOU!
SSSSSHHHHSSSSSTTTT

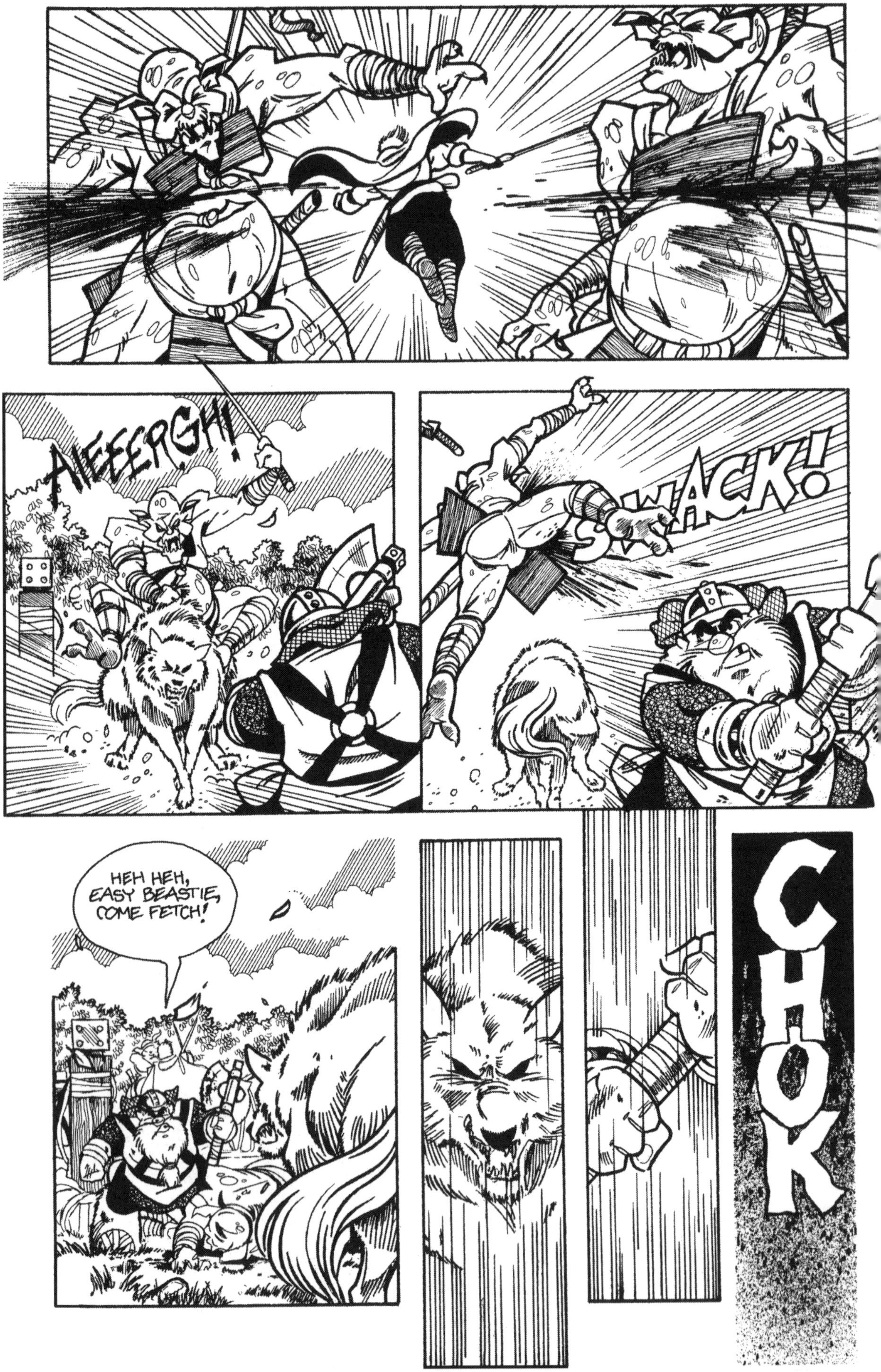
AIEEERGH!
SWACK!
HEH HEH, EASY BEASTIE, COME FETCH!
CHOK

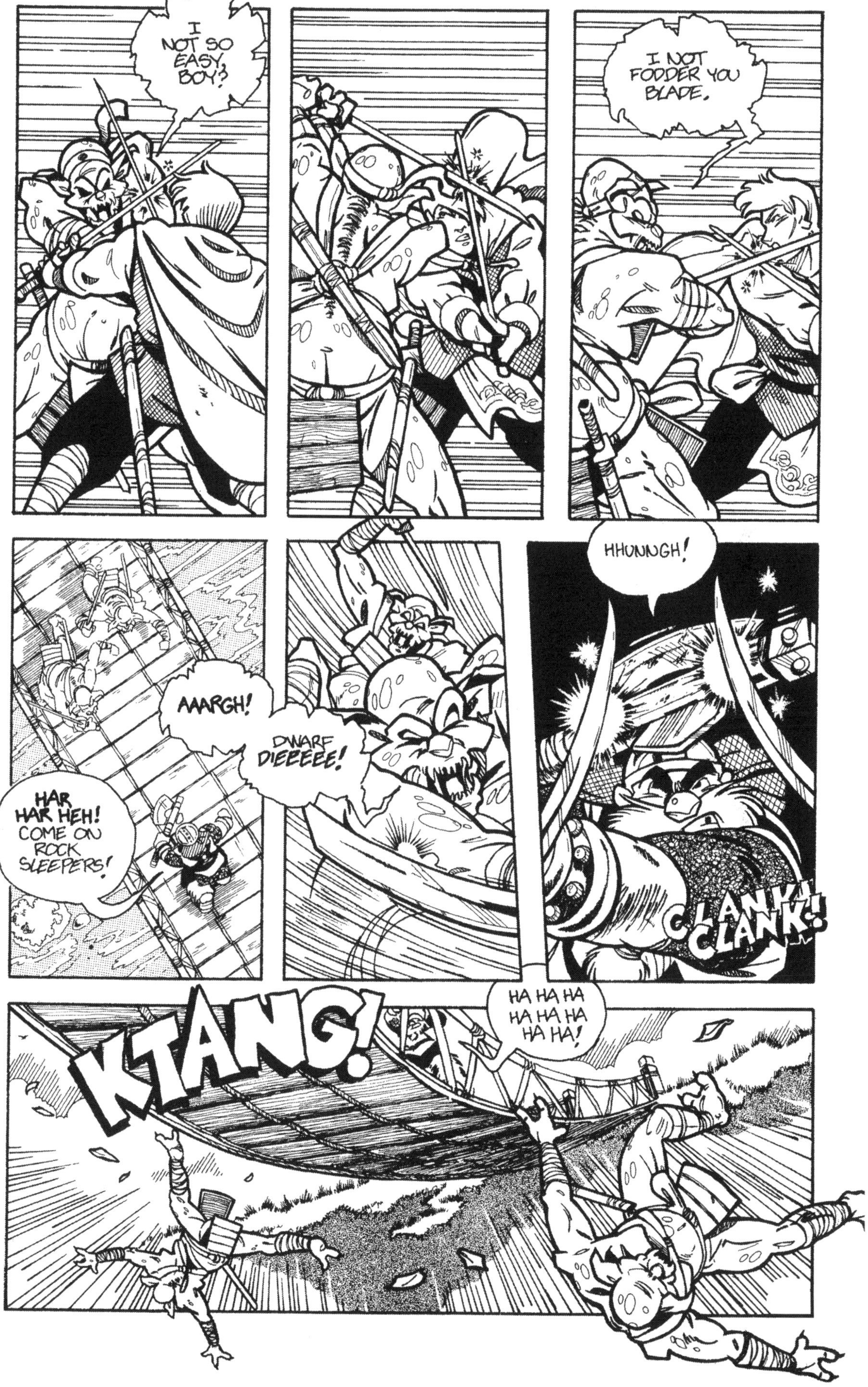

I NOT SO EASY BOY?
I NOT FODDER YOU BLADE.
AAARGH!
HAR HAR HEH! COME ON ROCK SLEEPERS!
DWARF DIEEEEE!
HHUNNGH!
CLANK! CLANK!
KTANG!
HA HA HA HA HA HA HA HA!

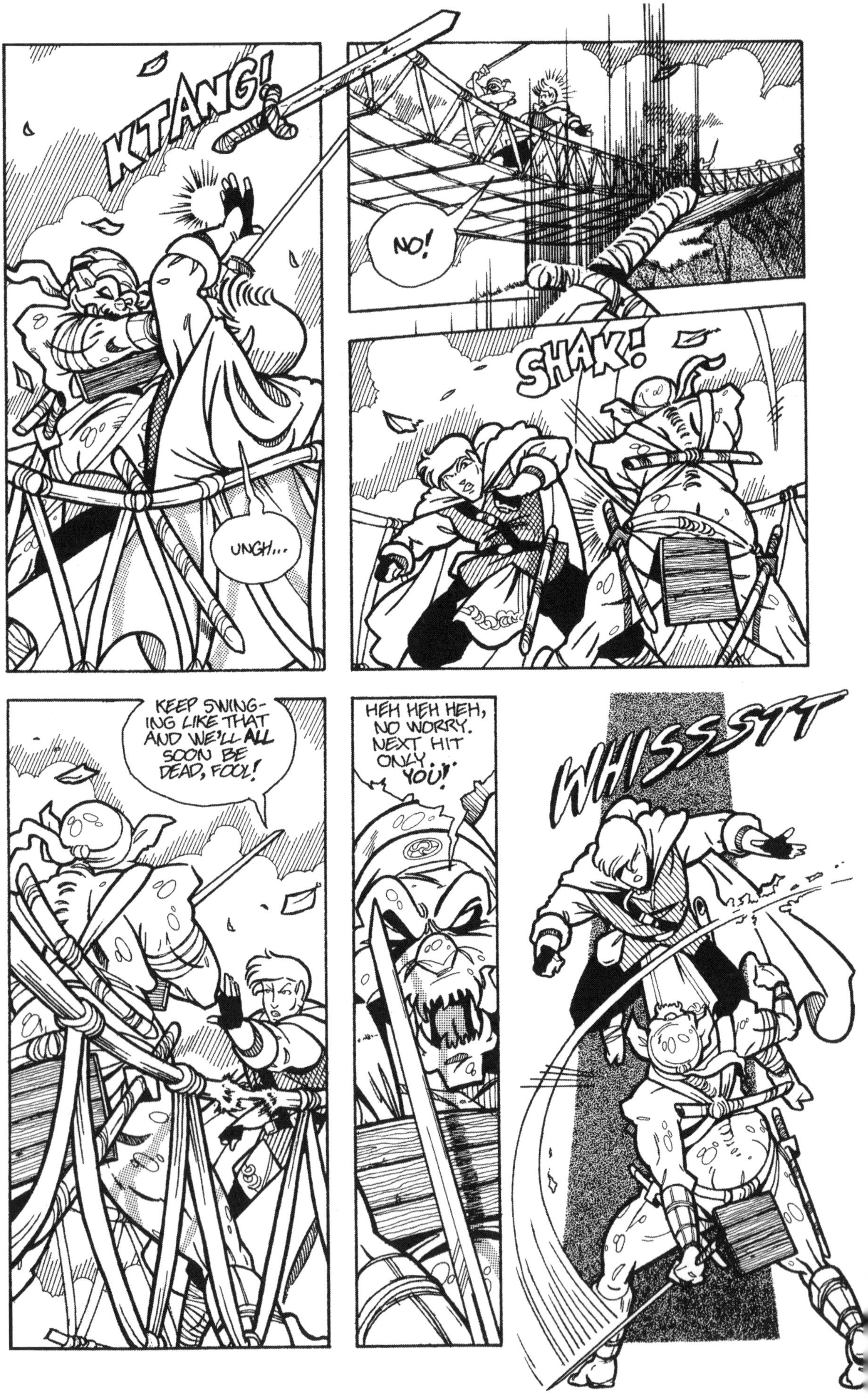
KTANG!
NO!
UNGH...
SHAK!
KEEP SWINGING LIKE THAT AND WE'LL ALL SOON BE DEAD, FOOL!
HEH HEH HEH, NO WORRY. NEXT HIT ONLY YOU!
WHISSSTT

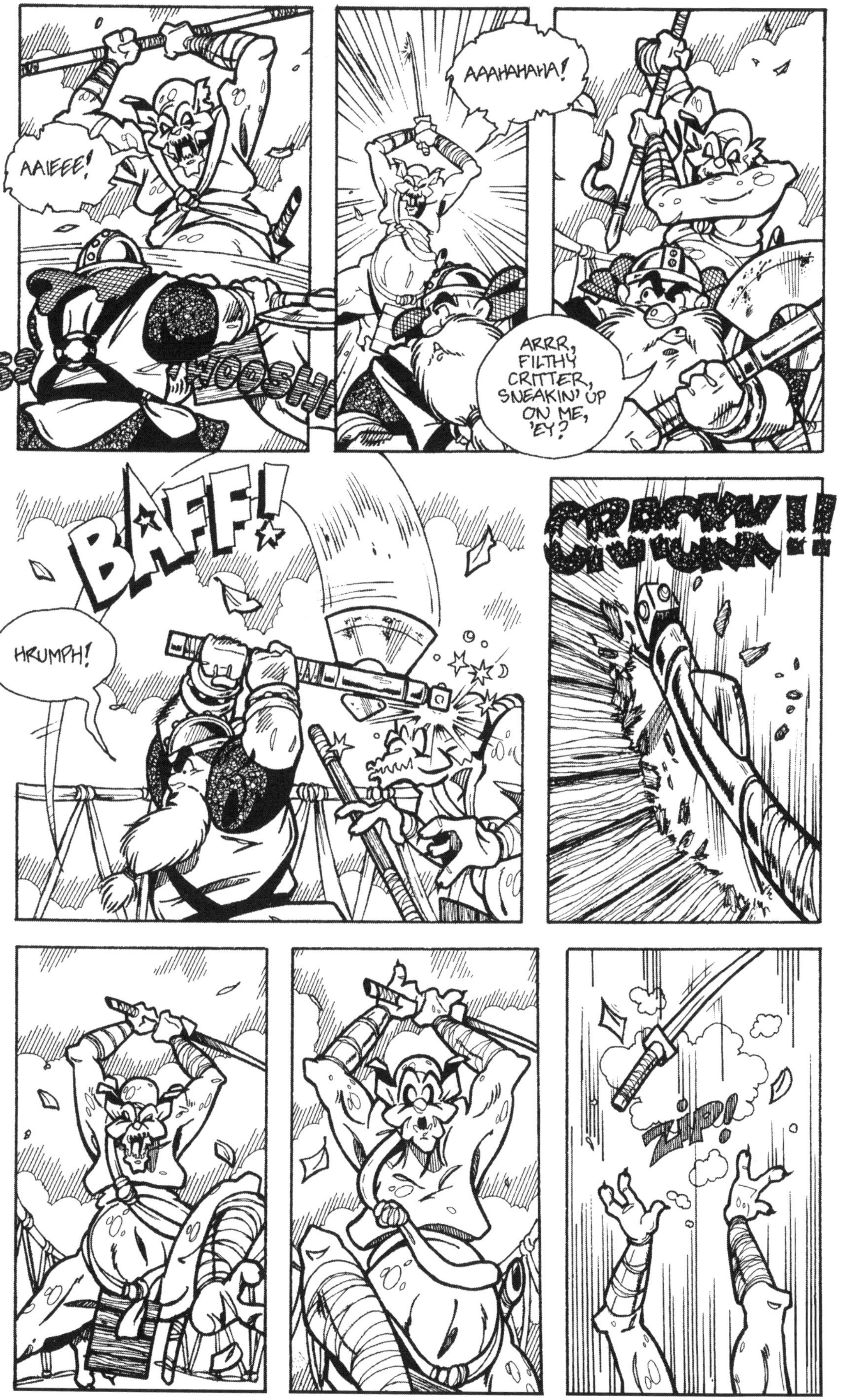
AAIEEE!
SSWOOSH!
AAAHAHAHA!
ARRR, FILTHY CRITTER, SNEAKIN' UP ON ME, 'EY?
BAFF!
HRUMPH!
CRACK!!
CHUNK!!
ZIP!!

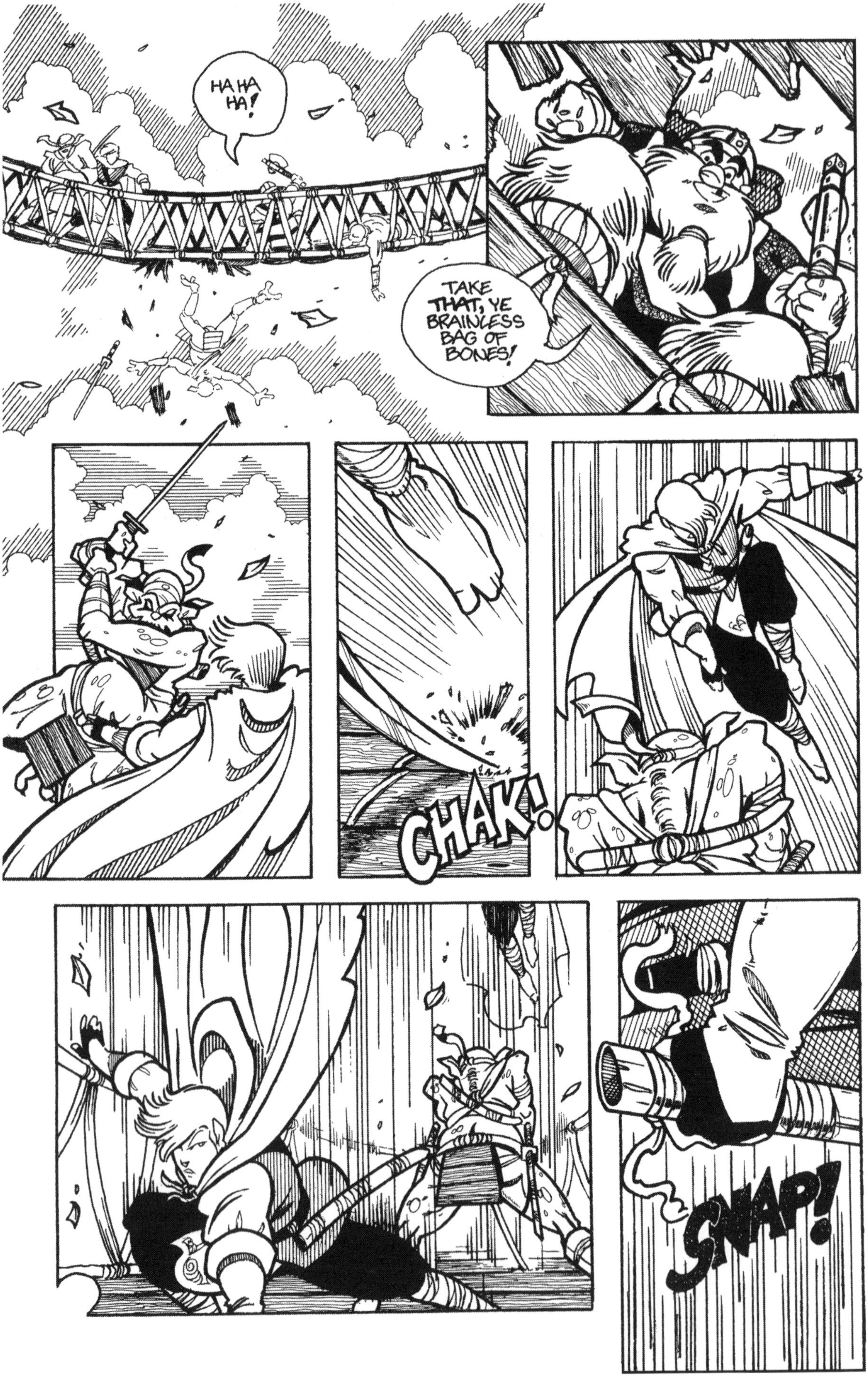
HA HA HA!
TAKE THAT, YE BRAINLESS BAG OF BONES!
CHAK!
SNAP!

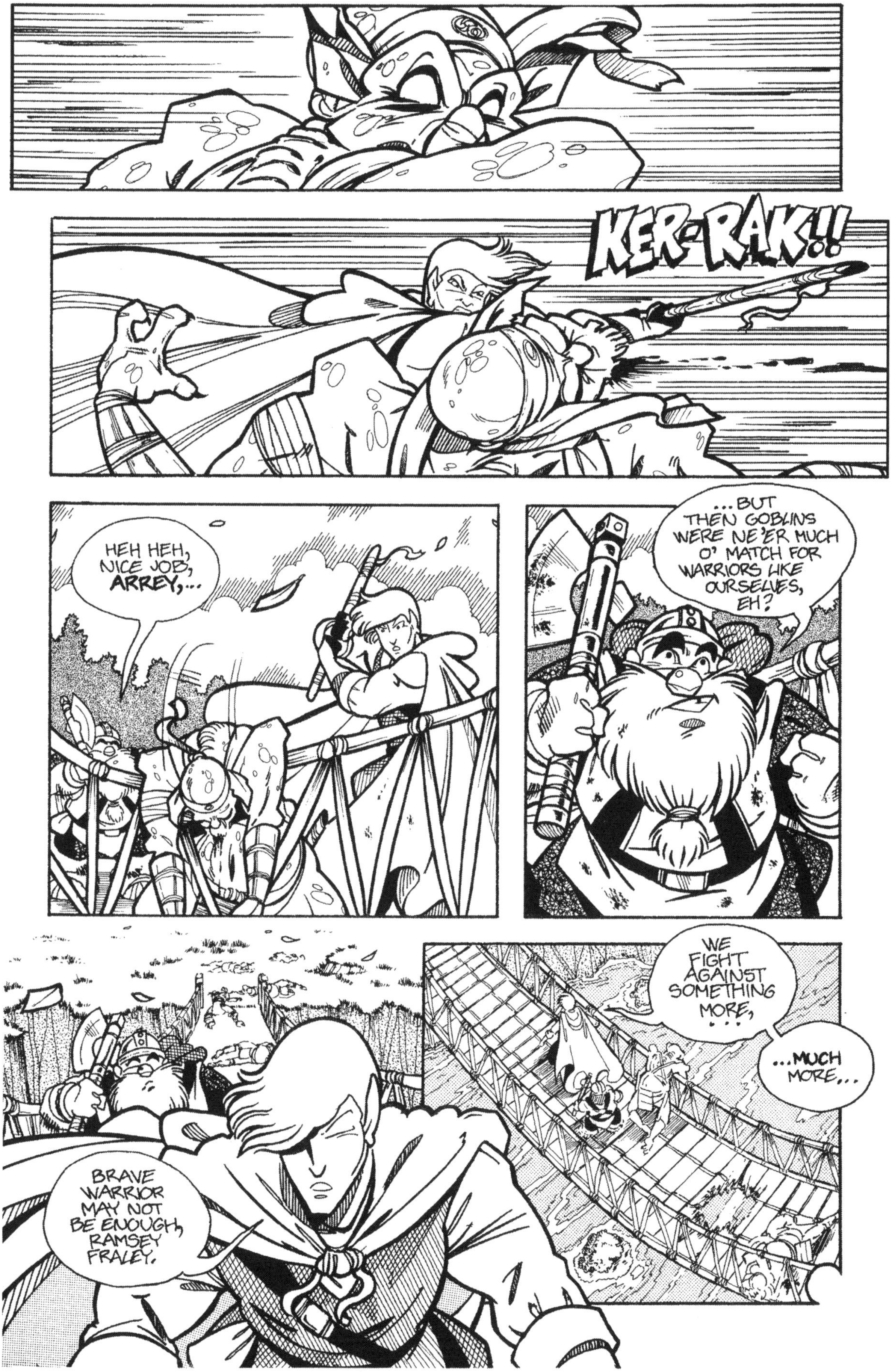
KER-RAK!!
HEH HEH, NICE JOB, ARREY,...
...BUT THEN GOBLINS WERE NE'ER MUCH O' MATCH FOR WARRIORS LIKE OURSELVES, EH?
BRAVE WARRIOR MAY NOT BE ENOUGH, RAMSEY FRALEY.
WE FIGHT AGAINST SOMETHING MORE, . . .
...MUCH MORE,...

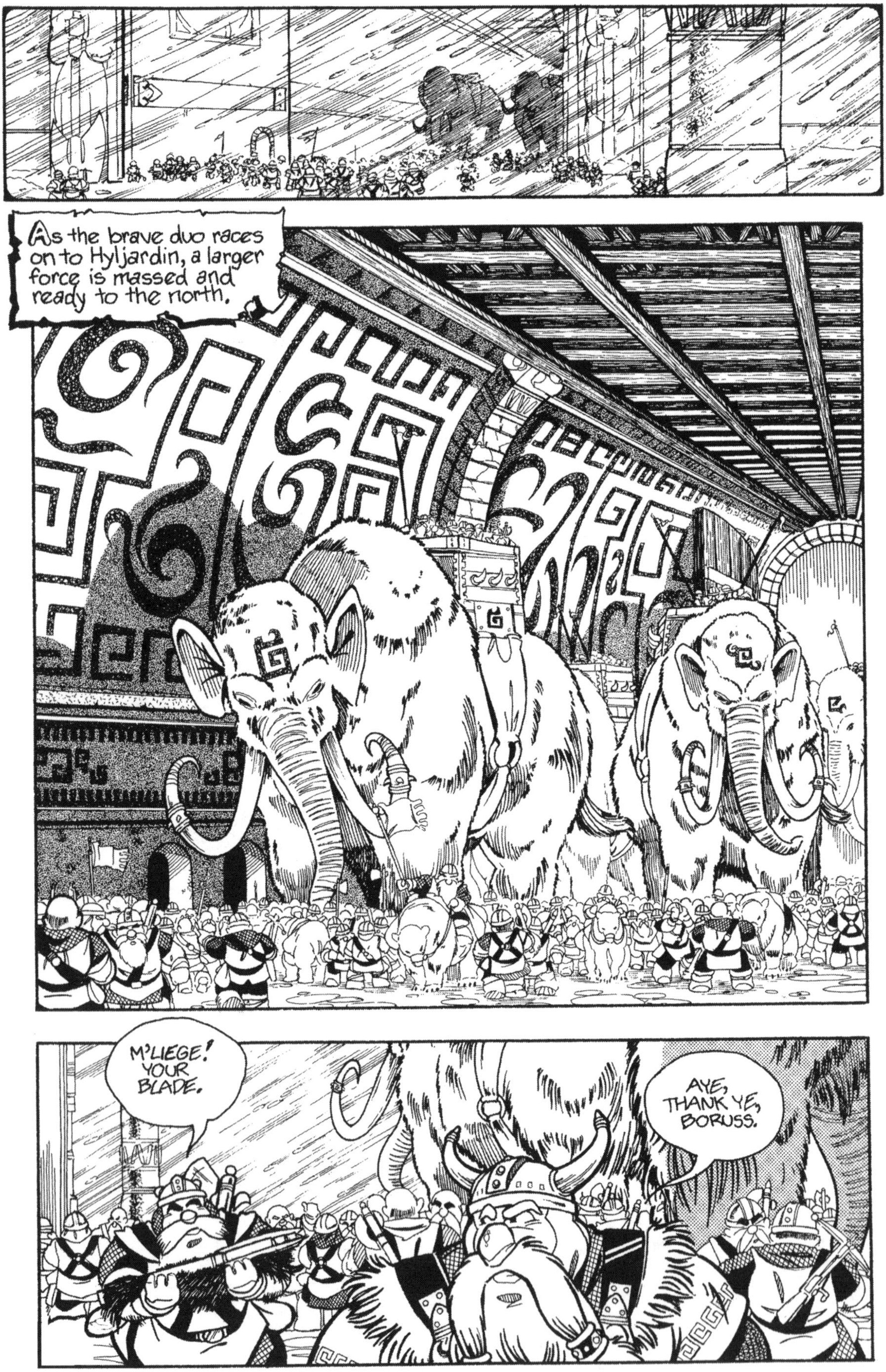
As the brave duo races on to Hyljardin, a larger force is massed and ready to the north.
M'LIEGE! YOUR BLADE.
AYE, THANK YE, BORUSS.

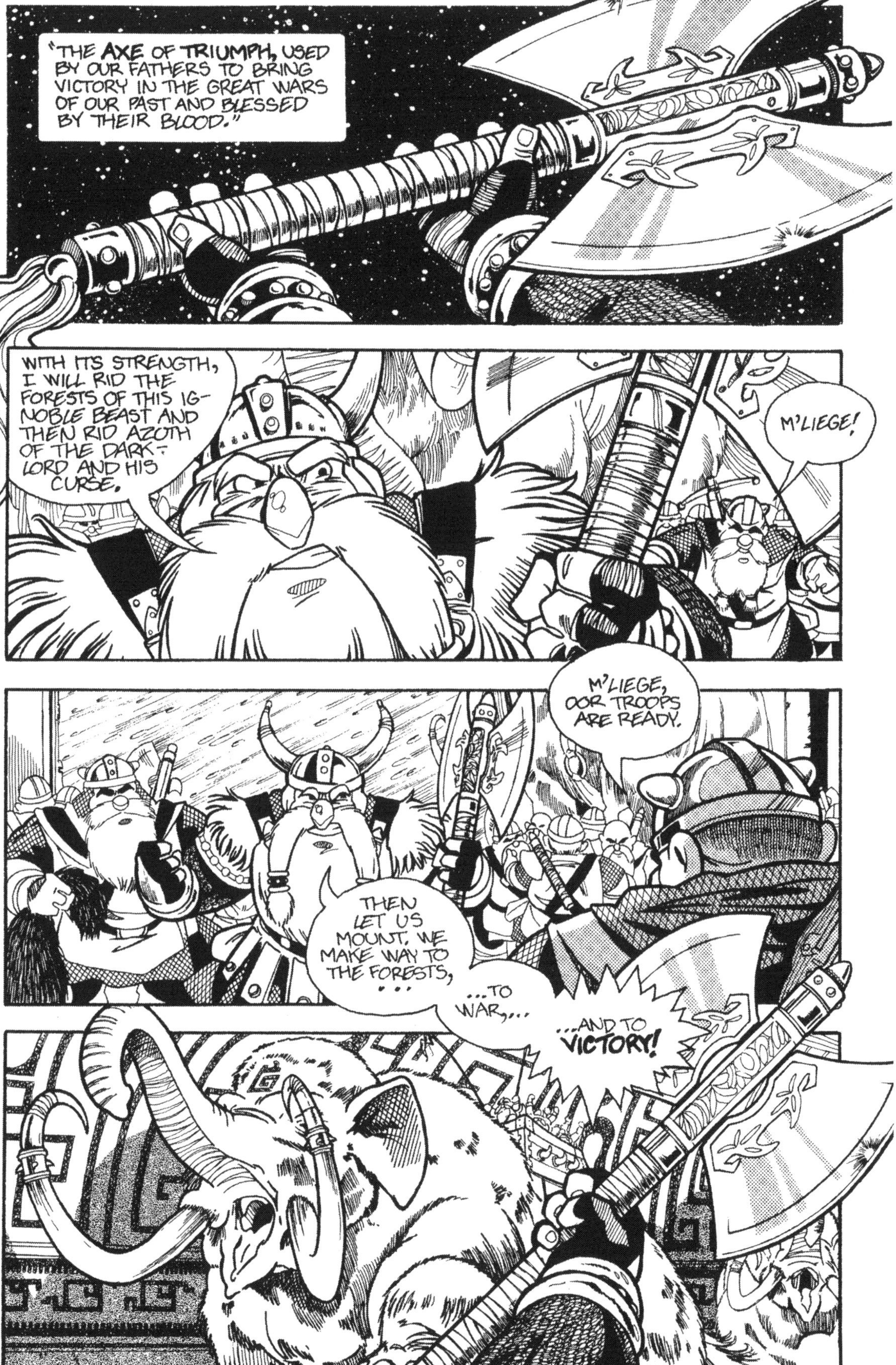
"THE AXE OF TRIUMPH, USED BY OUR FATHERS TO BRING VICTORY IN THE GREAT WARS OF OUR PAST AND BLESSED BY THEIR BLOOD."
WITH ITS STRENGTH, I WILL RID THE FORESTS OF THIS IGNOBLE BEAST AND THEN RID AZOTH OF THE DARK LORD AND HIS CURSE.
M'LIEGE!
M'LIEGE, OOR TROOPS ARE READY.
THEN LET US MOUNT. WE MAKE WAY TO THE FORESTS, ...
...TO WAR,...
...AND TO VICTORY!

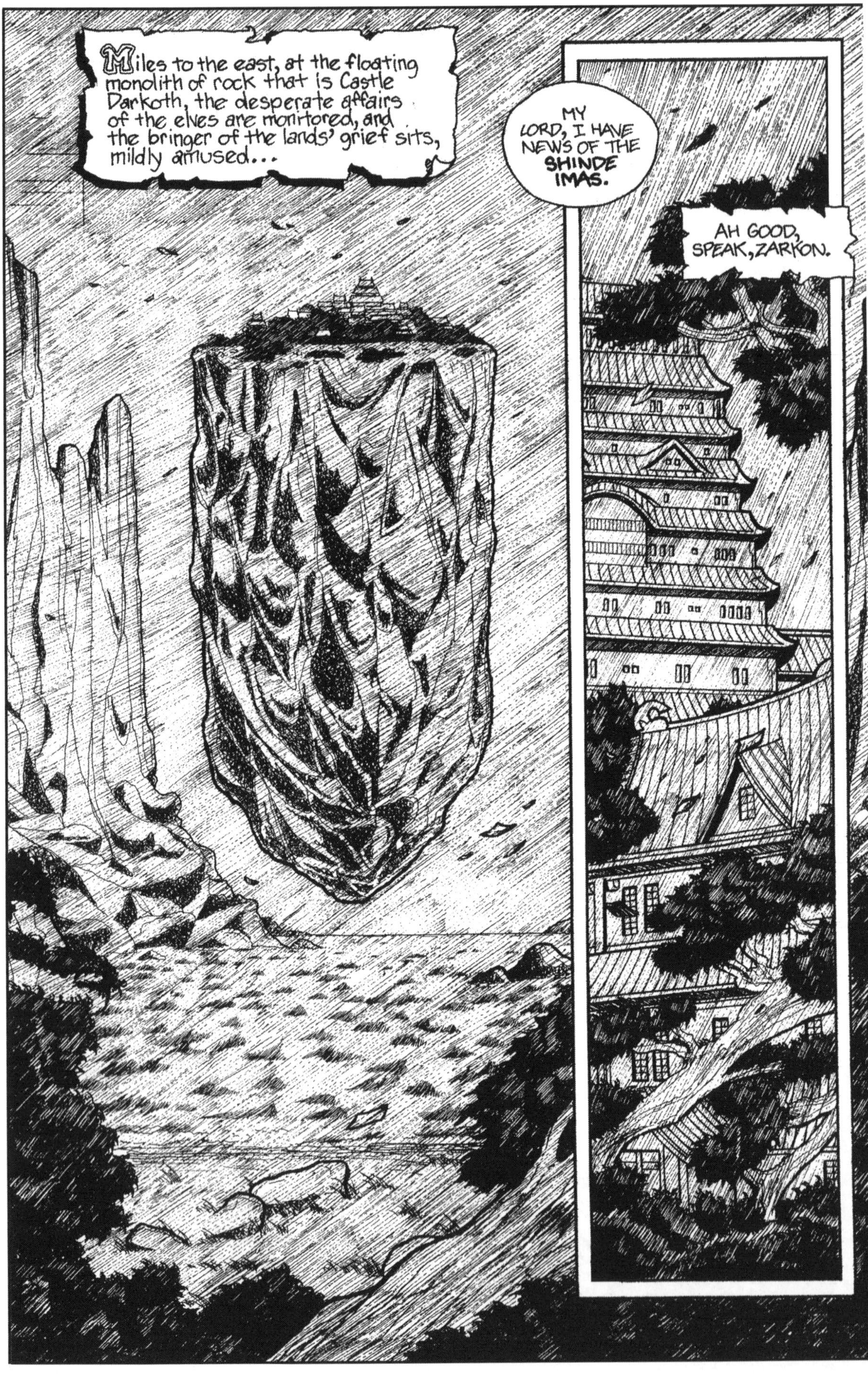
Miles to the east, at the floating monolith of rock that is Castle Darkoth, the desperate affairs of the elves are monitored, and the bringer of the lands' grief sits, mildly amused...
MY LORD, I HAVE NEWS OF THE SHINDE IMAS.
AH GOOD, SPEAK, ZARKON.

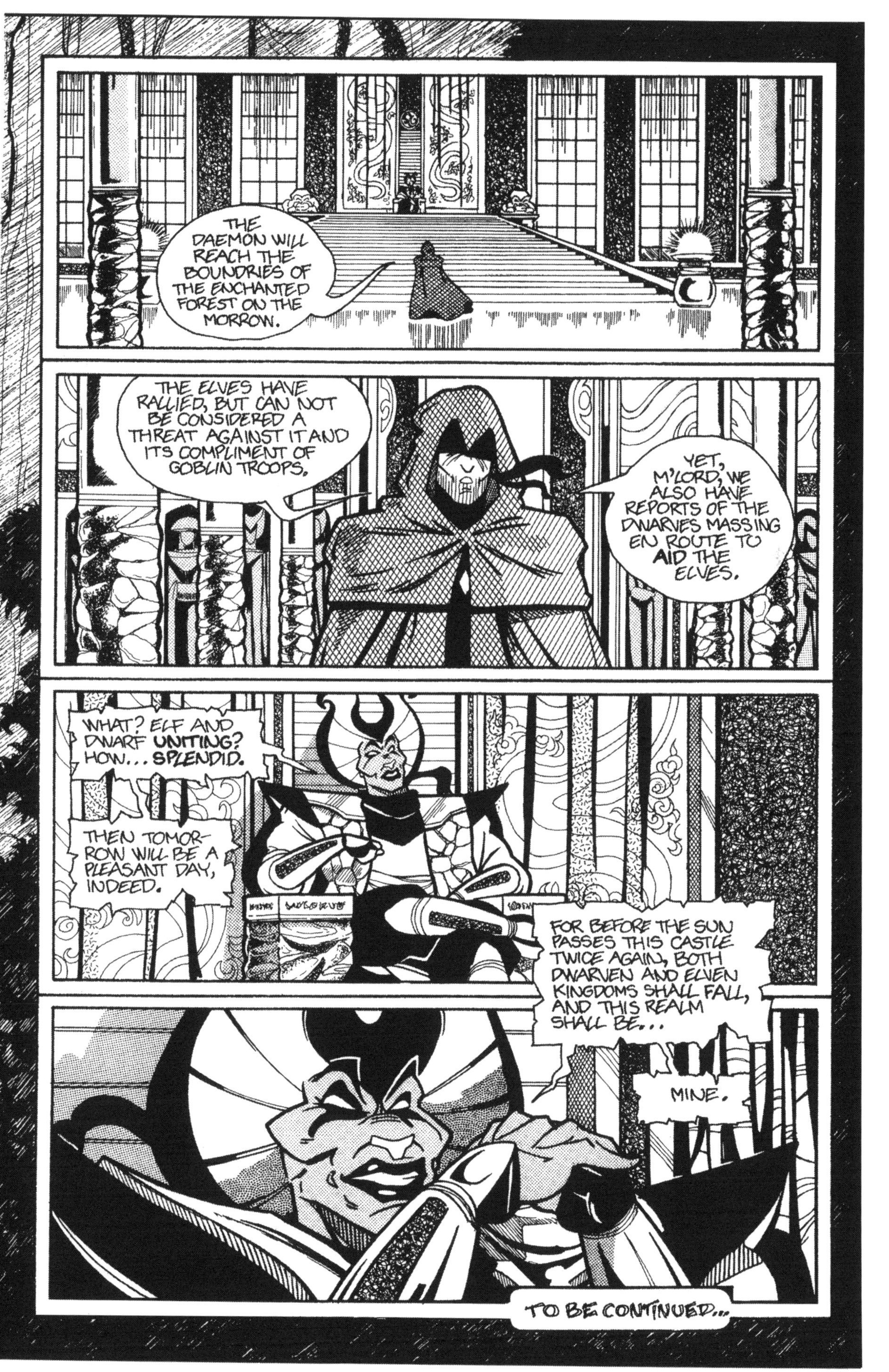

THE DAEMON WILL REACH THE BOUNDRIES OF THE ENCHANTED FOREST ON THE MORROW.
THE ELVES HAVE RALLIED, BUT CAN NOT BE CONSIDERED A THREAT AGAINST IT AND ITS COMPLIMENT OF GOBLIN TROOPS.
YET, M'LORD, WE ALSO HAVE REPORTS OF THE DWARVES MASSING EN ROUTE TO AID THE ELVES.
WHAT? ELF AND DWARF UNITING? HOW... SPLENDID.
THEN TOMOR-ROW WILL BE A PLEASANT DAY, INDEED.
FOR BEFORE THE SUN PASSES THIS CASTLE TWICE AGAIN, BOTH DWARVEN AND ELVEN KINGDOMS SHALL FALL, AND THIS REALM SHALL BE...
MINE.
TO BE CONTINUED...

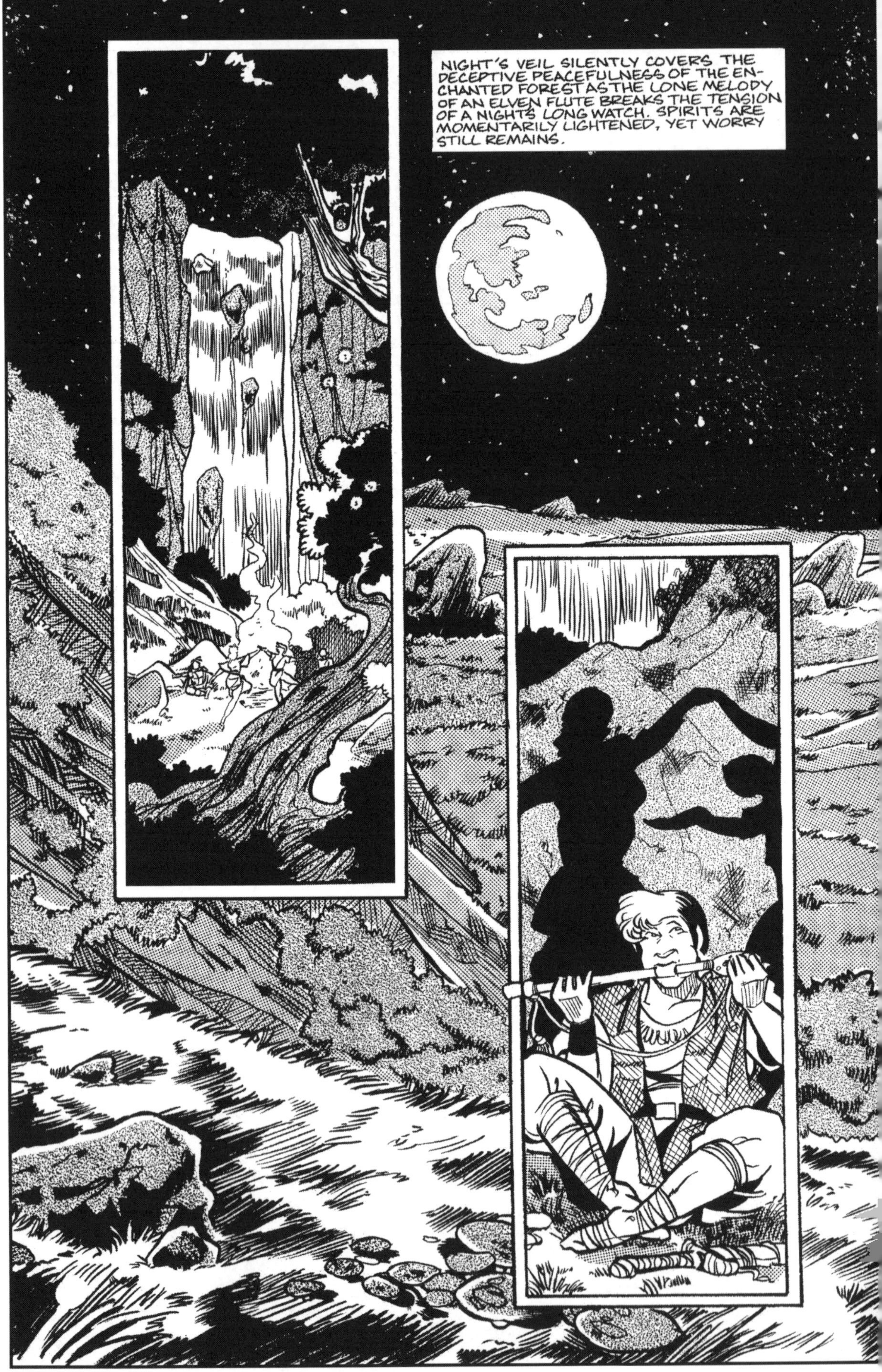
NIGHT'S VEIL SILENTLY COVERS THE DECEPTIVE PEACEFULNESS OF THE ENCHANTED FOREST AS THE LONE MELODY OF AN ELVEN FLUTE BREAKS THE TENSION OF A NIGHT'S LONG WATCH. SPIRITS ARE MOMENTARILY LIGHTENED, YET WORRY STILL REMAINS.

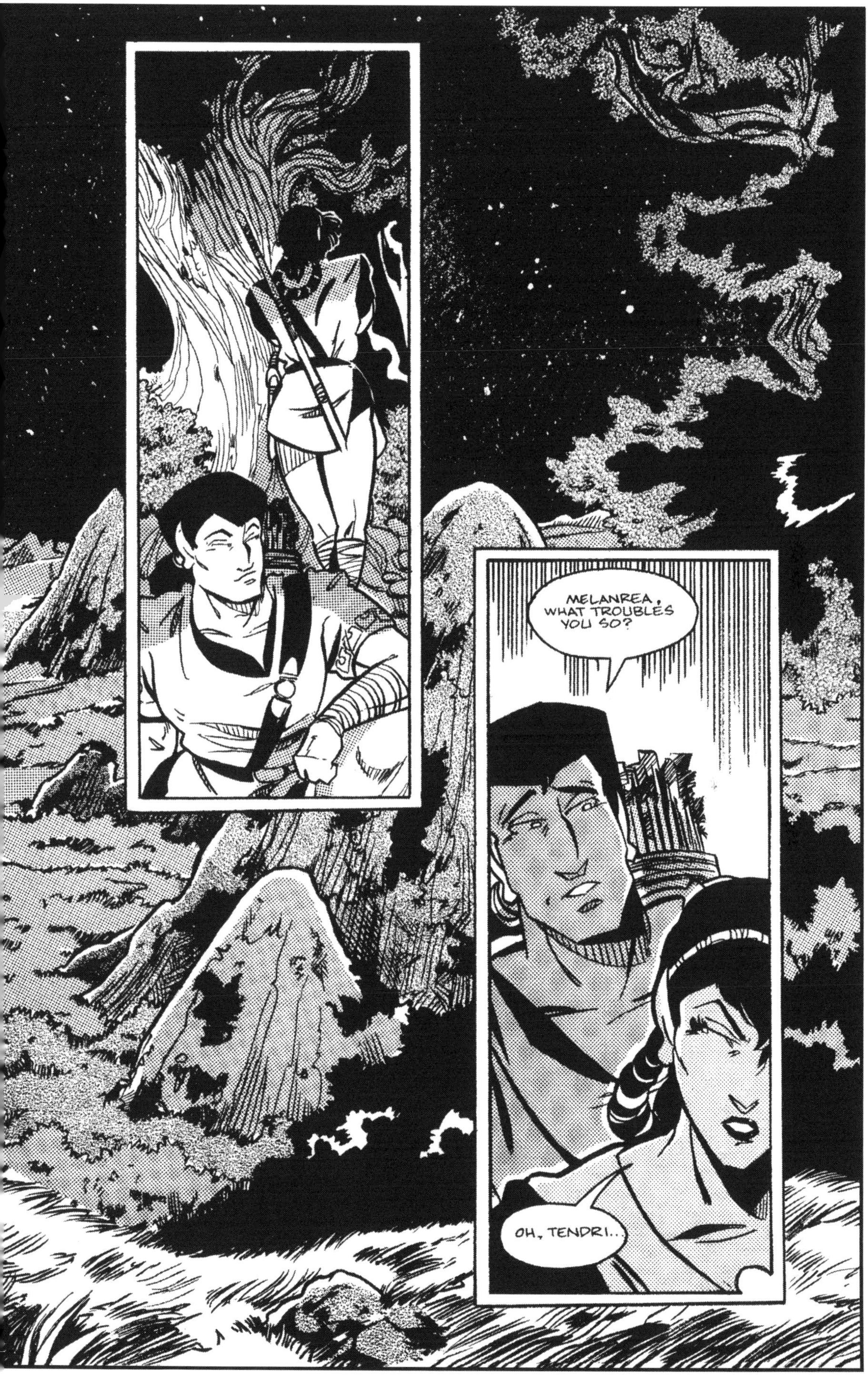
MELANREA, WHAT TROUBLES YOU SO?
OH, TENDRI...

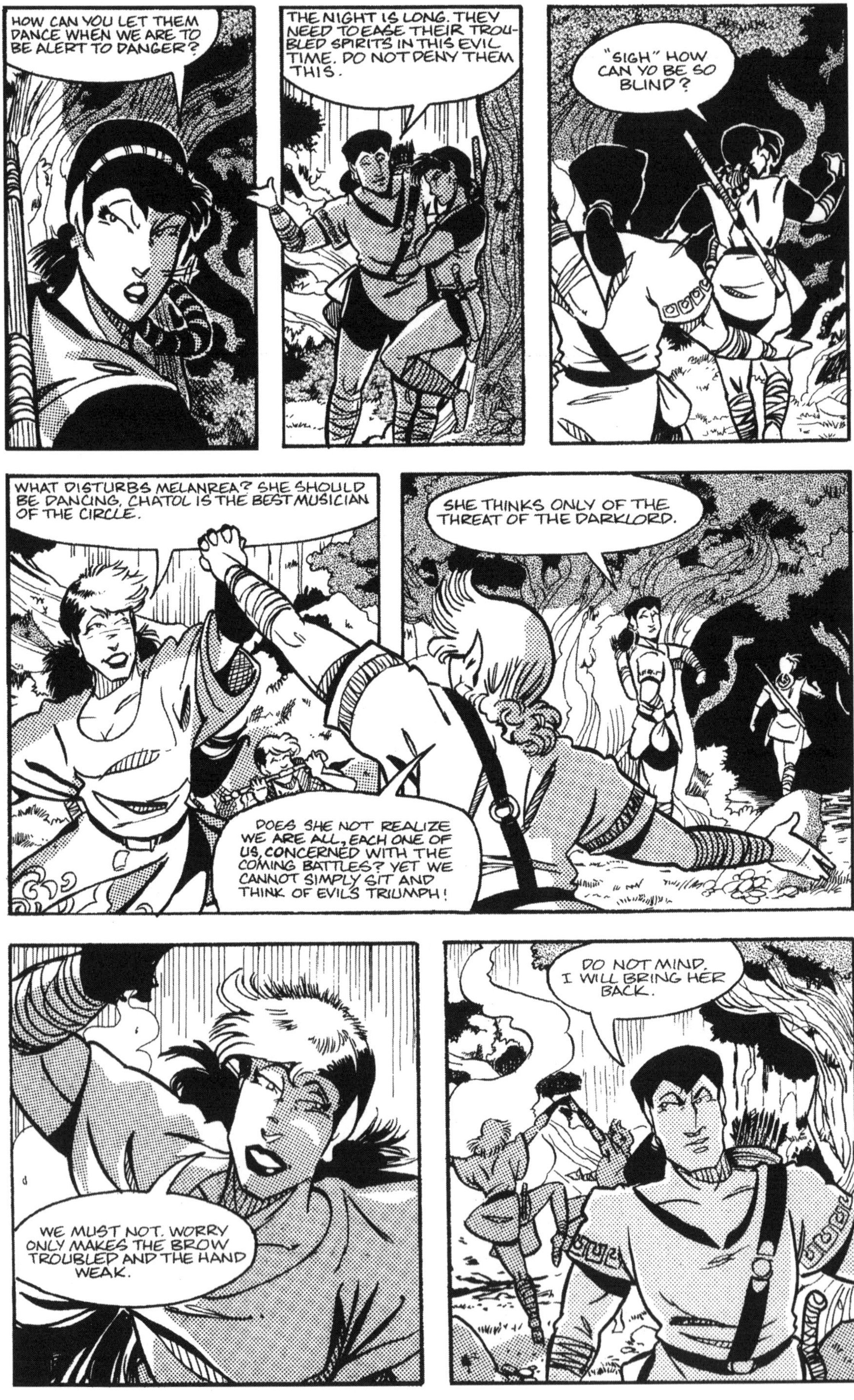
HOW CAN YOU LET THEM DANCE WHEN WE ARE TO BE ALERT TO DANGER?
THE NIGHT IS LONG. THEY NEED TO EASE THEIR TROUBLED SPIRITS IN THIS EVIL TIME. DO NOT DENY THEM THIS.
"SIGH" HOW CAN YO BE SO BLIND?
WHAT DISTURBS MELANREA? SHE SHOULD BE DANCING, CHATOL IS THE BEST MUSICIAN OF THE CIRCLE.
SHE THINKS ONLY OF THE THREAT OF THE DARKLORD.
DOES SHE NOT REALIZE WE ARE ALL, EACH ONE OF US, CONCERNED WITH THE COMING BATTLES? YET WE CANNOT SIMPLY SIT AND THINK OF EVILS TRIUMPH!
WE MUST NOT. WORRY ONLY MAKES THE BROW TROUBLED AND THE HAND WEAK.
DO NOT MIND. I WILL BRING HER BACK.

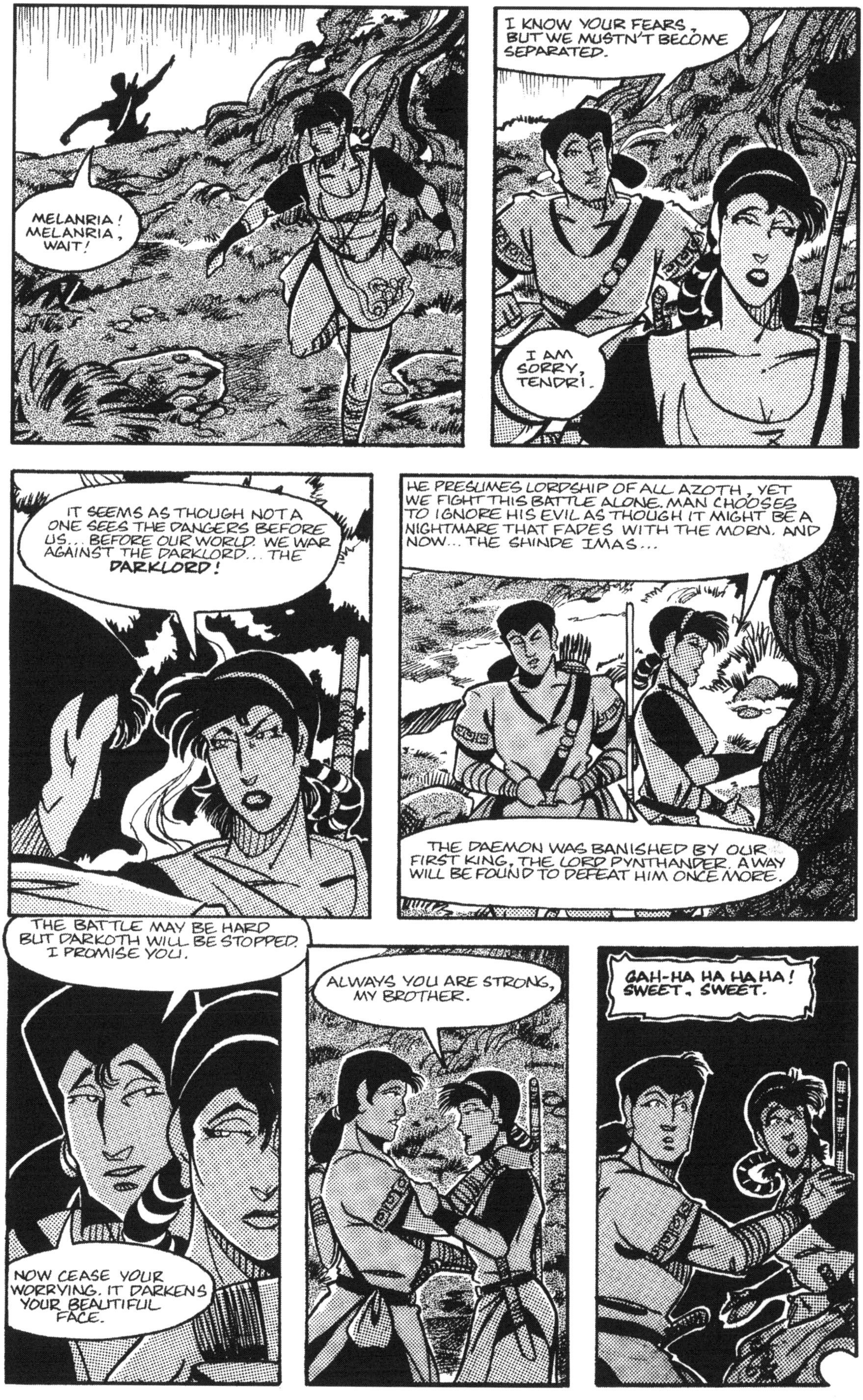
MELANRIA! MELANRIA, WAIT!
I KNOW YOUR FEARS, BUT WE MUSTN'T BECOME SEPARATED.
I AM SORRY, TENDRI.
IT SEEMS AS THOUGH NOT A ONE SEES THE DANGERS BEFORE US... BEFORE OUR WORLD. WE WAR AGAINST THE DARKLORD... THE DARKLORD!
HE PRESUMES LORDSHIP OF ALL AZOTH, YET WE FIGHT THIS BATTLE ALONE. MAN CHOOSES TO IGNORE HIS EVIL AS THOUGH IT MIGHT BE A NIGHTMARE THAT FADES WITH THE MORN. AND NOW... THE SHINDE IMAS...
THE DAEMON WAS BANISHED BY OUR FIRST KING, THE LORD PYNTHANDER. A WAY WILL BE FOUND TO DEFEAT HIM ONCE MORE.
THE BATTLE MAY BE HARD BUT DARKOTH WILL BE STOPPED. I PROMISE YOU.
NOW CEASE YOUR WORRYING. IT DARKENS YOUR BEAUTIFUL FACE.
ALWAYS YOU ARE STRONG, MY BROTHER.
GAH-HA HA HA HA! SWEET. SWEET.

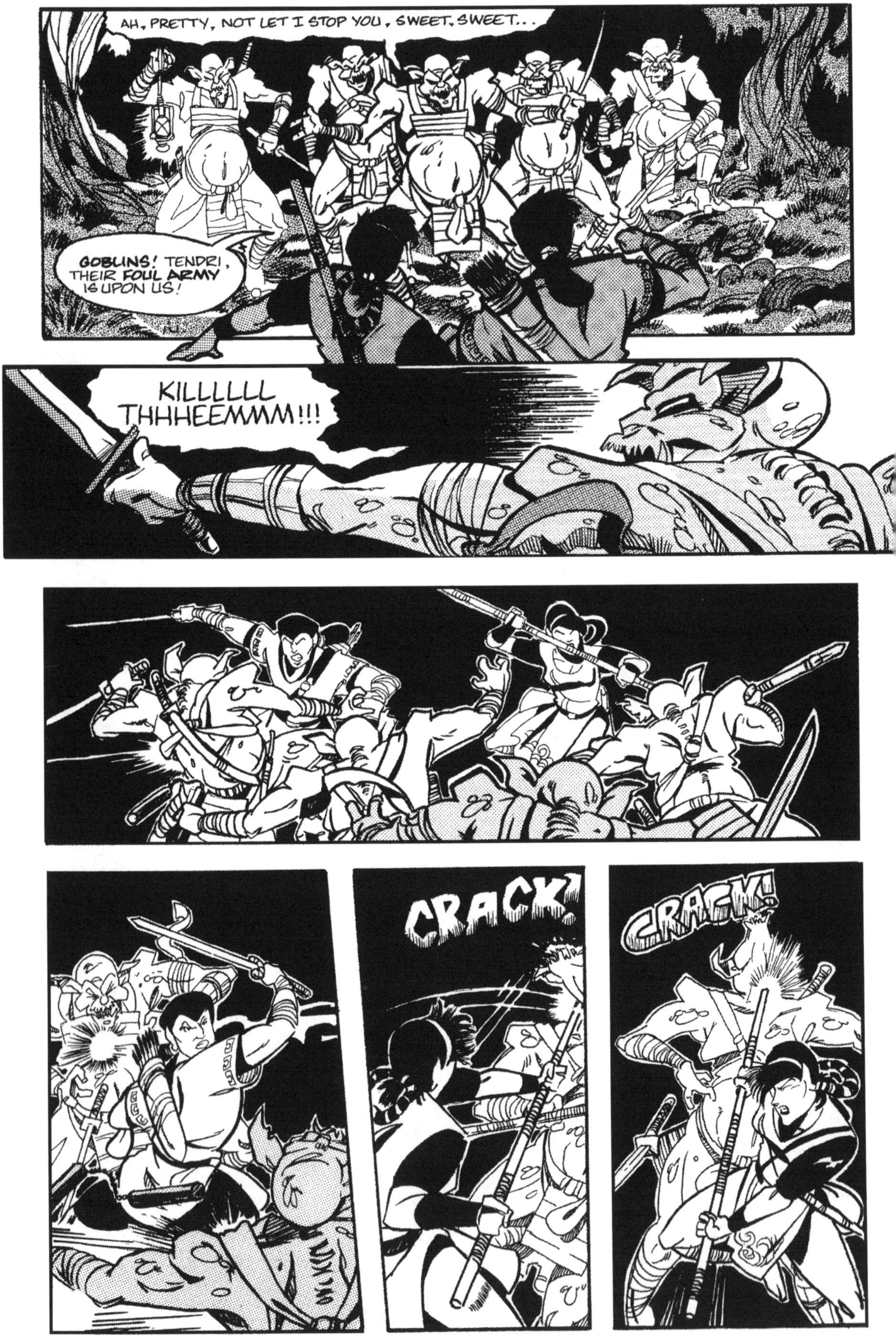
AH, PRETTY, NOT LET I STOP YOU, SWEET, SWEET...
GOBLINS! TENDRI, THEIR FOUL ARMY IS UPON US!
KILLLLLL THHHEEMMM!!!
CRACK!
CRACK!

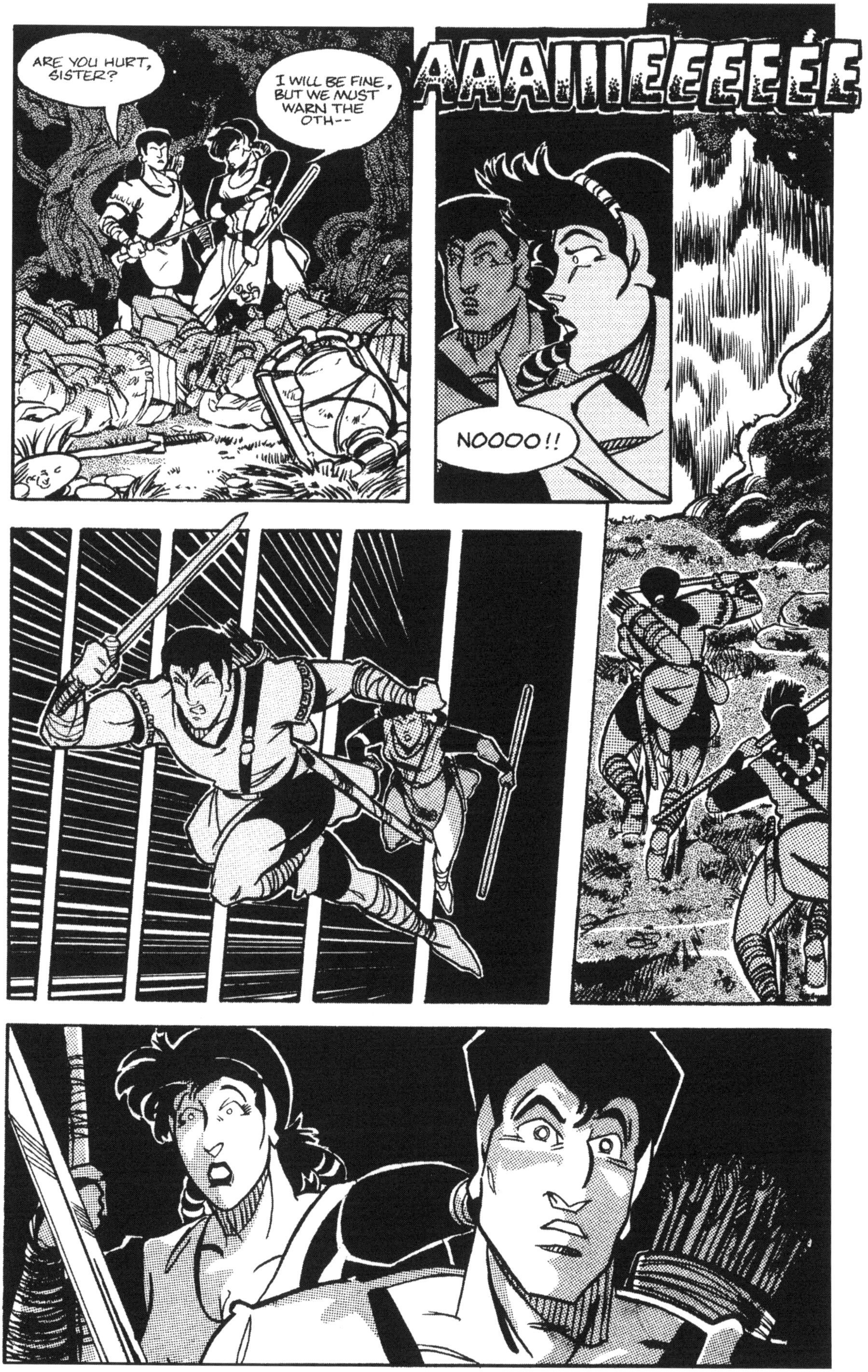
ARE YOU HURT, SISTER?
I WILL BE FINE, BUT WE MUST WARN THE OTH--
AAAIIIIEEEEEÉ
NOOOO!!

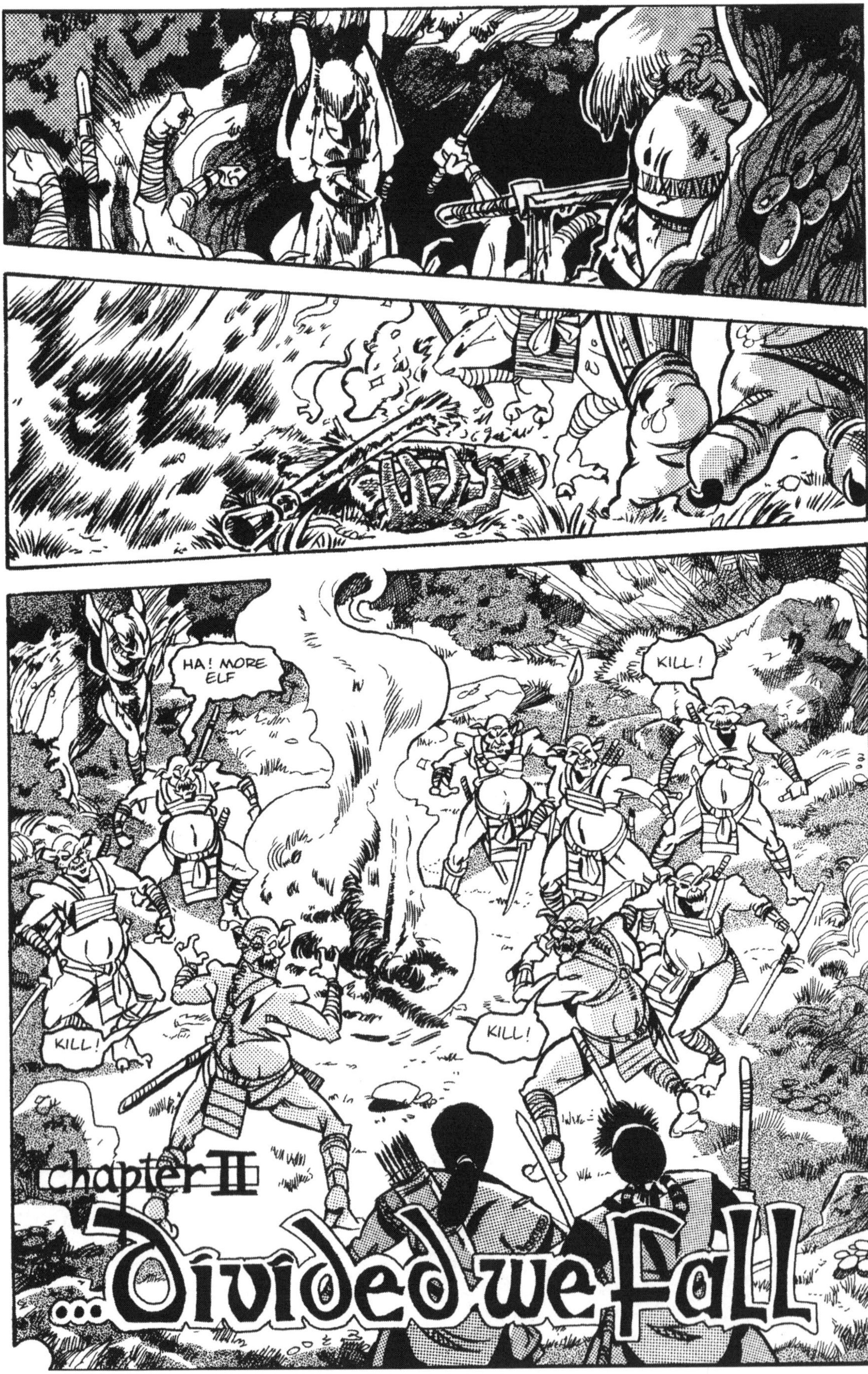
HA! MORE ELF
KILL!
KILL!
KILL!
chapter II
...Divided we Fall

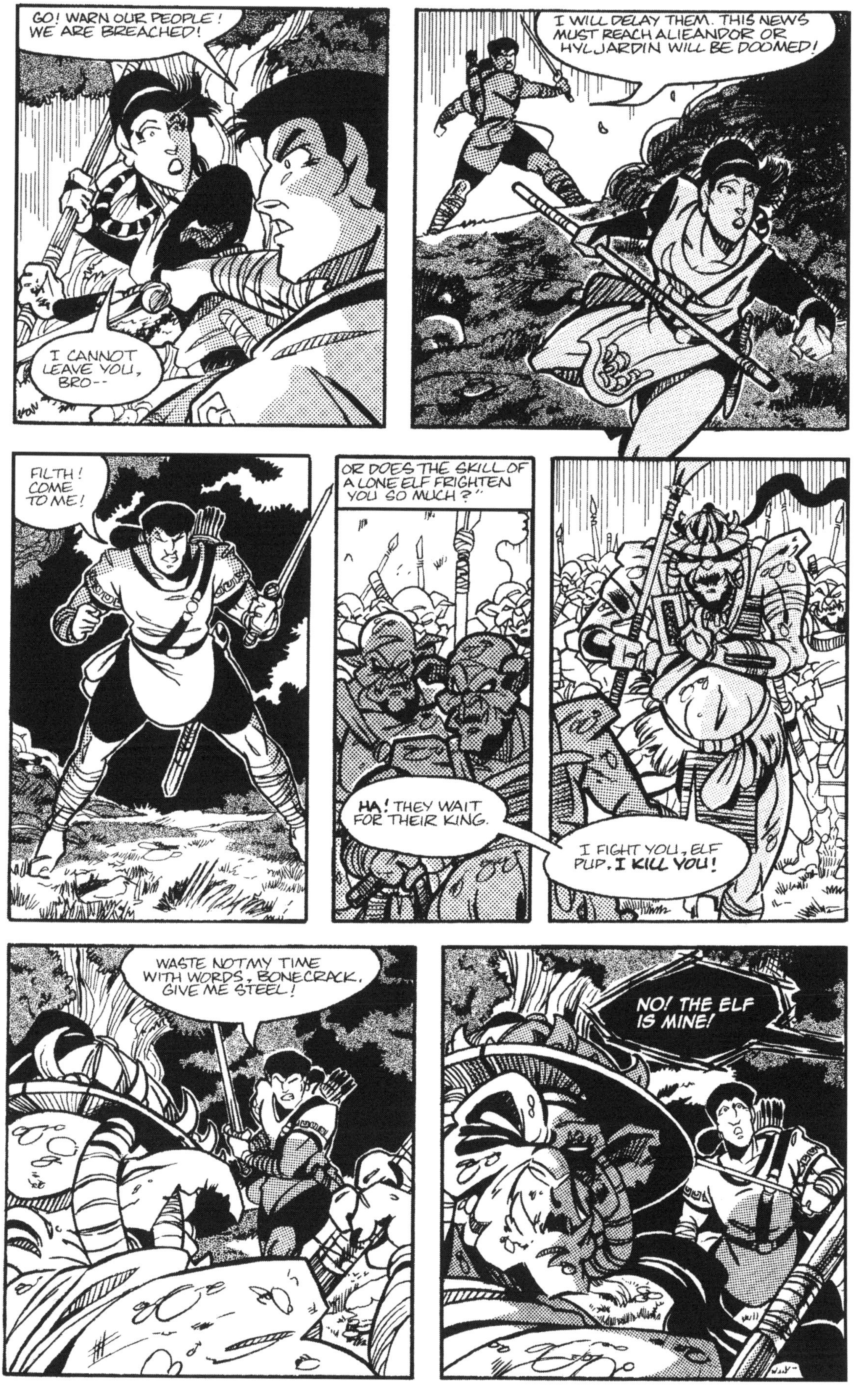
GO! WARN OUR PEOPLE! WE ARE BREACHED!
I CANNOT LEAVE YOU, BRO--
I WILL DELAY THEM. THIS NEWS MUST REACH ALIEANDOR OR HYLJARDIN WILL BE DOOMED!
FILTH! COME TO ME!
OR DOES THE SKILL OF A LONE ELF FRIGHTEN YOU SO MUCH?"
HA! THEY WAIT FOR THEIR KING.
I FIGHT YOU, ELF PUP. I KILL YOU!
WASTE NOT MY TIME WITH WORDS, BONECRACK. GIVE ME STEEL!
NO! THE ELF IS MINE!

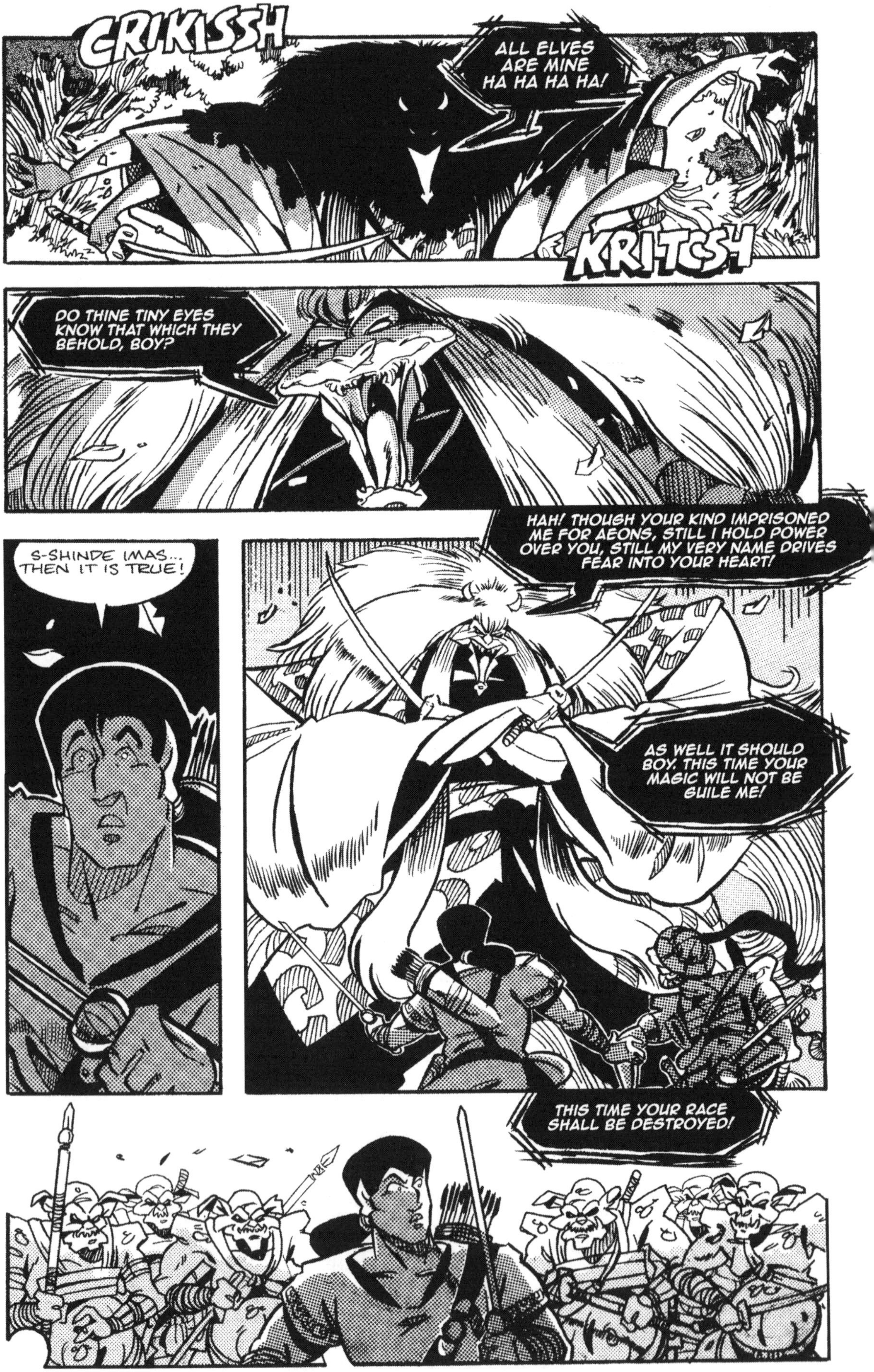

CRIKISSH
ALL ELVES ARE MINE HA HA HA HA!
KRITCSH
DO THINE TINY EYES KNOW THAT WHICH THEY BEHOLD, BOY?
S-SHINDE IMAS... THEN IT IS TRUE!
HAH! THOUGH YOUR KIND IMPRISONED ME FOR AEONS, STILL I HOLD POWER OVER YOU, STILL MY VERY NAME DRIVES FEAR INTO YOUR HEART!
AS WELL IT SHOULD BOY. THIS TIME YOUR MAGIC WILL NOT BE GUILE ME!
THIS TIME YOUR RACE SHALL BE DESTROYED!

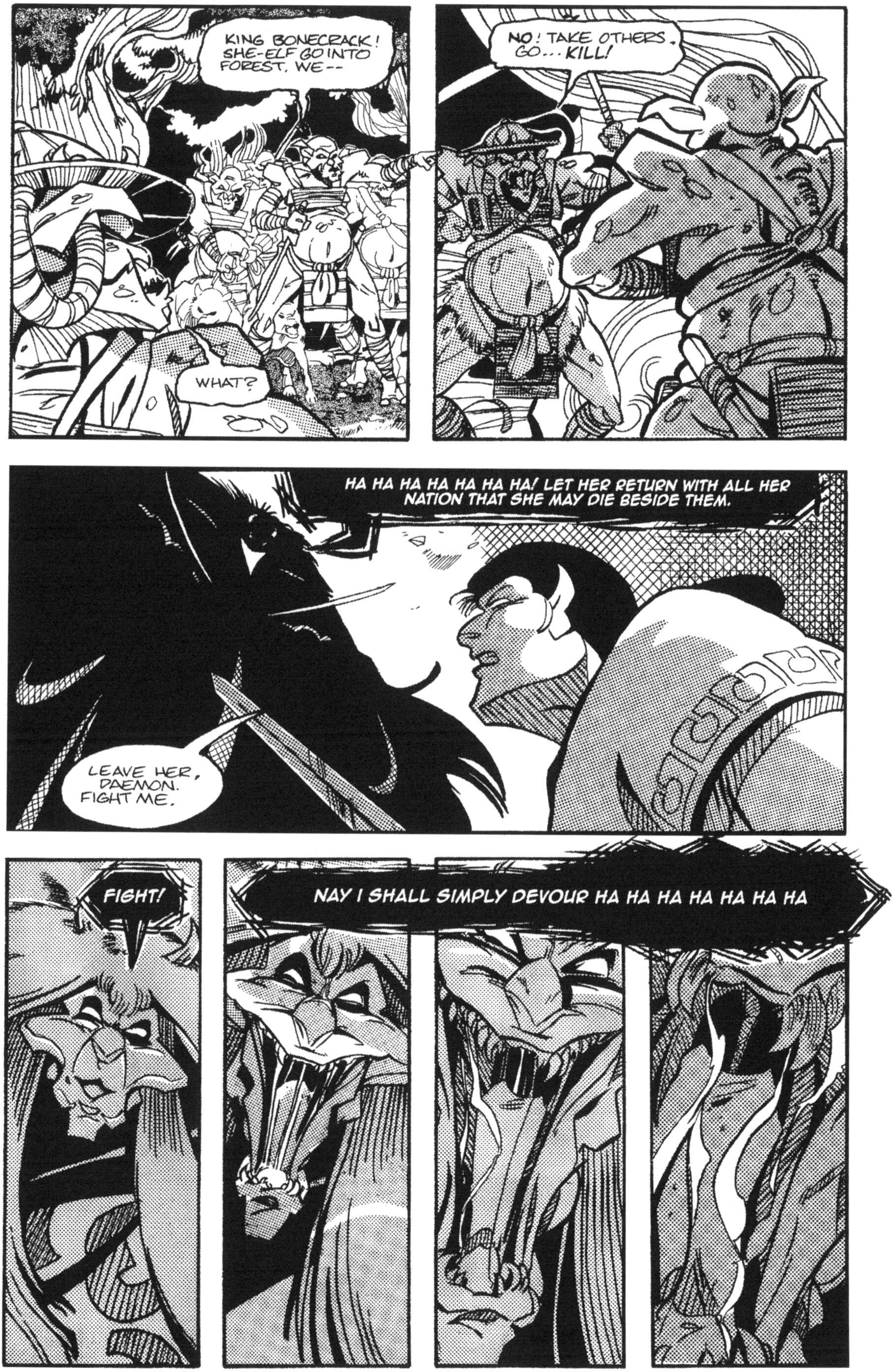
KING BONECRACK! SHE-ELF GO INTO FOREST. WE--
WHAT?
NO! TAKE OTHERS. GO... KILL!
HA HA HA HA HA HA HA! LET HER RETURN WITH ALL HER NATION THAT SHE MAY DIE BESIDE THEM.
LEAVE HER, DAEMON. FIGHT ME.
FIGHT!
NAY I SHALL SIMPLY DEVOUR HA HA HA HA HA HA HA

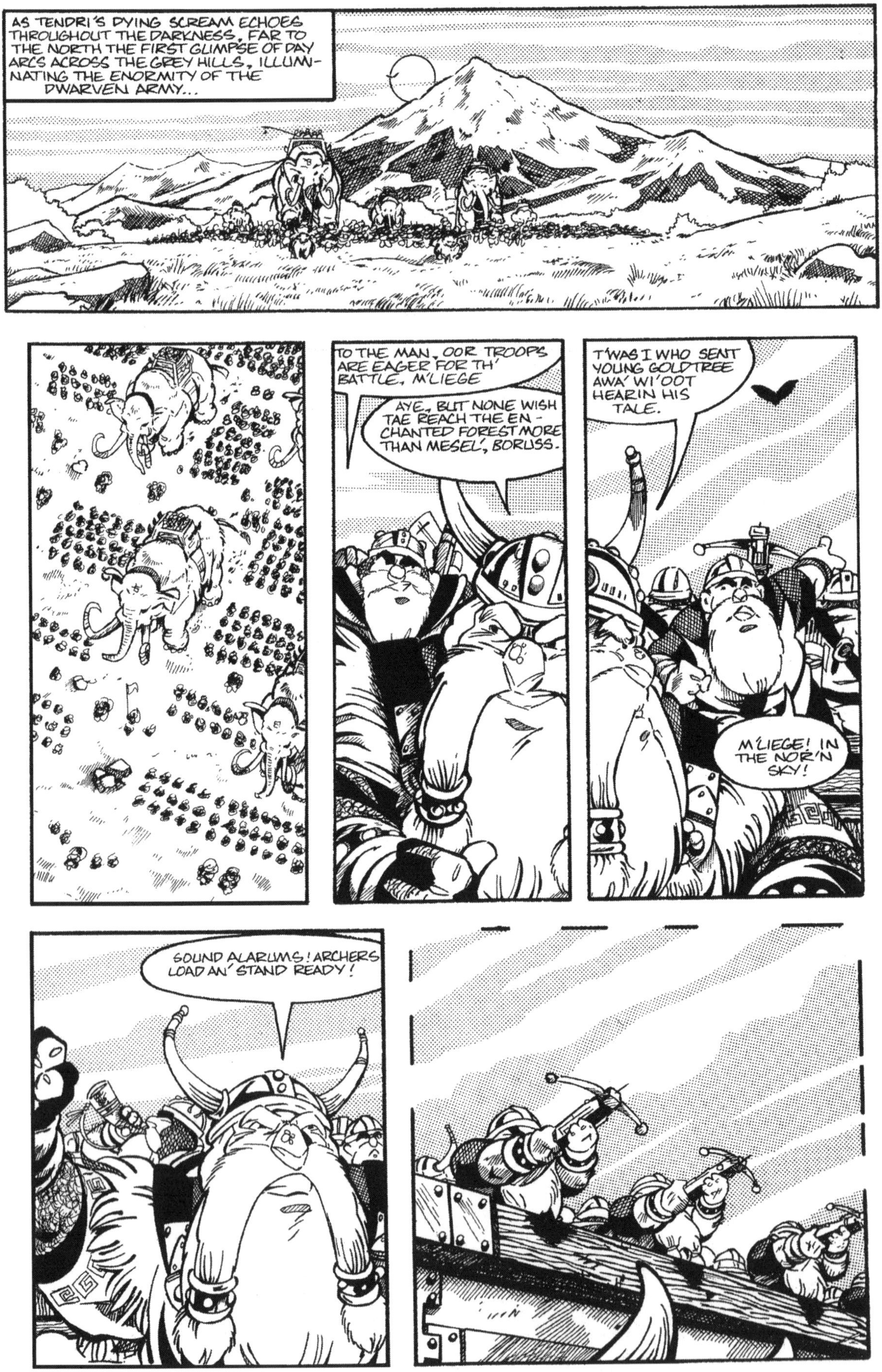
AS TENDRI'S DYING SCREAM ECHOES THROUGHOUT THE DARKNESS, FAR TO THE NORTH THE FIRST GLIMPSE OF DAY ARCS ACROSS THE GREY HILLS, ILLUMINATING THE ENORMITY OF THE DWARVEN ARMY...
TO THE MAN, OOR TROOPS ARE EAGER FOR TH' BATTLE, M'LIEGE
AYE, BUT NONE WISH TAE REACH THE ENCHANTED FOREST MORE THAN MESEL', BORUSS.
T'WAS I WHO SENT YOUNG GOLDTREE AWA' WI'OOT HEARIN HIS TALE.
M'LIEGE! IN THE NOR'N SKY!
SOUND ALARUMS! ARCHERS LOAD AN' STAND READY!

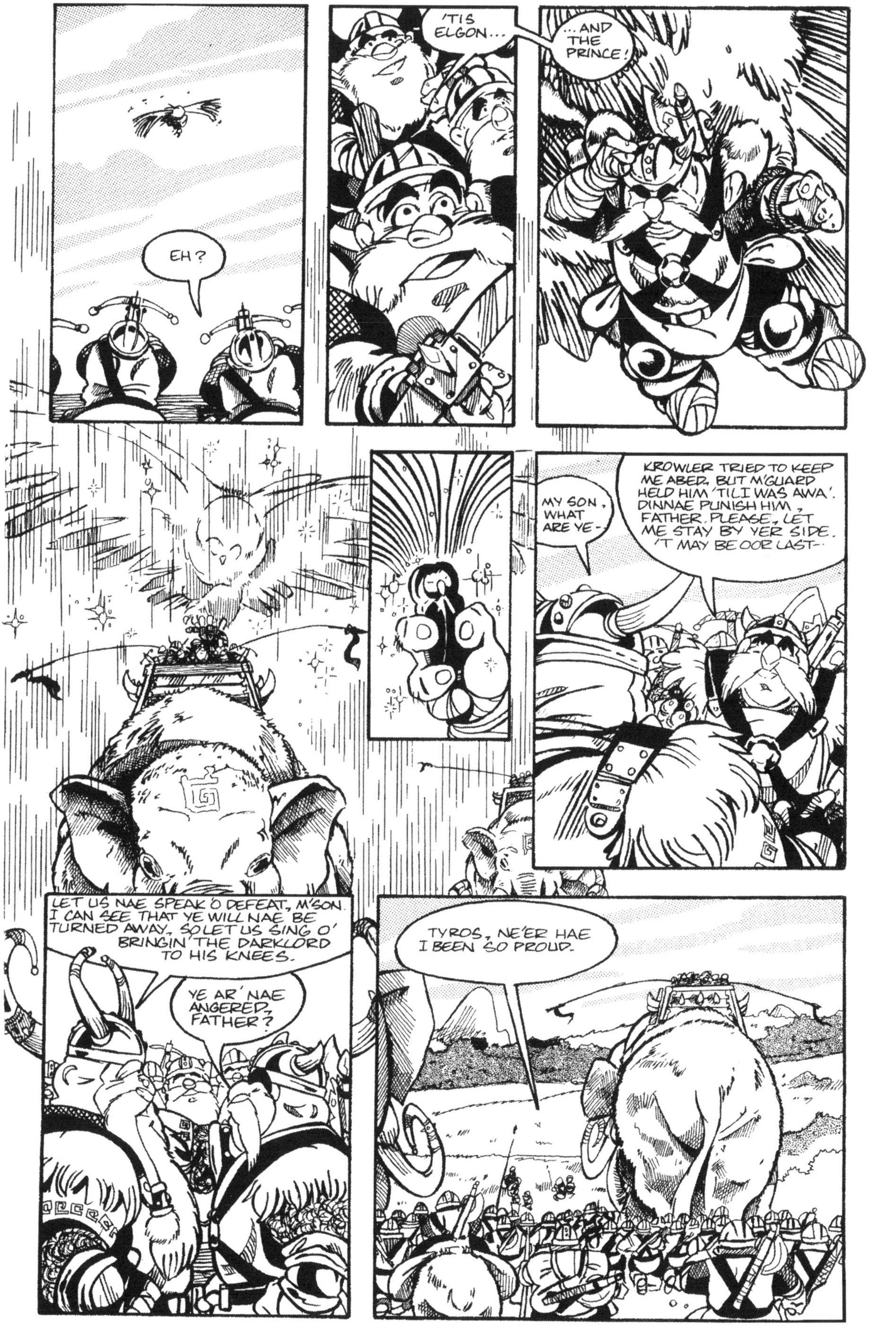
EH?
'TIS ELGON...
...AND THE PRINCE!
MY SON, WHAT ARE YE-
KROWLER TRIED TO KEEP ME ABED, BUT M'GUARD HELD HIM 'TILI WAS AWA'. DINNAE PUNISH HIM, FATHER. PLEASE, LET ME STAY BY YER SIDE. 'T MAY BE OOR LAST-
LET US NAE SPEAK O DEFEAT, M'SON. I CAN SEE THAT YE WILL NAE BE TURNED AWAY, SO LET US SING O' BRINGIN' THE DARKLORD TO HIS KNEES.
YE AR' NAE ANGERED, FATHER?
TYROS, NE'ER HAE I BEEN SO PROUD.

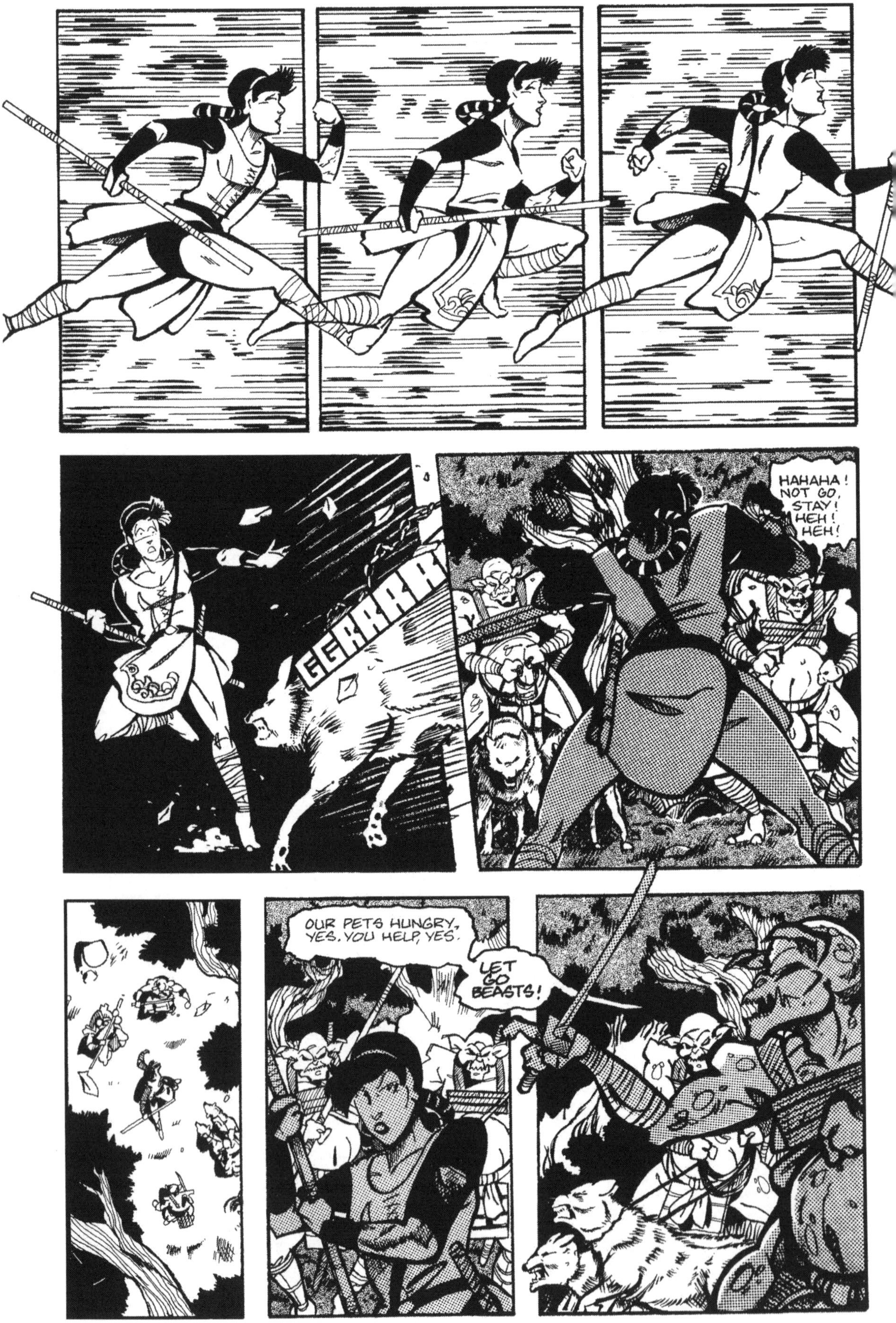
GERRRRR
HAHAHA! NOT GO, STAY! HEH! HEH!
OUR PETS HUNGRY, YES. YOU HELP, YES.
LET GO BEASTS!

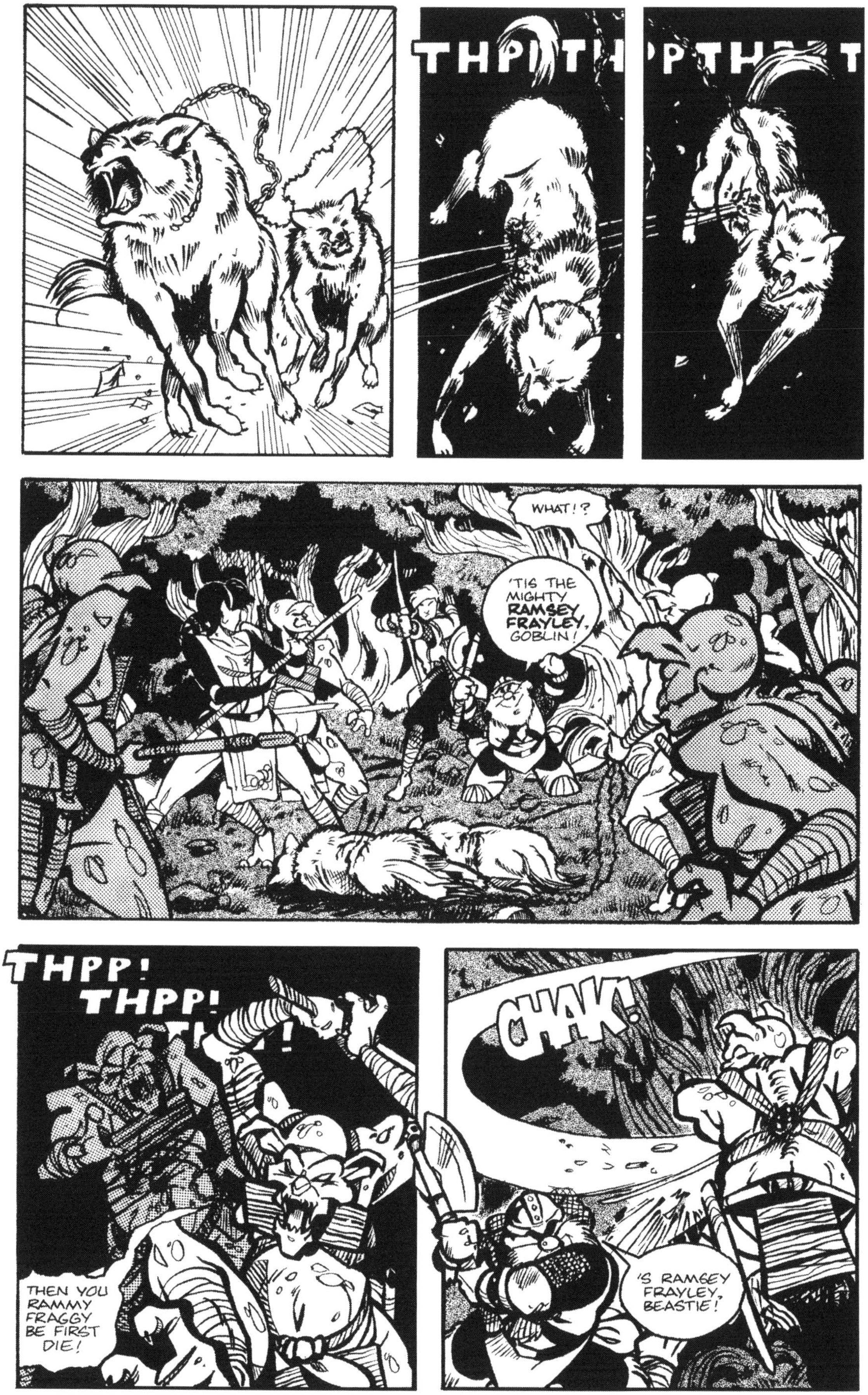
THPI THPPTHPPT
WHAT!?
'TIS THE MIGHTY RAMSEY FRAYLEY, GOBLIN!
THPP!
THPP!
THEN YOU RAMMY FRAGGY BE FIRST DIE!
CHAK!
'S RAMSEY FRAYLEY, BEASTIE!

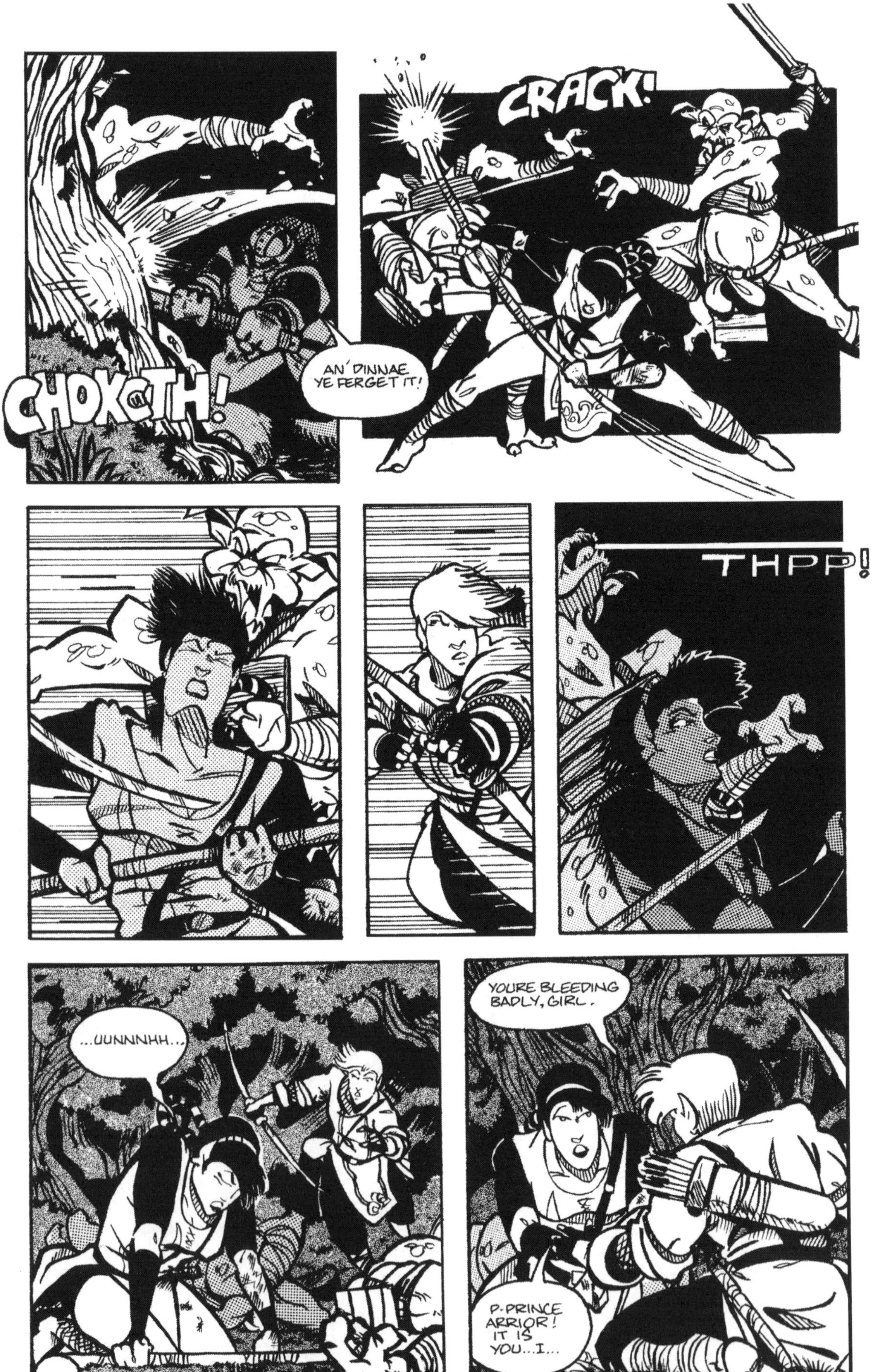
CHOKCTH!
AN' DINNAE YE FERGET IT!
CRACK!
THPP!
...UUNNNHH...
YOURE BLEEDING BADLY, GIRL.
P-PRINCE ARRIOR! IT IS YOU...I...

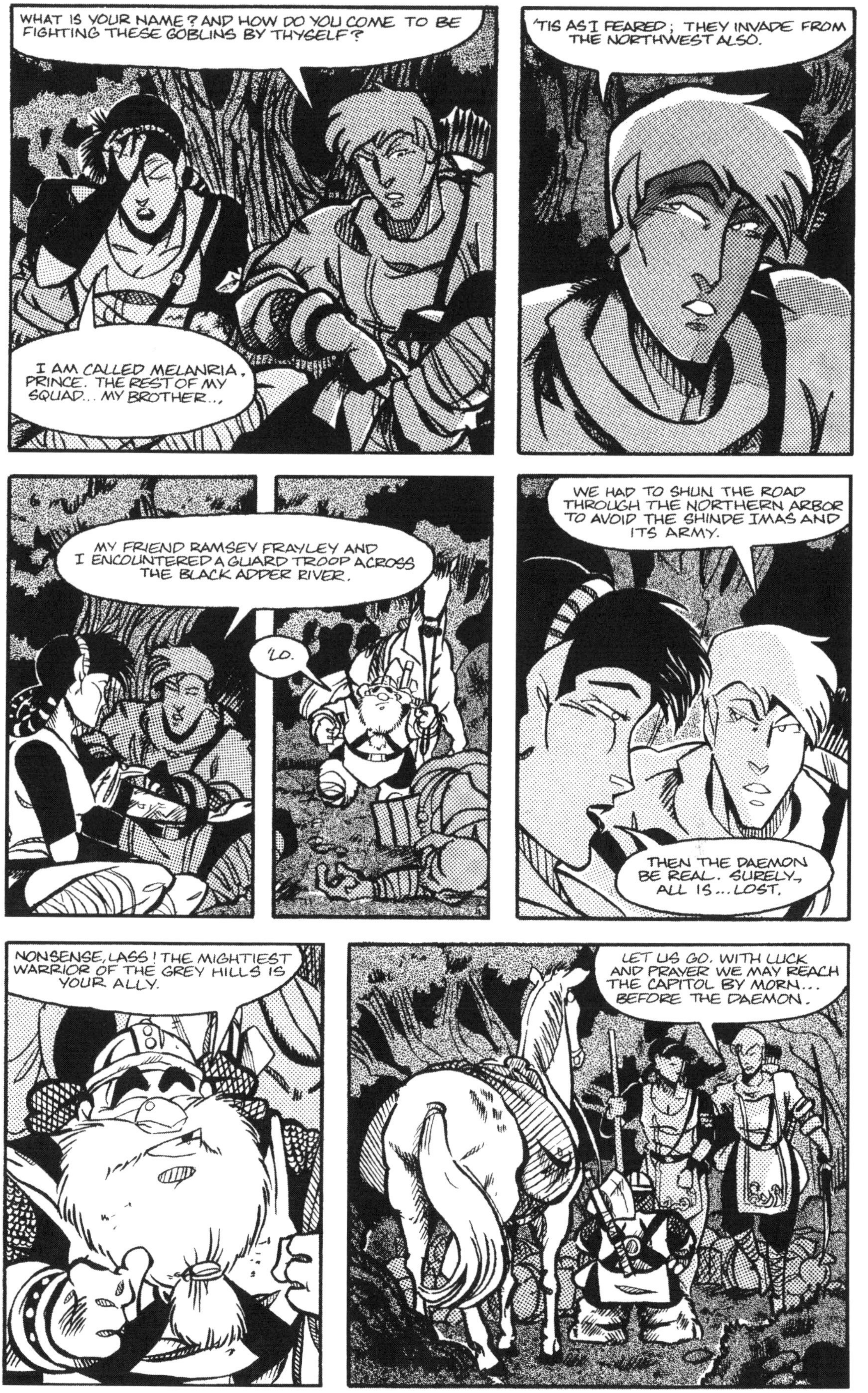
WHAT IS YOUR NAME? AND HOW DO YOU COME TO BE FIGHTING THESE GOBLINS BY THYSELF?
I AM CALLED MELANRIA, PRINCE. THE REST OF MY SQUAD... MY BROTHER...,
'TIS AS I FEARED; THEY INVADE FROM THE NORTHWEST ALSO.
MY FRIEND RAMSEY FRAYLEY AND I ENCOUNTERED A GUARD TROOP ACROSS THE BLACK ADDER RIVER.
'LO.
WE HAD TO SHUN THE ROAD THROUGH THE NORTHERN ARBOR TO AVOID THE SHINDE IMAS AND ITS ARMY.
THEN THE DAEMON BE REAL. SURELY, ALL IS... LOST.
NONSENSE, LASS! THE MIGHTIEST WARRIOR OF THE GREY HILLS IS YOUR ALLY.
LET US GO. WITH LUCK AND PRAYER WE MAY REACH THE CAPITOL BY MORN... BEFORE THE DAEMON.

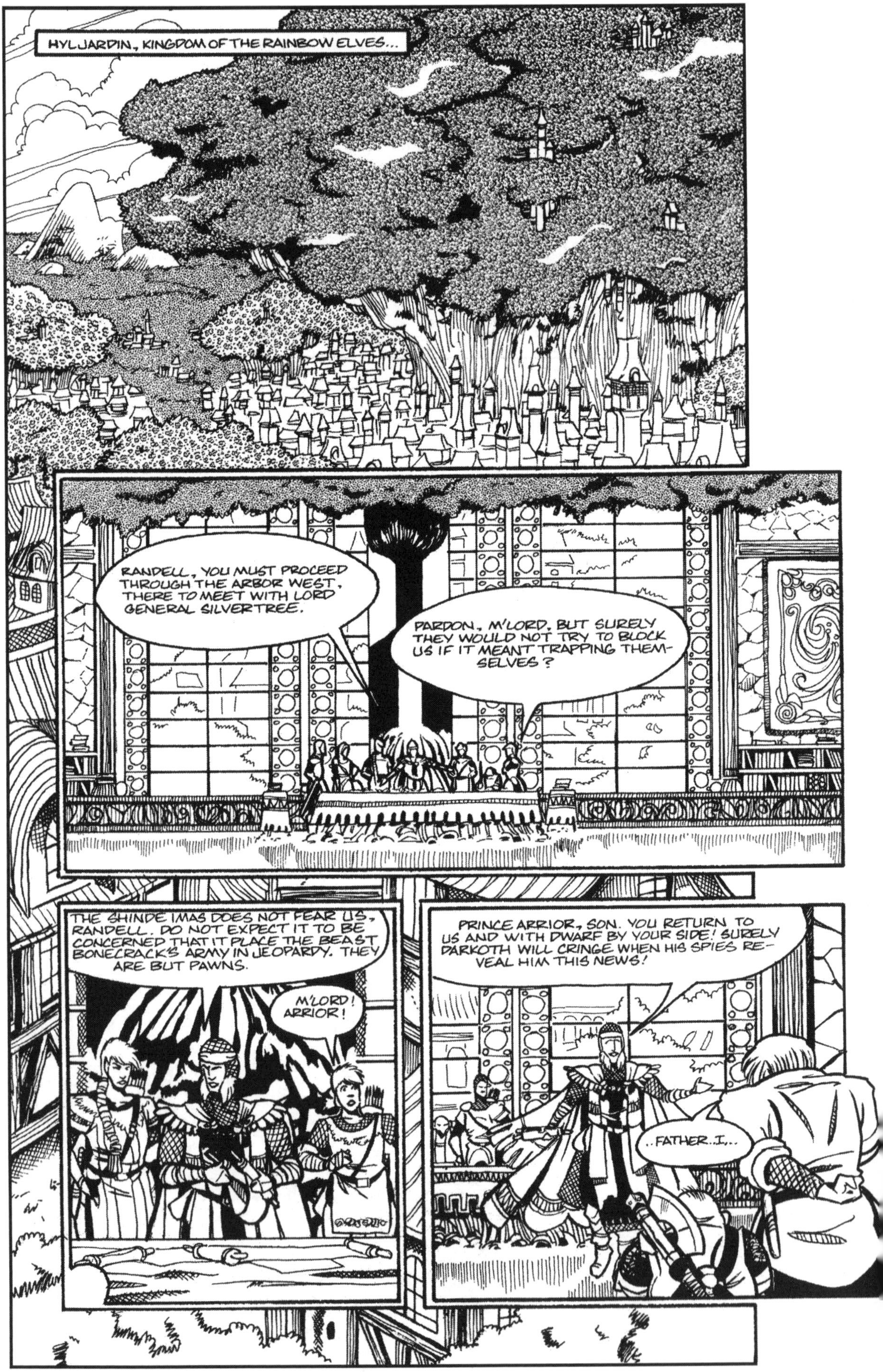
HYLJARDIN, KINGDOM OF THE RAINBOW ELVES...
RANDELL, YOU MUST PROCEED THROUGH THE ARBOR WEST, THERE TO MEET WITH LORD GENERAL SILVERTREE.
PARDON, M'LORD, BUT SURELY THEY WOULD NOT TRY TO BLOCK US IF IT MEANT TRAPPING THEM-SELVES?
THE SHINDE IMAS DOES NOT FEAR US, RANDELL. DO NOT EXPECT IT TO BE CONCERNED THAT IT PLACE THE BEAST BONECRACK'S ARMY IN JEOPARDY. THEY ARE BUT PAWNS.
M'LORD! ARRIOR!
PRINCE ARRIOR, SON. YOU RETURN TO US AND WITH DWARF BY YOUR SIDE! SURELY DARKOTH WILL CRINGE WHEN HIS SPIES RE-VEAL HIM THIS NEWS!
..FATHER..I...

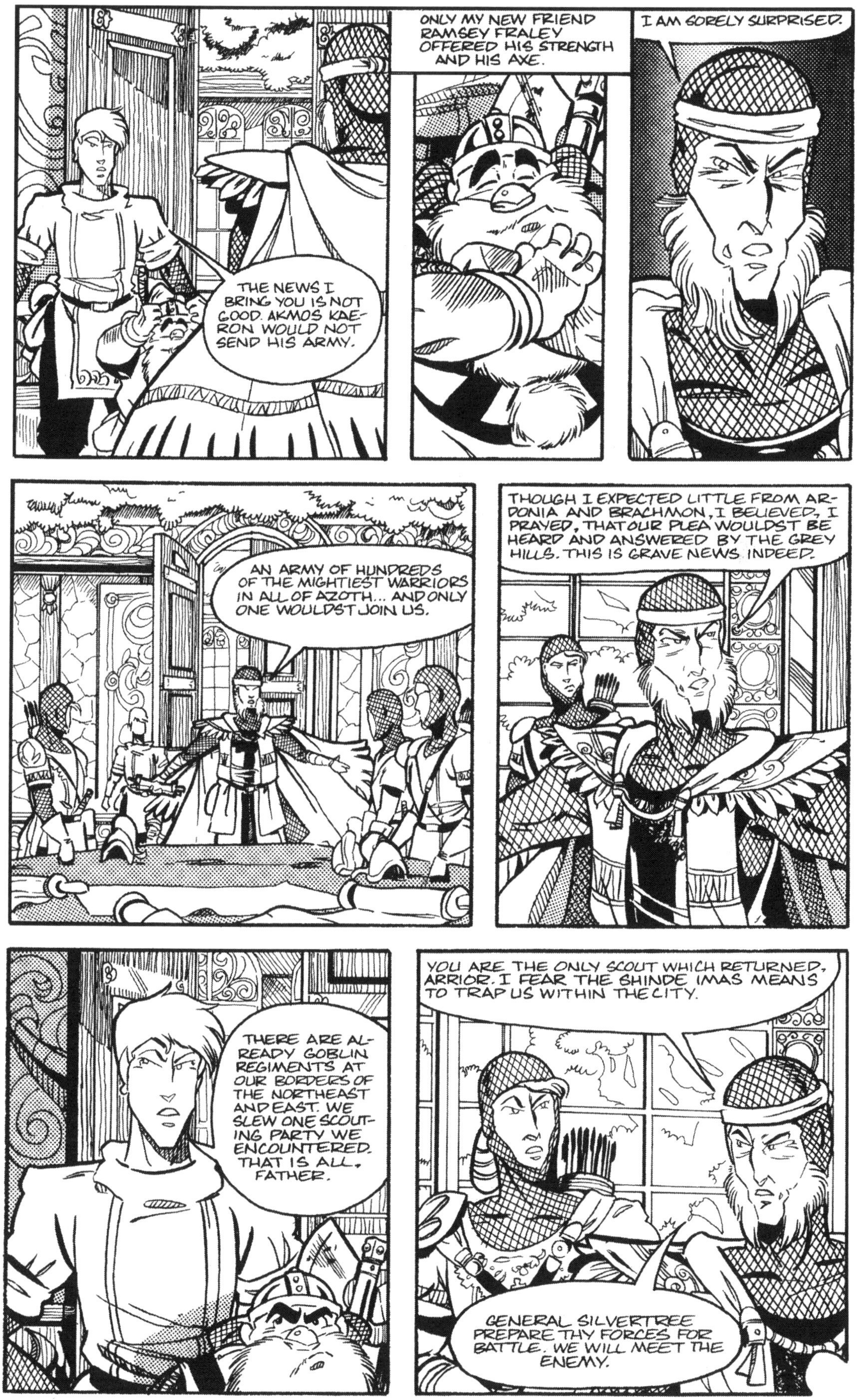
THE NEWS I BRING YOU IS NOT GOOD. AKMOS KAE-RON WOULD NOT SEND HIS ARMY.
ONLY MY NEW FRIEND RAMSEY FRALEY OFFERED HIS STRENGTH AND HIS AXE.
I AM SORELY SURPRISED.
AN ARMY OF HUNDREDS OF THE MIGHTIEST WARRIORS IN ALL OF AZOTH... AND ONLY ONE WOULDST JOIN US.
THOUGH I EXPECTED LITTLE FROM AR-DONIA AND BRACHMON, I BELIEVED, I PRAYED, THAT OUR PLEA WOULDST BE HEARD AND ANSWERED BY THE GREY HILLS. THIS IS GRAVE NEWS INDEED.
THERE ARE AL-READY GOBLIN REGIMENTS AT OUR BORDERS OF THE NORTHEAST AND EAST. WE SLEW ONE SCOUT-ING PARTY WE ENCOUNTERED. THAT IS ALL, FATHER.
YOU ARE THE ONLY SCOUT WHICH RETURNED, ARRIOR. I FEAR THE SHINDE IMAS MEANS TO TRAP US WITHIN THE CITY.
GENERAL SILVERTREE PREPARE THY FORCES FOR BATTLE. WE WILL MEET THE ENEMY.

BY THE CROWN!

THE FOREST BURNS!

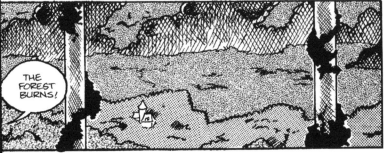

MY LORD! KING GOLDTREE! THE GOBLINS ARE OUTSIDE THE CIRCLE, BURNING THE FOREST AS THEY COME!

ALREADY THEY HAVE PASSED THE FIRST LINE!

YOVAN, RANDELL, PREPARE THE LEGIONS TO MARCH...WITHIN THE HOUR.

WE WILL NOT FAIL YOU, FATHER.

ACH, WHY SO GLUM, ARREY? LET'S GO WIN US A WAR!

WAIT...

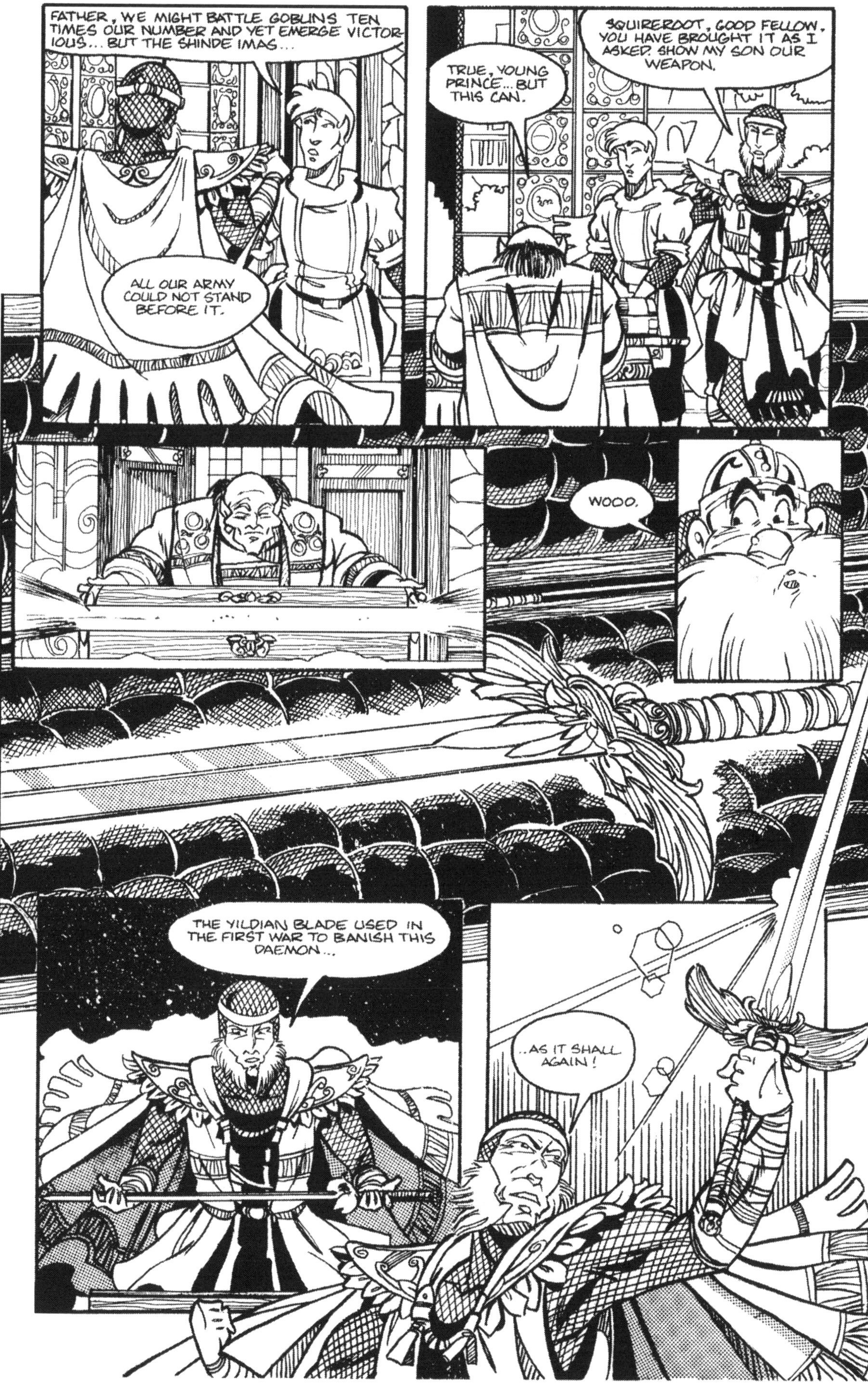
FATHER, WE MIGHT BATTLE GOBLINS TEN TIMES OUR NUMBER AND YET EMERGE VICTORIOUS... BUT THE SHINDE IMAG...
ALL OUR ARMY COULD NOT STAND BEFORE IT.
SQUIREROOT, GOOD FELLOW, YOU HAVE BROUGHT IT AS I ASKED. SHOW MY SON OUR WEAPON.
TRUE, YOUNG PRINCE... BUT THIS CAN.
WOOO.
THE YILDIAN BLADE USED IN THE FIRST WAR TO BANISH THIS DAEMON...
..AS IT SHALL AGAIN!

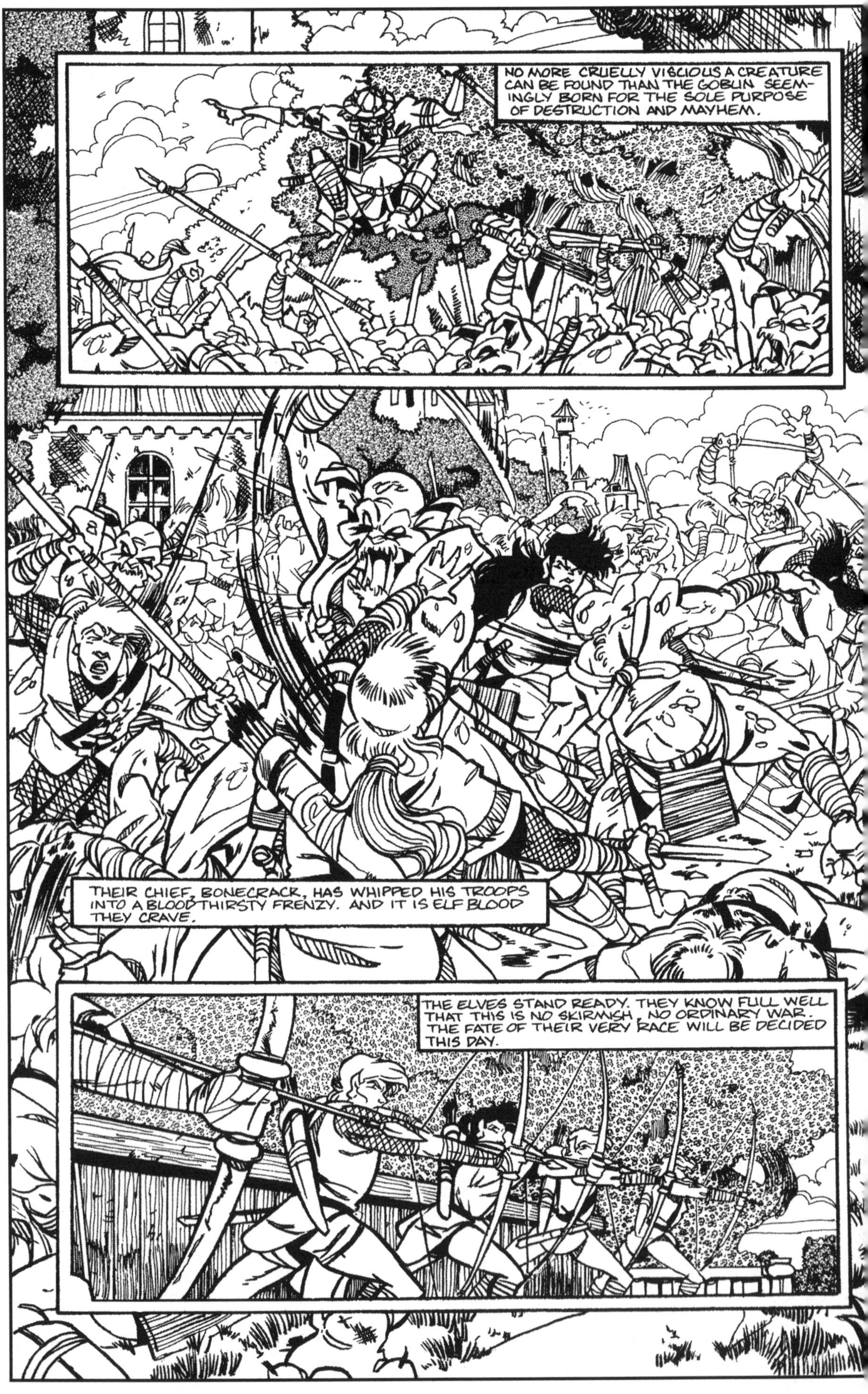
NO MORE CRUELLY VISCIOUS A CREATURE CAN BE FOUND THAN THE GOBLIN. SEEMINGLY BORN FOR THE SOLE PURPOSE OF DESTRUCTION AND MAYHEM.
THEIR CHIEF, BONECRACK, HAS WHIPPED HIS TROOPS INTO A BLOODTHIRSTY FRENZY. AND IT IS ELF BLOOD THEY CRAVE.
THE ELVES STAND READY. THEY KNOW FULL WELL THAT THIS IS NO SKIRMISH, NO ORDINARY WAR. THE FATE OF THEIR VERY RACE WILL BE DECIDED THIS DAY.

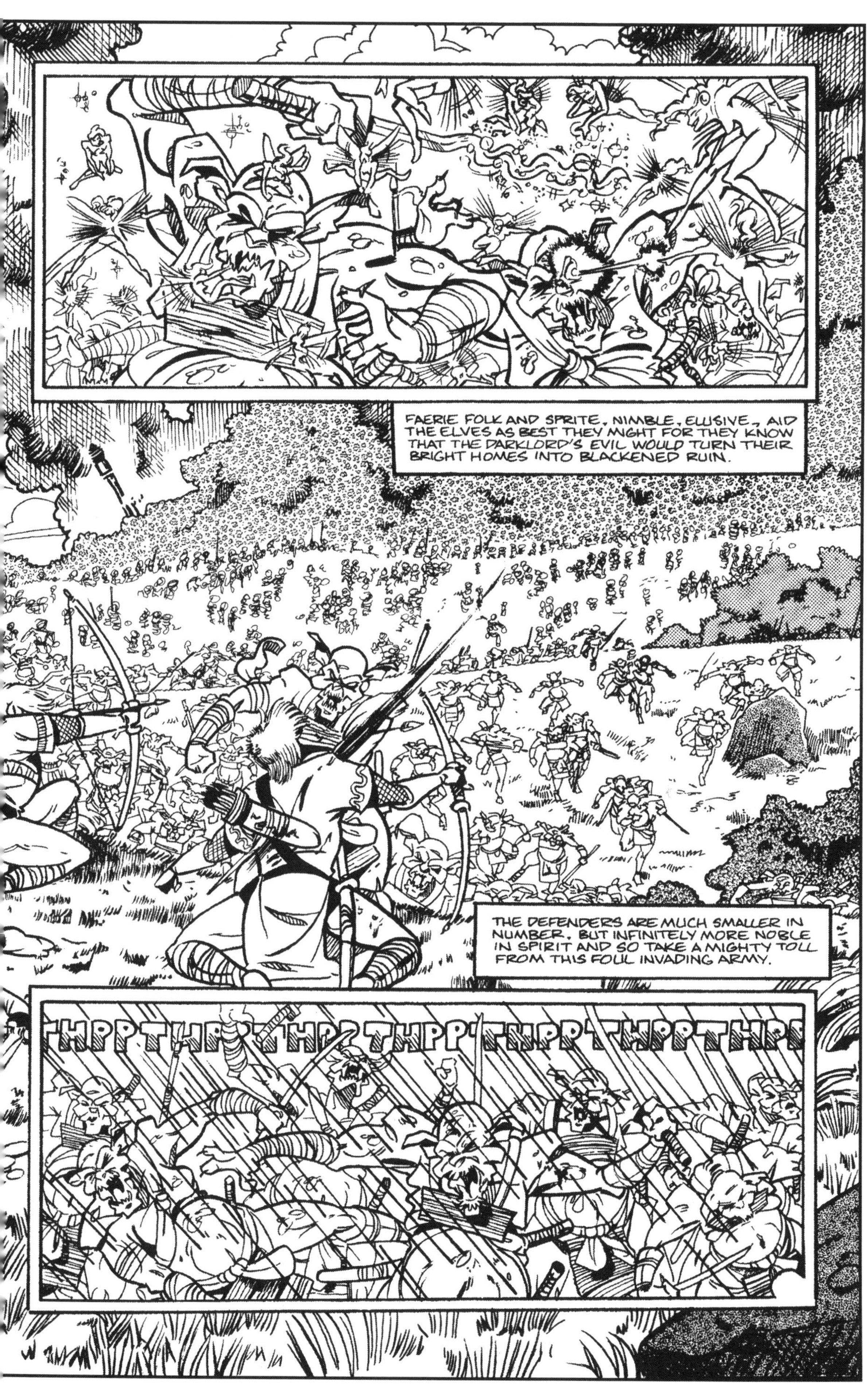
FAERIE FOLK AND SPRITE, NIMBLE, ELUSIVE, AID THE ELVES AS BEST THEY MIGHT FOR THEY KNOW THAT THE DARKLORD'S EVIL WOULD TURN THEIR BRIGHT HOMES INTO BLACKENED RUIN.
THE DEFENDERS ARE MUCH SMALLER IN NUMBER, BUT INFINITELY MORE NOBLE IN SPIRIT AND SO TAKE A MIGHTY TOLL FROM THIS FOUL INVADING ARMY.
THPP THPP THPP THPP THPP THPP THPP

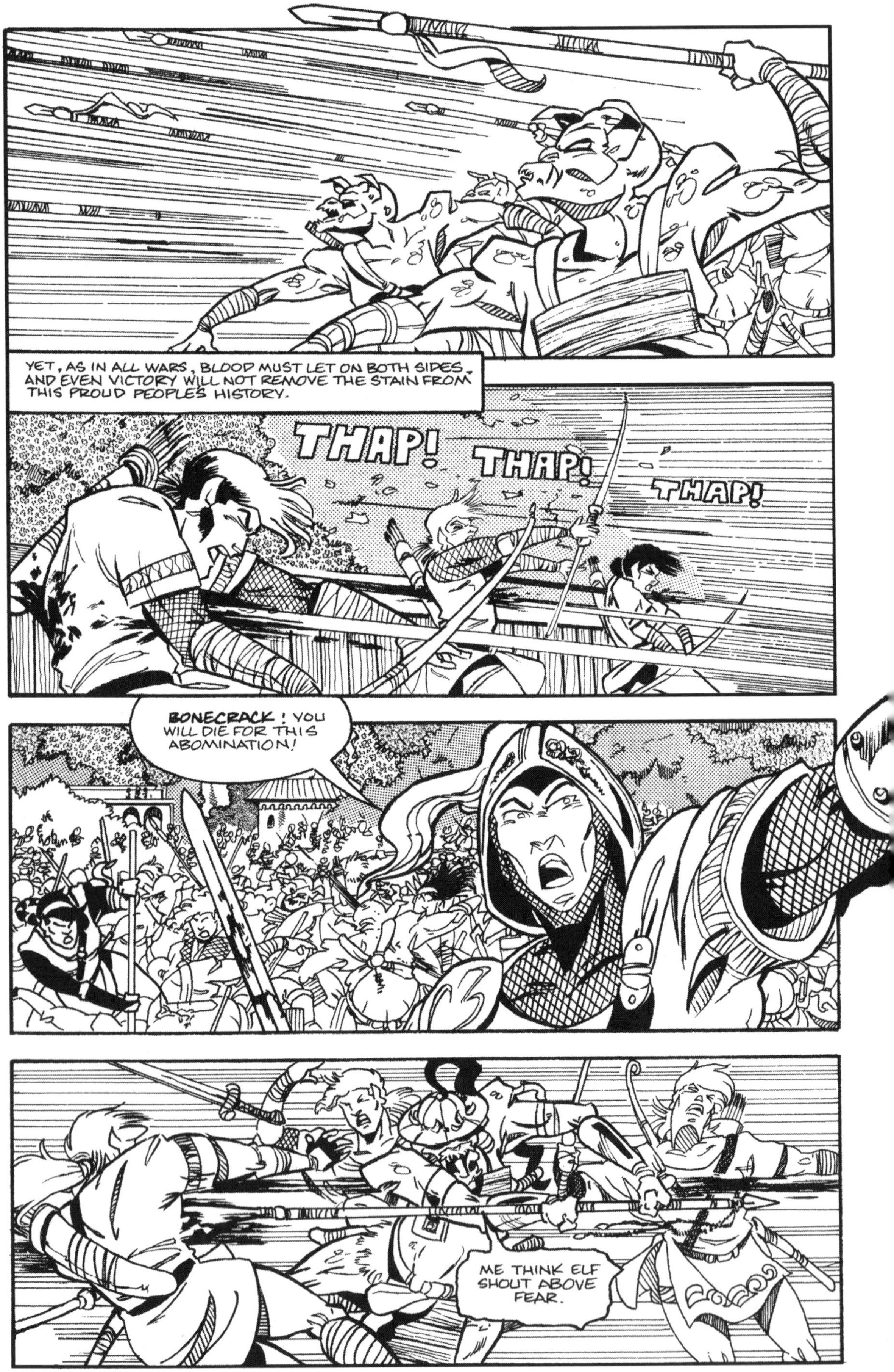

YET, AS IN ALL WARS, BLOOD MUST LET ON BOTH SIDES, AND EVEN VICTORY WILL NOT REMOVE THE STAIN FROM THIS PROUD PEOPLE'S HISTORY.
THAP! THAP! THAP!
BONECRACK! YOU WILL DIE FOR THIS ABOMINATION!
ME THINK ELF SHOUT ABOVE FEAR.

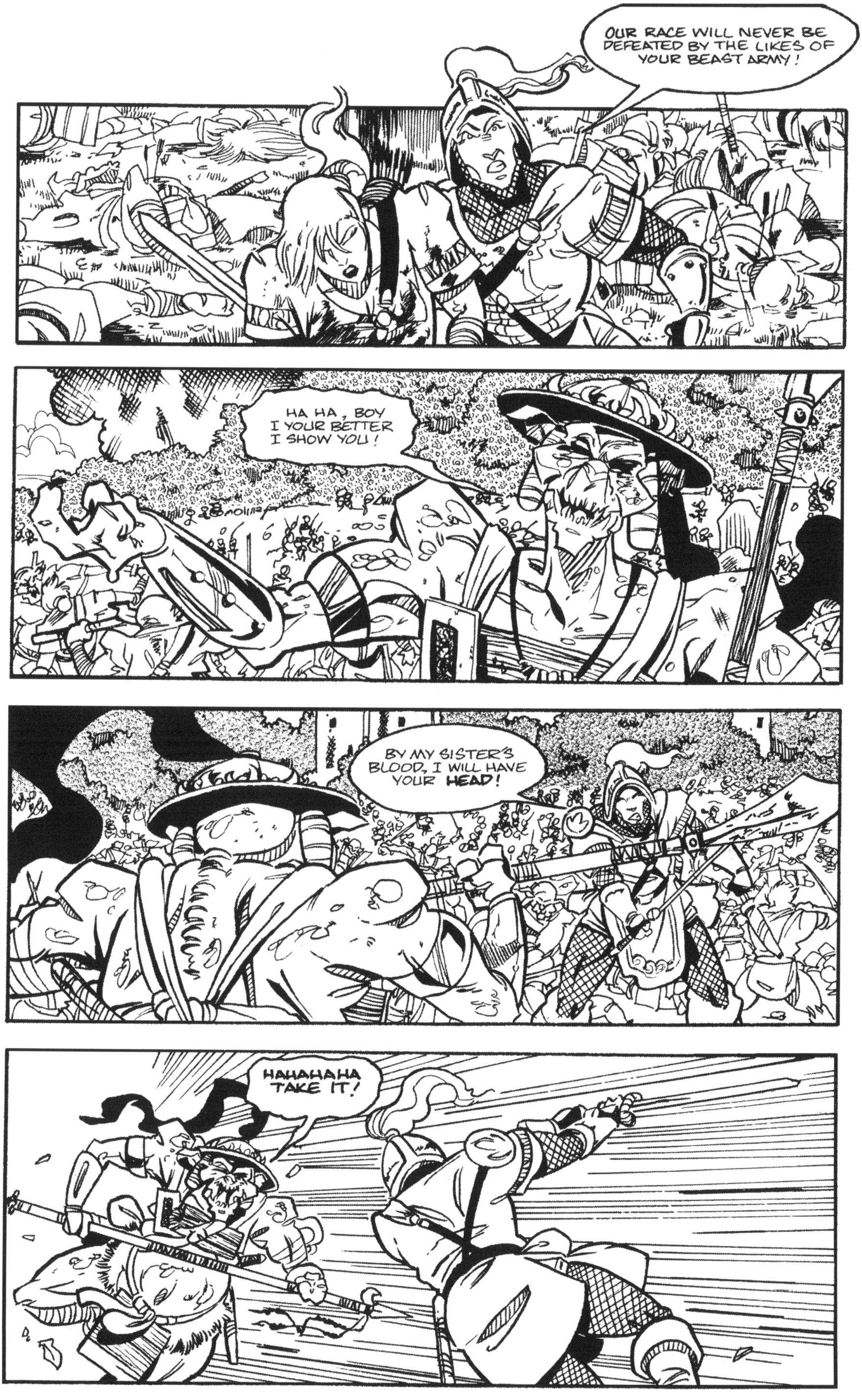
OUR RACE WILL NEVER BE DEFEATED BY THE LIKES OF YOUR BEAST ARMY!
HA HA, BOY I YOUR BETTER I SHOW YOU!
BY MY SISTER'S BLOOD, I WILL HAVE YOUR **HEAD**!
HAHAHAHA TAKE IT!

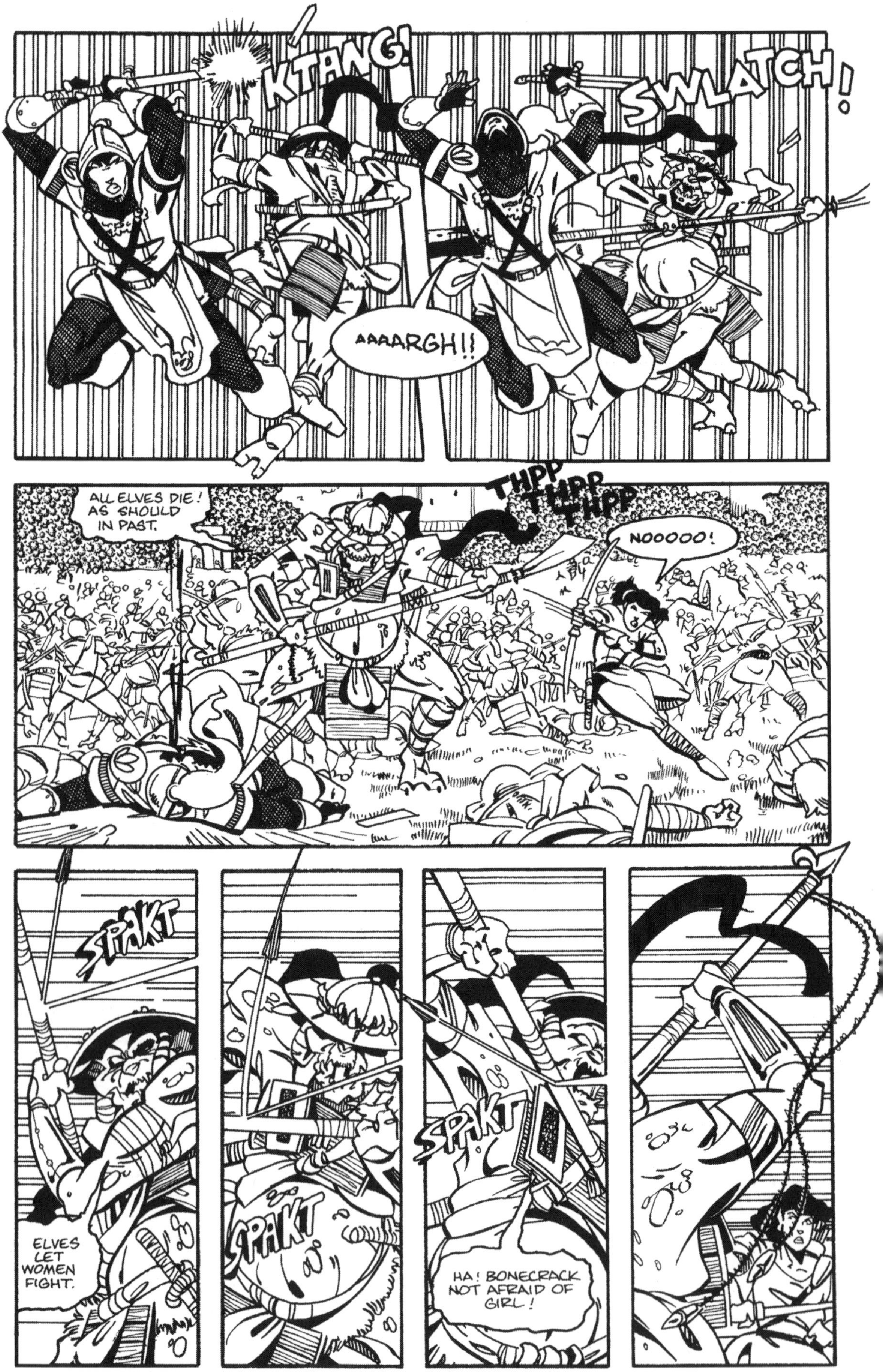
KTANG!
SWLATCH!
AAAARGH!!
ALL ELVES DIE! AS SHOULD IN PAST.
THPP THPP THPP
NOOOOO!
SPAKT
ELVES LET WOMEN FIGHT.
SPAKT
SPAKT
HA! BONECRACK NOT AFRAID OF GIRL!

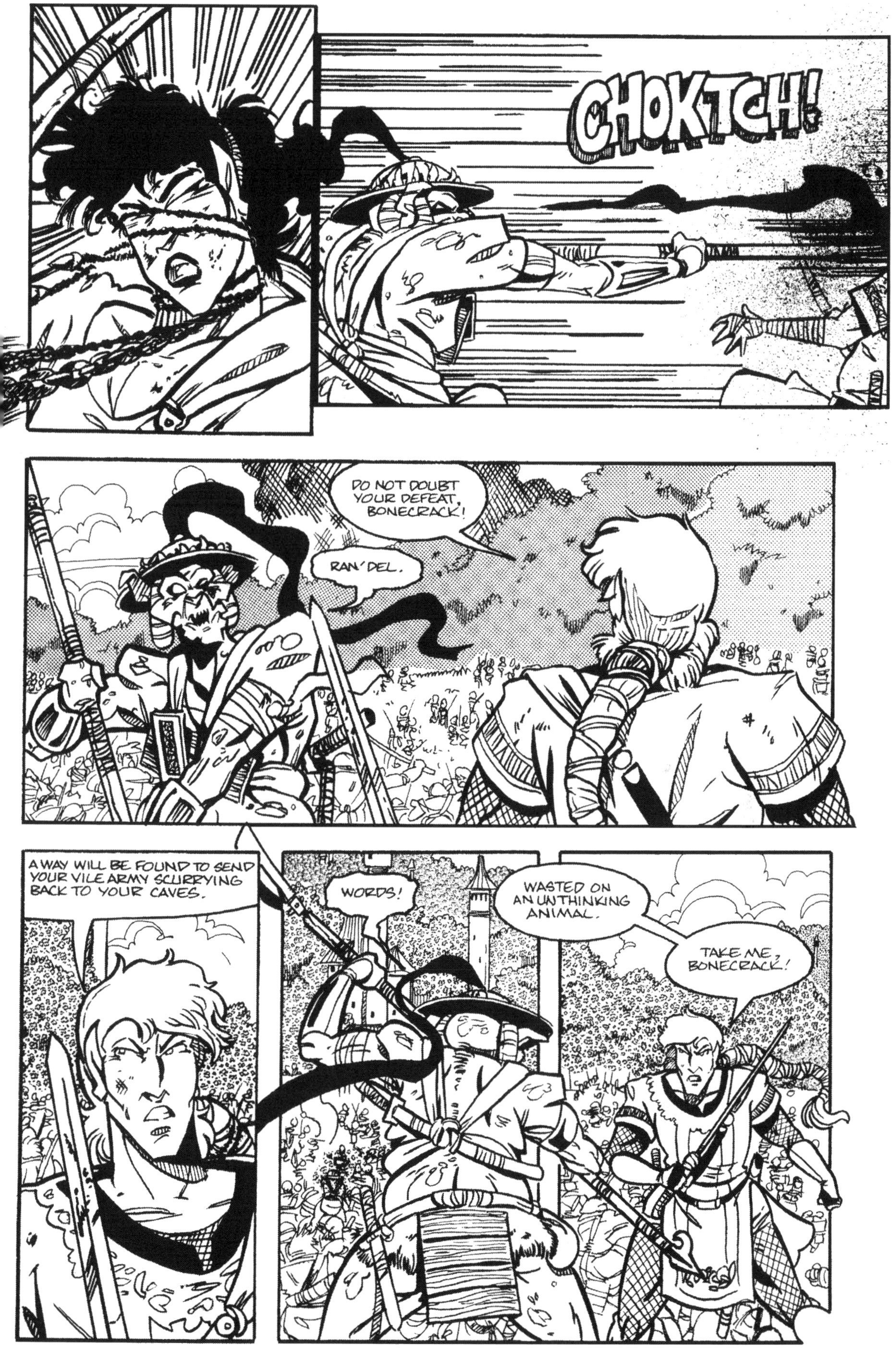
CHOKTCH!
DO NOT DOUBT YOUR DEFEAT, BONECRACK!
RAN'DEL.
A WAY WILL BE FOUND TO SEND YOUR VILE ARMY SCURRYING BACK TO YOUR CAVES.
WORDS!
WASTED ON AN UNTHINKING ANIMAL.
TAKE ME, BONECRACK!

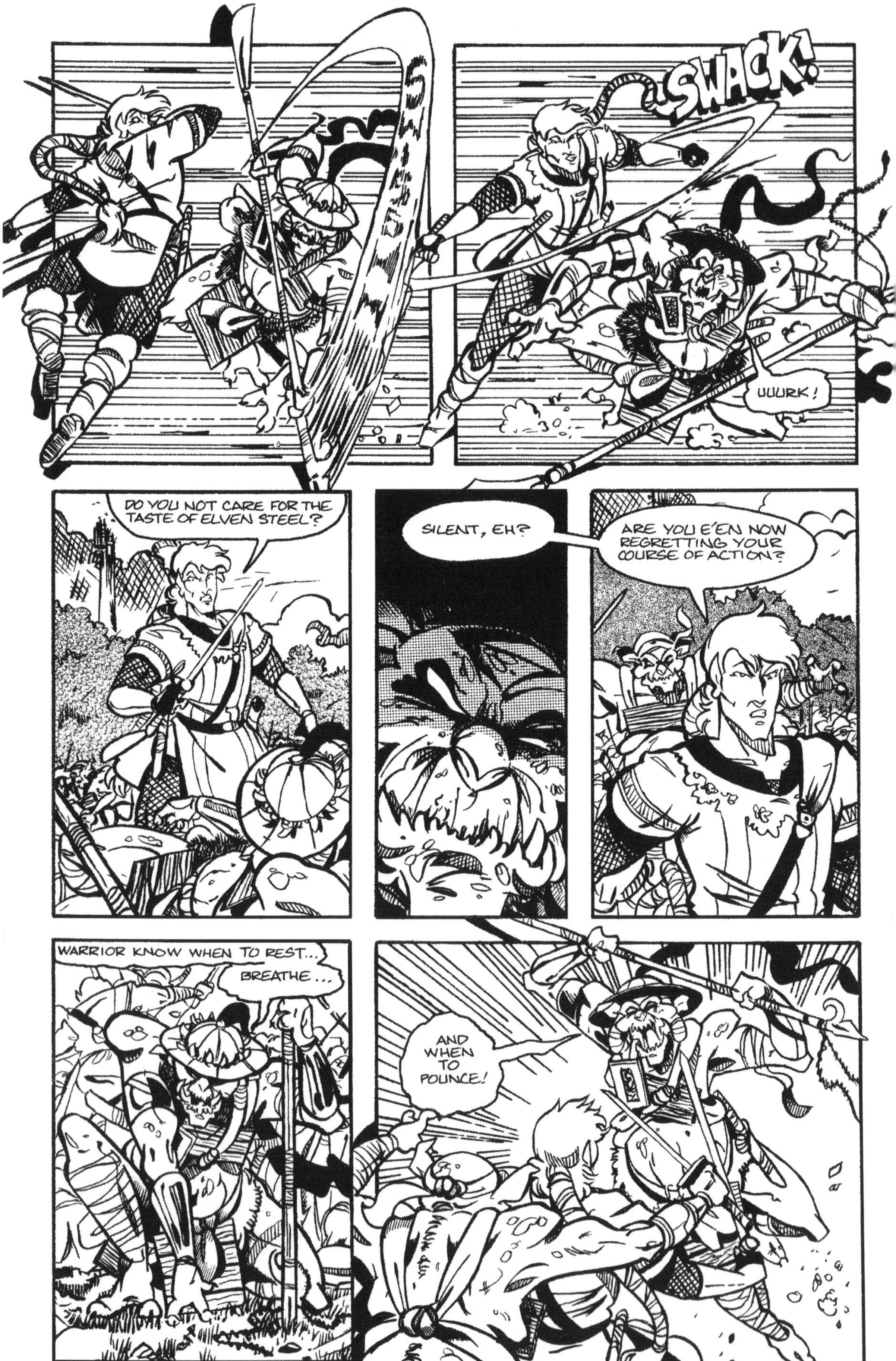
SWACK!
UUURK!
DO YOU NOT CARE FOR THE TASTE OF ELVEN STEEL?
SILENT, EH?
ARE YOU E'EN NOW REGRETTING YOUR COURSE OF ACTION?
WARRIOR KNOW WHEN TO REST...
BREATHE...
AND WHEN TO POUNCE!

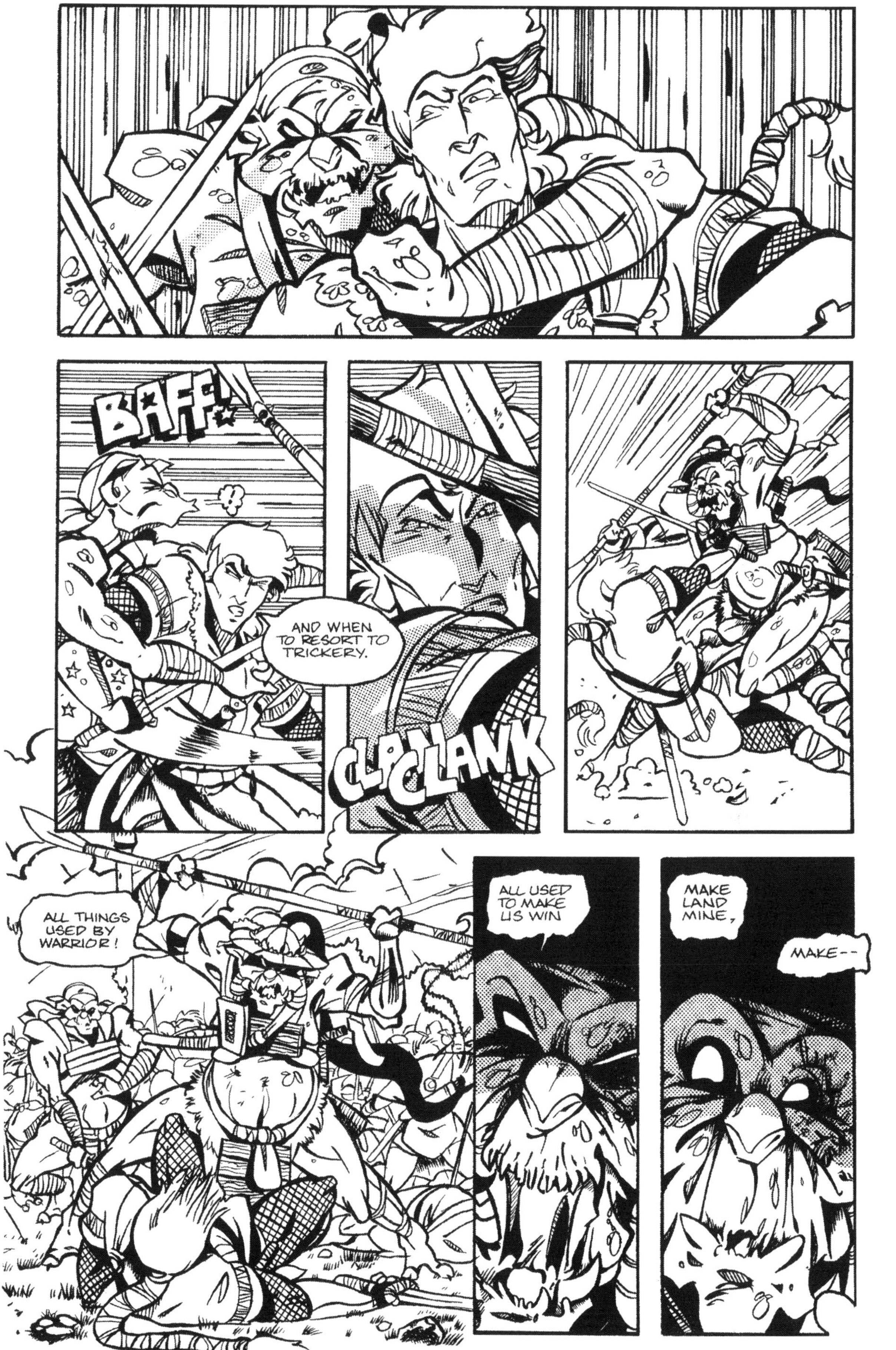

BAFF
!
AND WHEN TO RESORT TO TRICKERY.
CLANK
CLANK
ALL THINGS USED BY WARRIOR!
ALL USED TO MAKE US WIN
MAKE LAND MINE,
MAKE--

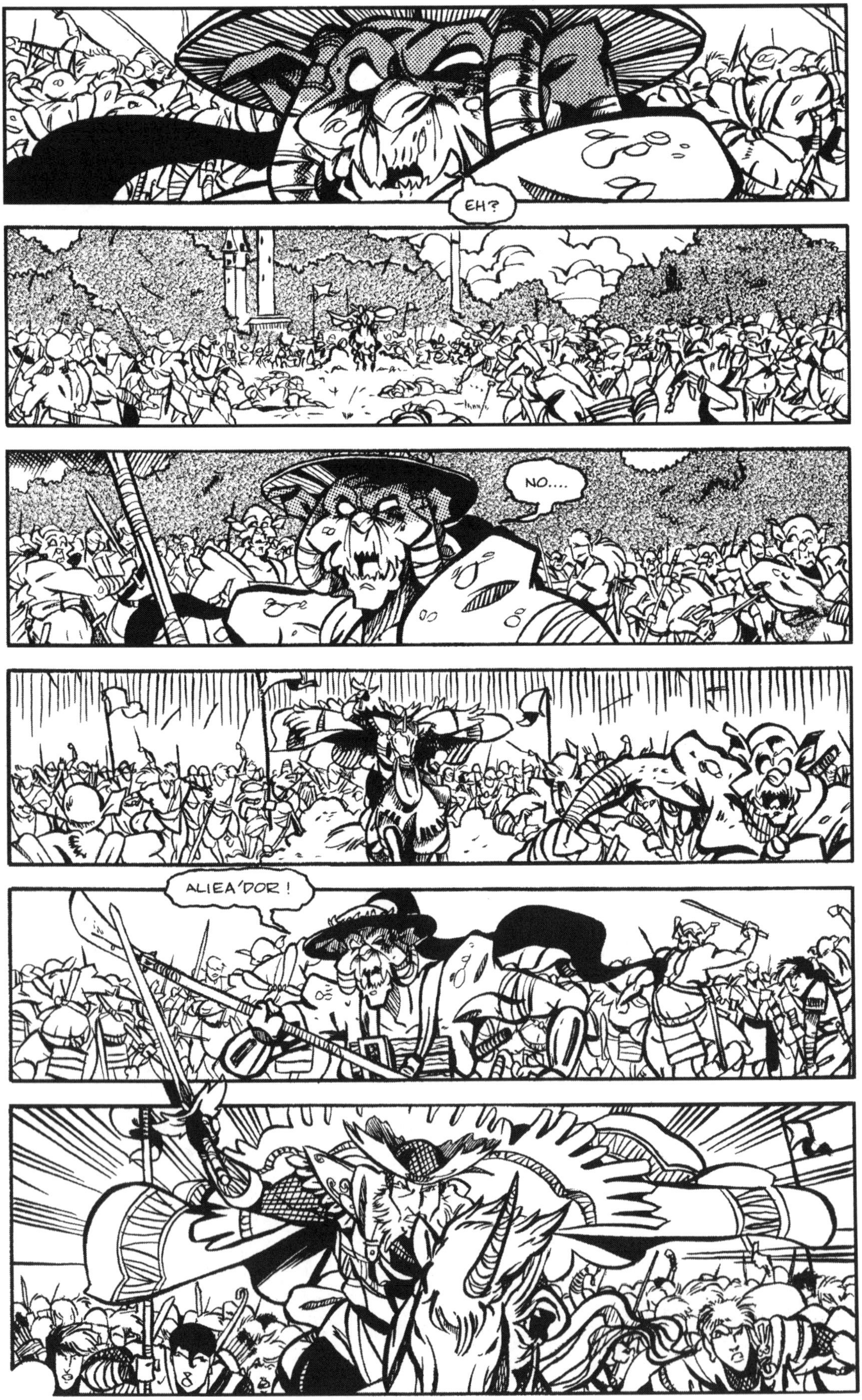

EH?
NO....
ALIEA'DOR!

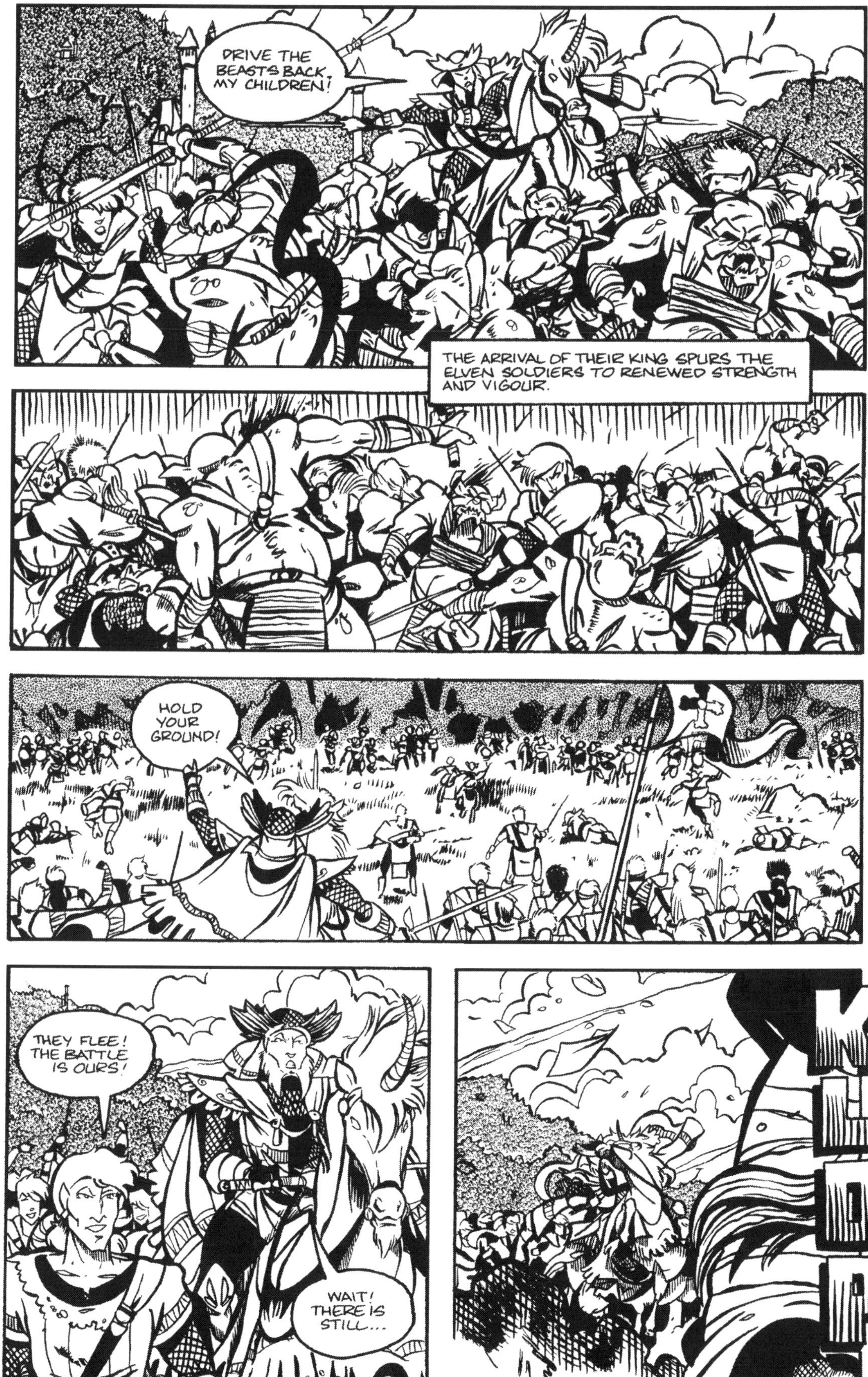
DRIVE THE BEASTS BACK, MY CHILDREN!
THE ARRIVAL OF THEIR KING SPURS THE ELVEN SOLDIERS TO RENEWED STRENGTH AND VIGOUR.
HOLD YOUR GROUND!
THEY FLEE! THE BATTLE IS OURS!
WAIT! THERE IS STILL...
KLOOP

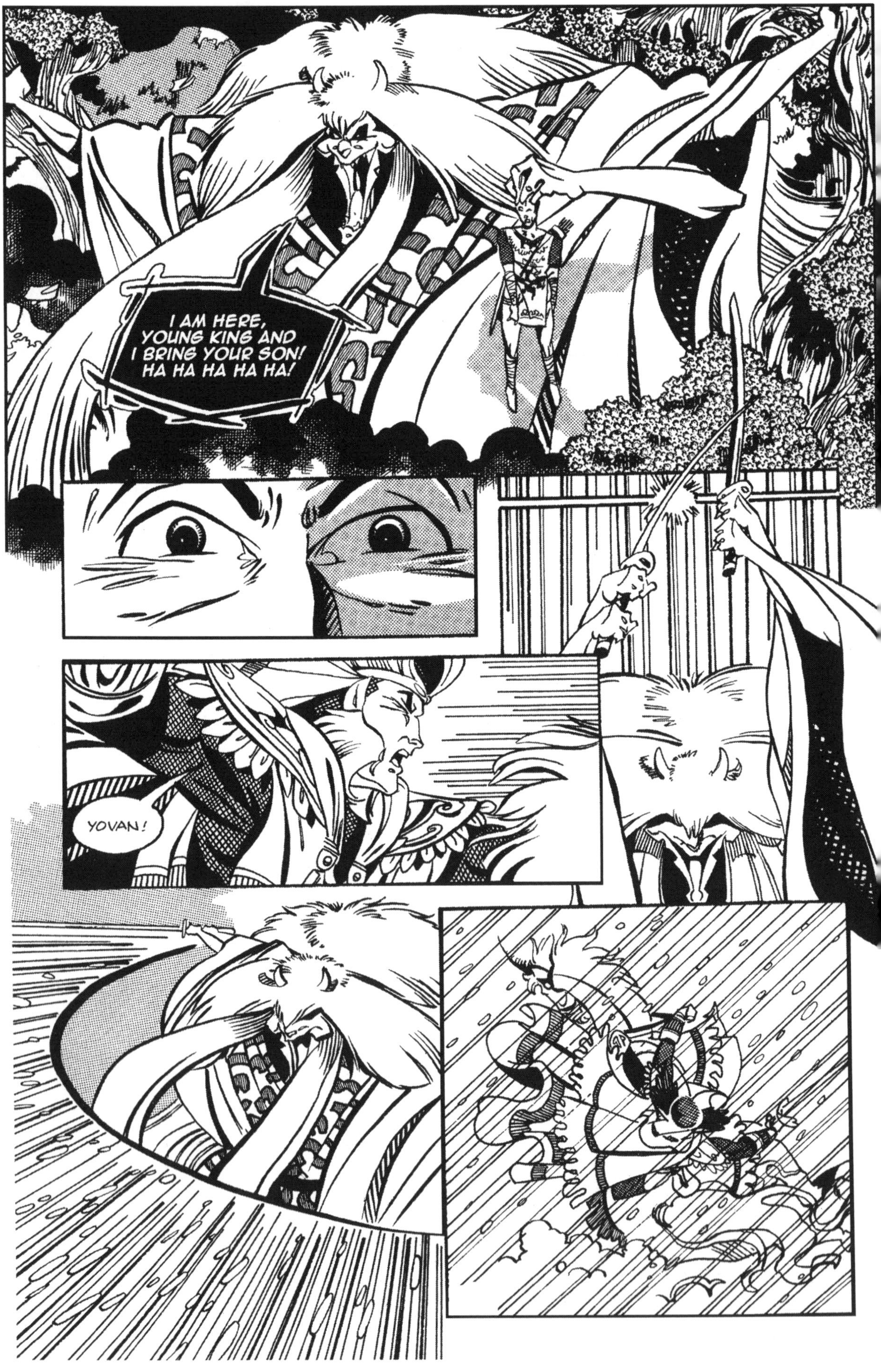
I AM HERE,
YOUNG KING AND
I BRING YOUR SON!
HA HA HA HA HA!
YOVAN!

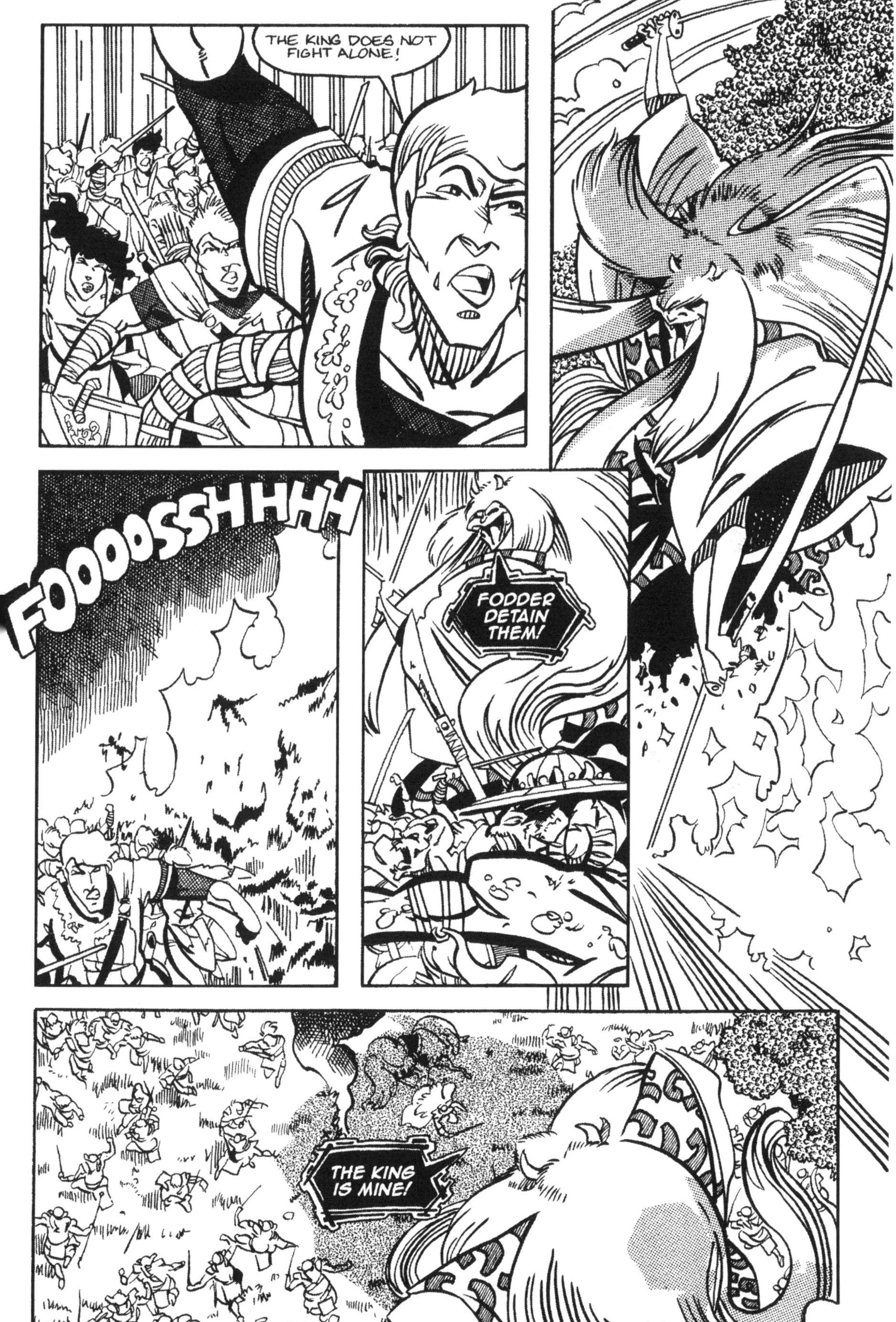
THE KING DOES NOT FIGHT ALONE!
FOOOOSSHHHH
FODDER DETAIN THEM!
THE KING IS MINE!

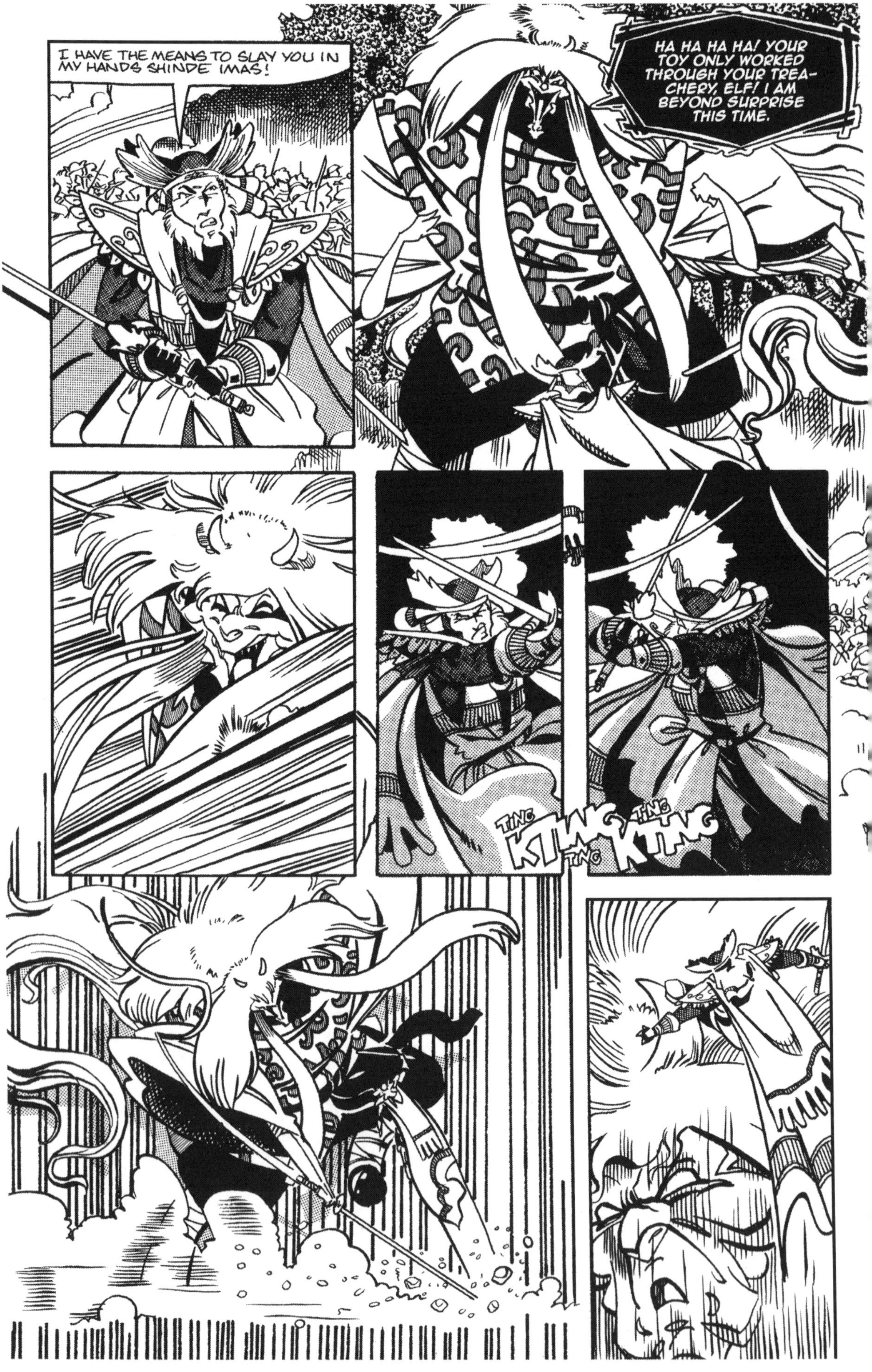
I HAVE THE MEANS TO SLAY YOU IN MY HANDS SHINDE IMAS!
HA HA HA HA! YOUR TOY ONLY WORKED THROUGH YOUR TREACHERY, ELF! I AM BEYOND SURPRISE THIS TIME.
TING KTANG TING TING KTANG

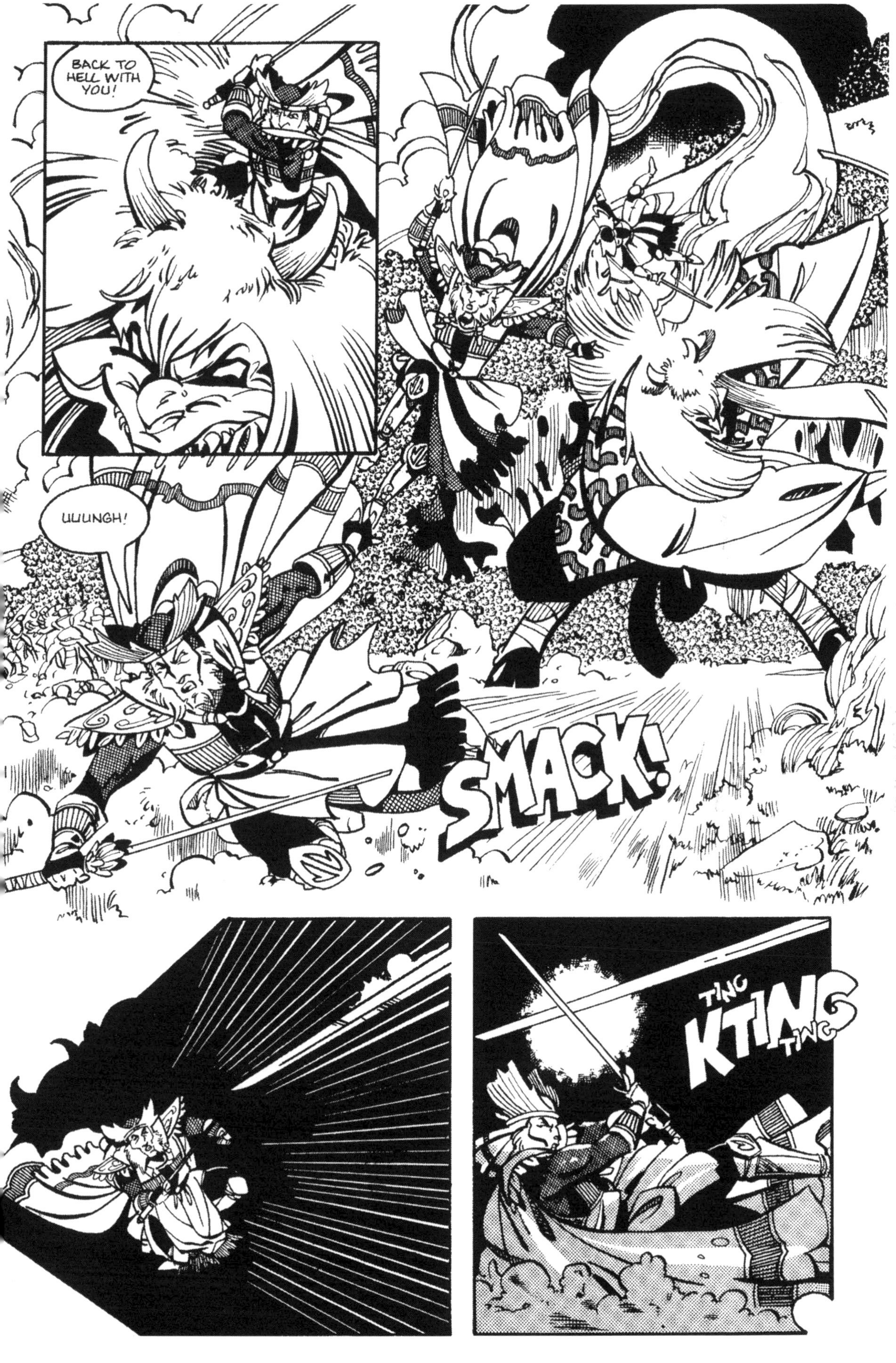
BACK TO HELL WITH YOU!
UUUNGH!
SMACK!
TING
KTING
TING

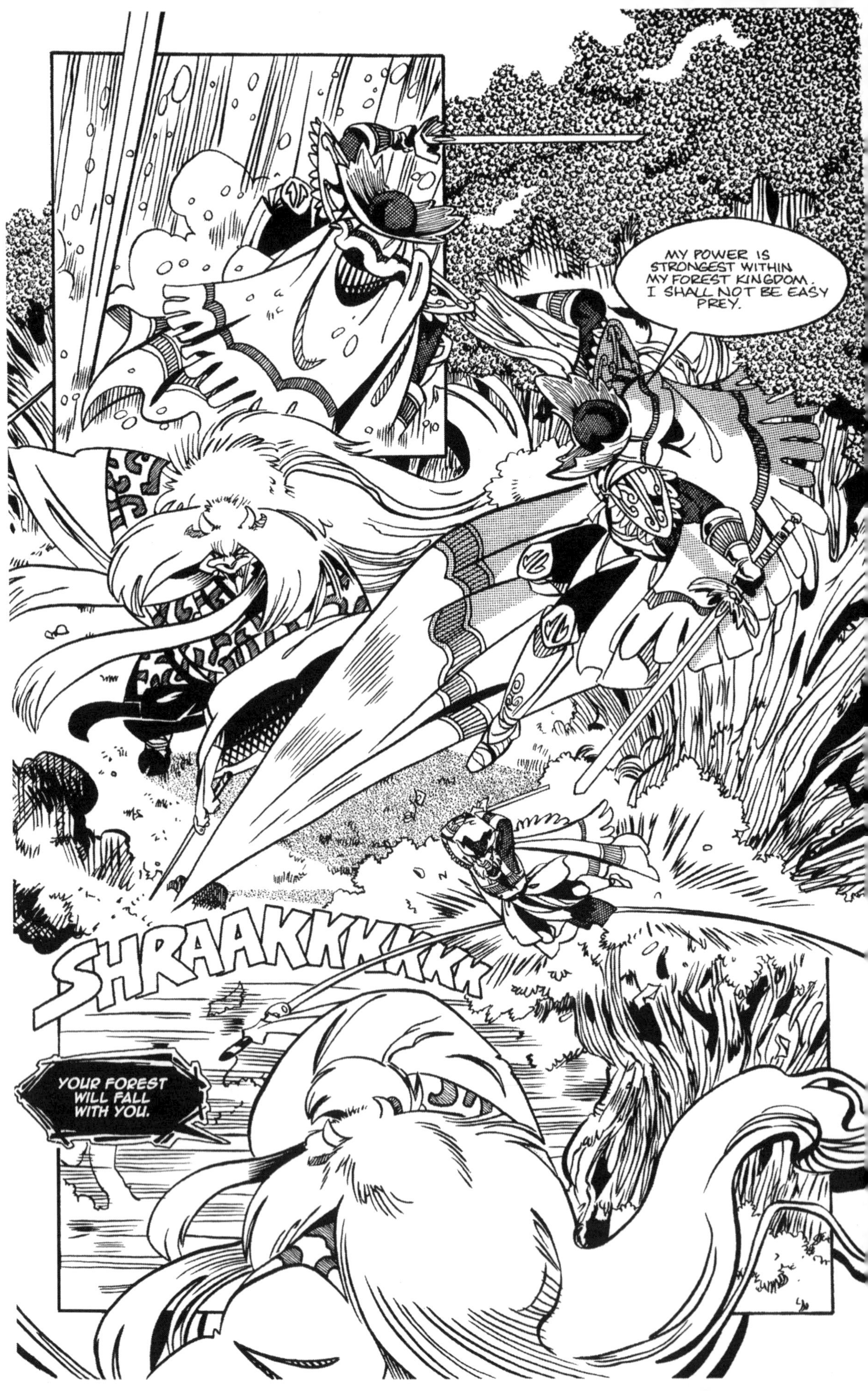
MY POWER IS STRONGEST WITHIN MY FOREST KINGDOM. I SHALL NOT BE EASY PREY.
SHRAAKKKKKKK
YOUR FOREST WILL FALL WITH YOU.

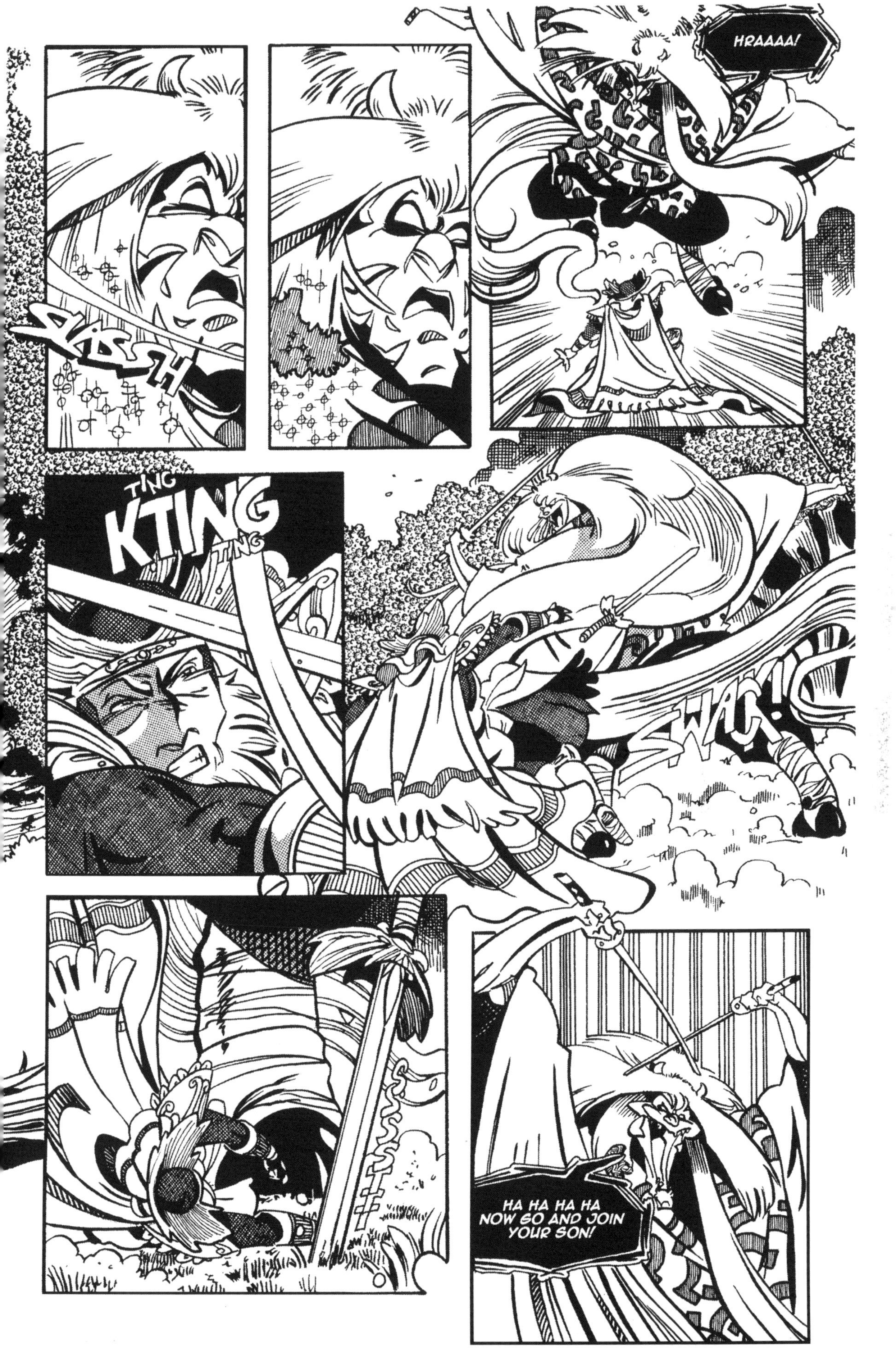
SHISH
HRAAAA!
TING
KTING
TING
SWACK!
HA HA HA HA
NOW GO AND JOIN
YOUR SON!

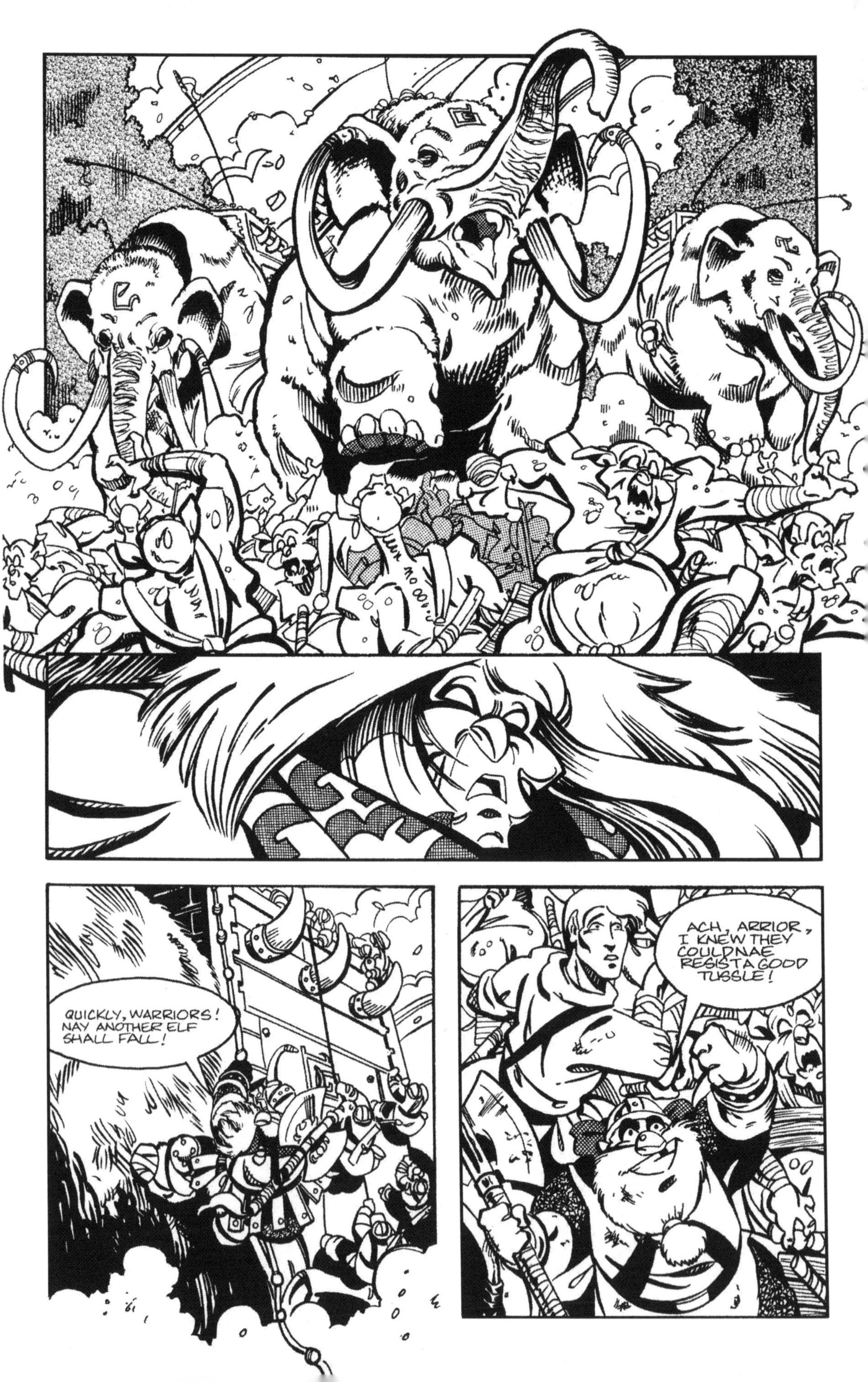
QUICKLY, WARRIORS! NAY ANOTHER ELF SHALL FALL!
ACH, ARRIOR, I KNEW THEY COULDNAE RESIST A GOOD TUSSLE!

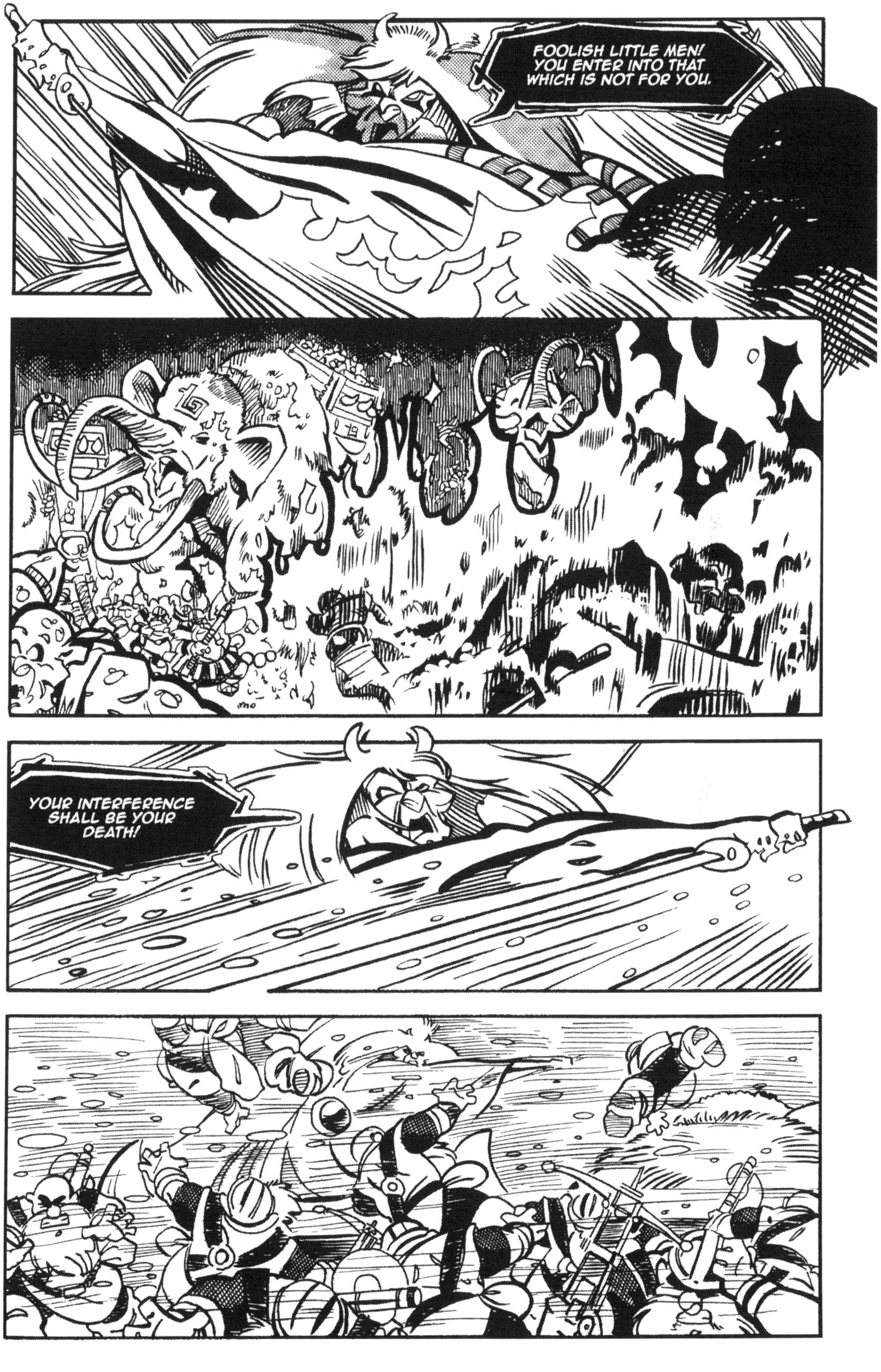
FOOLISH LITTLE MEN! YOU ENTER INTO THAT WHICH IS NOT FOR YOU.
YOUR INTERFERENCE SHALL BE YOUR DEATH!

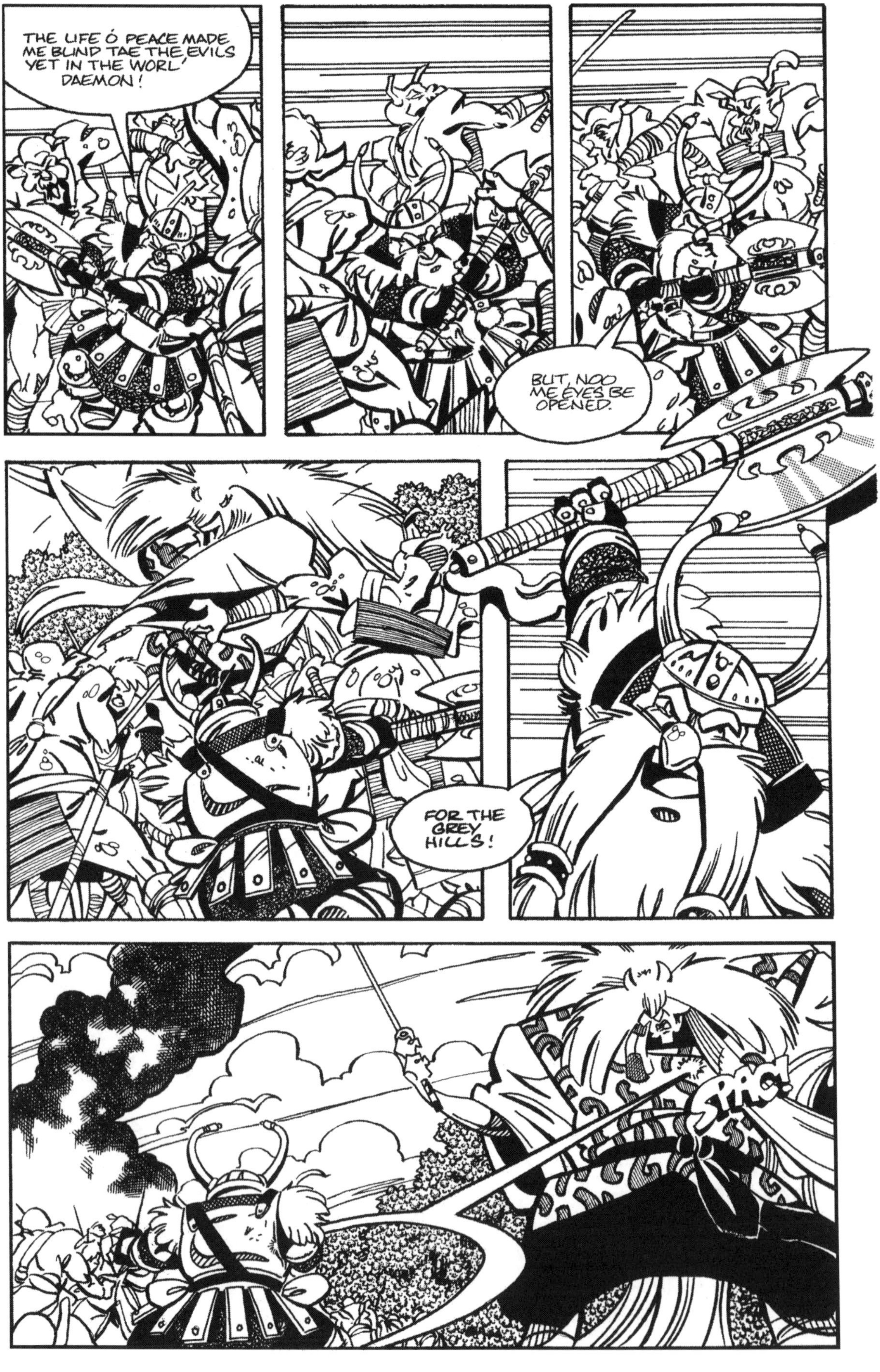
THE LIFE Ó PEACE MADE ME BLIND TAE THE EVILS YET IN THE WORL' DAEMON!
BUT, NOO ME EYES BE OPENED.
FOR THE GREY HILLS!
SPAG!

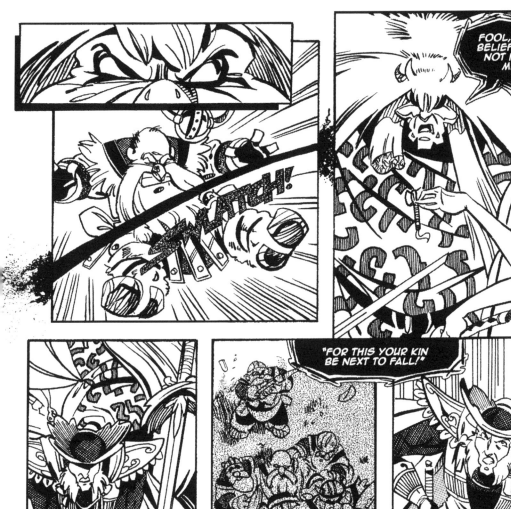

FOOL, YOUR BELIEFS CAN NOT HARM ME.

SKRATCH!

"FOR THIS YOUR KIN BE NEXT TO FALL!"

NO...

ENOUGH...

THIS HAS GONE FAR ENOUGH!

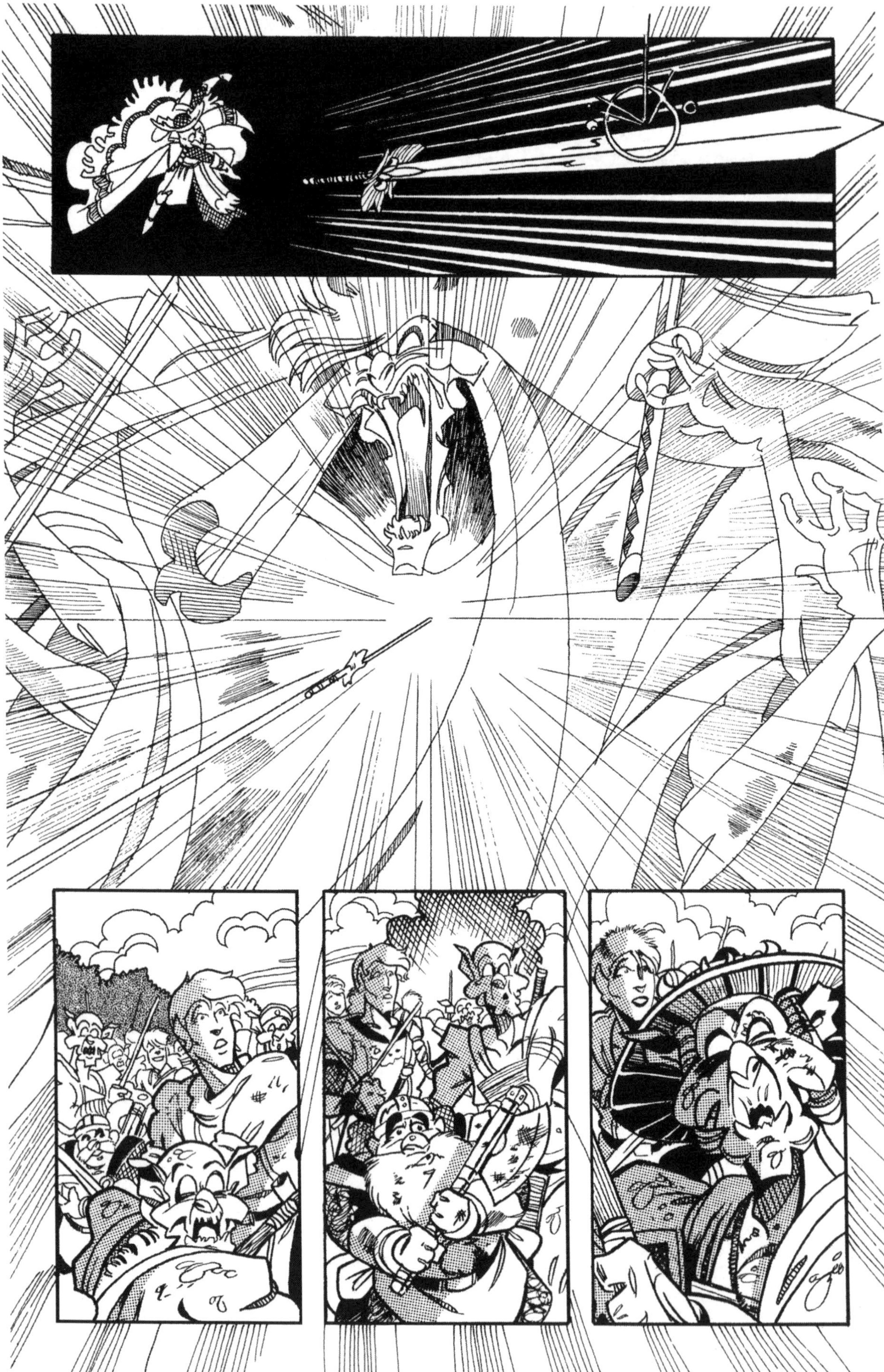

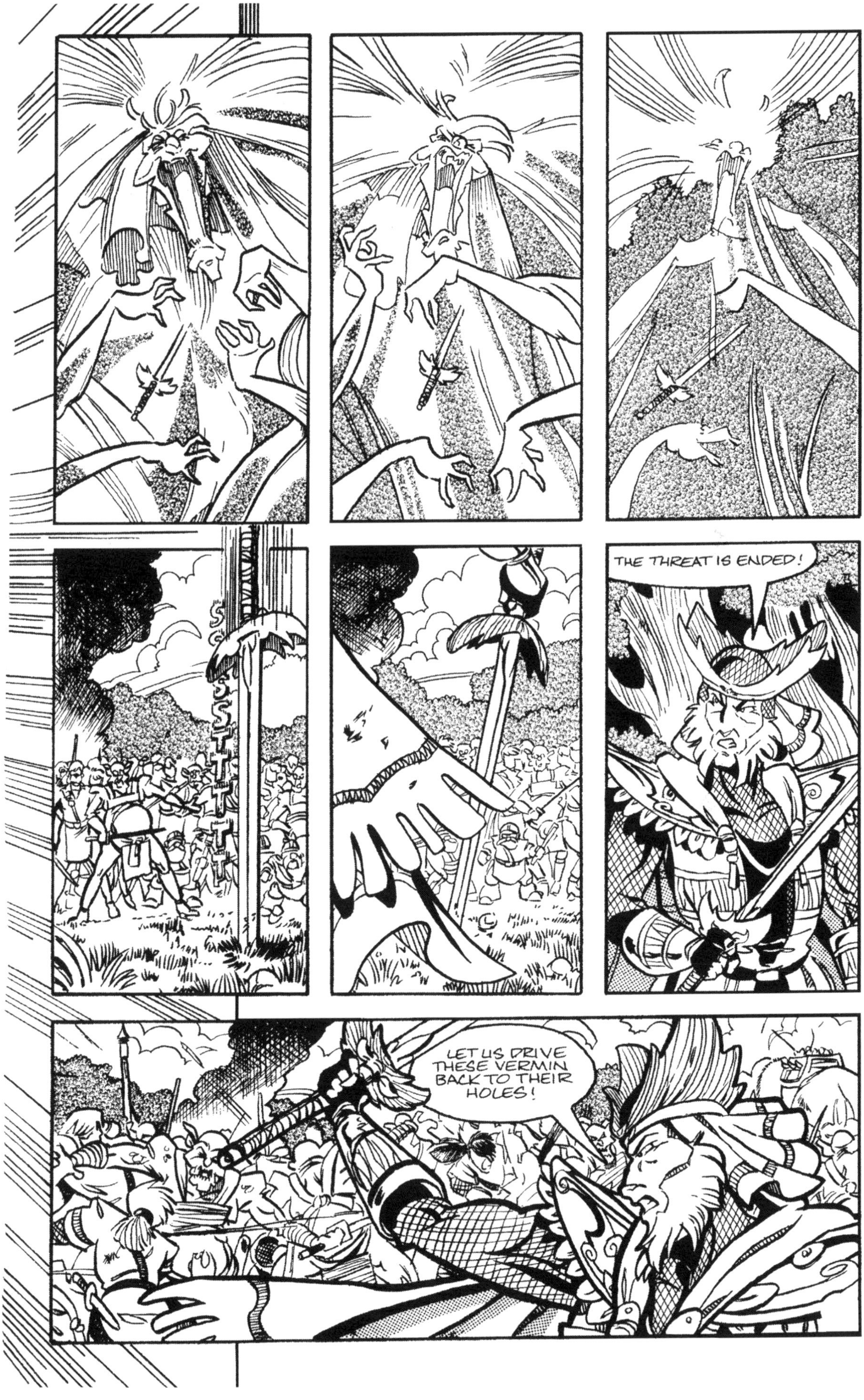
THE THREAT IS ENDED!
LET US DRIVE THESE VERMIN BACK TO THEIR HOLES!

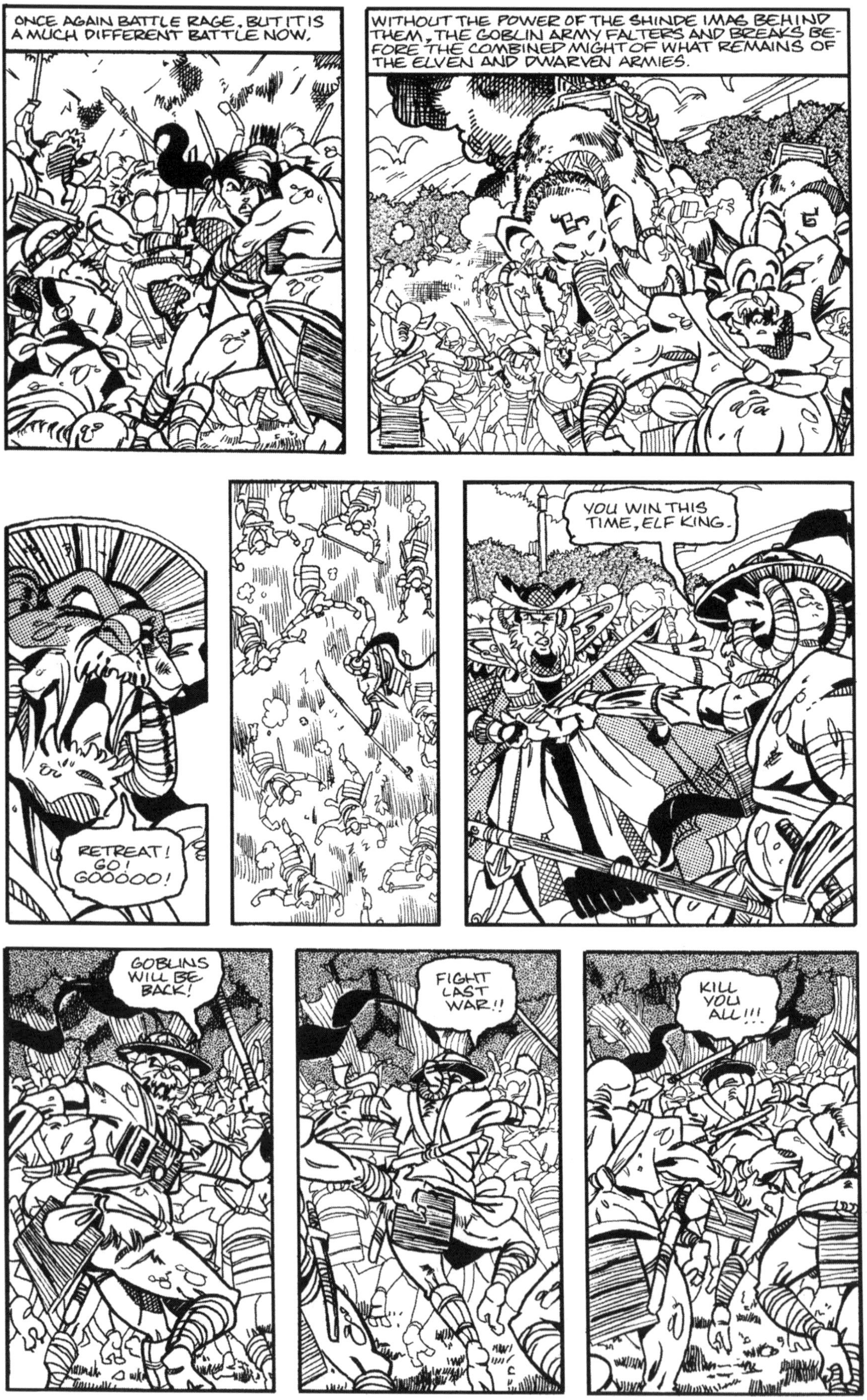
ONCE AGAIN BATTLE RAGE. BUT IT IS A MUCH DIFFERENT BATTLE NOW.
WITHOUT THE POWER OF THE SHINDE IMAS BEHIND THEM, THE GOBLIN ARMY FALTERS AND BREAKS BEFORE THE COMBINED MIGHT OF WHAT REMAINS OF THE ELVEN AND DWARVEN ARMIES.
RETREAT! GO! GOOOOOO!
YOU WIN THIS TIME, ELF KING.
GOBLINS WILL BE BACK!
FIGHT LAST WAR!!
KILL YOU ALL!!!

Epilogue...

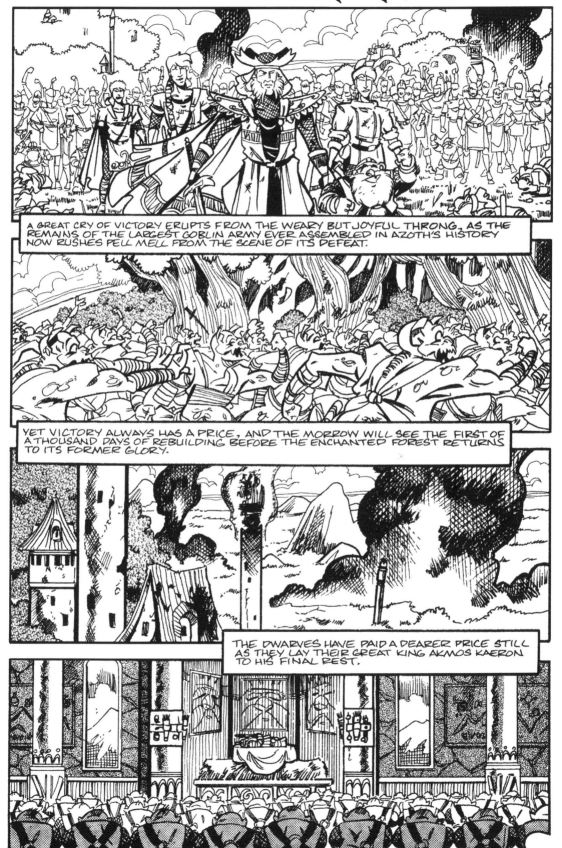

A GREAT CRY OF VICTORY ERUPTS FROM THE WEARY BUT JOYFUL THRONG, AS THE REMAINS OF THE LARGEST GOBLIN ARMY EVER ASSEMBLED IN AZOTH'S HISTORY NOW RUSHES PELL MELL FROM THE SCENE OF ITS DEFEAT.

YET VICTORY ALWAYS HAS A PRICE, AND THE MORROW WILL SEE THE FIRST OF A THOUSAND DAYS OF REBUILDING BEFORE THE ENCHANTED FOREST RETURNS TO ITS FORMER GLORY.

THE DWARVES HAVE PAID A DEARER PRICE STILL AS THEY LAY THEIR GREAT KING AKMOS KAERON TO HIS FINAL REST.

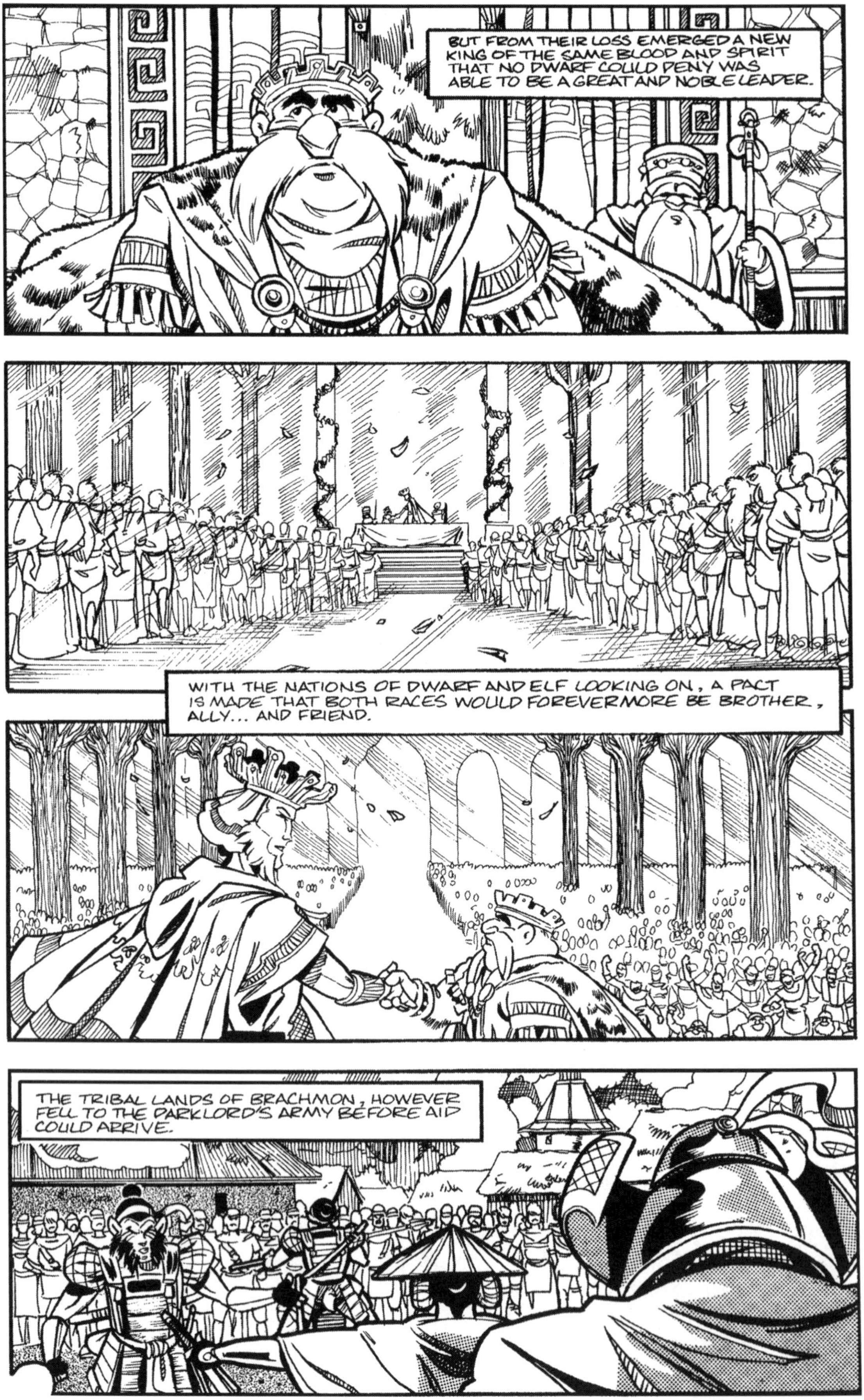
BUT FROM THEIR LOSS EMERGED A NEW KING OF THE SAME BLOOD AND SPIRIT THAT NO DWARF COULD DENY WAS ABLE TO BE A GREAT AND NOBLE LEADER.
WITH THE NATIONS OF DWARF AND ELF LOOKING ON, A PACT IS MADE THAT BOTH RACES WOULD FOREVERMORE BE BROTHER, ALLY... AND FRIEND.
THE TRIBAL LANDS OF BRACHMON, HOWEVER FELL TO THE DARKLORD'S ARMY BEFORE AID COULD ARRIVE.

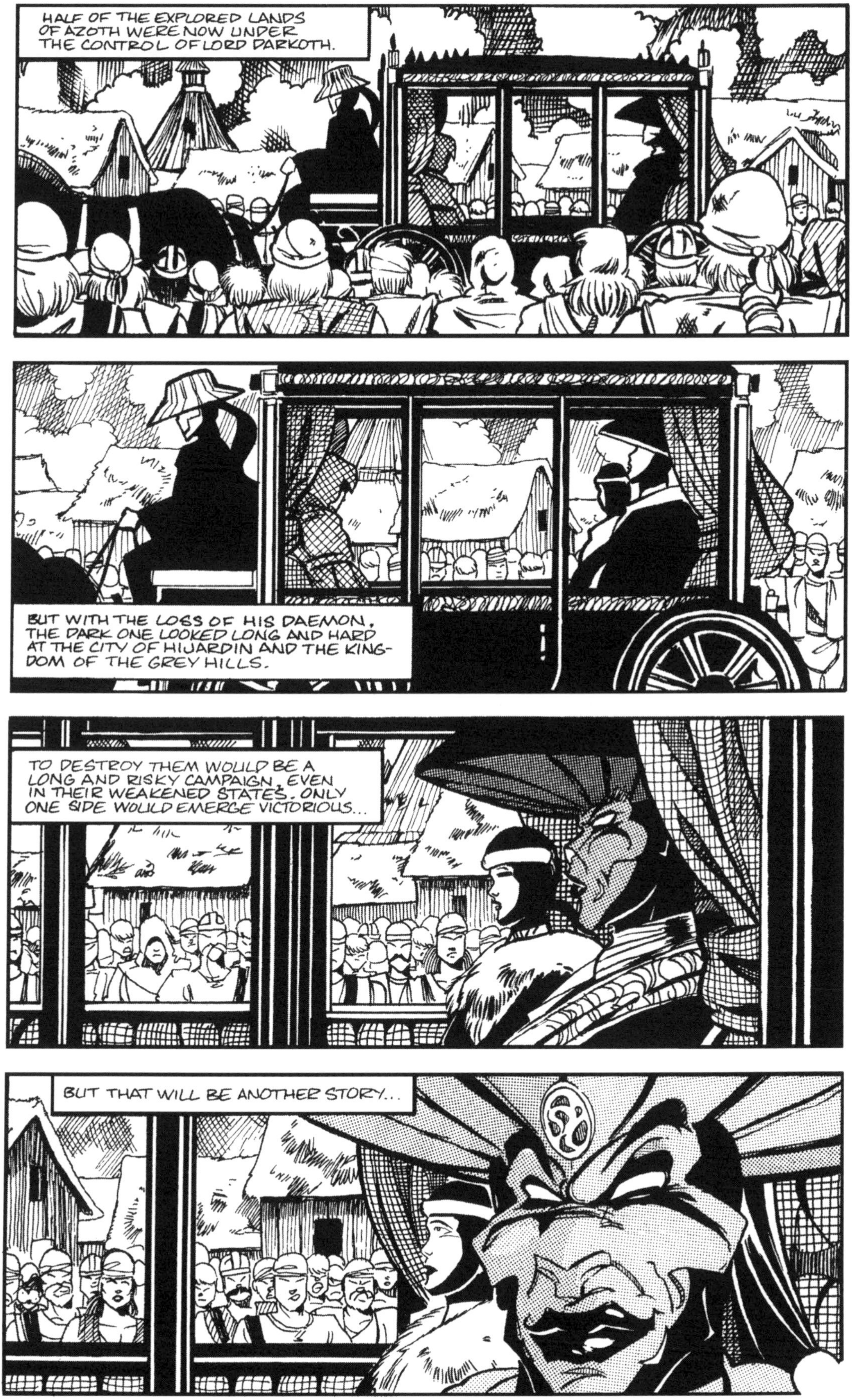
HALF OF THE EXPLORED LANDS OF AZOTH WERE NOW UNDER THE CONTROL OF LORD DARKOTH.
BUT WITH THE LOSS OF HIS DAEMON, THE DARK ONE LOOKED LONG AND HARD AT THE CITY OF HIJARDIN AND THE KINGDOM OF THE GREY HILLS.
TO DESTROY THEM WOULD BE A LONG AND RISKY CAMPAIGN, EVEN IN THEIR WEAKENED STATES. ONLY ONE SIDE WOULD EMERGE VICTORIOUS...
BUT THAT WILL BE ANOTHER STORY...

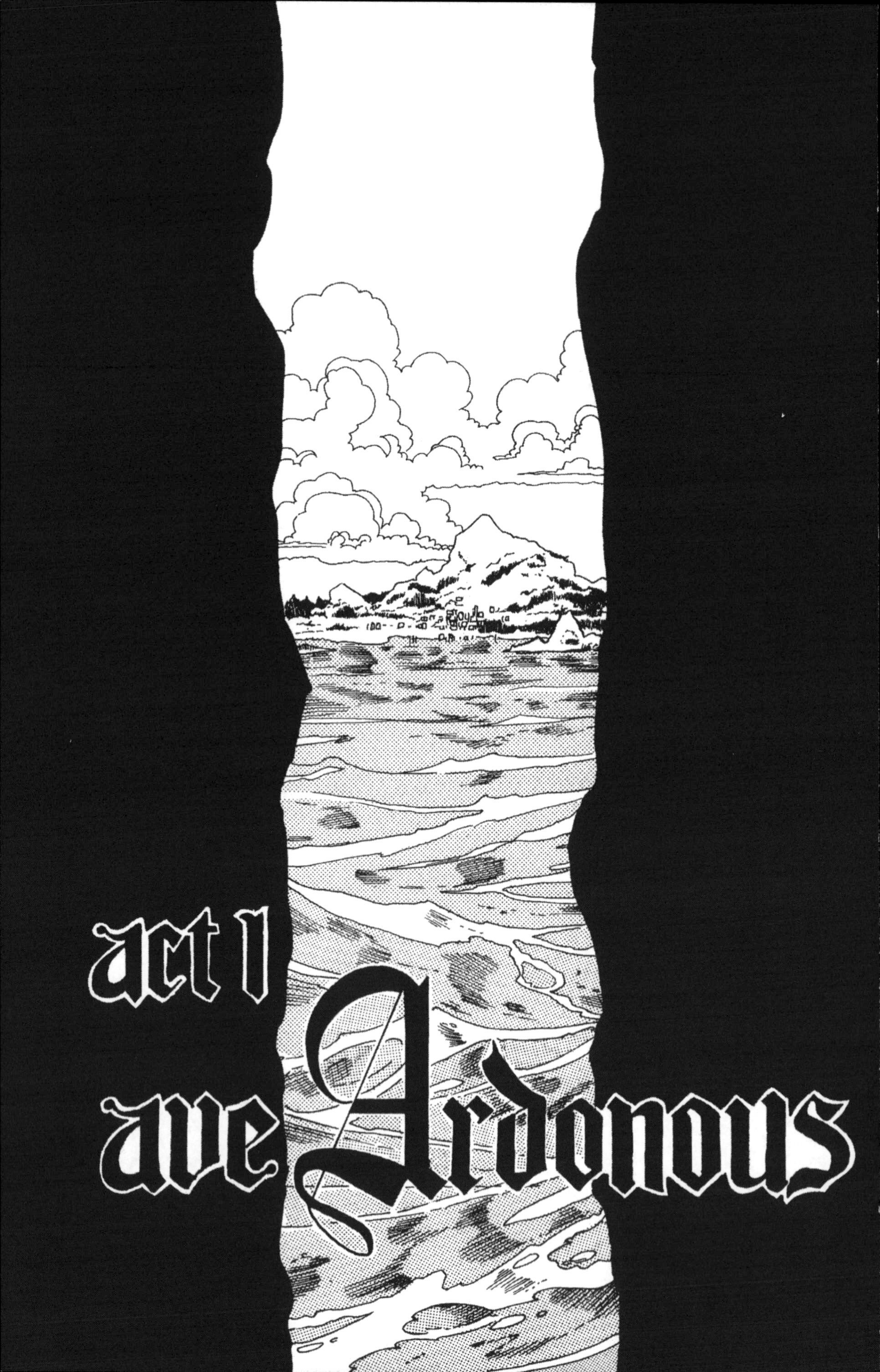
act 1
ave Ardonous

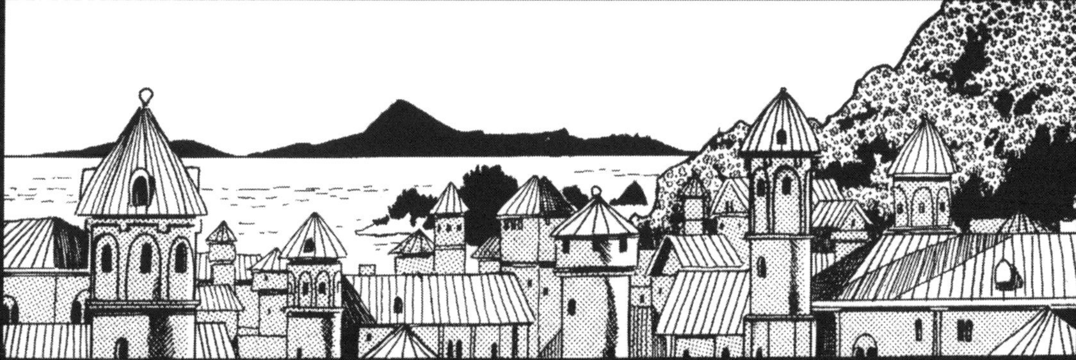

LONG AGO AT THE FALL OF MAGIC AND THE DAWN OF MAN'S CIVILIZATION ON AZOTH, THE HOLY LAND OF ARDONIA WAS NOT YET A PART OF THE GREAT CONTINENT, BUT INSTEAD A SMALL ISLAND OFF THE SOUTHERN COAST. CONTENT WITHIN THEIR SMALL LAND, THE INHABITANTS LIVED BLISSFULLY IGNORANT WITHIN THE BELIEFS OF OTHARRISS, A LIFE OF JOY AND HAPPINESS...

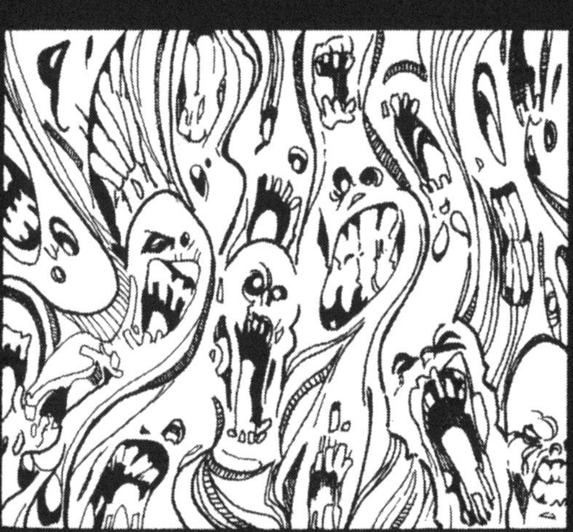

UNFORTUNATE WERE THEIR LIFE OF SUCH GAIETY THAT THE FORCES OF HELL WERE ENRAGED THAT ANY THING SO PURE EXIST. BUT, TRY AS THEY MIGHT TO DESTROY IT, THE BLACK GODS OF DARKNESS COULD NEVER MANIFEST THEMSELVES WITHIN THE LIGHT OF THE GOOD LAND'S RELIGION WITHOUT BEING SENT FURTHER BACK TO THE EVIL WHICH SPAWNED THEM.

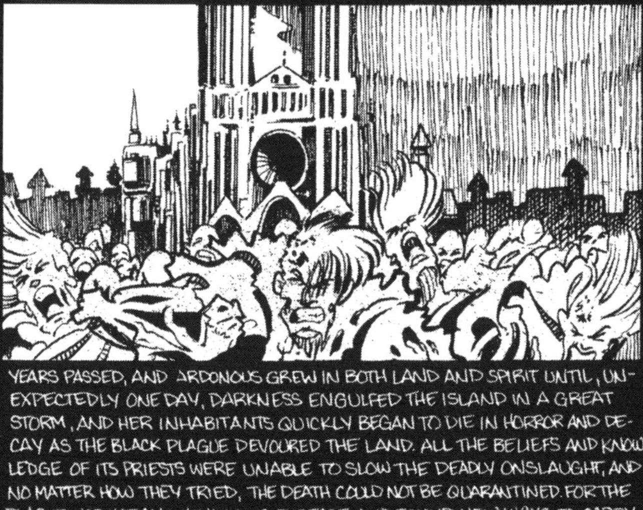

YEARS PASSED, AND ARDONOUS GREW IN BOTH LAND AND SPIRIT UNTIL, UNEXPECTEDLY ONE DAY, DARKNESS ENGULFED THE ISLAND IN A GREAT STORM, AND HER INHABITANTS QUICKLY BEGAN TO DIE IN HORROR AND DECAY AS THE BLACK PLAGUE DEVOURED THE LAND. ALL THE BELIEFS AND KNOWLEDGE OF ITS PRIESTS WERE UNABLE TO SLOW THE DEADLY ONSLAUGHT, AND NO MATTER HOW THEY TRIED, THE DEATH COULD NOT BE QUARANTINED. FOR THE PLAGUE WAS NOT AN UNTHINKING DISEASE, AND FOUND NEW WAYS TO CARRY ON ITS MISSION. FOR IT WAS, IN REALITY, THE DAEMON TERROREK WHO, THROUGH HIS EVIL AND TRICKERY, WAS ABLE TO RISE UPON ARDONOUS AND CLAIM ITS LIFE AS HIS OWN.

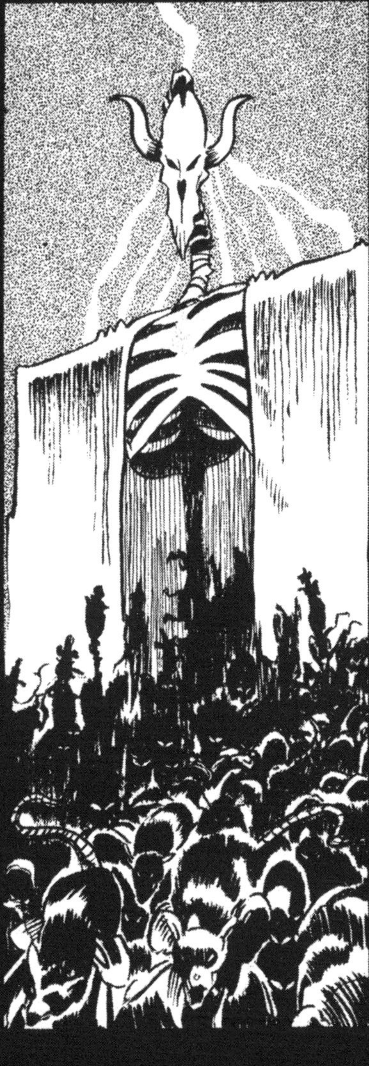

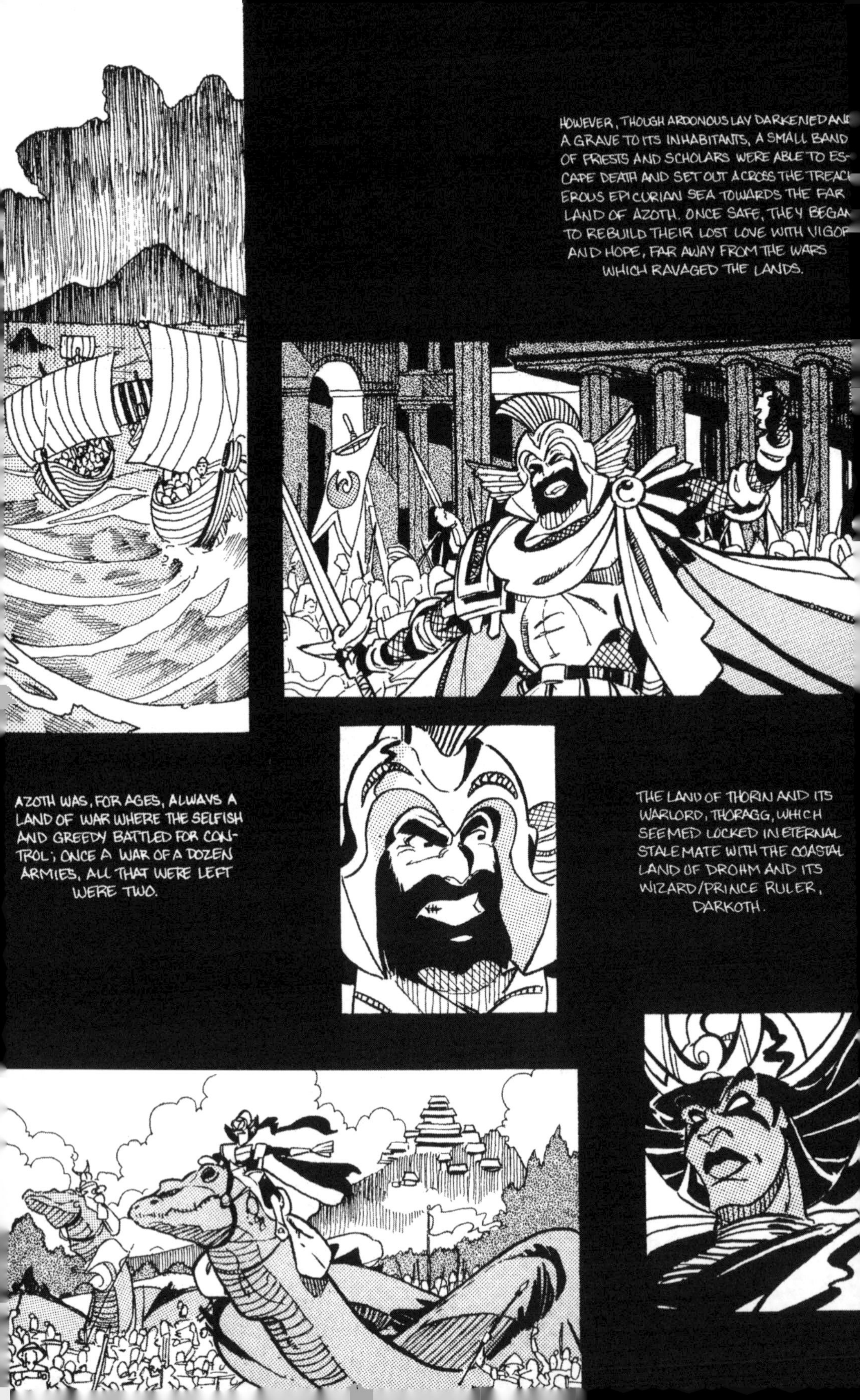
HOWEVER, THOUGH ARDONOUS LAY DARKENED AND A GRAVE TO ITS INHABITANTS, A SMALL BAND OF PRIESTS AND SCHOLARS WERE ABLE TO ES- CAPE DEATH AND SET OUT ACROSS THE TREACH EROUS EPICURIAN SEA TOWARDS THE FAR LAND OF AZOTH. ONCE SAFE, THEY BEGAN TO REBUILD THEIR LOST LOVE WITH VIGOR AND HOPE, FAR AWAY FROM THE WARS WHICH RAVAGED THE LANDS.
AZOTH WAS, FOR AGES, ALWAYS A LAND OF WAR WHERE THE SELFISH AND GREEDY BATTLED FOR CON- TROL; ONCE A WAR OF A DOZEN ARMIES, ALL THAT WERE LEFT WERE TWO.
THE LAND OF THORIN AND ITS WARLORD, THORAGG, WHICH SEEMED LOCKED IN ETERNAL STALEMATE WITH THE COASTAL LAND OF DROHM AND ITS WIZARD/PRINCE RULER, DARKOTH.

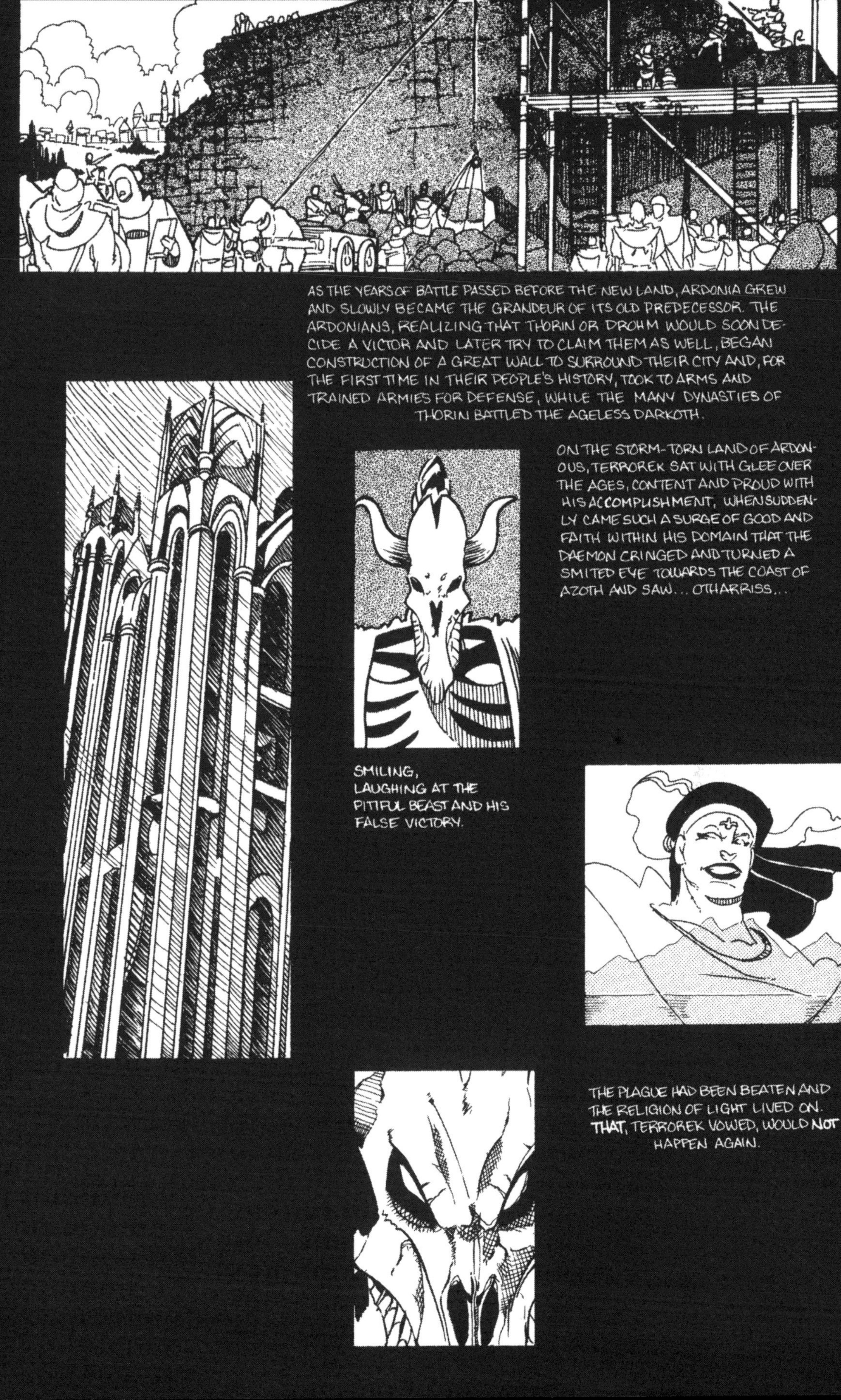
AS THE YEARS OF BATTLE PASSED BEFORE THE NEW LAND, ARDONIA GREW AND SLOWLY BECAME THE GRANDEUR OF ITS OLD PREDECESSOR. THE ARDONIANS, REALIZING THAT THORIN OR DROHM WOULD SOON DECIDE A VICTOR AND LATER TRY TO CLAIM THEM AS WELL, BEGAN CONSTRUCTION OF A GREAT WALL TO SURROUND THEIR CITY AND, FOR THE FIRST TIME IN THEIR PEOPLE'S HISTORY, TOOK TO ARMS AND TRAINED ARMIES FOR DEFENSE, WHILE THE MANY DYNASTIES OF THORIN BATTLED THE AGELESS DARKOTH.
ON THE STORM-TORN LAND OF ARDONOUS, TERROREK SAT WITH GLEE OVER THE AGES, CONTENT AND PROUD WITH HIS ACCOMPLISHMENT, WHEN SUDDENLY CAME SUCH A SURGE OF GOOD AND FAITH WITHIN HIS DOMAIN THAT THE DAEMON CRINGED AND TURNED A SMITED EYE TOWARDS THE COAST OF AZOTH AND SAW... OTHARRISS...
SMILING, LAUGHING AT THE PITIFUL BEAST AND HIS FALSE VICTORY.
THE PLAGUE HAD BEEN BEATEN AND THE RELIGION OF LIGHT LIVED ON. THAT, TERROREK VOWED, WOULD NOT HAPPEN AGAIN.

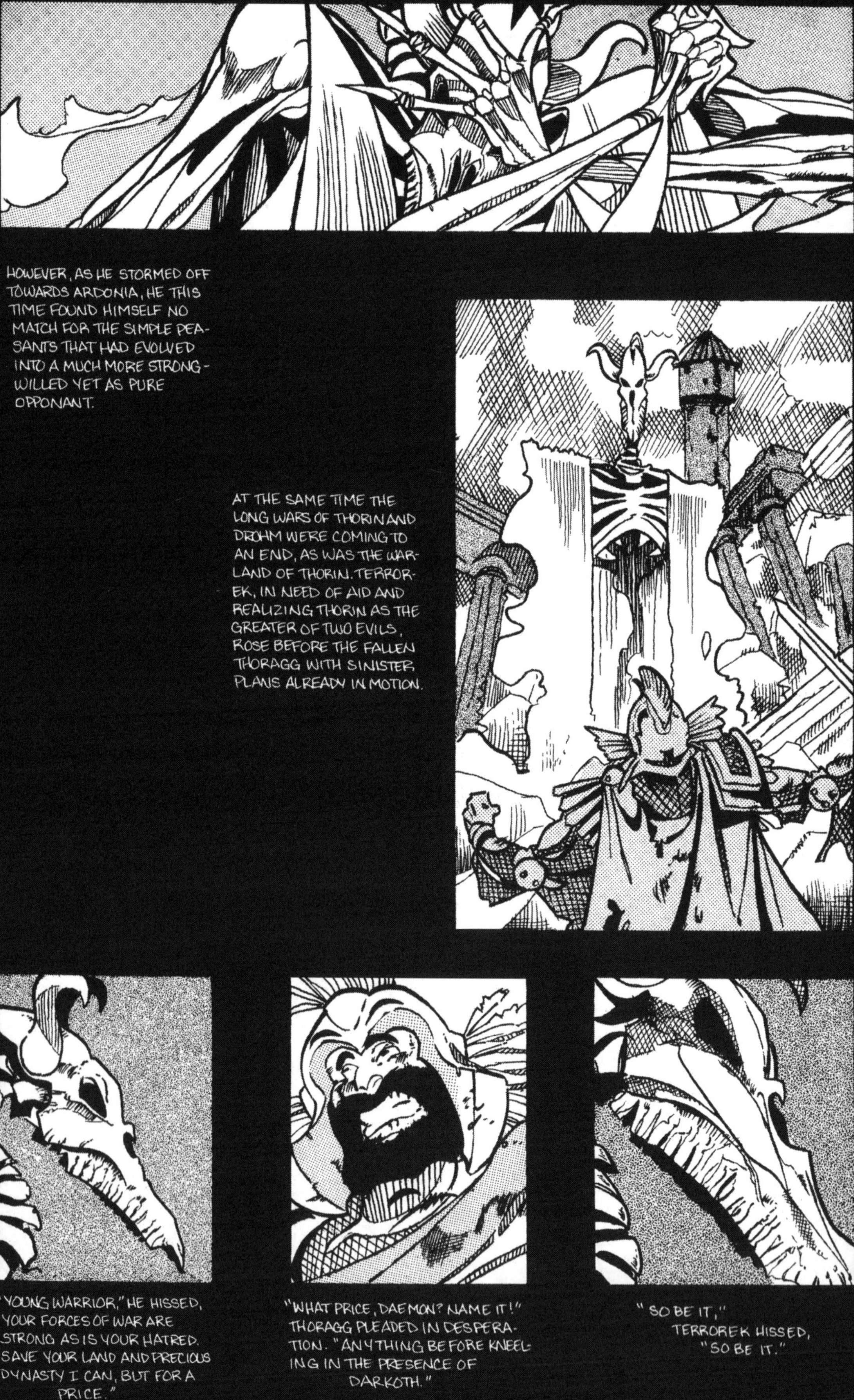
HOWEVER, AS HE STORMED OFF TOWARDS ARDONIA, HE THIS TIME FOUND HIMSELF NO MATCH FOR THE SIMPLE PEASANTS THAT HAD EVOLVED INTO A MUCH MORE STRONG-WILLED YET AS PURE OPPONANT.
AT THE SAME TIME THE LONG WARS OF THORIN AND DROHM WERE COMING TO AN END, AS WAS THE WARLAND OF THORIN. TERROREK, IN NEED OF AID AND REALIZING THORIN AS THE GREATER OF TWO EVILS, ROSE BEFORE THE FALLEN THORAGG WITH SINISTER PLANS ALREADY IN MOTION.
"YOUNG WARRIOR," HE HISSED, "YOUR FORCES OF WAR ARE STRONG AS IS YOUR HATRED. SAVE YOUR LAND AND PRECIOUS DYNASTY I CAN, BUT FOR A PRICE."
"WHAT PRICE, DAEMON? NAME IT!" THORAGG PLEADED IN DESPERATION. "ANYTHING BEFORE KNEELING IN THE PRESENCE OF DARKOTH."
"SO BE IT," TERROREK HISSED, "SO BE IT."

AND SO WAS THE PACT OF HELL MADE. FOR THE PRICE OF THORAGG'S SOUL AS WELL AS HIS LANDS, TERROREK, USING THE ORB OF DEATH, RAISED ALL WHO HAD FALLEN BEFORE THE DARKLORD WITH IMMORTALITY AND CURSED THE LAND WITH THE BLACK DEATH WHERE NONE COULD LIVE, SAVE HIS MINIONS. FOR ONCE DARKOTH FELL, THOUGHT TERROREK, THORAGG'S LEGIONS WOULD EASILY TOPPLE THE FLOCK OF THIS NEW ARDONIA.

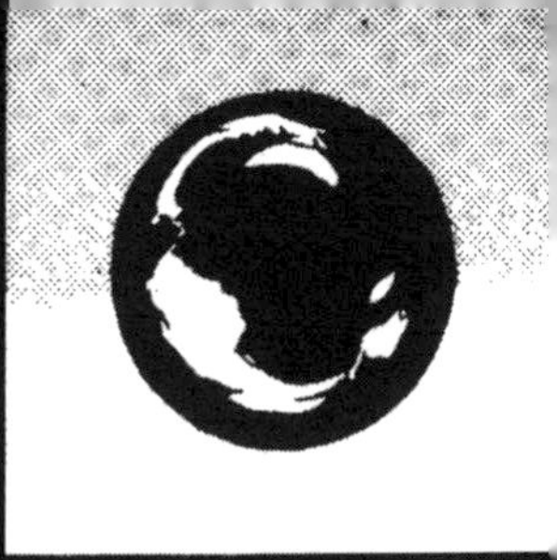

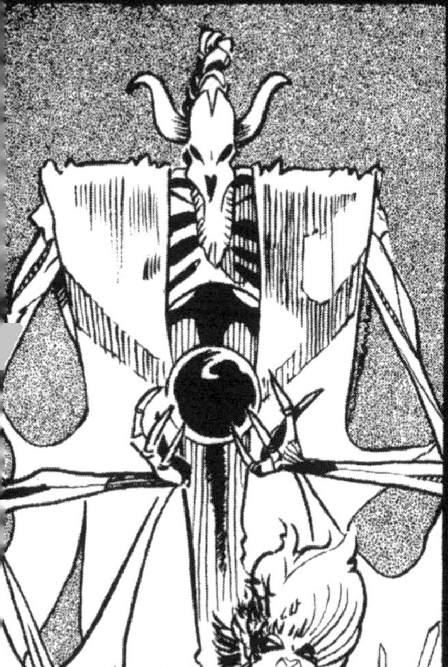

DARKOTH, SEEING THE DEAD RISE TO FIGHT HIM, WAS TRULY IMPRESSED, AND WHILE AS YOUNG AS HE WAS, HE WAS NOT NAIVE AND REALIZED HE WAS NO MATCH FOR THE POWER OF HIS ENEMY'S NEW ALLY...

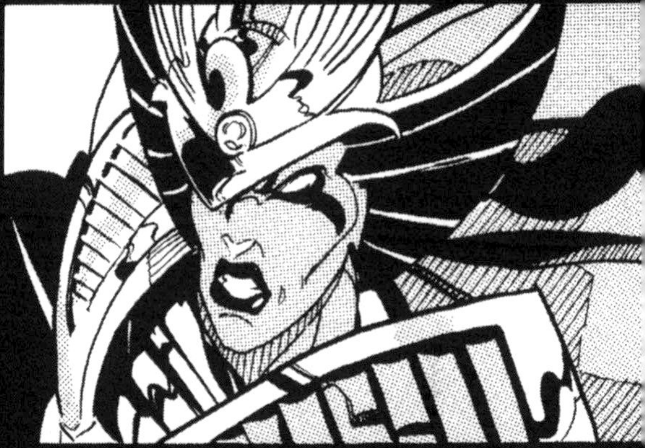

AND REALIZING HE, TOO, COULD NOT WIN THE NEW WAR ALONE, SENT HIS GENERALS OFF TOWARDS ARDONIA.

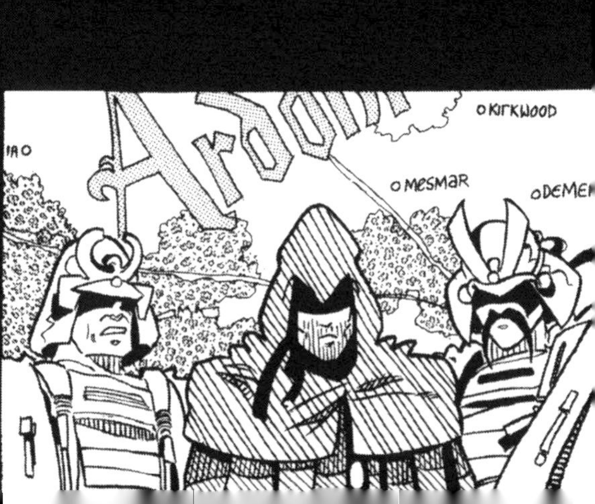

KIRKWOOD
MESMAR

TO BE CONTINUED...

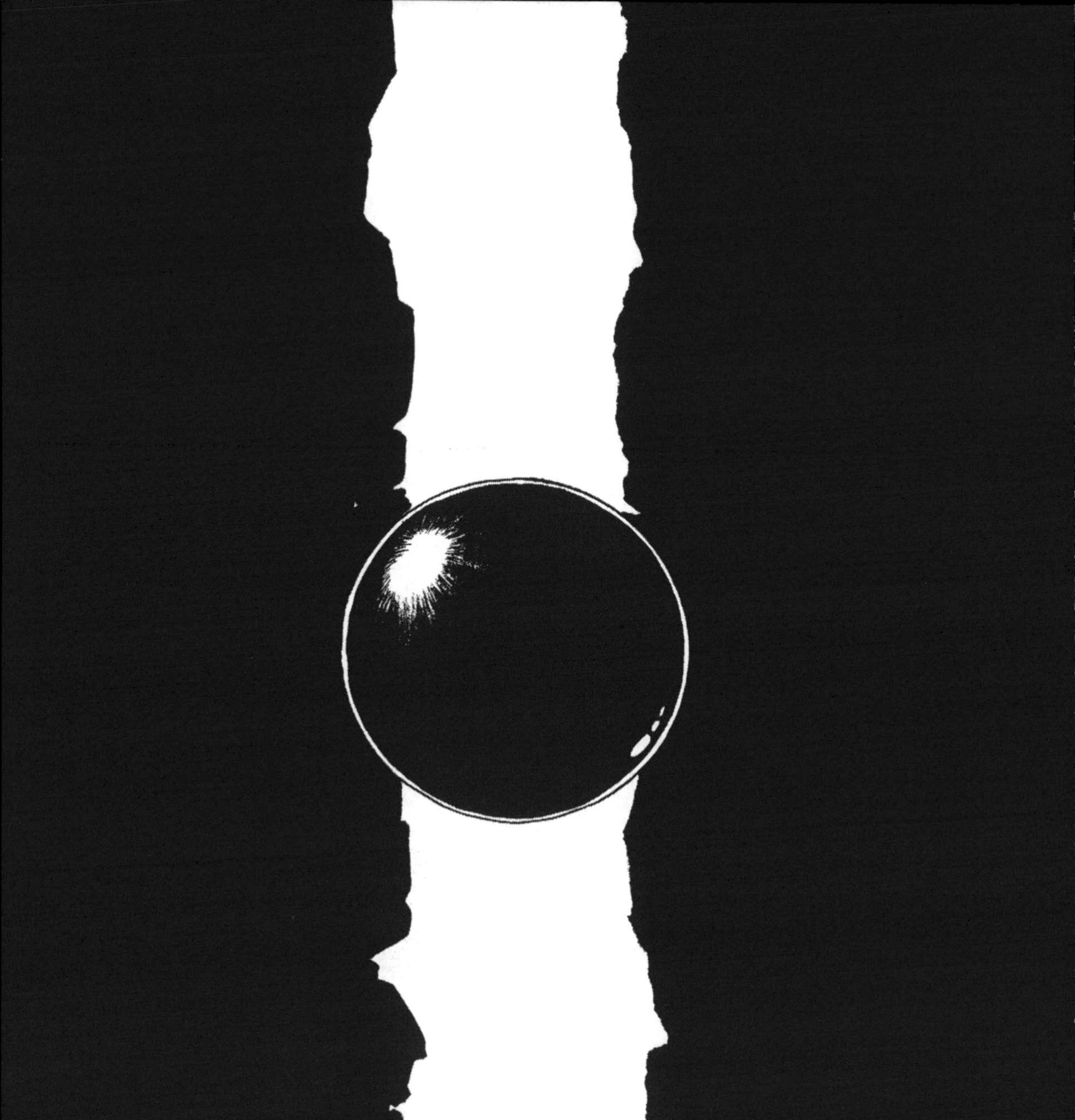

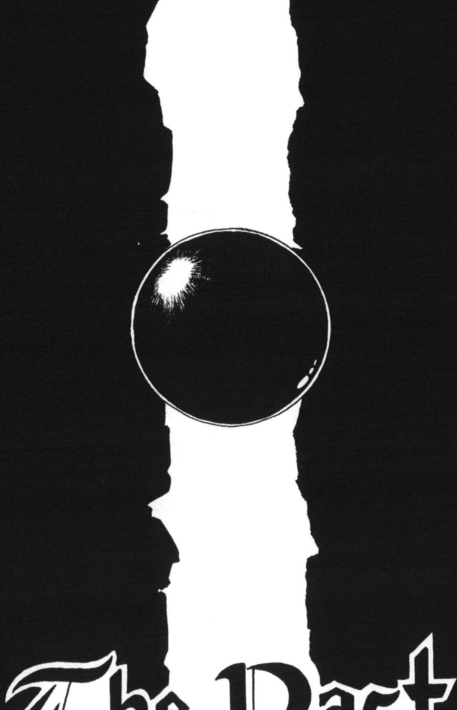

The Pact

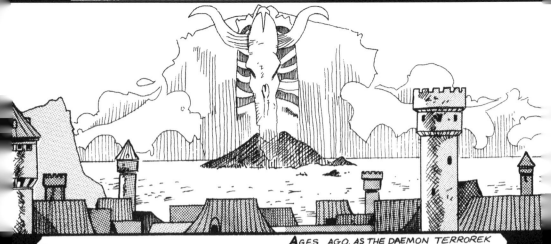

AGES AGO, AS THE DAEMON TERROREK SOUGHT TO ELIMINATE THE HOLY LANDS OF ARDONIA AND THE BELIEFS OF OTHARRIS, HE, WITH THE USE OF THE ORB OF DARKNESS, CLAIMED THE WARRIOS OF THE FALLEN LAND OF THORIN; TO AID HIM AGAINST ARDONIA'S GROWN STRENGTH.

AN UNHOLY ALLIANCE BETWEEN THE WARLORD THORAGG AND THE DEAMON WAS MADE. FOR THE PRICE OF HIS SOUL, AND THAT OF HIS LAND, THORAGG WAS MADE IMMORTAL. IN RETURN HIS SERVICES WOULD BE TERROREK'S FOREVER.

THE ARMY OF DEATH MARCHED AGAINST THEIR RIVALS; THE DARKLORD ARMY. DARKOTH FOUND HIMSELF NO MATCH AGAINST THE FORCES OF DARKNESS THAT SEEMED TO PIT THE VERY ELEMENTS AGAINST HIM. AS HIS FORCES DWINDLED BEFORE HIS EYES, HE SENT FORTH HIS GENERALS TO THE SECLUDED LANDS OF ARDONIA.

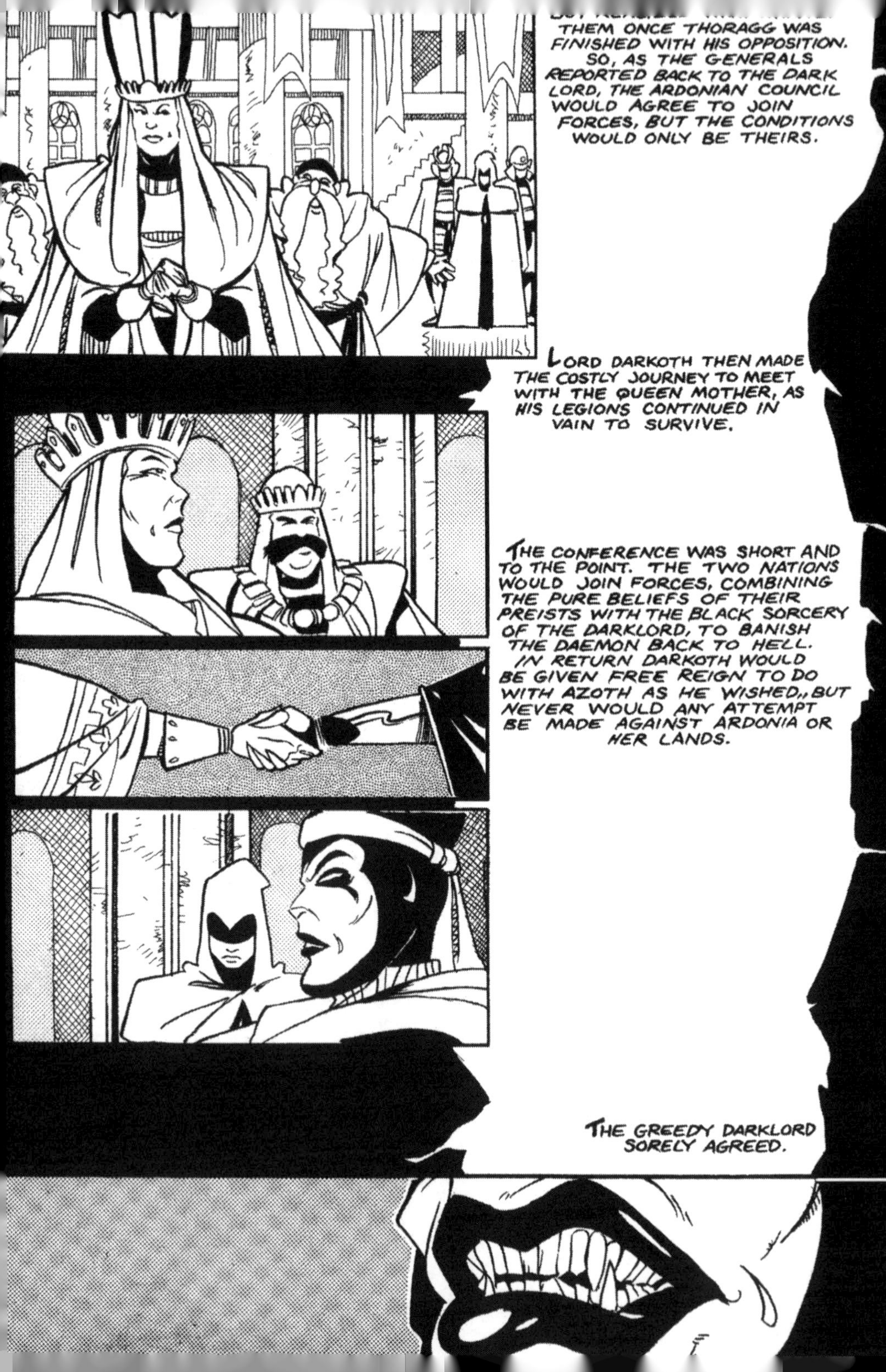
THEM ONCE THORAGG WAS FINISHED WITH HIS OPPOSITION. SO, AS THE GENERALS REPORTED BACK TO THE DARK LORD, THE ARDONIAN COUNCIL WOULD AGREE TO JOIN FORCES, BUT THE CONDITIONS WOULD ONLY BE THEIRS.
LORD DARKOTH THEN MADE THE COSTLY JOURNEY TO MEET WITH THE QUEEN MOTHER, AS HIS LEGIONS CONTINUED IN VAIN TO SURVIVE.
THE CONFERENCE WAS SHORT AND TO THE POINT. THE TWO NATIONS WOULD JOIN FORCES, COMBINING THE PURE BELIEFS OF THEIR PREISTS WITH THE BLACK SORCERY OF THE DARKLORD, TO BANISH THE DAEMON BACK TO HELL. IN RETURN DARKOTH WOULD BE GIVEN FREE REIGN TO DO WITH AZOTH AS HE WISHED,, BUT NEVER WOULD ANY ATTEMPT BE MADE AGAINST ARDONIA OR HER LANDS.
THE GREEDY DARKLORD SORELY AGREED.

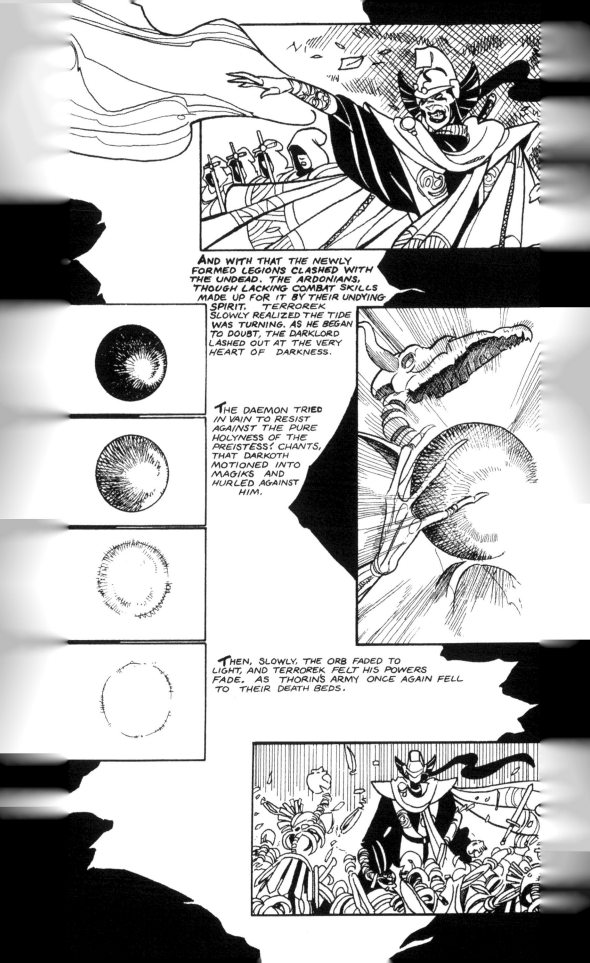

AND WITH THAT THE NEWLY FORMED LEGIONS CLASHED WITH THE UNDEAD. THE ARDONIANS, THOUGH LACKING COMBAT SKILLS MADE UP FOR IT BY THEIR UNDYING SPIRIT. TERROREK SLOWLY REALIZED THE TIDE WAS TURNING. AS HE BEGAN TO DOUBT, THE DARKLORD LASHED OUT AT THE VERY HEART OF DARKNESS.

THE DAEMON TRIED IN VAIN TO RESIST AGAINST THE PURE HOLYNESS OF THE PREISTESS' CHANTS, THAT DARKOTH MOTIONED INTO MAGIKS AND HURLED AGAINST HIM.

THEN, SLOWLY, THE ORB FADED TO LIGHT, AND TERROREK FELT HIS POWERS FADE. AS THORIN'S ARMY ONCE AGAIN FELL TO THEIR DEATH BEDS.

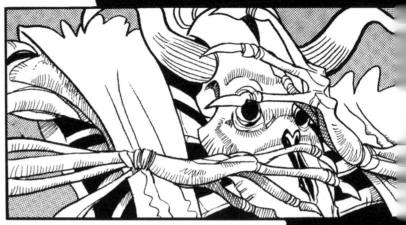

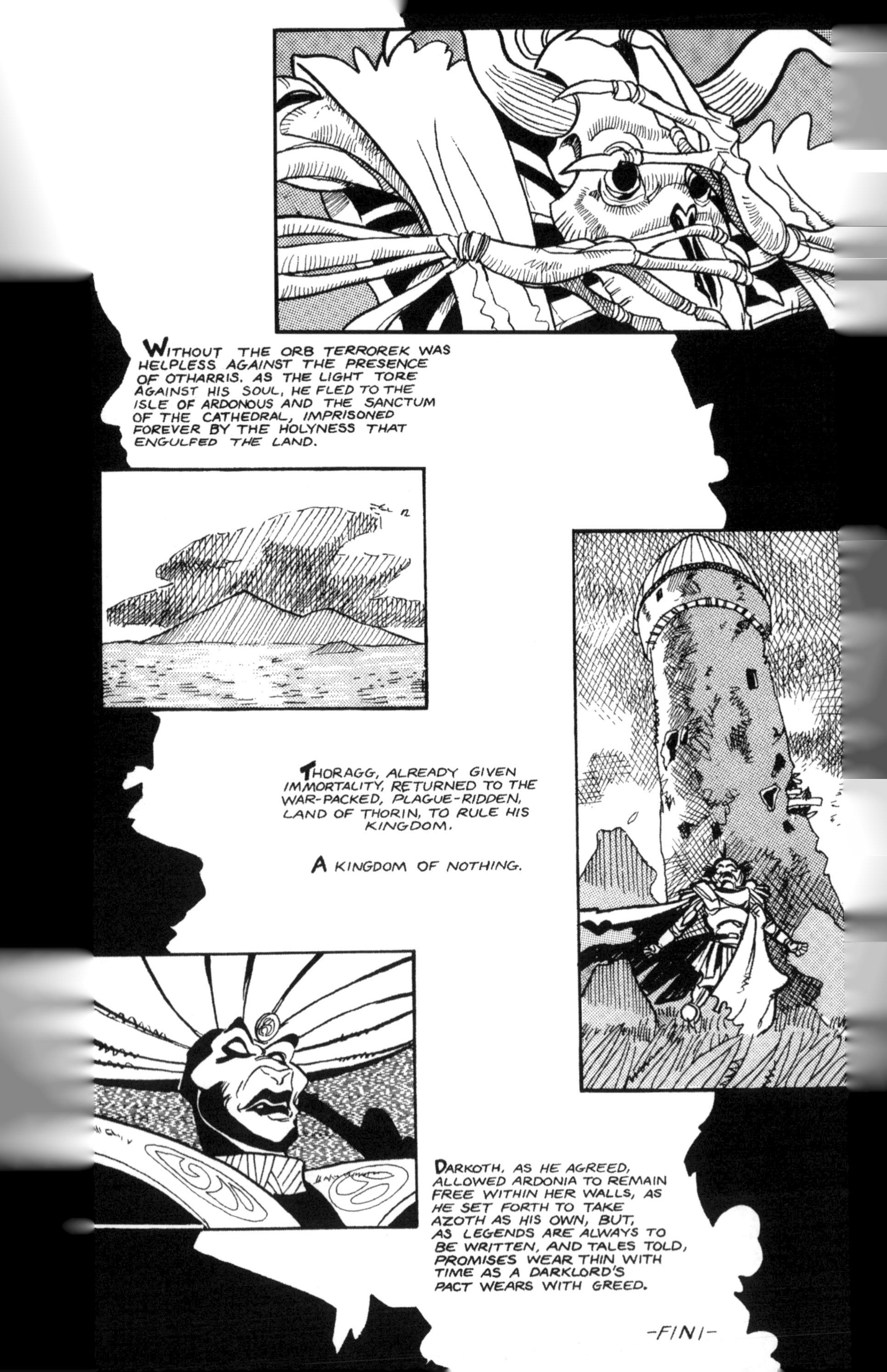

WITHOUT THE ORB TERROREK WAS HELPLESS AGAINST THE PRESENCE OF OTHARRIS. AS THE LIGHT TORE AGAINST HIS SOUL, HE FLED TO THE ISLE OF ARDONOUS AND THE SANCTUM OF THE CATHEDRAL, IMPRISONED FOREVER BY THE HOLYNESS THAT ENGULFED THE LAND.

THORAGG, ALREADY GIVEN IMMORTALITY, RETURNED TO THE WAR-PACKED, PLAGUE-RIDDEN, LAND OF THORIN, TO RULE HIS KINGDOM.

A KINGDOM OF NOTHING.

DARKOTH, AS HE AGREED, ALLOWED ARDONIA TO REMAIN FREE WITHIN HER WALLS, AS HE SET FORTH TO TAKE AZOTH AS HIS OWN, BUT, AS LEGENDS ARE ALWAYS TO BE WRITTEN, AND TALES TOLD, PROMISES WEAR THIN WITH TIME AS A DARKLORD'S PACT WEARS WITH GREED.

-FINI-

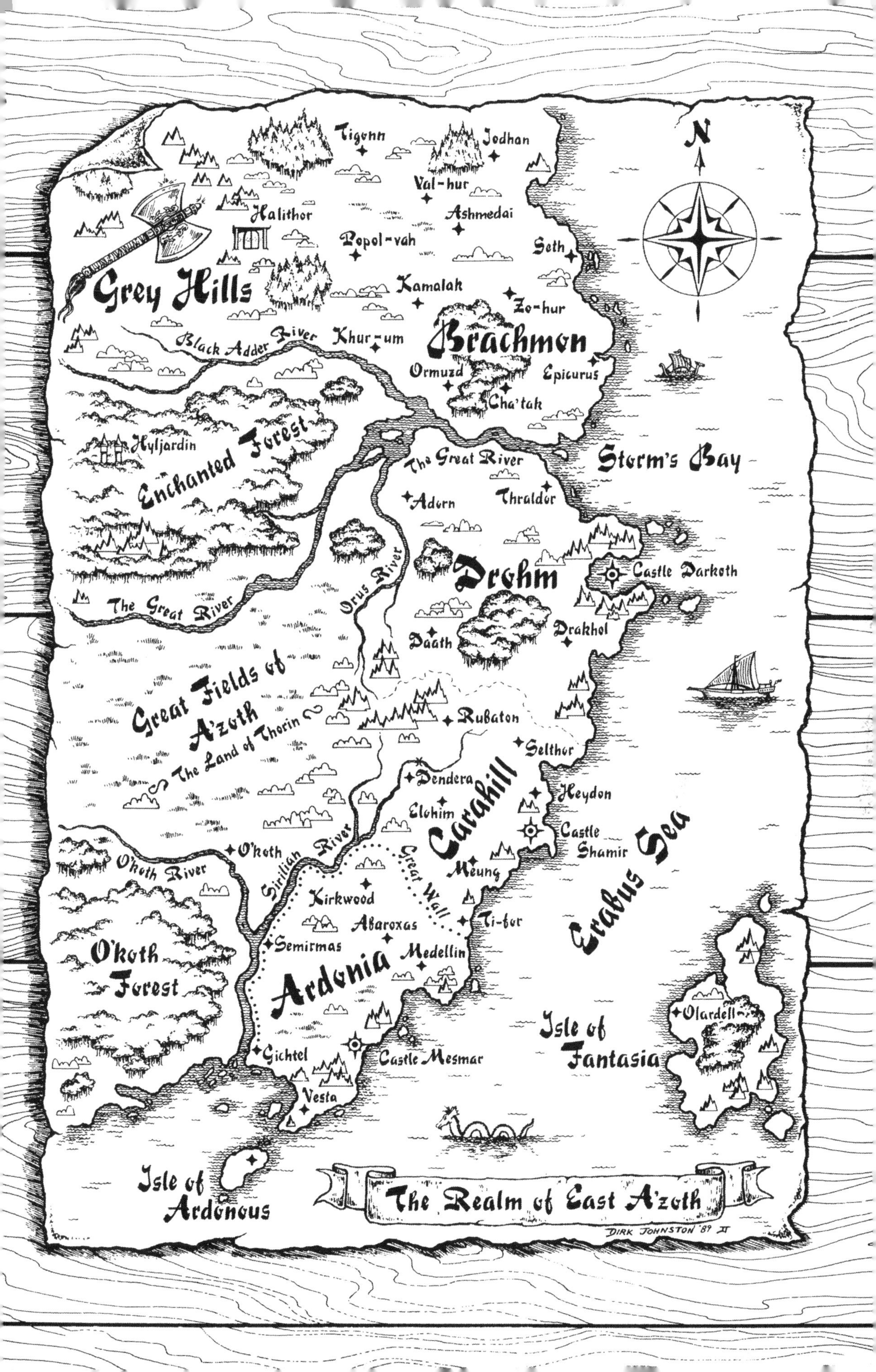
The Realm of East A'zoth
N
Grey Hills
Tigonn
Jodhan
Val-hur
Halithor
Ashmedai
Popol-vah
Seth
Kamalak
Zo-hur
Brachmon
Black Adder River
Khur-um
Ormuzd
Epicurus
Cha'tak
Hyljardin
Enchanted Forest
The Great River
Storm's Bay
Adorn
Thraldor
Castle Darkoth
Drohm
Orus River
The Great River
Drakhol
Daath
Great Fields of A'zoth
The Land of Thorin
Rubaton
Selthor
Dendera
Carahill
Heydon
Elohim
Castle Shamir
O'koth
Sirilian River
Great Wall
Meung
O'koth River
Erabus Sea
Kirkwood
Abaroxas
Ti-for
Semirmas
Medellin
O'koth Forest
Ardonia
Olardell
Isle of Fantasia
Gichtel
Castle Mesmar
Vesta
Isle of Ardonous
DIRK JOHNSTON '89 II

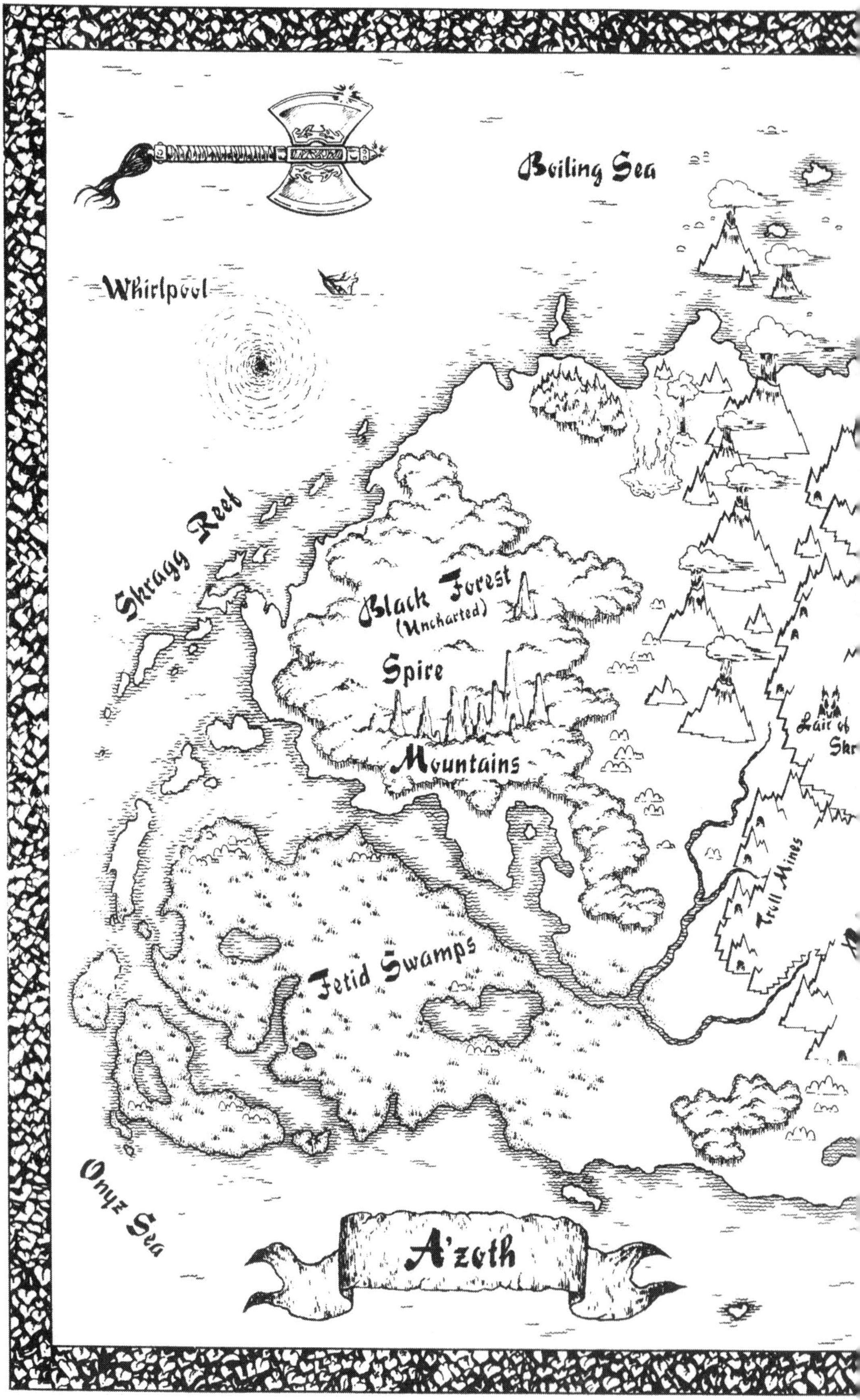
Boiling Sea
Whirlpool
Shragg Reef
Black Forest
(Uncharted)
Spire
Mountains
Fetid Swamps
Troll Mines
Onyx Sea
A'zoth

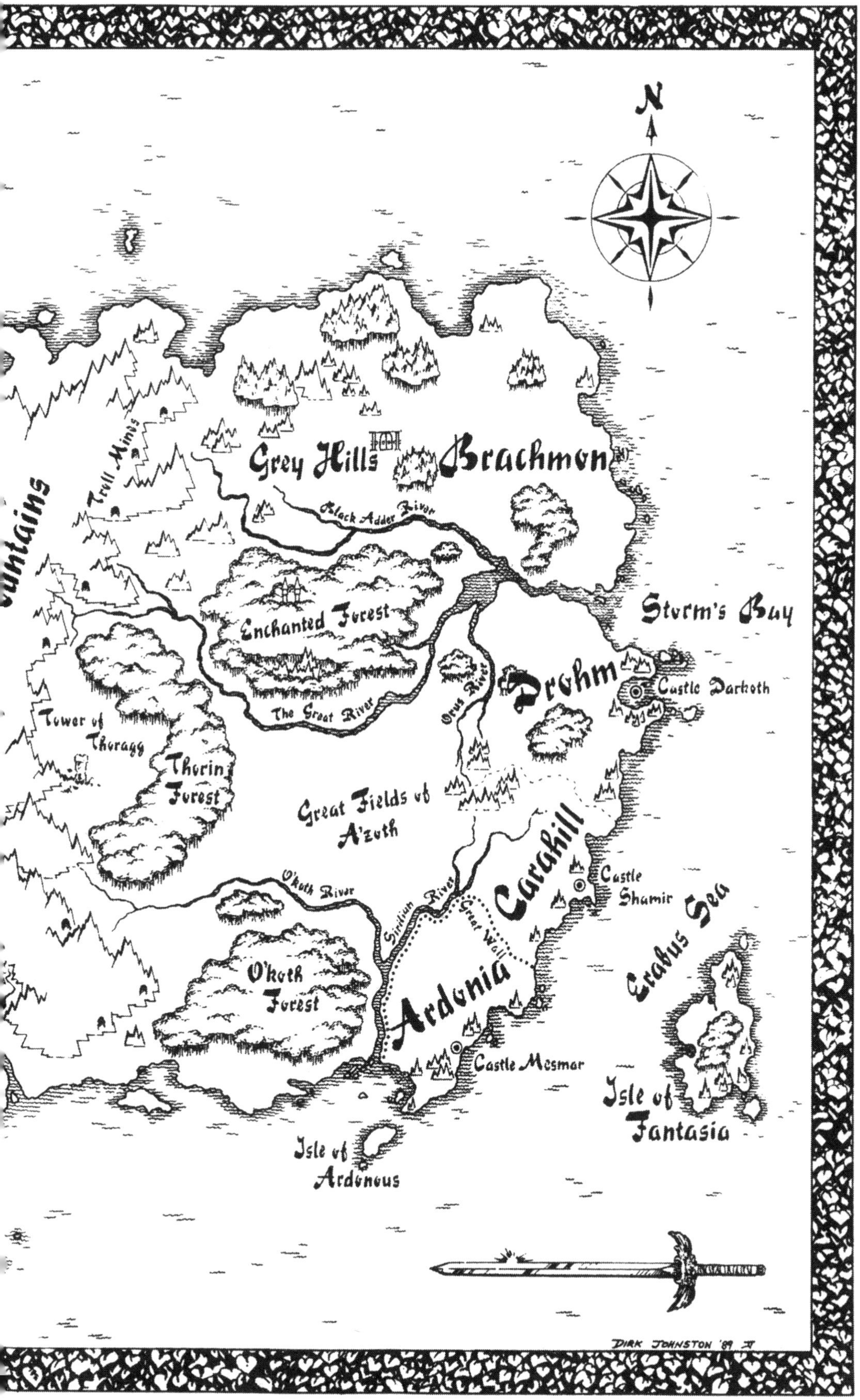
N
Grey Hills
Brachmon
Troll Mines
Black Adder River
Enchanted Forest
Storm's Bay
The Great River
Orus River
Drohm
Castle Darkoth
Tower of Theragg
Thorin Forest
Great Fields of A'zoth
Carahill
Castle Shamir
O'koth River
Sinilium River
Great Wall
Erabus Sea
O'koth Forest
Ardonia
Castle Mesmar
Isle of Fantasia
Isle of Ardonous
DIRK JOHNSTON '89

Made in the USA
Columbia, SC
17 February 2019